The Blessing of
Maharishi

The Wonderful Story of My Life

LOTHAR PIRC

An Autobiography written by Dr. Karin Pirc

1st WORLD
PUBLISHING

The Blessing of Maharishi

Lothar Pirc

Copyright © 2021 Kalyana Verlag – Lothar Pirc and
Dr. Karin Pirc GbR

Translator: Angela Mailander

Editor: Mark Hawkins

First Edition

Library of Congress Cataloging-in-Publication Data

Softcover ISBN: 978-1-4218-3680-5
Hardcover ISBN: 978-1-4218-3681-2
eBook ISBN: 978-1-4218-3680-5

All rights reserved to the author.

Published by 1st World Publishing
P.O. Box 2211, Fairfield, Iowa 52556
tel: 641-209-5000 • fax: 866-440-5234
web: www.1stworldpublishing.com

Most of the persons or institutions mentioned in this book are referred to by their real names. The names of persons or institutions from public life, however, have often been changed to maintain confidentiality. Fictitious names are designated with a *.

With Deeply Felt Gratitude

To my spiritual master, Maharishi Mahesh Yogi, who dedicated his life to the service of humanity and helped me to open my soul,

to Karin, who lent me her words for this book,

to our children, Aurel, Elisa, Lilian, and Daniel, who have enriched my life in countless ways.

Also:

To our friends who have encouraged us through word and deed: Stefan, Jan and Jan, Christoph, Bernd, and Dorothea.

And special thanks go to Angela Mailander for her dedicated translation services and her infinite patience and exceptional expertise in translating the original German text's deeper meanings into vivid English and to Silvia Hawkins for her outstanding assistance and support.

As well as...

...all the countless people who have supported me throughout my life: first, my parents and my siblings; my friends from the TM-Movement, as well my coworkers in our Maharishi Ayurveda Health Center, Bad Ems, Germany and also to the many who have trusted in me to teach them Transcendental Meditation, and those who have come to our clinic for treatment.

Table of Content

XI. Maharishi Ayurveda Clinic

XII. Hard Times

Vedic knowledge and its implementation by Maharishi is, in part, so revolutionary that, especially when first meeting it, it needs a deeper explanation. We cut some of the more comprehensive elaborations from the text and put them in the Appendix (on page xxx) so as not to interrupt the flow of the narrative, while also not depriving readers who are interested in more detailed background knowledge.

INTRODUCTION

This book describes the personal and subjective experiences of my life and the blessings I experienced in nearly four decades of contact with Maharishi Mahesh Yogi and his eternal wisdom. I was not an especially close student of Maharishi's, nor can my experiences pretend to cover Maharishi's activities anywhere near to completeness. In his work, Maharishi gave thousands of people the chance to work with him directly for a certain phase of their lives, thus giving them special attention. He often did this for many at the same time. Many were closer to him and for longer periods of time than I was. Despite this, I am taking the risk to allow my readers to partake of my life with Maharishi to allow those who had lesser privilege, or none, to experience this great saint and sense who he was and what he accomplished.

It is impossible to adequately describe with words how much the mere presence of a human being with such unbounded consciousness can uplift a person's own experience and subtle perceptions. I hope that I have succeeded anyway to allow the spirit of Maharishi to shine through my words and to communicate to my readers some sense of his greatness. Among the countless projects for the betterment of human life on this planet that he has brought into being, the great legacy he left us is the knowledge and the consciousness techniques of the Vedic Tradition. Through his work, these are accessible and easily learned by anyone under the name Transcendental Meditation™ and its advanced programs. They enliven unbounded consciousness, the experience of which sleeps within each one of us as a birthright. Through regular practice we enliven our awareness of this all-pervading consciousness more and more, so that every one of us can lead an increasingly happier, more fulfilled, and blessed life.

So Many Stories

The flames in the fireplace throw orange, flickering light onto the wall; someone has lit candles, and the mood is peaceful. A few men and women are sitting together, and I, among them, am in some far away country far from home. During the day at the conference, in my capacity as the managing director of a private health center in Germany, I spoke about the amazing success of the Maharishi Ayurveda treatments for our patients, also citing scientific studies; I also had conversations with doctors, influential politicians, and sometimes even with a minister of health.

As usual, generous people, in whatever city I happened to be, had supported me in preparing for these contacts, people who, like me, were intent on spreading this knowledge, knowledge humanity so desperately needs. And now, we were all sitting together in the evening, in comfort and peace, thinking about the next steps or celebrating the successes achieved that day. Stories and anecdotes made their rounds, and, sooner or later, I began to talk about how I, personally, experienced Maharishi, the great sage of the last century. Often smiling, I told of the amazing events of my life, including some unbelievable experiences. And then one of my listeners, deeply moved or sharing laughter would say, "Lothar, why don't you write all this down; these are such wonderful stories!"

I'd continue telling stories, from the most diverse countries of our earth. People loved it; I loved it. And again, and again, a new friend would suggest, "Lothar, you should write all that down; write a book, there are so many people who would love to read it!" At some point, I asked a jyotishi, a Vedic astrologer, about that; he looked at my horoscope and then said with conviction, "You will write this book, and many thousands of people will read it!" A few years passed, and I asked a second one. "Yes, Lothar, you will write this book, and it will inspire tens of thousands!" For sure encouraging, but could I really do it? And he then expressed what I was feeling instinctively: "But you're not such a good writer; it would only be good if you write these stories just as you tell them."

A few years later, the desire to assemble these stories into a whole grew stronger. I kept putting it off as everyday concerns devoured me with a thousand inconsequential details. But at some point, the time had come. I began to speak into my little Dictaphone, telling how things began from the start. Right away, I showed the first print-out to my wife, Karin. As soon as she had read it, she looked up and said cautiously, "Hmm, that's not really a fascinating read. You can tell it in such lively and compelling ways. And that's the way it has to be put down on paper!"

Well, expressing myself in writing really is not my main strength. I have to get into the flow of things, and for that I need real listeners. "Let me try and see if I can do it!" My dear wife agreed to be my audience, and, soon enough, she really had fun articulating my thoughts and writing them down. I told her my experiences. She asked questions about this or that to the tiniest detail, lured out the feelings that had moved me back then with further questions, subsequently researched many fascinating details, and then expressed all that in lively words—only to read it all to me anew, so that we would for once (and not just once) agree. And so, finally, this book lies in your hands, with the highest possible accuracy possible in hindsight.

Dive right in, dear reader, into my eventful and varied life with all its twists of fate and miraculous events through which the blessings of my spiritual master Maharishi Mahesh Yogi run like a golden thread.

I.

THE VILLAGE

For the space of the spirit,
there where it can spread its wings,
that is silence.

Antoine de Saint-Exupéry
(1900-1944; French writer and pilot)

A Head full of Crazy Ideas

That river was my flow. I loved it. I loved sitting motionless on its shore, taking in its small, whirling movements and its peaceful flow. I knew the silence all around intimately, it was a part of me, sometimes lively with the far-away voices of neighbors, who, further down river, tended community gardens. Once every hour a steam locomotive with its puff-puff-puff rattled along the shores of the Lahn River. Other than that, our village lay in tranquil peace that even the monotonous tones of the marble factory or the joyful calls of children on our unpaved streets could not disturb. Barely 200 single family homes from various epochs cuddled against the slope on one shore, with the lofty walls of the 900-year-old Schaumburg castle towering above them. On the opposite side of my river stood the motionless, tall trees of a great and untouched forest.

My idyllic hometown Balduinstein on the gently flowing
Lahn River as it appeared in my childhood

I knew almost every home inside and out, as I also knew their inhabitants. My mother and my father showered us three boys with their love and attention. They were protectively intent on keeping us from harm. My two brothers and I grew up in the certainty that Father and Mother would be there for us no matter what to give us a good start in life. So, as a little boy, I felt love and protection all around me.

We lived in our own house, yet we were strictly frugal and we learned early that every penny had to be turned over twice. One of the high points of the year were the family trips to Koblenz, where we let ourselves go bargain hunting and to clearance sales.

"Kids, put on your jackets, let's go!"

My mother's voice gave the starting signal. Six skinny boys' legs ran down the hill of our street, and jumping crossed the railroad tracks, past the sign with its black letters that carried the name of our village *Balduinstein*, and then, after excited and impatient waiting, climbed the tall steps of the train car. The locomotive pulled its cars right along the shores of the Lahn River. The high-rising shores covered with trees on both sides allowed us to watch trees rushing past and the few houses of small villages and train stations in the valley.

Just before getting to the outskirts of Bad Ems, I'd rush to the window and press my snub nose flat onto the pane. Excited and completely spellbound I'd look around. With every trip my inner suspense rose anew. Soon the city with its huge white house would come into view. With its one hundred-fifty barred windows, its three-story height, and its tile-covered angular roof decorated with several pointed towers—all this was for me the essence of harmony and grandeur. Every time, I was overcome with inexplicable and inescapable fascination. The breath of a far-away intuition animated me.

Even as a small rug rat I loved to be outside in free and wide-open nature. I spent much time playing with my friends and wandering through the forests and meadows of the untouched surroundings. This idyll was dimmed by the daily walk to school, in which I had no special interest. This drove my father, who wanted the best future for me, up the wall with wonderful predictability. He had built most of our house for us with his own hands; he worked the nightshift at the railroad company and, during the day he earned a bit more as a master tailor. His life had taught him that you couldn't get anywhere without hard work and dedication. And with this, the deep and constant conflict of my childhood years was already programmed into me. As soon as I got home from school, the neighborhood boys would dribble a ball in front of our dining room and yell, "Lotha, c'mon, let's play soccer!"

Then nothing could hold me down; I'd fidget and want to go. And who, in the face of such temptation, could still want to do homework? When my father lost all patience and, fearing for my future, his admonitions always culminated in a standard sentence: "If you don't try harder, you'll work construction with a shovel and a hoe."

Well, if that isn't a hell of a threat for a worry-free boy!

Not infrequently, I'd decamp after such dark prophecies to brood somewhere about the threatening future that seemed to throw its dark shadow over me. One afternoon, on the balcony of our house, I let myself go into those gloomy thoughts. It became quieter and quieter within me, and the boundaries of my small, narrow boy's form seemed suddenly to dissolve. I felt myself become infinite and all-pervasive, merging with the hills and the heavens above into one being. The whole environment seemed wrapped in dazzling light, and I felt these words rise from within me: "You don't have to worry, because you'll have a very special vocation and you'll accomplish great things, things that don't even exist today." I heard these words not in the way people normally spoke to me; instead it was a super-clear thought that sprang from deep inside and without any contribution on my part. Yet it was completely different from all the thoughts that normally flowed through my head. I felt this inner voice as if someone had shared something with me in a gentle, quiet, and yet unmistakable way. At one with the infinite feeling of liberation that came with it, I felt deeply calmed and secure within this infinite space.

Another time I escaped from the familiar, thundering tirade of my father's scolding into my parents' bedroom and, forlorn, looked into the three-part mirror. There stood an eight-year old boy in shorts, with skinny legs, blond, short hair, and somewhat dreamy and sad blue eyes. Completely unexpected and in the same way as before, that familiar voice came from deep within me, "You will be king in a realm yet unknown." The deep gentleness and unshakeable strength with which these words came together with my child-like trust in them consoled me completely.

This inner feeling of security had been part of me since my earliest childhood. Always when friends and relatives asked full of love, "Hey, Lotha, whadduya wanna be when ya grow up?" the answer came from deep within, "I'll be something that doesn't exist yet …"

And a clear, gentle certainty would come with these words that felt good and true.

My father was often displeased, and not just because of my somewhat lacking enthusiasm for school. Now and then, he'd receive a summons from the principal because I didn't want to learn or had gotten into something. Our contact with the outside world was confined in those days to the daily newspaper and the wooden radio that was covered with cloth, sported three big dials and that could be found in nearly every house. Other than that, there was nothing happening, so that energy bubbling over and a good portion of unused creativity regularly forged us some path. Not only our teachers were targets for our pranks and plots, of which we devised many.

"Lotha, you in?"

My friend Joachim had whispered something to me grinning. Wow, did that ever sound tempting! A done deal. We got a long thread from my mother's sewing basket, a thumbtack and some rosin—and we chose our victim. In a moonlit night we stole outside and sneaked quietly to our classroom teacher's house.

From the bedroom of the clueless couple we could hear loud snoring, a clear sign that we could proceed. I wound the thread around the thumbtack and made a tight double knot while my stomach made somersaults and my legs trembled with excitement. Quickly, I pushed the thumbtack into the window putty in such a way—and this was important—that the metal point touched the glass. And then we were off as fast as could be.

Another one of us little rascals stood at a safe distance of five meters away. He transformed the innocent thread into a ghastly-sounding violin string by covering it with the rosin, and which, in combination with the dull vibrations of the window pane, produced a loud, blood-curdling sound.

In a few spots of our teacher's front yard several of us little devils stood guard and listened. At last came the frightened voice of the teacher's wife: "Guenther, somebody is sawing away at our house! Oh God, those are burglars! Should we turn on the light, or maybe not?"

We, little scoundrels that we were, held our stomachs with suppressed laughter and kept right on sawing.

"Elli, don't turn on the light, I'll surprise them!"

Suddenly, the front door opened and the teacher showed himself in all his glory wearing a floppy night cap and a white night gown shimmering in the moonlight, while we boys in unspeakable terror took flight and spread out in all directions. The teacher pursued one of us for more than a kilometer and a half, until he, huffing and puffing, finally gave up and had to let the terrified and trembling boy get away.

We worried terribly about the uncertain fate of our friend but were reunited an hour later—thank God it was all of us—in the pitch-black center of the village, where we couldn't stop laughing. Oh, what a terrible, delicious fright that, naturally, after many repetitions, urged us to include more victims.

After the village baker had laid the bags full of rolls in front of everyone's door, and the village lay deep in unsuspecting sleep, we were already out and about. With thin and quick fingers, we'd bore a hole in the yet warm crusts, enjoyed the still somewhat sticky insides we'd dug out so carefully and chuckled at the perplexed faces that the rightful owners of these biscuits would make when they cut them open at the breakfast table.

One the eve of Walpurgis Night, the night of May 1st, a

night in which any kind of prank could be pulled off without punishment according to ancient tradition in our village, we dumped a double-sized load of manure in front of the teacher's, as well as the priest's, door. Or we sang provocative songs all over the village. The priest didn't allow tricks to be played on him and always had ten buckets of water ready to defend his territory.

When we were older, my big brother and I used our brand-new tape recorder to document the loud scolding of a neighbor lady who regularly complained about us kids all the way across the street and at the top of her lungs. Then, with smirking faces, we'd play it back, maybe even a little louder than the original—and, of course, at safe distance—from the window of our room. And then we'd record her subsequent screams of rage and play them back to the delight of all the kids around. We kept repeating this until a letter from an attorney was delivered.

To save my father's honor, it must be said here that he, too, enjoyed making fun of people. So, he often protected us and often had to suppress his own laughter when my brothers and I had played a mischievous trick on someone and he'd caught us at it.

All the above was one side of my life: I was a completely normal, wild, and mostly happy boy with a head full of crazy ideas.

But the other side was my carefully guarded secret.

My First Secret

It was a warm and sunny summer's day. My sandals carried me lightly up a steep hill; I was happy and content. The village sounds were far behind me. The air seemed almost to stand still under the blue summer skies; only now and then you could hear the thin humming of a mosquito.

At one point of the stony footpath and completely unexpectedly, I heard the peaceful inner voice I already knew so well, and it gently but firmly told me, "Sit down right here on this rock!" So persuasive was this impulse that I obeyed instantly. As soon as I was seated, a second quiet request made me repeat the name of a friend in a soft murmur. I didn't ask why, I just did it, slowly, innocently, just so, several times. The syllables transformed themselves, became softer and subtler and more reverberated gently within me. I surrendered to it, while I had the feeling that the top of my head opened and received an energy yet unknown to me. It became bright and crystal clear, while two gentle syllables came from above and entered my head. Instinctively, I repeated them again and again, until the sound faded away. I rested fully awake within myself, and my body became almost rigid with the blissful sensation that I had finally come home. Here the world was alright and all my everyday problems paled.

In that way, I sat there for perhaps a quarter or half an hour. Happy and gently moved, I finally made my way home. I knew that what had just happened to me would remain my secret and that I could call it back any time. It was instinctively clear to me that I could speak to neither my friends nor my parents about this because they would not understand. And yet a deep joy came over me for having this one and wondrous secret.

From that moment on and in my wanderings through nature, I felt drawn again and again to my favorite benches: the one at the edge of the forest near a bee hive or the one next to a weeping willow at the river's shore whose softly swaying branches gently stroked the water flowing gently by. Unnoticed by my parents or my siblings, I was drawn there. How could I have found words to describe sinking within myself when I repeated the syllables that had been gifted me in the stillness of my thoughts? And that I perceived the water and nature in such a way that only silence and detachment surrounded me until my breath almost ceased? This inner world, that opened for me and for which I now had a key, attracted me with its magic. It was so beautiful, so quiet, so perfect—it seemed to me that what I experienced within myself was much more meaningful and important than anything happening in my small life. Surprisingly, other people seemed to know nothing of this inner kingdom. So, I let it be and took joy in it quietly and secretly. It was impossible to forget it because regularly the gentle inner voice reminded me to go there again and let myself fall into this emptiness that was nevertheless a fullness.

Through this sinking into my inner self, it was completely clear to me that there must be other knowledge that was not taught in school. So, convinced was I of this, so unshakably certain, that one day at home—I was perhaps eight years old—I grabbed our big encyclopedia with its green cloth covered back and its embossed gold letters and put it on my lap, leafing through it at length. Systematically, I searched for a picture of a great personality who had brought new or different knowledge into the world and who could explain my inner experiences to me. I had a clear idea how this person should look and was, after long searching, confused and disappointed for being unable to find this important significant person in the encyclopedia.

"Well, okay then, if I can't find him in there, I have to go look for him!" Many times, I came to this resolution, but my mind always kept me, a little munchkin, from going out into the big wide world; after all, I was just a kid. And so, the two souls within my breast argued,[1] until finally—reason be damned—and, following my inner desire, I simply went into the forest to look for him. I went further and further until, finally, after almost three hours and six kilometers, almost to the next town and with dusk coming, my mind won the upper hand: "What are you going to do? You've got nothing to eat, and where would you sleep? And your parents are going to worry big time if you don't come back!" Back and forth these urges struggled until I gave up and turned to go home with a heavy heart.

And so, I had to be content to create this state of boundless peace for myself alone. When I'd sit somewhere in the pristine countryside, I directed my attention to it, let go completely, and then saw and felt how this deep silence suffused all of nature, the trees, the meadows, the houses, and the people. Its gentleness spread within me and all around me. This state of palpable peace and respite at last became such a part of me that I often felt it even while horsing around with my friends on the streets. Even then, I felt the soundless blessing that warmed my heart.

And sadly, in my last years at the village school and during

---

[1] Goethe's Faust: "Two souls, alas, are housed within my breast, / And each will wrestle for the mastery there."

my business training, as well as my daily work in the textile shop in the neighboring city, this conscious contact with my inner world was lost more and more. Never again in daily life was I aware that everything was suffused with light. Then, too, the quiet admonitions of my inner voice that had always drawn me into nature to repeat the magic word that moved me within me were silenced. A growing and dense veil of forgetfulness spread over it. Finally, I didn't even remember it.

I was still drawn into nature. But the untroubled, long ramblings of my childhood had yielded to cruising by motorbike, which I enjoyed a lot. On weekends, I camped with my friends or slept under the open skies during warm summer nights. Without noticing and gradually, I looked for happiness in the outside world. Like my contemporaries, I began to smoke, drink alcohol, go to nightclubs, and become stressed out looking in vain for the ideal girlfriend.

During the week, I drove to the neighboring city daily and finished my training in a textile shop. Even as I was in my second and third year as an apprentice and became more and more independent and responsible at advising customers while selling suits and coats, learning bookkeeping and all the other activities that went with it, the prospects of having to do this, or something similar, for the rest of my life scared the wits out of me. My heart wasn't in it; it all seemed too empty and monotonous. But I didn't know anything better to do with my life. All in all, my life back then didn't give me much joy. I was often frustrated and depressed.

Cut off from the magic of my childhood, I knew only one thing: I'm not in the right place. This is not the life I want; this day-to-day boredom, always the same treadmill, and without sense or meaning.

The Die is Cast

One evening after work, I wandered as usual to the station to take the train home and—

there he was,

the man whose image I'd searched for in vain in our encyclopedia and who I'd wanted to track down even when I was still just a boy on that wild escapade into the deep woods: a face that was completely familiar to me at first sight and that, for me expressed wisdom, goodness, and inner peace—the man who I'd known with unmistakable certainty, even back then, would give me the knowledge and truth for which my soul was thirsting.

Maharishi on a poster announcing the 1973 lecture on
Transcendental Meditation

His face was prominently displayed on a billboard and announced a talk about Transcendental Meditation for that same evening. It was totally obvious that I should go—in fact, absolutely *had* to go. I hesitated briefly—and took the train home.

What a colossal mistake! Again and again I tried to shake

off the feeling that I'd missed something extremely valuable and that I had made a grievous error in my life. Even two weeks later, I was distraught about this, and months later, I was still occasionally sad.

A year later I went to night school to get my high school diploma. In desperation, I talked to my history teacher after class because I felt that he might know how to deal with my elusive longings. But I couldn't find the words; I had no name for what I was seeking. Even so, he gave me good advice, and I got a book about Socrates. Through the dialogues of this great man, with his students and other contemporaries, dialogues which are woven into Plato's writing, it became clear to me for the first time that there was such a thing as pure Being and that it could be experienced. Everything I read in Plato was familiar to me from my own experience. And I tried to discover this pure Being through the questions Socrates asks. A distant echo of this pure Being came to me through my interest in these texts but something central was missing: the possibility to experience this pure Being for myself. My seeking and my longing remained.

A short time later, a friend let me borrow the book *Siddhartha* by Hermann Hesse. Like lots of guys, I'm not too crazy about reading, but this story of the wealthy son of a king culminating in his enlightenment totally hit bull's eye for me. Contrary to my usual laziness when it came to reading, I devoured that book all at once. It held me spellbound till five in the morning, and I had to read a few passages two or three times to take it all in—that's how fascinated I was. Here, finally, was what I'd been searching for but couldn't find the words to express. Afterwards, I tried to meditate now and then as Siddhartha had done, and long-lost intuitions from my childhood came back to life.

Through this great book, I now understood that there were higher states of human consciousness and that the sources of this knowledge were alive in India today. I sensed that I needed a teacher; I needed someone to guide me. Whenever I wanted to go within myself, something just didn't seem right.

Back then, something decisive changed as well. Suddenly I no longer wanted to eat meat. Even the smell of it was disgusting to me. And the thought that innocent animals had to give up their lives to nourish mine was even worse. But how could I communicate this to my parents, when my mother, tirelessly and with much love, day-in and day-out prepared and then brought to our dining room table that great-tasting, plain German fare? I sensed clearly that such a change in my diet would fall on deaf ears.

"I don't want to eat meat anymore!"

There. It was out in the open. My father's response was instant: "Who put that bug in your ear?" As a united front, both my parents tried to talk me out of this crazy idea with all the counter arguments they could muster.

But I was stubborn. And Mom and Dad were extremely worried.

How can you change the mind of a determined boy of eighteen? Especially one who, meanwhile, had let his wavy hair grow down to his shoulders and who'd diligently and resolutely been pursuing night school despite all difficulties? A boy who, wanting to go his own way, slowly slipped through your fingers? Professional advice was imperative here!

And so, just a bit later, my father stomped into the office of the village doctor and reported our dilemma. The doctor was a good doctor and up on the cutting edge of his profession back then. "You can't let the boy do that; meat is the only thing that has all the essential amino acids. Without meat, he will miss vital proteins that the body can't produce by itself."

My father delivered the doctor's bad news: "If you quit eating meat, the doctor gives you one more year to live at most."

That was the end of the discussion. But my aversion remained.

I was still drawn to the outdoors. A special, intimate feeling united me with the cows on the long pasture far from town on the meadows on the other side of the Lahn. When I wandered there, the cows liked to walk alongside me on the other side of the enclosure, while they looked at me with their big and gently melting eyes. Often, we walked together in silent harmony for the whole kilometer of their pasture and to its end, where they could go no further and so stood and watched me go.

How could you eat the flesh of these wonderful gentle beings? And yet I was forced to do it, though it felt all wrong to me. I was so sorry about it that, often, I silently asked their forgiveness.

It didn't help much, but it did lighten my heart.

On the way home on my motorbike after night school, I sometimes visited the youth center in the neighboring small town of Diez. Young people sat there in the dim light and in small groups in various corners. I would get a seat somewhere in the room or at the bar near the entrance, drink a coke or some other drink, listen to pop music for fifteen minutes, and then stroll off.

One time, I noticed a few boys and girls my age, who seemed especially relaxed and happy. These young people had such an open vibe that I had to look at them again and again. Clearly, something about them was different.

The next few times, when I went up the stairs in that old timber-frame house, I was expectant: would they be here today? If they were, my eyes, all by themselves, would seek out these young people to learn what it was they had going for them. They didn't smoke, didn't drink alcohol; and yet they were happy. Their eyes shone, and they laughed with each other. As much as I wanted to, as much as I longed to be a part of this happy group, I didn't have the nerve to talk to them.

Five or six times I went there, and every time my courage deserted me. I knew that they had something that I was looking for. Every time, I went home depressed because, due to the fear that I'd make a fool of myself, I again couldn't say a word to them.

One evening only one young man of this group was still there, lean and lanky, with brown eyes and long dark hair—a young man who radiated enormous peace and harmony, which drew me to him. Thank God, he was alone at the bar. Unobtrusively, I sat down on the stool next to him. And we got into a conversation. At one point, he said, "Man, I haven't eaten anything in forever; I'm really hungry!"

That was my cue! Glad to be able to do something for him, I offered him my sandwich, "You are welcome to it; I don't need anything else today!"

Smiling, he asked, "What's in it?"

"Salami."

"That's too bad; then I can't eat it. I'm a vegetarian."

"How long's it been since you've had meat?"

"Two years." My God, the dude looked like the very picture of good health!

"And you're totally fine?"

"I feel better than ever!" In that moment, I decided never to eat another piece of meat. But my curiosity was not yet satisfied.

"What motivated you to become a vegetarian?"

"Since I've been meditating, the appetite for meat just got less and less by itself."

I kept at him. "What kind of meditation do you practice, and where can I learn it?"

Jochen seemed glad to have found such an interested listener, and he eagerly told me all I wanted to know.

That night and in this way, I heard about Transcendental Meditation for the first time. Jochen called it simply TM. I learned that this kind of meditation was especially easy to practice. But it could only be learned from a qualified teacher who had been trained by Maharishi himself and who had brought this method from India to the West. Now it dawned on me slowly. I asked Jochen about his friends who were usually with him in this youth center. "Yes, they all meditate twice a day."

So, it was this I'd noticed right away! Was it possible that, in this big room in the youth center, I unexpectedly found exactly what I'd been seeking for so long? A little later Jochen's brother, Frank, joined us, and, with great enthusiasm, he wanted to tell me all about the scientific studies and the positive effects of TM. But my mind was already made up. I didn't need any persuasion. All I wanted to know was when and where I could learn this meditation. And as fast as possible.

The brothers knew two teachers of Transcendental Meditation in the immediate vicinity. One was a lawyer, a respectable man, with great charisma, whom they praised to the skies—but his schedule was so full that I'd have to wait four weeks for my initiation into TM. There was also a student in Koblenz who probably had time right away. I asked only, "Does it matter in terms of the quality of my meditation with whom I learn?"

"No, they're both equally well-trained to initiate you into TM. It's independent of the personality of the teacher."

My First Meditation

On my red Honda 250, I rattled to Koblenz—for my first proper meditation! With Frank on the seat behind me. Just like that, for the fun of it, for accompaniment. My heart sang. I was excited, full of joy and anticipation.

On a beautiful street in Koblenz and in a seminar room decorated student-style with chairs upholstered in colorful patterns, my breath almost stopped with amazement. There hung a picture of Maharishi Mahesh Yogi, whose eyes, full of love, gazed at me. How could this be real! It really was the same man! Without the slightest clue as to where my life would lead me, I was about to learn the meditation of the wise man on the poster I'd seen a year and a half ago. Back then, I'd missed my chance. Now I was more than ready to grasp it with both hands.

But, oh, well, what a disappointment! Instead of learning to meditate, there were first two lectures. The young teacher gave me an overview of the effects of TM. Ralf-Otto explained that brain researchers in all over the world took it for granted that human beings normally only use three to ten percent of their mental abilities. So far, no one knew for sure what the remaining subdivisions of brain function were good for and how they could be used. He claimed that, through regular meditation, the remaining 95% could be accessed little by little. Finally, he had my undivided attention; I was fascinated. He went on about the improvement of health, in social conduct, and even about the effects on society.

I practiced patience, and learned that it is possible to measure various changes in the body during meditation. For real? All that was much too boring and I could not have cared less. I simply longed only for the practical experience. Yet finally, I was impressed that, within twenty minutes even beginners could experience a level of peace that, on average, was twice as deep as deep, dreamless sleep. Dr. Keith Wallace, a young American physiologist, had determined this, and in a recent study, he had measured the oxygen consumption in the blood, the breath rate, and the heart rate in test subjects, and had found that these physiological activities were spontaneously reduced.(1) Researchers had even used a polygraph to study people during the practice of TM. They found that the skin-resistance, which is high in relaxed people with dry skin, shot up immediately and significantly during meditation. This also happens when a subject simply sat still, eyes closed, or while listening to music. However, the state of rest experienced during TM was seven times as deep as it is while reading, five times as deep as while listening to music, and four times as deep as it is while simply sitting with the eyes closed.[2]

All that was well and good, but I wanted to start to meditate right here and now. But all my pushing was useless and I had to go home with nothing accomplished.

On the way back home, I stopped once again in my favorite place, Bad Ems, so I could show Frank the majestic health resort at the Lahn River; the big, white house, whose façade with its big pillars had fascinated me since childhood, and which, again today, inexplicably drew me into its spell.

Next day, I again drove to Koblenz, where my young TM teacher, Ralf-Otto, this time explained to me the differences between Transcendental Meditation and other methods for personal growth: "The technique of Transcendental Meditation requires no effort because it just uses the natural

Maharishi Mahesh Yogi (1917-2008) taught the simple, natural technique of Transcendental Meditation from the tradition of the Vedic Masters as transmitted by Guru Dev.

Maharishi's enlightened master Guru Dev (1870-1953), Swami Brahmananda Saraswati, Jagadguru, the Shankaracharya of Jyotir Math,
the spiritual head of Northern India

tendency of the human mind to seek levels of greater joy," And he added, "On the one hand, TM comes from a valued tradition thousands of years old; on the other hand, a series of scientific studies show that this ancient technique is successful with normal people like us who are active in daily life." Well, in my fiery zeal, I was convinced of that already.

I learned that the Autogenous Training, developed by Heinrich Schulz as a relaxation technique was widespread in Germany back then. When Transcendental Meditation became better known, Christa Kniffki, a psychologist in Kiel, recorded changes with a psychological questionnaire. A group of people learned Autogenous Training; the other group learned TM. In the first eight weeks, the effects in both groups moved into the same positive direction. But thereafter everyone who practices Autogenous Training (with one exception) lost the improvements of those first weeks. In contrast to this, TM meditators became increasingly relaxed, fearless, and less stressed; nervousness and depression continued to decrease during the sixteen weeks of this study.[3]

Additionally, Ralf-Otto confided in me a bit more about "my big day." "Tomorrow you'll get a mantra. This is a pleasant sound without meaning, that's been used for meditation since time immemorial. This mantra serves as a kind of vehicle for leaving your animated daily thinking and sinking into the quieter realms of your consciousness. However, the mantra alone is not enough. To meditate successfully, you also need a technique for using it appropriately —you'll learn all this step-by-step tomorrow during your personal instruction." Though I now knew on an intellectual level approximately what to expect, but my soul hungered even more for the practical experience.

Finally, the following day the moment had come. My meditation teacher led me into a quiet room. For the initiation, I'd brought a small bouquet of flowers and some fruit. On the table, I saw a picture of Maharishi's Master, Bhagavan Swami Brahmananda Saraswati, Guru Dev for short. He, like Maharishi, wore his hair long. Briefly, a worry flashed through me, "Oh boy, are you running away from Jesus and Christianity?" But then my sunny sense of trust won out. I no longer judged it and began my first meditation with the help of my young teacher.

Already while he, according to ancient custom, sang a traditional melody in a language I'd never heard before— Sanskrit, the centuries-old language of India's advanced civilization—my awareness changed. The picture of Guru Dev suddenly seemed to be three-dimensional and the colors began to shine. And when I began to meditate with closed eyes and according to the instructions of my teacher, the state of consciousness that manifested itself was deeply and completely familiar. There were phases without thoughts, I was wide awake and felt that everything became soft and bright. I sat on a chair, my hands relaxed on my lap. My body became so heavy that I had the impression I could no longer move and my spirit became light and expansive. Quietly, the teacher left the room. An inner peace flooded me in such a way that I felt completely sunken within myself and I perceived everything within and around as a quiet observer.

I could have sat in that way for a long time. When Ralf-Otto came back, he had a bit of trouble with me. He told me gently that I should gradually come out of the meditation. But I didn't want to, I wanted to remain in this quiet condition of complete happiness and security. Only after several attempts on his part did I slowly open my eyes.[2]

I drove to Koblenz three more times to check my meditation and to discuss my experiences—that was part of the course. I wasn't entirely enthusiastic about this because, after the resounding success the first time, I thought I could do it and already knew everything. But it was to be otherwise. I soaked up the ensuing explanations and deepening of my experience like a dry sponge. I sat there, my eyes big, and listened to the expositions of my meditation teacher, who knew so much that he had me mesmerized.

Now, I heard for the first time where the name Transcendental Meditation came from. "The expression comes from the Latin word, *transcendere* ("trans" – across and "scandere" – climb) and it means to go across something. During TM we naturally transcend our normal conscious thinking level and the thoughts that spring constantly from our innermost being. These naturally become refined and quieter until they are so vague and unexpressed that we dive into a level where there are no longer any thoughts. We rest in the realm of absolute silence while our consciousness is wide awake without the movement of thoughts."

Yes, exactly this is what I had experienced, again and again, even if just briefly most of the time. It felt so familiar to sink into this unbounded silence within me that I asked myself why this didn't happen by itself. Presumably we are so awestruck by new and ever-changing distractions and absorbed in continuous thoughts and ruminations through

---

[2] The personal experiences in meditation are, of course, subjective; they are determined by the condition of the nervous system. Therefore, they are different not only from person to person, but also normally differ from one meditation to another in the same person.

26

our absorption in external things that this natural ability was just lost with all the hectic activity.

As far as I was concerned, I finally again had the key to this realm in my hands.

I was literally beside myself with joy when my meditation teacher told me on the third day of checking that "If you practice this technique regularly twice a day, consciousness accustoms itself to the silence of transcendence that, gradually, this state becomes permanent even while pursuing our daily activities. Once that peace and silence in meditation is established even during daily activity, then that is a state of enlightenment or what we call "Cosmic Consciousness." Siddhartha—Hermann Hesse! He knew it! He knew and empathized with the Indian wisdom tradition—and so for me it came full circle.

As part of the technique, my initiator chose a certain meaningless sound, my mantra. I used this systematically with my eyes closed, just as he had instructed me. Meanwhile, I knew that similar spiritual practices were well-known in India. During the second introductory talk, I understood additionally that the choice and use of a mantra should be taught by a specially trained meditation teacher so that the time dedicated to meditation is most fruitful. When used appropriately, this sound helps a restless spirit to become peaceful gradually and to expand consciousness itself. This truly is the birthright of every human being.

For human consciousness functions for everyone according to the same principles and allows this spontaneous and effortless sinking within.

After a few days, something so completely unexpected and unbelievable happened that it knocked my socks off. As

I was sitting in my room at home with closed eyes and my mantra like a distant sound within me, a nearly lost and faint memory came over me. It bubbled up unexpectedly from the depths of my awareness as if a veil had been lifted from it. This sound for meditation that I used daily was deeply familiar. I sat there speechless, awestruck, and shaken. How could this be possible? I knew that sound! It was the same sound that I had received as a boy at the cliff on the stony path above our village and with which I had often "meditated" in my childhood without even knowing the word "meditation!"

Despite all this, it was different now that I was a young man. When I meditated the same childlike innocence and dedication came to me. But now I also had detailed knowledge about the technique and had learned how to use a mantra appropriately and what kinds of experiences could arise during meditation and how to handle them. Above all, I learned what kind of growth processes would be enhanced through the practice. This gave me confidence and trust—and now I could and wanted to use all of it regularly and consciously.

A New Life

I was nineteen and because there were so many holes in my high school record I had to bone up on things and go to night school. In addition to that, I worked half days to support myself. I was completely tied down with all that. Even so, I guarded my new treasure; I meditated twice every day. And I loved it. Mornings, I looked forward to meditating again in the evening, and evenings I looked forward to the morning meditation. I never missed one.

One day I caught myself as I bounced like a rubber ball down the steep street from my parents' house to the train station. Where did this unexpected joy come from? I was fascinated by the lightness and the feeling of joy that always showed up all by itself when I meditated. That this feeling also flooded my daily life after a few days and weeks; that was just marvelous. From the depths of my heart and all by itself came a quick prayer: "Dear God, help that I can keep this for the rest of my life!"

These unexpected blessings of meditation showed up not only during the time I rested within myself, eyes closed. Little by little, my outer life changed. I clearly became more conscious. Where, earlier, I had to overcome my shyness to connect with other people, it suddenly seemed easier and happened all by itself. I'd always liked making jokes with my friends and entertaining others but now I could be relaxed and easy even among strangers, as if a merciful and magical hand had removed my inner blockages. Slowly, I became as I'd always wanted to be but had not been able to pull off.

I felt my mother's moods and those of other people more

clearly than before and could empathize better. Even my perceptions had changed. Often colors seemed brighter, shinier, and I could enjoy the beauty of nature more intensely. I was especially impressed with the changes while listening to music. I heard instruments and tones on my favorited records that I'd never heard with such discrimination. This was true for all kinds of music, for pop and rock, but especially for the nuances of the classical pieces I loved so much. And something else, something decisive, happened. With this newfound joy of life, I also had the feeling and desire for orderliness. Much to my mother's delight, the mess in my room and in my school supplies vanished. With newly awakened pleasure, I showered daily, and, when necessary, even twice a day, and I took satisfaction in the cleanliness of my body, something my parents had tried and failed to instill in me before.

Even my body became healthier. When I was a kid, I'd had an accident in which a grown-up ran over me with his bike and injured the vertebrae in my neck. Since then, I was often plagued with mild headaches. These would increase during puberty and became more and more intense until I suffered from them almost daily. And even this curse was lifted after some time. Before, I'd had to have excuses from the doctor for these headaches and, additionally, had to miss work five or six time a year due to the flu. But now, it happened at most once a year.

Within a few weeks and months, my whole life had changed. I'd found something and I knew that with TM, a new and better life had begun for me.

Like a bee to honey, I was attracted to everything that had anything to do with meditation. For me, a door had opened wide, and in my glowing enthusiasm and youthful naiveté, I wanted only one thing: to see the people around me equally relaxed, free, and happy as I was in the moment. I loved my parents and my brothers, and my many relatives and friends in my environment and had received much good from them in my life for which I was thankful. Now, I finally had something valuable, something wonderful that would help them too.

To the people that were especially close to me, I raved about the blessings of this meditation technique, completely convinced that whoever was listening would dive into the thing as enthusiastically as I did. With my three best friends in the village, I was met with deaf ears, much to my amazement; the spark just didn't jump over to them. At the same time, I found their lifestyle, that I'd shared with them earlier, increasingly unattractive. I no longer wanted to empty many bottles of apple wine with them in one evening; or to impregnate the air with pipe and cigarette smoke, or, in conversation, to blow my own horn about heroic deeds on the motorbike, or enthuse about a new car, or tear down a boss or a neighbor at great length. Our meetings became less frequent.

In contrast to all that, I felt happy as a lark and content in the company of other young meditators who I gradually got to know. In my spare time in my attic room in my parent's home, I started to read Maharishi's book, *The Science of Being and the Art of Living* [4] in which, step-by-step, he describes the spiritual background of TM and the changes that regular practice of meditation will bring with it.

Jochen gave me a booklet that described the yoga poses that Maharishi had recommended, and he demonstrated them. From then on, I practiced them daily in addition to my evening meditation. I even did them several times on weekends, before and after my meditations. I learned pranayama, a simple exercise that refines the breath gradually and allowed me to dive more deeply into my consciousness.

I also loved listening to a record, *Love and God*, on which Maharishi recited wonderful verses about human and divine love, accompanied by the melodic chords of a sitar. He expressed his unending love for our Creator with a devotion and openness that I'd never heard before. His voice sounded so tender and full of humility that the intimacy he had with God communicated itself to me as well. Worshipful silence sank into my heart, which opened wide, full of reverence and love for my Creator and his Creation. I'd keep my eyes closed for a long time. I'd never in my life perceived something so beautiful and clear, not even in the most beautiful church services, not even at Christmas time. I bathed in an atmosphere of sanctity in my room under the roof.

On the back of the record cover you could see Maharishi among a group of young and older people, laughing joyfully. For me, they were all radiant like angels. There were no people with such vibes in our village—not even one. I looked at them for a long time, again and again, and thought, "I want to experience this vibe at least once in my life!" And one day, the answer came up from within me: "Don't worry, that desire will be fulfilled."

For longer and longer periods of time, a colorful sign I'd painted lovingly was hanging on my door with a red ribbon: "*Please do not disturb; I'm meditating.*"

The scent of incense sticks pervaded my room—in fact, the whole house.

Slowly but surely, all of it rubbed my father the wrong way.

Seelisberg

"I'm going to Switzerland soon, to Seelisberg! I'm really excited!" Beaming, Frank dropped this news on me while leaning casually on the bar at the Youth Center. "Maharishi lives there and trains TM teachers."

"Well, do you want to be a TM teacher?" I asked with surprise.

"Naw, I can't afford it right now, but they are always looking for people who can help. I'll probably work in the kitchen as an assistant cook and I'll get to enjoy the great atmosphere—close to Maharishi."

Aha.

But he wasn't finished yet, "Seelisberg is a dream, just above Lake Lucerne. The surroundings are really beautiful, and there are two or three hundred people from all over the world that all meditate and are high on it."

All the bells within me started to ring: "Tell me, can anybody just go there?" All kinds of new and auspicious images came up, and the summer vacation of night school was imminent.

"Well, do you feel like visiting me there and see for yourself? That would be fab, I'll find a place for you somehow."

Frank knew that the rest of my stash of cash had shrunk from learning to meditate and that I was short—or, more accurately, I was as poor as a church mouse. "You could camp around there; that wouldn't cost you anything. Yes, that's what we'll do!" I could see him warm up to the idea.

And I did too.

Yes, I did want to meet the great Master. But I didn't want

to drive those 500 kilometers on my motorbike since I wasn't feeling as strong as usual. Never yet in my entire life had I worried about me physical strength; it had, of course, always been reliably there. But in recent times energy and strength had gradually diminished. After my decision to go vegetarian, I only ate the white bread from my parents' kitchen, potatoes for lunch, and, occasionally some vegetables. Even as a child I wasn't crazy about milk and cheese, and so I only had the side-dishes. I was always hungry!

And so, I hitchhiked to Luzern a couple of weeks later, loaded down with a big backpack and then, relaxed, leaned on the railing of the white cruise liner that was crossing the big blue Lake Lucerne. And then from Treib, I took the cogwheel railway up to Seelisberg. Finally, I stood in front of the luxurious building that Frank had already shown me on a postcard. I stood in awe. It really was the most beautiful place I'd seen. The hotel was an old, magnificent building with high ceilings, and whose big windows looked onto the Lake Lucerne far below. On the opposite side, a massive rock, shaped like a pyramid, rose from the gigantic mountain range that surrounded the lake. It glowed orange-golden in the evening light.

I kept going. In my backpack, I had a small tent and a sleeping bag, and so I camped in the wild by the 'Seeli' ("small lake" in the local Swiss dialect) a bit lower down. In full measure, I basked in my marvelously free and uninhibited life of a drifter, swam in the clear water of the mountain lake, and for tea. dried wild peppermint on the lines of my tent.

Frank, like an old friend, took me under his wing. In exchange for two hours of work per day in the kitchen with him, he provided me with two hot meals and led me directly

The former Grandhotel Sonnenberg, Seelisberg, Switzerland
where Maharishi founded the Maharishi European Research
University (MERU) and lived there with his international
staff from 1972 to 1983

into a fairy tale land. In the dining hall, my eyes teared up.
For the first time, I experienced how various and delicious
vegetarian cuisine could be. I didn't even know the names of
most of the dishes piled high. Never yet had I seen avocados,
zucchinis, broccoli, or artichokes; or eaten kiwis, persim-
mons, fresh pineapple, pine nuts, or Brazil nuts. I got to know
new milk products such as cottage cheese and creamy fresh
Swiss yoghurt. And everything was tempting with its
abundance. Of course, I wanted to take away many new suggestions. All this was unthinkable at home, where only the
most inexpensive things were bought. And I blossomed. After
a few days, I felt physically strengthened in unbelievable ways,
and only now it became clear to me why I'd been so weak
before—my body had suffered from the malnutrition imposed
by my ignorance.

Of course, I wanted to meet the man with whom I'd been connected since childhood in unfathomable ways: the wise man, who allegedly lived in this hotel with its many rooms and hallways—the Maharishi who had so much knowledge and who was the source of this meditation that I'd begun to practice recently. As a young man, he had not only completed his degree in physics in Allahabad, in addition, he had also lived in the presence of his Master, Guru Dev, Bhagavan Swami Brahmananda Saraswati, and had served him, a man who was held to be the embodiment of Vedic wisdom.

Dr. Rajendra Prasad, the President of India, at the feet of Guru Dev. Subtitle of the newspaper article: "Dr. Rajendra Prasad, the President of India, enjoys the divine splendor of the lighthouse from the Himalayas".

Afterwards, Maharishi had lived for two years completely withdrawn in the caves of the *Valley of the Saints* near Uttar Kashi, high in the Himalayas, where Guru Dev had spent his apprenticeship with his own Master. In this deep and withdrawn silence in the highest mountains of the world, he finally received again and again the impulse to go to the south of India. And so, he just left without any money in his pocket, with profound trust in divine guidance, and out of this nothingness, he'd created a world-wide movement and all that was before me. Impressive—and soon I would meet him personally!

"Every night," Frank told me, "There are lectures in the big hall. Normally you need a course I.D., but if you use the back door, you can just come in."

Full of anticipation and very quietly I sneaked into the last row in the back. But Maharishi could only be seen on a big TV screen, and he spoke only in English. I didn't understand much of it—my knowledge of languages, I had to admit to myself, was not exactly great. I stayed anyway. At the end of the seminar, someone started a tape recorder and two velvety and evenly flowing deep men's voices filled the room, and, like everyone else, I listened with closed eyes. These thousand-year-old *Sama Vedas* drew my awareness deeply within. I was wide awake, and, at the same time, I sat in unbelievable peace, like an especially good meditation. I never wanted to open my eyes again. But then, someone gently touched my shoulder. It was the course leader. "What are you doing here? And how did you get in?"

Naturally, he'd noticed me: I was not wearing a suit and tie like his course participants and, on top of that, I had thick, shoulder-length curls, while every other guy here wore his hair cut short. The course leader had unbelievably bright eyes, was nice to me, and explained to me, the newcomer, that course participants had to be properly registered. Then he took the time to tell me a little about the content and aims of the four-week course that he was leading as preparation for future TM teachers.

I immediately took advantage of this opportunity: "Is Maharishi in the building? And can I see him?"

"Yes he is. But he's meeting in another room with scientists and the government representatives of various countries, and unfortunately, you can't go there."

The meeting hall of MERU in Seelisberg, Switzerland. Here Maharishi held major conferences with scientists from various disciplines, government officials, and educators to solve contemporary problems through the development of consciousness.

We talked for a while like old friends, including about my education and plans. I also learned from him that I could earn my education as a TM teacher through a work-study program. In any case, he added that I should first finish my vocational training and my degree in my night school.

Pleased with all I'd experienced and seen in these last four or five days, I knew I wanted this quality of life. I wanted to be here when I was done with school.

On the same evening, I got a big downer. Frank knew

that I—if I wanted to participate in such a program—would have to cut my glorious curls because Maharishi wanted TM teachers to look neat. Well, that did it for me! No way! And so my rosy future that was about to pass before my inner eyes was pushed far away.

But it was working within me.

The Chasm

A few months later, I had my high school diploma in my pocket. And it was even pretty good because transcending regularly in meditation had also had a good effect on my efforts at night school. Clearly, I could concentrate better than I'd been able to in the months before, and, within a short time I could also understand and retain the information better. Whereas at the beginning of night school, I'd found all my subjects relatively boring and I did only what was necessary to get the diploma, I now found the content of my courses significantly more interesting. And I could see connections between them that had been hidden before.

My good results gave wings to my father to fly higher. I should finish my *Abitur*. "Abitur" is the name of the German high school graduation diploma. It takes thirteen years to complete and it is required for admittance to any university.) It is necessary to become a doctor or a lawyer. My father gave it his all. In the few hours of his free time, he spoke to the administration of several different schools, spoke well of me everywhere, emphasized my obvious successes, got me registered at the College of Koblenz, and even saw to it that I got money through the "Federal Education and Training Assistance Act."

Meanwhile, I went to weekend courses—in meditation. In a remote house in the woods, we did group meditations—not just twice a day, as usual, but several times daily. That was my life!

During this time, not only did my inner experiences become deeper, but the qualities of my heart began to unfold: I began to revere Maharishi more and more and felt great admiration for him. Who was this extraordinary man who'd come from India? When the diving into the depths of our consciousness was so sublime and delightful, even for us small "lights" out here in Westerwald as we could fathom more and more of what lay within and all around us, what enormous vastness of consciousness must be his, a man who'd been meditating for decades? A man who'd spent many years in the sacred presence of his Master, Guru Dev, whose unlimited consciousness Maharishi had imbibed. Guru Dev, who, in turn, had withdrawn, alone for many decades, into the impenetrable forests of India and there had lost himself within his own silence. Only in his later years had he—though reluctant in the face of years of pleading with him—agreed to take over the empty position of Shankaracharya, the spiritual head of Jyotir Math in the north of India—a position that had been empty for 150 years. This highly respected position had been empty so long because in one and a half centuries no one could be found who was worthy of the responsibilities that attend the spiritual guidance of humanity. And now his number one disciple, Maharishi, had gone into the world and had settled, of all places, in our neighboring country of Switzerland.

In the delightful experiences of these weekends, the tender, almost bashful wish to experience Maharishi for myself surfaced. And I felt a longing grow to be one of those who Maharishi knew personally.

Often on these weekends, there were newbies who learned to meditate in the forest house. I found it extraordinary how changed the TM teachers looked after giving personal instructions. In the meantime, I'd gotten to know their little problems and personal uniqueness. But when they came from the door of the initiation room, they seemed to shine, every one of them. Not only did their eyes shine, but even through their skin a hidden light seemed to shimmer. In what other profession could you open the door to happiness and joy of life to others, while you, yourself, are given so much for your own development?

But at home things became more and more constrained. I didn't want, or even could, simply sit at the family table and eat side dishes. No. At least I occasionally wanted to prepare my own food in our small kitchen. But that was too much! My mother, whose big heart was full of love for everything and everyone, would certainly have found a way to be fine with this. As open and understanding as she was, she would have loved to learn to meditate in the first months, had my father not suppressed this desire so vehemently.

My father, on the other hand, lost his cool more and more over my excesses. Soon the once beloved son was just "the yogi," who, through being "different," insistently rattled the underlying assumptions of all his values and views on life. And he was so hurt that he was often resentful. And, for the first time, a deep and insurmountable chasm that hurt us both opened between me and my father, with whom I'd always felt close—a chasm that in this current state we could not bridge over.

This catastrophe had been predestined. I wanted out. I could and would no longer live like this. Most likely, the dice had fallen already. At some point, I confided in my parents that I no longer wanted the Abitur or the life plan that they'd designed for me with all good intentions. I wanted to be with Maharishi and become a TM teacher. At the very least,

I planned to go there for a year to see if I liked it there and if it was the right path for me.

My parents were devastated and frightened; they feared for my future. And I am sure, especially about my father, that back then his world was destroyed.

II.

NEAR THE MASTER

Outside is the joy of a drop of water
Inside is the joy of the ocean.
In the inner core of one's own personality
Is the ocean of joy,
The ocean of wisdom,
The ocean of creativity,
The ocean of peace.

Maharishi Mahesh Yogi

First Time

I was ready. My glorious locks had fallen. Jochen and Frank put the phone number of the coordination office into my hand. "If you want to go there, you have to call them. Maharishi is currently in France."

I only had a single DM coin with me, and dialed the number from the phone booth in the Limburg train station. I asked bluntly, "Do you need any more staff?"

I heard only, "Yes, but you have to bring a letter of recommendation from your local TM teacher." Then it went "click" and the connection was broken.

But that was enough for me. Next day I packed my suitcase, said good-bye to several friends, hugged my parents, and gave both my big and my little brother a last kiss on the cheek. A new life was beginning.

The summer sun shone auspiciously into the windows of the high-speed train. My destination: the winter sports resort of Courchevel, where the TM movement had rented several hotels that normally stood empty during the summer. To save on costs, the TM organization managed these hotels by itself. In Courchevel, they ran six-month advanced courses for experienced TM teachers; that's pretty much all I knew.

Frank had told me that there was a hotel for men only, in which you could meditate especially well. Obviously, I wanted to get into that very hotel more than anything else. But when I got to the coordination office in the first hotel, somebody put me in a totally different one. A hotel worker from that place came to get me in with a car. Well, that didn't go too well! After driving further and further up in the mountains, my driver put me into a bright state of ecstasy:

"Man, are you ever in luck. Do you know that I'm taking you to Annapurna, the hotel where Maharishi is staying, and it's the most beautiful hotel in the entire city?" Halleluiah. My fate loved me. Would I soon get to see Maharishi?

When we got there, we seemed almost to touch the heavens. The long, four-star hotel with its wooden façade with elaborate carvings and countless balconies was located on a plateau with an elevation of 1,850 meters. On the ground floor, picture windows went all the way around to expose a view of the impressive panorama of the surrounding mountains.

In the elegant wood-paneled lobby, I waited a bit later in front of the hotel elevator to ride to the staff room assigned to me. Sweating, my clothes wrinkled, and worn-out from the long journey, I stood there. From the other side of the lobby a bunch of people came towards me—I was stunned and could hardly believe it—Maharishi came directly towards me. He looked exactly like the pictures I'd see of him. A small man in a white, floor-length Indian gown, and with long hair, a full beard, and big peaceful eyes. And he had an aura of great dignity and authority. Exactly one meter away, he stood still. He didn't say anything, just looked at me, and took me within himself. I was still and looked back at him. I can't say if his eyes rested on me for one or four minutes. I felt his loving, but at the same time, stern attention; he had the effect of an incorruptible observer. I had the feeling that he could see the depths of my soul and penetrate every cell with his gaze. I felt the breath of omniscience and I knew, "You can't keep any secrets from this man; he knows everything about you." Even so, I did not feel appraised or judged, but just accepted as I was. And he liked what he saw. At the end, he smiled almost impalpably, and I felt: "Now he has accepted me as his pupil." The elevator came, opened, and I saw the small yet great man for whom I'd waited for so long vanish along with his close co-workers. When I got to my room, I just had to just sit down.

A little later, the hotel director took me to the kitchen where, in the presence of the chef, he directed me to wash the pots. And he had a special reward for me. As a co-worker in the house, I could attend Maharishi's lectures and discussions in my free time. Great! And with all that, I now participated in a work-study program and could work for course credits in this wonderful environment that I could later use for a variety of TM training courses. I had reached the goal of my dreams!

At twenty years old, I was small and delicate. The work was brutal. But the meditations were wonderful—at least when I got to meditate; not used to the physically demanding labor, I was often so exhausted that I'd doze off in meditation. The body demanded its rights. Not infrequently I slept through the time, until I woke to the impatient banging on my door pulled me out of the depths, and the loud, rough voice of the Australian chef blustered at my door, "Lothar, come on, you gotta wash pots."

The gigantic, stainless steel pots had to be scrubbed vigorously. The rubber gloves that were supposed to make my life easier and protect my busy hands all too often had holes due to the forks that were in with the dish water so that the boiling hot water got into the gloves. My hands were often as red as lobsters.

But, once again, my fate was merciful. After only ten days I was promoted to dishwasher! Someone, apparently, had had an insight about my short stature and my not exactly packed upper arms. To clean salad greens and wash dishes three times a day every day for 250 people was still exhausting work, but now I at least had machines to help me.

Daily I was rewarded because I was allowed into the gigantic and flower-decorated lecture room for two to three hours. There Maharishi sat on a stage so that everyone could see him clearly. He sat cross-legged on the traditional deer skin on a sofa covered with a white sheet.

Maharishi's radiance was just unbelievable. It was bright, and sometimes I could see that he was surrounded by a silvery light. He was full of love, power, and a great sense of humor. While explaining or commenting on something to his audience, he often made brilliant word plays and then laughed full-throated. Many in the audience laughed with him. Sometimes it was like a joyful choir, sometimes the sparkling silvery laughter of the women exploded into the air, supported by the deep bass of happy men. It wasn't just his joyfulness that seemed catching, but in his presence, I felt light and unburdened.

Of course, I had no clue about the unwritten rules and customs in his presence—at least not yet.

One afternoon Maharishi had a meeting with some generals and the head of the Swedish Air Force, who'd had his pilots instructed in TM. Of course, these gentlemen sat in the first row in front of the platform, where the guests of honor always sat to speak directly with Maharishi. I listened as the head of the Air Force reported enthusiastically on the successes with TM. I learned for the first time that many years ago eighty percent of the fighter pilots who'd been trained nevertheless quit their jobs after a short time. This was because their deep-seated fears that in everyday life were never visible now came to the surface and made flying impossible. Obviously, the Swedish government was throwing tons of money out the window and was looking for help. So a scientist developed a sophisticated psychological test that revealed these subconscious fears in aspiring pilots even before their training. Evidently this test was effective because 30 years after its use, there was not a single pilot who was ill-suited for duty.

But this only partially solved the problems of the Swedish Air Force because fighter pilots, due to the extreme stress they had to endure in their work, could only do their job for a few years. After that they could only do ground duty. And it didn't matter what they did, what psychological methods they used to help them deal with their fears, nothing helped. Because of the high costs of training the pilots these problems still led to great economic loss for the government. How the head of the Air Force got the idea to try TM was beyond me, but he did it. With the dozen or so pilots who now meditated regularly within the framework of their duties, the diagnoses, using the same tests, showed such a reduction of deep-rooted fears that these pilots could be re-deployed for duty. [5] No other method in the world, not even years of psychotherapy had yet been able to achieve such results. That had never yet happened in the entire history of the Air Force and it saved the Swedish government a lot of money.

When these dignitaries finally said their good-byes, and left their chairs empty, I used the rare opportunity. I got up from my place and surreptitiously sat down in the first row and directly in front of Maharishi. Some people were grinning, but I didn't know why. Time flew by. Someone tapped me on the shoulder and asked me to turn around. About fifteen rows behind me the chef was waiting and brought me back to reality.

People grinned even more—including Maharishi.

My first buddy in the hotel was Maharishi's personal chef, a small, skinny Indian, who always sang or smiled as he was doing his work. Rarely have I met a person so radiant with happiness. On our days off we would go out into nature together and climb up the French Alps. He hardly knew any English, but we understood one another very well. Beaming at each other or nodding and smiling from time to time we just enjoyed our silent company and the breath-taking beauty of nature. We couldn't talk to one another, and we didn't need to.

After only two more weeks, I got another "promotion." I became the night watchman! Now I was responsible for security and during the night I had to walk around the hotel with a flashlight every two hours to make sure everything was okay. The rest of the time, I had to sit at the elegant telephone switchboard in the lobby, which was paneled with light cherry wood and equipped with brass spotlights, and where, as was customary back then, each room had its own connection. Well, it sure was a peaceful job and I was all for it.

Right on my first shift the phone rang in the middle of the night around 2:00 a.m. Who could that be so late? To my great surprise, I heard the voice I'd come to know so well. Maharishi said into my ear, "Can you please connect me to this number in America?"

Oh, man, my English! I had crammed it at the night school, but it evidently was not good enough. I gave it my best. When I had the number written down after repeated questions from my side and the most patient master teacher on the other side, I got all my courage together and asked carefully, "What is 'connect'?"

It was beyond comprehension and surreal. Full of love and angelic patience, Maharishi the saint, Maharishi who was worshipped by everyone, explained to me, the small and insignificant light in this hotel and linguistically challenged night watchman, how to operate the telephone switchboard and how to connect the individual plugs.

From then on, I joyfully anticipated every shift because Maharishi often worked through the night with international calls, and I, naturally, could make the connections easily after a short time. Every time I was excited again when I could see because of the room number that lit up on the switchboard that Maharishi would now ask me to connect him—and I loved doing it.

Bigger Responsibilities

"Lothar, we're moving to Switzerland today!"

On a clear, sunny fall morning, the manager of the Hotel Annapurna knocked at my door. "Please pack your suitcase, Lothar. Be ready with it in one hour and be at the entrance, where all of us will meet."

Well, I didn't have that much to pack, and I was ready on time. At the entrance to the hotel, several busses were already waiting to take the course participants and the working staff to their new destination. Spontaneity ruled the day; it felt alive and I loved it. It suited the adventurer within me.

In 1976, Maharishi held huge courses with thousands of people from all over the world who came up with the course fee to stay six months to further their spiritual growth with experience in deep meditation. To make it equally comfortable for everyone and to make it as economically feasible as possible, the organization rented the winter sports hotels that stood empty during the summers back then. In winter, for that same reason, we went to awesomely beautiful spots for summer vacationers. No matter where we went, the surroundings and nature all around us were always dreamlike; until this day, I still love the Swiss mountains and lakes.

Now the staff had to help prepare for the opening of various hotels around Lake Lucerne. After arriving in Weggis, we learned that at least fifteen hotels around the lake had been rented for the winter and that the course participants from France would shortly move into these hotels. I was surprised with a special assignment. All by myself, I had to prepare Hotel Hertenstein for the opening! The six-storied complex, all covered in white stucco, was located on the peninsula Hertenstein that reached out into the lake. A park full of trees and a lawn for sunbathing went down right to the water where boats still bobbed up and down.

I grew into these big shoes surprisingly well. The owner of the hotel was a very pleasant and nice man who liked me. We spent several days together to take inventory of all the facilities as well as noting and documenting any damages in the elegantly appointed rooms before he let me take control of the place—he a wealthy and experienced hotel owner, and me, a green boy. I grabbed the big chance to develop my abilities in this domain; I was given enormous responsibilities and wanted to be worthy of them.

I placed the first order for groceries and got the storeroom ready. What sort of course would be moving in? That would reveal itself soon enough. In the meantime, I trained myself with stoic ease in every situation, a super-training for my life to come!

One late afternoon three busses arrived, and—oh how great—they were the residents of the Hotel Annapurna, with whom I'd already lived in the months before. And, a little later—oh how even greater—Maharishi also moved in. What colossal and outrageously good luck I had again!

I was responsible for all purchases for the hotel and, as time permitted, also worked with reception. Meanwhile, I was familiar with the routines of Maharishi and his co-workers, and felt like a super lively fish in water and had the feeling that I'd gotten a big, new family.

Time flew by; every day I learned highly interesting new things. The people in Maharishi's surroundings were fascinating. They radiated light and seemed to be very happy—as was I.

I also got some insight into Maharishi's work and got

a feeling for the magnitude of his world-wide movement. New and very interesting guests came regularly. The national leaders of his global organization reported on the successes in their countries; they shared experiences and Maharishi inspired them with his knowledge, new courses, and projects.

Professors of physics, mathematics, chemistry, and biology worked with Maharishi on new courses that were all documented with professional TV cameras and video recorders. Maharishi gave interviews on TV and for the press. International symposia were prepared and held in the areas of education and rehabilitation.

Now and then, Maharishi flew somewhere by helicopter. As soon as the sound of the helicopter became audible, all co-workers knew that they'd now have a chance to see Maharishi because he always walked from the nearby landing strip. So we let everything just lie and rushed towards him. The loving gazes of his closest disciples and Maharishi's response created a special atmosphere. Often, he took the time and looked lovingly into each person's eyes. He took note of each one of us, and everyone felt blessed. My heart beat louder every time I heard the approach of the helicopter.

In this environment, where so many people enlivened their connection to the realm of inner knowledge, my intuition became markedly clearer, just as it did for the other meditators here. In today's daily life, access to this realm is buried for most people, though it sometimes surfaces in especially happy moments or in crisis situations, only to vanish into obscurity. But here we experienced wondrous "coincidences" or precognitions almost daily.

"Oh, what a beautiful carnation," it sprang into my eyes on one of my walks along the lake. I just had to buy it, but not for myself. Its petals were finely chiseled and gently curled. It was suffused with a silver light, and I knew right away: "You'll give this flower to Maharishi." I bought it. But one day followed another, and no opportunity to do so presented itself. I trimmed it, and cared for it with fresh water every day and took joy in the glowing, deep rose color of the petals. One night, while I had been sleeping deeply, I woke around 2:00 a.m. and had the impulse to get up right away, to freshen myself and dress properly. I got ready, slipped into my best suit and, as I was leaving the room, took the carnation with me. Then I went through the deeply sleeping hotel to the entrance—and at this precise moment, Maharishi arrived by himself with just his driver. I opened the heavy, big glass door of the hotel entrance, and we beamed at one another. "Oh, so late, and still up?" And he took my carnation.

How great, how unbelievably great to have him here just for myself! I'd anticipated this! My heart skipped a beat with joy.

When I wanted to get the elevator for him, he smiled, "No, no, not we don't want to wake anyone this time of night!"

How gentle his voice was, how much he loved his pupils, and how considerate he was…I accompanied him; silently and in shared harmony that required no words, we went up the stairs step-by-step and to his room. I even went in with him for a short moment, then put my hands together in front of my chest and said, "Jai Guru Dev." With this greeting Maharishi regularly thanked his Master for the knowledge he had given him, and we all did it too. I bowed slightly and so silently bid him good night.

I went with a feeling of immense gratitude and with a light and dancing heart.

The Blessing of Maharishi

Since the founding of his movement in 1957 at the Indian Madras[3], Maharishi spent the first seven days of every year in silence. He *went into silence*, as we called it, and stayed alone in his room, didn't speak or eat, and nobody disturbed him during those days. For the rest of the year he was indefatigable, and, without a single day off, he was there for others and for the whole world. He slept at most two to four hours and held one conference or meeting after another, while, at the same time, working on innumerable projects with his disciples; or he was on the phone with people from all over the world, even at night. He kept three shifts of secretaries on the go continuously, young men in their prime, who helped him with his efforts; nobody could come even close to keeping pace with his energy and his countless activities. He gave of himself and his energy without end—but this one week every year belonged to him alone.

All course participants who meditated here in Switzerland in those more than twenty hotels used the precious opportunity of this carefully planned week of silence to join him. In our hotel at that time, there were about 120 people that belonged to his inner circle of co-workers. They too remained in their rooms for those seven days and went into silence with this spiritual technique from the Himalayas, which had stood the test of time for thousands of years. Only three times a day, they came into the dining-hall and drank fresh juices. All world religions and traditions recognize the healing power of fasting and of silence to deepen the connection between the

---

[3] Chennai

individual and the Divine. But what I was fortunate to experience here went beyond anything I could have imagined.

It was so far beyond all words, so deep, so boundless, that our human mind cannot grasp it. A silence, unbelievably gentle, descended upon the entire hotel, a silence so deep that it condensed into a field that was palpable and felt like cotton wool. Never in my entire life had I experienced such concentrated quietness and energy as in that silent time. Even the walls vibrated with joy. And it became clear to me what Maharishi meant when he spoke of the power of silence. It wasn't just rhetoric—the power of silence is a lively level of life and a concrete experience.

The doors of my perception opened. In supreme clarity, I experienced all-pervasive Being. I was overwhelmed by this silence that inspired reverence; it was something I had only experienced in my deepest meditations. I felt a powerful, yet at the same time, a gentle stillness and unboundedness. This force field of infinite energy that I'd never known, penetrated the armchairs, the walls, the carpets, and the air with its powerful silence. Eternity and peace touched me and my environment; it was a heavenly silence. I was at home; my heart sang.

And I made juice.

I was one of the few who, in those days of silence, still did physical work. The kitchen was closed and instead, I ordered and received trucks full of purple and green grapes. Directly under Maharishi's room, I made liter after liter of fresh and delicious grape juice that I served three times a day to everyone in the dining hall. The only loud sound was the big machine that cut through the silence with its droning. But even this could not disturb the silence. I made more than a thousand liters in those days for all those who so enlivened this field, this web woven of consciousness that I could see and feel even while working. My soul blossomed and I bathed in the waves of eternity.

As he did every year, after those seven days—at midnight on the 7th of January—Maharishi ended his silence in his room. That week was the highpoint for many of us because he let us partake of it; any of us who wanted to dive into his deep silence, and all of us wanted it—those 120 people in our hotel and the 300 who in neighboring hotels had come for their six months' course—were part of the shared silence. They'd already been waiting patiently on the street for Maharishi to *come out of silence*, wrapped in their heavy parkas and their woolen caps.

My legendary good luck was with me once again. I was permitted as one of the first in a group of about 30 to step quietly into Maharishi's room. Every fifteen minutes a new group was allowed in. Maharishi saw all of us until the early hours of the morning.

Somebody would open the door from the inside. You could only hear the muted sound of socks against the carpeting; and everyone sat down on the floor cross-legged. The light in Maharishi's room was so dim that my eyes took a while to make out his silhouette on the sofa.

How to express the inexpressible in words? How to even just suggest the awe-inspiring greatness that we saw here? The cumulative power of silence in this room was unimaginable. We knew that Maharishi's silence was so deep that he'd need two or three days for his expanded consciousness to take possession once again of his human body and his metabolism to be as active as before. Whispering, some of us expressed their joy that they were so privileged to be here and thanked him for all he did for humanity—and he answered lovingly, softly, and extremely slowly. He was still so far away, only coming back slowly to this gross and dense world.

We felt the unboundedness and the holiness of this man, who had come to us from India, from the country where great masters held inwardness to be more important than the outside world. A friend had previously explained to me that through this deep silence the consciousness of the world would be cleansed—and we partook of it up close and personally.

In this hotel room, at the feet of my Master, I got a hint of all this and felt the extent of his great consciousness that he radiated upon all of us. I was deeply moved.

All of us felt the boundless, selfless, and universal love that he had brought back from those realms he had visited. And so there we sat, reverend and silent, taking it all in with gratitude and devotion. And he enveloped us, each one of us, and fulfilled our wide-open souls—the blessing of Maharishi.

More and More

My work assignment at the Hotel Hertenstein bore fruit. The bosses seemed satisfied with my work and now asked me to visit all the hotels that the organization had rented in Switzerland and to train and guide their respective buyers on site. What an honorable and, at the same time, wonderful assignment! I traveled through magnificent Switzerland to the most beautiful vacation destinations and only had to deal with relaxed and nice people. In every hotel I spent a few days, trained co-workers, and then off I went to the next one. Now and then I saw Maharishi from a distance as he visited the course participants in the different hotels.

All course locations were meanwhile covered with a clean, white, and shining blanket of snow. I reached the Park Hotel Vitznau that looked like a modern fairy tale castle with tall, arched windows and its white, decorated façade, right next to the water of Lake Lucerne—one of the three best hotels of Switzerland.

Soon after my arrival, I quietly snuck through the door of the seminar hall, whose big windows provided a dream-like view of the water of the big lake and the surrounding mountains rising high above it. Maharishi was just meeting with his close co-workers. Oh dear, I had entered just from the side! All eyes were on me, except Maharishi's who sat to the left of me on a sofa—I stood there in my corner, quiet as a mouse.

"Lothar can do it!" It was Don's* voice, Maharishi's closest secretary. Maharishi turned his head to the door where I stood, looked at me briefly and repeated, "Yes, Lothar can do it.

I was in seventh heaven! He had addressed me by name! All the same, I didn't have not the slightest clue what this was all about and I was as curious as a cat. Only after Maharishi had left the hall, I learned about my unexpected assignment: the extremely valuable collection of videos with recitations of the Vedas was to be safely taken to a new destination. And this was about the most likely only collection of its kind world-wide until now. More than twenty years later, the Vedic recitations were declared by UNESCO to be a "masterpiece of an orally transmitted cultural heritage of the world." Already in 1976, the best Vedic scholars and pundits had recited the entire Vedas according to Maharishi's wishes, and these had been recorded on video. The Vedas are thousands-of-years-old recitations of enlightened seers who cognized in their own refined consciousness the primordial sounds of creation. Since those times of advanced Vedic culture, these sounds were transmitted from master to disciple. And traditionally, they were not just read but instead were recited in an established sequence of sounds with a well-defined rhythm. In this, the exact pronunciation is most important. From early childhood on, various pundits learn specific parts of the Vedas that—when recited appropriately—have the effect of expanding the consciousness of the listener. It was exactly this which I had experienced myself on my very first visit to Seelisberg as listener of the Sama Veda that drew me into a deep, meditative silence. These videos were a special treasure because they represented around 2,000 hours of recordings sung by the very best pundits of India, who Maharishi had personally chosen and won over to the project. So, it is understandable that this valuable collection had to be guarded most carefully.

What unbelievable proof of trust in me, a young guy, who had to organize and protect that move. Of course, it was also a drudgery. So, I had those fifteen heavy steel boxes, closed tight with steel bands and big locks, each one numbered and three times as big as a suitcase lifted into cars and then loaded onto the alpine railway. The last part of the way went via bulldozer through the snow to the hotel in Melchsee-Frutt, where I would finally hand over the steel boxes with its valuable videos unharmed.

But it did not happen as fast as I believed it would. After those monsters had been stowed away safely in the basement room set aside for them, it turned out that the lock on the door was broken. Now what? There and then, the ladies, who were living in this hotel and had been entrusted to lead courses and deal with administrative duties, put down a mattress in the room in which—right next to my monstrous companions made of steel sheets—I served for two days and nights as a living alarm system. Well then, I slept in the basement on a mattress on the floor; I didn't care, my tent next to Seeli had not been any less comfortable.

This whole time I felt a kind of loving attention around me: the special blessings of Maharishi. It was a feeling of benevolence, a velvety protection that accompanied me, even when the Master was not physically present. Later, I spoke about that with some of his closest co-workers. They were all familiar with this. So here I lay stretched out on the mattress on the floor hurriedly thrown on the floor in this storeroom and slept. That is, my body slept; I heard it breathe softly and evenly, interrupted now and then by a couple of snores. My consciousness was awake, crystal clear, and rested in silence without thoughts and was one with the expanse of the universe almost for the whole night.

When the door had been repaired, I continued to do my tours through the many hotels, I schooled the purchasers on site with great zeal. Finally, I got to Arosa, a dreamy spot in eastern Switzerland high up in the Alps. The last one of about five hotels that I visited there was situated above the town, directly in the sparkling mountains covered with snow. The Hotel Prätschli was a huge, angular complex; on both sides of the entrance hall, visitors were greeted by gigantic and dark pine trees. The view of Lake Obersee of Arosa, deeply covered with snow, the panorama of the mountains, and the silence all around were breathtaking. I liked it immensely. "Here, I'd love to become the hotel manager!" was a thought that popped up, to my own surprise.

As soon as I got close to the entrance, a tall man in a blue suit and a red tie came towards me—the creases in his pants were flawless. He was the hotel manager, and he'd been expecting me. In English, with a strong Dutch accent, he confided in me shortly afterwards: "I would like to take the TM teacher training course, and I'm looking for a successor, a new hotel manager. I've already discussed this with the co-ordinator of all the other employees. He's on board with it. I just have to find a good replacement."

Here, apparently, an invisible hand was at work.

I got the job.

Maharishi 1974 in the mountains above Arosa, Switzerland

The Visit

"We'd love to visit you. Next week your father will be on vacation, so we can come down to Switzerland and see how you're doing!" My mother's voice was pleasant and loving as always.

So, my parents would show up.

Of course, they'd been worried that whole time because our family doctor had prognosticated that their son would live at most another year if he kept up his vegetarian diet. Now they wanted to see for themselves how I lived here, how I was doing, and see to it that all was well. They also entertained some hope of convincing me to get a "real" job. Naturally, they'd also been missing me. Presumably it was a mixture of all the above.

I'd been at the Prätschli Hotel for several months and loved my work. The course participants who lived under our roof were a special group who, in their experiences of higher states of consciousness, were exceptionally advanced. The entire hotel was filled with a subtle yet powerful energy that opened new worlds for me.

Maharishi often came by helicopter and I had the honorable assignment to prepare his room and to clean it again when he traveled to other courses. When he was in the hotel, I often saw him come out of the lecture hall with measured steps and go to the elevator. Every time this was a sublime vision for me, as an incredible dignity radiated from him. Once, when he was going through the hallway to the elevator, a short distance from me, there was an aura of bright silver light all around his whole body. Shining brightly, this aura contrasted with the background of the surroundings.

I closed my eyes tightly and then looked again. Yes, it was still there, a penetrating, glistening, bright light, a good meter wide all around his form. It was visible in a completely natural and obvious way, and I was suffused with reverend and gentle bliss. Fascinated and grateful, I realized that the doors of my perception were beginning to open. Many times afterwards, I saw this heavenly aura around Maharishi when he'd come into my view anywhere.

An important part of these courses, designed to deepen experiences, was that the TM teachers from all over the world would share their experiences daily during the hour for the discussion of these often-overwhelming experiences. This was in order to enliven further this ancient world, new to them, that opened before their marveling and blissful eyes. All of us were totally fascinated with this new world of experience that our parents and earlier generations had never been able to experience in this way.

Hungry as we meanwhile were for enlightenment, we were more than ready to glorify India and everything that came from there. Legendary tales from the far-away Himalayas made their rounds: about yogis whose state of consciousness was so highly advanced that they, in a second, completely living body, could instruct their disciples in far-away places, while at the same time, they went about their tasks in their hometowns, clearly visible to everyone. We devoured Yogananda's *The Autobiography of a Yogi* in which the most unbelievable stories about levitation, spiritual healings, clairvoyance, and other unbelievable and miraculous deeds were described in detail. What exciting experiences were suddenly possible in our future!

But Maharishi exhorted us to remain strictly with our

own personal practice. He promoted no infatuation and no mood-making. He instructed us not to believe, but to approach our inner experiences with the clear and scientific understanding of the 20th century because the translation of the word "Veda" is "knowledge."

When he came for his regular visits in the different hotels, the course participants would share their experiences and describe them in the smallest detail. It was inspiring to see how much joy Maharishi took in seeing that his pupils had advanced into new spiritual realms. Not only did his eyes shine, happy that the fire of the Himalayas had lit up people from completely different cultures, East and West. The enthusiasm and the joy of these meetings was indescribable.

Maharishi also brought out why the enlivening of these inner experiences was so important. The silence of the consciousness of the individual, especially when it was intensified through group practice, was transferred to the consciousness of the whole world and relieved it of stress. I had already heard about Carl Gustav Jung, the great student of Sigmund Freud, who had discovered the same eternal truth, the realm of the collective unconscious, in which all of mankind is connected. In the writings of Plato, who transmitted the dialogues of Socrates, I found the same thing expressed in different words: he described the realm of Being which is the basis of everything and which connected everything to everything else. While Socrates and Jung and with them many outstanding philosophers and theoreticians of the Western World only postulated this realm, the rishis had immediate access to experience this realm directly.

Hardly noticeable, Maharishi prepared the ground for a new era in human history with his six-months courses. For us, who were working in these hotels, a magical air of the highest mystery surrounded these courses. Something was happening, something new and thrilling. But how could we surmise that, behind carefully locked doors, something was going on that would soon touch us all?

It was rumored that those course participants who had the clearest inner experiences were gathered in our hotel and therefore, the consciousness that bound us all together was being cleansed intensively through their deep silence.

All the guests in the hotel were older than I was. I showed my best manners and had the feeling that they enjoyed the fact that a twenty-year-old took on such a responsibility. I blossomed and gave it my best. And, by the way, I lost my shyness there, since now and then I had to make announcements in front of the approximately 100 guests in the lecture hall. It all ran like clockwork. Even the representative of the hotel's owner was most happy with me and with the work of the other staff members.

How would my parents react to these things that were so completely unfamiliar to them? Especially my father, who'd had such problems with my behavior back when I left? My father, who'd seen my Maharishi poster as the symbol of everything that scared and shocked him back then, and who tore it off the wall of my hermitage under the roof and shredded it in his impotent desperation?

I didn't worry about my mother with her big heart. She would feel the positively charged atmosphere and would appreciate the shining faces—of that I was certain.

They came by train. I went and got them and my little brother Rainer with a car. Mother and father were eminently pleased to see me so well nourished, beaming, and in such a good position as the boss of thirty co-workers. The course leaders at the Prätschli Hotel and I were on very good terms and so they greeted my family cordially and treated them like special guests and good friends. Even Mr. Ritterstaedt, a retired and licensed engineer, a grey-haired man in his mid-sixties who was the leader of the German TM Movement, took a lot of time with my parents. They were deeply moved—their previous stress and deep disappointment fell away.

And there was something else that was exceptionally lucky for the three of us. In those few days of their visit, there was a summer celebration in another one of the hotels rented by the TM organization, which was attended by about 2,000 course participants. Maharishi came personally by helicopter, and well-known scientists sat on the stage next to him. Swiss alphorn players blew their horns loudly at the beginning of the celebration. There was a whole row of honored guests, among them the famous Canadian magician, Doug Henning, who was not only a course participant but who also took us into a magical wonderland with his performances. A few groups of artists among the course participants presented various and almost professional concerts and read their own poetry, both funny and profound. Maharishi, with his unbelievable sense of humor and surprising word-plays, always made everyone laugh.

So, torn from their village and its completely normal life, my parents and little brother sat there among strangers in the first row reserved for honored guests and directly in front of Maharishi. They were dressed to the nines like everyone else in this classy and expensive hotel—an utterly different environment for them—among my big, new family.

The next morning, I took them to the train station. As we

were saying our good-byes, they delighted in telling stories about the celebration with Maharishi. My short and somewhat rotund mother's eyes shone excitedly as she saw again with her inner eye the events of the previous night. She smiled. And my father, standing on the platform next to the railway tracks, had an unexpected gift ready for me. "Maharishi is really different from what I thought. So normal, full of humor, and intelligent—I'm totally impressed!" And a little later: "Lothar, I'm sorry. I want to ask your forgiveness for raging about him! I see everything differently now; you sure do know what you're doing!"

We hugged one another, the four of us. My mother, the peacemaker who was often too tired and had lately been plagued with headaches, was once again happy. And there he stood, my strong, good-natured but stubborn father, with his gentle face in which his life had begun to carve deep lines and who'd been so skeptical; tears shone in his eyes. He was moved to his bones; the greatness of Maharishi had touched his heart.

When the train disappeared in the distance, a big weight was lifted from my heart.

Disciplinary Transfer

I continued to work as the director of the Prätschli Hotel. I meditated mornings and evenings, had a lot of work to do, and was relaxed and happy—my life was beautiful. Again and again, there were new challenges and unusual assignments that were given to me. Everything was easy here that would have been an extravagant and complicated process in the normal life outside. We didn't have to fill out any application forms, conduct job interviews, or do the same work for years on end. Everything was always in flux and I had the feeling that my evolution, and that of everyone else in this environment, went at express train speed.

Nowhere else would I have gained knowledge and experience in so many different and often taxing activities. How could I have guessed that all that I was learning in Maharishi's presence would later be so useful? I didn't think about any of that. Here and now, it was just plain fun, and it enlivened me from the top of my head to the bottoms of my feet.

Meanwhile, I took a two-week course that the coordinators had organized for all hotel managers. When I came back, rejoicing to be allowed to work in my beloved Prätschli Hotel again, I got a big shock. During my absence, half of my co-workers had been taken away. It was preposterous. How could I go on leading this huge hotel complex in an orderly fashion with the fifteen people who were left? How could I see to it that everything was kept clean, that food for almost 100 people was ordered, unloaded, cooked and served, and that the various management and coordination tasks were synchronized and successful? All that was too much for me who had basked in the approving recognition of the representative of the hotel's owner and kept the house in great shape with the help of my "staffies," as I called them lovingly.

In the lofty heights of the Swiss Alps above Arosa on a walk with Maharishi's singing cook, with whom I communicated without words

Even though I had been in seventh heaven that whole time, I now became really upset and even angry. I grabbed the phone and complained—in a friendly way, as is my nature: "Where are my people?"

"They were needed elsewhere!"

Decisive, as is my nature also, I said, "Then I must insist I get them back, otherwise I will no longer take the responsibility for this hotel!"

The reaction was immediate: "Then we shall find someone else!"

Everything moved really fast, for sure. And the power of evolution carried me on its wings. But I felt nothing of that; instead I grieved for having to leave my Prätschli and learned the high art of letting go quite reluctantly.

A day later I was given a disciplinary transfer; at least, that's how it felt to me. The hotel I now came to was only half as big, was closer to the city, and was less demanding in terms of its standards. I now had to take care of about fifty people—with a team of only three co-workers! And to top it off, right after my arrival, I learned that this was the cook's day off and that, to fill in for him once a week, the manager of the hotel had to do the cooking. In other words, me. I was pretty good as a hotel manager, but as a cook, I was a total flake. With courage, I explored the kitchen supplies—the course participants were meditating—and I decided on a mixed vegetable soup. I was even ignorant of the fact that carrots had to cook longer than zucchini to be done at the same time. In the dining hall, the course participants waited for their food at the usual time—they were extremely patient. Fifteen minutes later, they sensed that something wasn't right. The first ones peeked into the kitchen, and taking pity on me, they lovingly came to my assistance. The food tasted somewhat acceptable. That was my debut!

Here, a joyful group of carefree individualists had come together. Some of them took a bit of getting used to, but each one of them was lovable in their own way. For example, there was the American bagpipe player, who spent every free minute—except for meditation time—putting the whole house into swing mode. Others felt really at home for the six-month course. They rearranged the furniture in their rooms and even dragged them into the hallway to make more space for their yoga exercises. Like my friends at the Prätschli, they had scraped together their savings and arranged for an unpaid vacation to attend this special course to deepen their experiences. They, too, were inspired by meditation but they took life lightly, sometimes too lightly.

To intensify the experiences of the course participants, Maharishi had carefully designed a special "rounding program;" several meditations alternating with breathing and yoga exercises, as well as rest periods. He knew that when many people together did the same spiritual practice within themselves this would foster the effect of coherence. The nervous system would rest because of early bed-times so that more subtle levels could open. Just before the especially early bed-time, the course participants would listen to Sama Veda to expand consciousness through these Vedic sounds on the one hand, and on the other, these relaxing sounds would prepare them for deep and restful sleep. After that, everyone went quietly to bed.

In these courses, everything went according to a set routine. Times to eat and to sleep were fixed, as were short walks after the mid-day meal. The TM teachers in the

Prätschli Hotel had been very focused: during meditation times and at night, the entire hotel was as quiet as a mouse. They'd held tightly to regulations to get the utmost benefit out of these precious six months.

My non-conformists in the new hotel followed the routines most of the time. However, often they couldn't tear themselves away from the exciting conversations during afternoon tea times to vanish into their rooms for the afternoon meditation. Punctuality for the evening lectures was not a thing for them. Or, after listening to the evening Sama Veda in exemplary fashion, some of them gathered afterwards in joyful rounds of discussions. Now and then, I even found some of them in the kitchen in the middle of the night, where, in relaxed togetherness they enjoyed the food supplies in the huge white refrigerator or to the mutual joy of everyone they watched popcorn jumping in the pan. It was a joyful atmosphere down there, and I had to laugh with them when I found them. They took life easy, even here on this intensive course. Despite everything, the atmosphere in this hotel was great, and during meditation times a deep silence spread. The energy was high and outside of meditation they were joyful and relaxed; their laughter sparkled in the air.

Here too I did everything as well as I could. The hotel owner looked in on me occasionally and was satisfied. Every time he came, he chatted with me and tried—as sure as the "amen" in church—to win me over as hotel director for the coming season. For a really good salary, of course. As tempting as it was, I was drawn to other shores.

In this new hotel, I didn't have as much work as I'd had at the Prätschli. So I found time for longer meditations and enjoyed the increasing silence and bliss that came with them and was, at last, very satisfied here.

And yet, more and more often, the dream that had made me leave house and home behind appeared in my thoughts. Silently at first, and then louder and more persistent. I began to figure out how many course credits I'd gained with my various activities. For close to a year and a half you could get a five-months course, including the course fee, the food and the housing. So that would leastways be enough for the four-week course in the Science of Creative Intelligence (SCI) and the first part of TM teacher training. That was for sure something and afterwards I'd see what to do next.

The power of evolution would carry me!

III.

THE STUDY OF CONSCIOUSNESS

The whole world submits to him whose spirit is silent.

Zhuangzi
Chinese Philosopher

New Horizons

I dialed my boss' number at the Office of Coordination. "I'd like to join the next SCI course…I want to become a TM teacher. Is there a course starting soon?" The voice on the other end of the line was relaxed. "There was one that started last night!"

I looked at my watch. If everything went smoothly, I could slide right into it even today. As soon as I thought it, it was done. I organized a successor, who was happy to fill in for me and grow in this job. I packed my stuff and once again shook hands with all those who'd been close to my heart, slapped others on the shoulder, and gave, as well as received, hugs—and a few hours later I sat on my chair as a course participant in Mürren, the Swiss winter resort across from the summits of **Eiger**, *Mönch* and *Jungfrau*—yet another heavenly place.

With his SCI Course, Maharishi systematically introduced us into the art of life. In 33 video lectures that built on one another, we learned something new every day about the *Science of Creative Intelligence,* in which Maharishi gave us the essence of the thousands-of-years-old Vedic knowledge in a form easy for us Westerners to understand. We were a colorfully diverse group of about 40 people of different ages and occupations. Some of us, like me, wanted to become TM teachers; others wanted to deepen their experiences in meditation and to learn more. We studied, lived, and ate together in the same hotel and, as always, it provided excellent and various vegetarian cuisine.

But, sadly, as soon as we were comfortable in our new home that first day, we were suddenly told: "Unfortunately, you have to move to a different hotel, to Leysin."

Too bad. It was an unwelcome interruption for all of us. In a most friendly way, the bearer of these news asked to be forgiven for the inconvenience. We grumbled briefly, sighed, packed our stuff, and got ready for the 100 km bus ride to our new home. There, we were met with pure awfulness. Even from the outside, the small inn didn't exactly look inviting. As soon as we'd stomped up the wooden stairs and were standing in the entry hall, we were petrified. None of us had seen such unkempt filth before. Our high spirits took a heavy blow. Depressed and desolate we went to our rooms, where things didn't look a bit better. The hotel hadn't been used for a few years; everything was covered with grime.

What do most people do when they meet with circumstances contrary to their expectations? Exactly! We were upset and began to gripe. A wealthy businesswoman from Hamburg was enraged: "I refuse to even unpack my bag! If we have to stay here, I'm going home right now!"

Others also got really upset and complained; we felt badly treated—and of Eastern peace, there was not a trace. In any event, we needed some redress and we wanted to complain to those responsible. We for sure could not and would not spend four weeks in this place. But, oh, well, disgruntled as we were, we sat down on our suitcases. The two course leaders and a few of us to accompany the ladies trudged into town to get some things and figure out some remedial measures.

And now a miracle began to take its course—I'd often seen these kinds of "coincidences" in awe as I'd been around Maharishi. Our little group was next to a gas station when we saw Maharishi's car drive up. He was just coming from another course and he was sitting in the back. Curious, they all looked at him. Maharishi rolled down his window. He smiled like they were old friends that he was seeing again after a long absence; he reached behind him and then, to welcome them, he offered a flower through the open window. Bernhard from Bavaria, a thin young man with straight blond hair and enormously bright blue eyes was standing nearest to Maharishi. He didn't hesitate; clueless that in India greetings were done differently, he automatically reached for and took the hand of the great Master. He shook the Master's hand vigorously and at length: a big fat faux pas, because Indians bow slightly with their palms together at heart level and they say, "Namaste", or, in the case of Maharishi mostly, "*Jai Guru Dev*". For anyone around Maharishi, it would have been unthinkable to just touch him like that. But Maharishi's reaction was completely calm, as if this was the most normal thing in the world, and the smile on his face deepened—in case that was even possible.

And then one of the course leaders just blurted things out. She described our misfortune and told him that many were angry and wanted to leave if they couldn't get other accommodations, recounting the whole unpleasant story in detail. And Maharishi sat there in the middle of this gas station and had all the time in the world for our needs. "Yes, I've already heard about this. The people in charge had made every effort to find another hotel, but hard as they'd tried, they couldn't find one. Tell the course participants that they should stay. Use it as an opportunity. When you're about to gain the highest knowledge, as all of you soon will, then there are always some obstacles on the path that you have to overcome. All of you just get together and clean the place, and you'll see—it will be a wonderful and special course for you!

But if any of you still want to go home, feel free to do it."

When the group came back to our inn, those who'd remained behind listened to the breathless account. The people who'd been there at the gas station had to repeat every single word Maharishi had said many times and had to describe every one of his gestures. When they got to Bernhard's handshake, everyone was bent double with laughter. That was just too priceless!

The businesswoman from Hamburg and her son decided despite everything to go home. The rest of us rolled up our sleeves. For a whole day we swept, cleaned, wiped, and polished, while laughing, joking, and out of breath, we became a group of friends as if we'd all known one another forever. And it turned out to be an especially wonderful course, just as Maharishi had predicted.

In a few weeks, we became a tight-knit troop, hungry for knowledge. We laughed often and stood in awe, as the well-informed video-taped lectures of our Master from the Himalayas showed him to be an accomplished scholar. They revealed to us the richness of the laws of nature that governed life and that had largely been hidden from us until now. We began to see the infinite intelligence behind all of creation. The universal laws behind the processes of life were brought to light for us. From every possible point of view, Maharishi described for us the workings of this silent intelligence that created all things but that most people could not see at first sight. Despite the most detailed descriptions, his word choices made every course participant free to imagine and understand the effects of this intelligence in his or her own way without necessitating any belief system. We learned new facets of life and we learned much about ourselves.

This course was appropriately named. It was a science and it imparted knowledge about consciousness, about life; it was systematic and verifiable. In this peaceful and remote environment, we could meditate twice each morning and evening, and, between each meditation, we did our yoga exercises. We studied two to three hours, mornings and afternoons, and met yet again in the evenings. We wrote down the main points and made drawings for each lesson so that the new knowledge could take hold more deeply. We learned that, step-wise, evolution allows life to become more blissful and that it is the nature of life to grow. Aha, so it was the evolution of life that had kept me going so much so that I had to burn the bridges behind me to spring into a new and completely unknown life.

It is the nature of life to grow!

Here we learned that human consciousness never stops developing. And for me, the most exciting parts were the explanations of different states of consciousness. Everyone knew the three main states of consciousness, the basic human starter kit so to speak, of waking, dreaming, and deep, dreamless sleep. In each of these three states, the functioning of the body is so different that any doctor can unequivocally know by means of brain waves, breath rate, blood chemistry, eye-movements, and other bodily signals whether a person is awake, in deep sleep, or dreaming—without even having to see the person but just on the basis of these data. But in addition, there was also a ground state of human consciousness, a state of complete silence and without thoughts. This was so different from the three known major states of consciousness, that the scientists who discovered it in the sixties in meditators during the practice of TM classified it as a fourth major state of consciousness.[6] In this state, the body was significantly more relaxed than it was in deep sleep, but awareness was wide awake and resting in silence without thoughts.[A]

In his video-taped lectures during the course on SCI, Maharishi described the higher states of consciousness that would unfold with the regular and systematic experience of transcendence—the state of restful alertness—leading to the various states of enlightenment. A person in Cosmic Consciousness is so completely relaxed and peaceful that he or she experiences this powerful, eternal, silence of the transcendent as a gentle continuum even as he or she is engaged in activity during the day. It remains while dreaming and even in deep sleep. When I heard this, I instantly remembered my night in the storage room with the valuable videotape boxes and now understood that I'd had caught a glimpse of Cosmic Consciousness. My body was in deep sleep, while my spirit was completely awake in undisturbed silence, free of thought.

Through further practice, the human senses refine themselves so much that, in the state of God Consciousness, one can spontaneously perceive more subtle states of creation. I sensed that Maharishi was only suggesting the details because he didn't want to force us into a specific direction, but instead wanted us to have our own experiences without any preconceived ideas. In any case, I joyfully anticipated perceiving the divine shimmer in everything and everyone possibly soon in my own life. The sparkling and bright aura that I sometimes saw around Maharishi, and, less so, around people in his environment—these observations for sure belonged to these refined perceptions. Would I eventually see the heavenly world with angels and other subtle beings—or would I, like

St. Francis of Assisi understand the language of animals? Were these completely normal human abilities on the path of spiritual evolution? I was amazed and at the same time expectantly joyful.

Maharishi called the crowning glory of the evolution of human awareness Unity Consciousness, which would develop because of further refinement. In that state, human beings don't just experience pure Being, the all-pervasive silence within themselves, but also within everything else—in people, animals, plants, and objects. For such people, there is nothing that is not an expression of absolute and heavenly silence. The feeling of separateness vanishes and people feel one with everything and suffused with divine love.

I was deeply moved and I surmised that Jesus most likely meant exactly this experience when he said, "Love your neighbor as yourself." It wasn't just one of his commandments, but it was his own self-evident experience of reality that he communicated to us.

Clearly and systematically, Maharishi described the smallest details. This is only possible for someone who knows what he is talking about. And it was crystal clear to me that Unity Consciousness was the state of consciousness in which Maharishi lived day-in and day-out.[B]

Things transpired exactly as Maharishi had predicted; this course gave us the highest and most deeply blissful knowledge, which became an extremely enriching experience for our whole group.

And with that, it finally spread out before me—the clear and richly faceted, and unbelievably fascinating knowledge that I glimpsed even in childhood but that did not exist as an ordinary field of study.

Bus Ride without a Destination

Once again, I packed my bags and got on a bus. It was packed with people; every seat was taken. All of us were going to a four-months course, the first phase of TM-teacher training. But no one knew where we were going. Rumor had it that our destination was somewhere in France.

Even our bus driver was clueless. Once every hour, he had to find a place to park and get in a phone booth for new instructions about where to go next. Back then, there were always hundreds of people on various internationally mixed courses in Switzerland or in France. And I suspected that the organizers of the courses tried to get the best prices for seasonally empty hotels until the very last moment. Luckily, the bus driver was a laid-back guy. Laughing, he'd say every time, "Well, I've never seen anything like it."

He enjoyed the trip with us beaming and constantly chattering folks whom he was driving to their uncertain destination, which, no matter where it was, would be a milestone in their lives.

Again and again, there were situations in our TM Movement that changed quickly and things turned out differently than expected. Maharishi was the master at upsetting the apple cart or making a decision only at the very last moment. Since this happened so often, he liked making one of his funny word plays: "Movement means it is meant to move!"

In this way, we always got some flexibility training, which was invaluable schooling for our future. We learned to take the unexpected easily and to live in the here and now.

Only when we'd arrived at our destination did we know

where we'd landed: the French spa Vittel in the Vosges Mountains, fortunate in its altitude and its forested environment. But we'd not get to see all that much of it in the following months.

All told, 200 people had come together here, people from all parts of the world. The daily routine followed that of the SCI courses: longer meditation programs in the mornings and afternoons and, during the day and in the evenings, we learned. It went from early, 7:30 a.m.., to late evenings, 10:00 p.m., six days a week. Our days were so packed that the one day off each week was necessary to just let our spirits hang loose a bit—and to wash our laundry.

We watched countless videos, heard many, many lectures by Maharishi and lots of speeches by scientists in the most various fields. Maharishi, who'd earned his degree in physics, was intent on connecting the discoveries of modern science with the thousands-of-years-old knowledge about the evolution of consciousness; he wanted to draw parallels between them and, thus deepen our understanding of the rules and the lawfulness of creation. We were absorbed in the basic knowledge of quantum physics. Our physics lecturers compared the qualities of the unified field of all the laws of nature—the energy-rich, yet quiescent ground state of matter that physicists had discovered only a few years earlier—with the silent levels of our own consciousness. We heard about the various laws of thermodynamics which allowed us to better understand the cleansing of our nervous system which took place during the deep rest during TM.[C] All that was exciting, demanding, and challenging.

During those lectures, we sat in a gigantic hall. My English had become so fluent in the last two years that I liked translating almost simultaneously for other Germans, but only the tapes by Maharishi. With the technical languages of the various fields of science, I couldn't keep up. Even so, it made me more consciously aware and happy. It is the nature of life to grow!

In my entire life, I have never again taken so many notes as I did with both TM teacher training courses. We wrote down every lecture. We recited the main points that one of us had compiled and then we discussed everything in the whole group. We also practiced giving lectures on the effects of Transcendental Meditation. For that, we had to familiarize ourselves with the scientific research that, even back then, was already extant about the spiritual, physical, and societal effects of this spiritual practice. We learned what cortisol and growth hormone levels are, how the breath rate and the brain waves changed during the practice of TM, that the symptoms of sleep disorders and asthma were reduced and why that was—there seemed to be no end to it. We learned how to read the graphs of research studies and deepened our knowledge of technical terms. One thing was clear: the restful alertness during meditation was reflected in all the possible physiologically measurable parameters. Naturally, we had to know all that in detail and understand it.

On this course, I learned the deeper meaning of the name "Maharishi." "Maha" is Sanskrit for "great"; "rishi" means "seer." And so, a maharishi is a great seer. An enlightened rishi of the Vedic tradition can see, hear, and understand the hymns of the Vedas within himself. Beyond that, a maharishi, as a great seer, can give a life in that same state of consciousness to his students. I was amazed: even among enlightened masters there were evidently profound differences! Shortly after that,

I heard to my joy in a lecture by Maharishi that this title was not elitist—quite the contrary, because Maharishi's mission was to make a maharishi out of each one of us, as this ability was a natural potential within all human beings.

We especially loved role-playing. After we had mastered the theoretical knowledge about meditation, we learned to correct the errors that could have crept into the practice of others. Toward the end, there were many tests that we could only pass when we no longer made a single error. Everyone had to be perfect in everything because, back home, we would have the responsibility for the correct practice of our meditators. Thank God we could take those tests as often as needed and, in the end, all of us passed the tests despite the stringent criteria.

Mornings and evenings, we experienced our deep inner awareness and, by way of a side-effect, this improved our receptivity; it was an ideal mix of theory and practice. It was highly effective and, because of the course structures developed by Maharishi, we really could remember an unbelievable amount. Even today, three decades later, I can remember many of the details.

After four months, the time had come: highly motivated, I had completed the first part of my TM teacher-training course and, once again, sat in a bus. We were going to phase II of our instruction, where we would practice what we had learned under the supervision of experienced TM teachers.

The First Downer

I wasn't all that enthusiastic about this internship. If I'd had my own way, I'd have wanted to keep learning and have my TM-teacher certificate in my pocket as soon as possible. What was the point? However, I must now first use and implement what I had taken in during the last four months. Only after successful completion of this internship could I register for the third and last part of TM teacher training, which would encompass another four months of intensive study.

On the spur of the moment, I went back to my homeland and into the arms of my family. The joy of seeing one another again was great: my father, my mother, and my little brother, Rainer, who was six years younger than I was and who lived at home. My big brother, Jürgen, had meanwhile moved out.

Soon after my return, my father blurted out at supper: "Lothar, imagine. I just met the doctor on the road. Dr. Ilch asked about you explicitly. He'd seen you a couple of days ago and he really wanted to know what you've been doing all this time. He said that never in his whole life had he seen anyone who changed in such positive ways, and in such a short time! And he said to say hello to all of you!"

So, I was the prodigal son coming home, and in no way deceased in the meantime because of his "highly dangerous malnutrition." On the contrary, he looked even better than before. I was rehabilitated; what a great feeling!

I was full of energy. The good fortune that had been my constant companion since starting to meditate three years before had slowly and surely become even deeper. The silence of meditation was meanwhile gently present as a background to activity; I was relaxed, calm, and I felt in tune with myself and the world. Life was a joy for me and only rarely in that time were there any hours in which my elation subsided. There were still situations that were uncomfortable for me, above all the discussions with my father that gradually re-asserted themselves. He felt that he, his life-style, and the loving togetherness of our family were under attack because I was not happy with our traditional family meals and because I checked out twice a day to meditate in my attic hermitage. The "yogi" was back! My father began again to grumble, and I withdrew within myself. Despite all that I was in a good mood; life was beautiful, even when it was just this life with all that went with it.

I registered at the Transcendental Meditation Center in Montabaur, a small town near us with about 6,500 residents at that time. It had a very active TM Center on the first floor of a beautiful one-family house. The big seminar room with its glass front allowed a view of Westerwald. Many learned and practiced meditation here, and came to evening and weekend events. They shared their experiences during TM and the many good changes that resulted in their lives. They discussed things animatedly or were busy with Maharishi's knowledge.

In one-on-one meetings, I checked the correctness of the meditation of many people, and this brought me unbeliev-able joy. In the small meditation room, we'd both close our eyes, and, systematically and step-by-step, I reminded them of the effortlessness and the naturalness of meditation, and then, together, we sank into the unifying silence that is such an intimate feeling for everyone who experiences it. With peaceful or radiant eyes—whichever—they'd say their good-byes. And I knew more and more: this is my true profession that I'd been waiting for. How would it be if I could teach others to meditate?

During that time, I gave many lectures and presentations with information presentations to interested parties about the many and various positive effects of TM. I organized talks in smaller neighboring towns, hung posters for them, and was grateful that I could share the good I'd experienced with other people. Every new meditator was a joy to me because I was convinced that his or her life would turn towards the positive in a short time. As with me, that person too would become happier, more relaxed, and healthier, lose his or her fears, and, with new enthusiasm, be able to follow his or her personal goals in life.

Even so, in my normal life a part of my high spirits that I had been fortunate to experience these last years while in the immediate vicinity of Maharishi and in the hotels with many course participants was lost. In Switzerland and in France I'd been surrounded continually by people who, in this vacation setting were far from the worries and the needs of normal life and were almost always beaming and pleasant in their dealings. All the people in my surroundings there didn't just meditate the regular 20 minutes morning and evening—they did it for many hours a day. The hotels were suffused with silence, energy, and joy. Almost automatically, I expected this even here in daily life—that's how accustomed I was to this joyful life. It was not clear to me that this inner bliss I'd been taking for granted was enhanced by the heightened levels of consciousness of the people in my surroundings and that I could not maintain it by myself—at least not yet. So now here, in "the real world," I noticed this clearly. I had personally heard Maharishi say in the last years: "Don't expect perfection in the relative."

But this was exactly what I'd been doing, and I landed hard on the ground. I was disappointed by the behavior of many people. Their set ways and troubles that I'd been accepting as God-given—after all I didn't know anything different—now hit me hard. And not only with people who did not cultivate contact with that source of natural harmony within. Those I met aplenty in my various part-time jobs that I worked in those days to earn a living. To my disappointment, I also saw meditators, who, though they often spread joy more than other people, still made vicious remarks or got all worked up in angry tirades about politics or the world in general.

I'd totally pushed it into the back of my mind that meditation did not create a peaceful world overnight, but was primarily an effective technique to remove stress and old "programming" from the nervous system. This was a systematic and natural process that obviously took some time until the harshness and sharp edges of a person were smoothed out and the fundamental and loving nature underneath came into view more and more. Given my impatience, I would have loved to see a peaceful world a lot quicker. Instead, I again first had to get used to some of the roughness I encountered when dealing with other people.

Of course, the essentially unique character of each person did not change when he surrendered to the healing effects of deep rest. I noticed that personal likes and idiosyncrasies became even more pronounced when someone began to let go of the deeply embedded stresses he'd held for so long. In the end, the person became more aware so that he or she could create a life as was thought to be right, rather than simply yield to social pressure. Each one of us carried within ourself an individual load of undigested and long-stored experiences of life that brought with them stresses and blockages in body and mind. And TM uses a natural law, according to which the weaknesses and negative programming dissolved little by little through deep rest. I understood all this most clearly through an image that Maharishi liked to use for this. According to the nature of this programming we each have, every person wears his or her very own and special pair of glasses through whose colored lenses the view of the world is distorted. Someone would see everything in blue, another would see red, and yet another green. So, inevitably, meditators in crisis situations would give expression to old behavioral patterns and injuries. However, these would be triggered with increasingly less frequency. Unconscious reactions became weaker; the soul only frees itself little by little. In the course of meditating for months and years, the originally intense color of the lenses became more and more transparent until everyone would see everything as clearly as it really was, and without the earlier individual distortions.

Though I'd learned about these interrelations in theory during the first part of TM-teacher training, but now, in practice, everything had to be put into its proper context. After my blissful time around Maharishi, who had shown me how effortless, pleasant, and joyful everything could be, I had again landed in the societal quality of life of our times with all its light and dark qualities. For this reason, it made total sense that in my TM teacher training this practicum was a necessary part of it.

The Cops Couldn't Believe It

"Montabaur has reached the 1% threshold!"

I heard this rumor again and again. It meant that in this small town one person in a hundred had by now possibly learned Transcendental Meditation. Friends from many parts of Germany called me and wanted confirmation of this. It was rumored that when this percentage was reached, something exciting and unheard-of could have happened in Germany. Because I didn't want to pass on speculations or unproven rumors, I wanted to check this out. But what was it that was so exciting about this magical number?

The 1% effect; this term was the epitome of a new dimension in scientific studies about the social effects of TM that we had already studied thoroughly during our TM teacher training. How could I have anticipated at this point that everything connected to it would have such huge influences on my life to be?

Already in his first TV interview in the U.S. in the early sixties, Maharishi had said that, for a peaceful world, it would be enough if only around 1% of the population in every city would meditate. He illustrated this with one of his many analogies: "The power of light is stronger than the power of darkness—a few street lights drive away the darkness of a whole street. Exactly in that same way, negative tendencies such as argumentativeness and crimes, traffic accidents, illnesses, economic misfortunes, yes, even natural catastrophes—they will all decrease when at least 1% of the population meditates. If 5% do it, then a new phase transition will take place in the direction of an ideal society."[D]

That the scientific concept of *phase transition* was being

used for a social phenomenon was the result of many discussions by Maharishi with various scientists. They looked for parallels in their own areas of expertise—and indeed, in biology, physics, and chemistry, there were analogies to this revolutionary concept.

Already during TM teacher training I'd learned that if you want to bring some disorderly substance into a state of higher coherence, it is enough, amazingly, to bring only a small percentage of its components into that orderliness. Even the size of this coherent component is known: For this effect, the square root of the total number of components is enough. If this critical number is reached, then the phase transition is automatic, and all other components fall into place as if by themselves in a ripple effect. This principle can be found everywhere in nature: the coherent elements of any system have a stronger influence overall than disordered components. Put simply, order takes over if it is extensive enough.[E]

So far, so good—but what percentage would be big enough for this effect to take hold in the case of human consciousness? Of course, it would be wonderful if everyone were to meditate and people were mostly nice and loving to one another. Wars and hostilities would end. We would no longer systematically exploit and destroy our beautiful planet because respect for nature and insight into the whole would be re-established. But everyone meditating is most probably not a realizable dream! But then I learned something amazing, namely that this utopia could well be made palpable and real. In analogy to the scientific phenomenon, researchers of consciousness start from the premise that the necessary number of TM meditators only need to be one percent of the total population to be effective. That was exactly the number that Maharishi had predicted—I'd have to get used to these "miracles" in the next few years.

As unusual and strange as these new ideas were for many people, there were a few sociologists who nevertheless took Maharishi's statements seriously enough so that, in 1973, they began to verify them scientifically. As early as 1972, there were eleven cities in the U.S. with more than 10,000 people in which 1% of the population had learned TM.[4] These researchers took the government crime statistics and compared them with controls in eleven other cities of the same size. Of course, they saw to it that these cities were comparable to one another to ensure the validity of their results. They were rigorous; they compared the geographic locations, the percentage of students compared to the general population, the median education of the citizens, and the per capita income, as well as the proportion of the population of 15-29-year-olds. With all that information, they ensured from the get-go that their results would be irrefutable and air-tight. Only then, did they evaluate the crime rates five years before and five years after reaching the 1% mark.

Even back then in the U.S., there was a worrisome tendency for crime rates to increase. In the first five years, the average increase in all 22 cities was identical at almost 8%. Immediately after reaching the 1% mark, this unfortunate trend reversed itself. In the following five years, the crime rate dropped by 8% while, in the control cities it climbed

---

[4] According to this theory, 100 persons who, in a community of 10,000, meditate each for himself is enough to establish coherence and to locally stem the emergence of negativity. In more exact terms, the necessary percentage is lower as the population of the city under consideration rises. Though it is scientifically not quite correct, we nevertheless call it the 1% effect for the sake of simplicity.

unhindered by yet another 8%, meaning overall, the crime rate in the 1% cities fell by a total of 16%. The statistical likelihood that these changes were purely coincidental was one change in a thousand. There were three surprising aspects to this research: first there was no city in which crimes rates had failed to drop significantly after reaching the 1% mark, and, second, there were no cities in which the crime rate failed to rise if there were not 1% meditators.[7, 8] And these numbers held true even though, it was highly unlikely that people who'd committed any kind of misdeeds had begun to meditate, but, instead, simply one hundredth of the population had done so. The third point was almost even more amazing. When the 1% had been reached, a phase transition had clearly taken place just as a completely normal piece of iron changes into a magnet, or when laser light is produced[E] What was fascinating was that many people learned TM in those cities that had not reached the 1% mark but the percentage fell too far short of 1%. The researches named this phenomenon that they had established for the first time in human history, the *Maharishi Effect*, after the founder of the TM movement.[F]

Maharishi was not just happy about the results of these studies, he also used them as an opportunity to publicly proclaim what he'd foreseen for a long time. In 1975, he formulated this poetic sentence: "Through the window of science, we see the dawn of the Age of Enlightenment."

He saw (like other wise men in the last decades) that humanity had begun a revolution of consciousness—a never-yet-seen transformation toward the realization of the full human potential. Slowly but surely this would lead to a life without hatred, conflict, and wars; instead, there would be more unity, more mutual support, and love in all aspects of life on this planet. Through these new scientific analyses, at the very least a practical and easily implemented way out of thousands of years of tyranny and suppression had been shown. Maharishi's expression about the dawning of the Age of Enlightenment was spread all over the world with much fanfare. To many people this seemed so exaggerated, or it sounded somehow suspect and religious, that even a few meditators of the TM movement were shocked and—at least officially—wanted nothing to do with all that.

In public, Maharishi never spoke about his own inner experiences and insights. He was willing to conform to the usual habits of analytical thinking and intellectualizing of modern times. He even went further. He wanted to subject the knowledge of the Vedas to scientific testing, for he knew that this systematic and thousands-of-years-old proven knowledge would stand the test. He began with the assumption that we would be able to take it in and accept it more easily in this way.

A few years later, teams of researchers corroborated these early data even more solidly. They had compared what had meanwhile become twenty-four cities of 1% meditators with 160 small and similar small towns; in other words, a quarter of the rural municipalities of this size in the U.S.! There was not a single town in which the crime rate declined unless it had 1% TM meditators. At the same time, there was a reduction in hospital admissions and traffic accidents as soon as the 1% mark was reached—just as Maharishi had predicted.[9]

And now, was this same process going on and possibly right in front of my nose here in Germany? Was this completely new perspective on solving the problems of modern society unfolding even here? I really wanted to get to the bottom of this. We did have files in our Meditation Center, but not all TM teachers had been conscientious about keeping them up to date; they were incomplete. We only knew that many in Montabaur and environs had learned TM—possibly one in a hundred. Wouldn't it be great if, even here in Germany, we could demonstrate with official statistics that we had a practicable solution in our hands for solving many problems? And, on top of that, as well as contrary to existing measures, downright cheap to implement and in a short time? Full of trust in the American research results, my logic was as follows: In Montabaur the crime rate must have declined through the power of silence if enough people practiced TM. Of course, this new concept required people, who'd never heard of the 1% effect, to rethink things radically. It was new for them, really new, and took some getting used to—as I was to learn soon enough.

I made a beeline to the police station in mid-town and stepped into the dark brick building. "My name is Lothar Pirc, I'm from the training center for Transcendental Meditation."

In a few words, I explained what TM was, and I was then taken to an office where I quizzed the officer one rank higher, "Is it possible to look at the records of the crime rate for the past five years?" I explained why to him.

Obviously, however, these concepts went over his head. I told him that in the past few years hundreds of people in Montabaur had learned TM. But that made things worse. The more I explained, the more dubious the thing seemed to the officer: "Unfortunately, we can't give out our records of the crime rate!"

A few hours later, a police car rolled up in front of the Meditation Center. Two uniformed officers got out, rang the bell, and soon stood in our hallway. "Our boss said we should take a look here and make sure everything's okay!"

In one of the lecture halls, I gave him a short overview of the activities in our center and summed up some of the studies on the effects of TM. I presented the 1% effect to them and explained the relevant graphs in detail, hoping all that time to get the stats I wanted. They listened, friendly but distant. And I could feel it: I was dealing with a complete lack of understanding—an experience I was to have quite often in my life.

In any case, they'd convinced themselves with their visit that there was nothing untoward going on here. And despite all the information, they vamoosed, all but convinced.

I never heard from them again.

Vagabond in the Mayor's Office

I was extremely intent on completing my TM teacher training as soon as possible. But where to get the money? The course fee for the four-months teacher training course, including room and board, was not exactly chickenfeed for a young dude like me.

One thing was certain. I needed a new job, an especially well-paying job, obviously.

I started to look. After a short time, a newspaper ad jumped into view: well-paid position on a commission basis at a city-map publishing house. It didn't sound bad and soon I had the phone in my hand and got an invitation.

First, I would have to learn how to work the thing. So, as instructed, I drove to Bielefeld and accompanied an experienced representative, squeezing myself into a phone booth with him, while he made appointments with potential advertising customers and thus surrounded me with cigarette smoke for half of the day. Of course, the whole enterprise lived off selling ads in the city maps, but to be crushed in a phone booth day in and day out was abject horror for me. I was not going to earn my money like that!

After three days, my needs had been met. I went to see the boss of this enterprise and soon came to the salient point: "I'd love to work for you, but can't I have my own city?" He hesitated briefly; after all, I was the inexperienced new guy who didn't have much to show for himself. "Hmm," he said slowly, "That might just work. We've got a small town right between Cologne and Bonn that doesn't yet have a city map...."

Wow, that did sound downright hopeful!!

"Our company had the cartography done, and the mayor has promised his support."

Well, then, that was exactly what I was looking for! The boss let me use the company's rickety old VW bus, and off I went into a new field of responsibility.

Certain of success, I asked to speak to the mayor on the phone. I got an appointment, and, dressed to the nines, I went into city hall and explained my plan to him. He was extraordinarily kind: "Young man, can I help you?"

"Well, I'll need an office and my own telephone connection."

The mayor hesitated at my suggestion, as had my boss not long before. But I got both, right here at the city hall, together with a letter of recommendation from the mayor himself to the corporations to buy the ads that would support the creation of a city map.

I was as poor as a church mouse, dead broke, and I needed every penny, but I didn't have to trumpet this to these pre-eminent gentlemen at the mayor's office. I saved every dollar for my course fee, and renting a hotel room while on the job would have been a real waste! Thank God it was summer, and so I could once again refresh my experience as a gypsy. I immediately rented an off-road space a few kilometers from my new workplace, one that was wonderfully situated right by the Rhine. Close to my beloved river, I pitched my big frame tent in which I'd spent vacations as a child with my parents and my brothers.

Every morning the ducks and the swans on the Rhine could observe the miraculous transformation of a tramp into a business man. Neat as a pin, I stepped out from the entrance of my tent in a three-piece suit, my tie adjusted just so, and was off to make money and get closer day-by-day to my longed-for course. I took great joy in this work and sat in a bright, modern office in a super location with a terrific view of the city. As I called potential clients, I made my sales pitches look very attractive while, of course, mentioning discreetly that I was calling from the mayor's office and that I had a letter of recommendation from him.

I sold a thrilling number of ads, and the cash piled up. Often, the clients for these ads showed up personally in my office at city hall. I loved my new job. Now and then, I met with colleagues from the publisher, who, after years on the job, were still on the treadmill of phone booths and out-of-office appointments. They and my boss had to pick their jaws up off the ground with amazement; none of them had seen anything like it—and I was the youngest one there.

After a short time, things went so well that I needed my own assistant. And with that, I could finally do something for my family ties. My brother Jürgen was a master electrician and the father of a young family, and to the great concern of our parents, he'd just lost his job. So, I got a job for him and notched up a few brownie points with my dad. And, incidentally, I got a lot closer to my older brother. We both lived in the big frame tent, and little by little, he caught my fever for meditation. He, his wife, and two kids learned to meditate back then; he still does it to this day.

Often in the evenings we drove my car to the TM Center in Cologne. "Lothar, have you heard the news? There are now TM-Sidhi courses in Germany!"

The TM teachers there had come up with some brand-new information, as Maharishi had again created something new.

I had noticed in Switzerland and in France that something exciting relating to consciousness was being planned behind closed doors. But back then, only TM teachers could do whatever it was because their consciousness was used to intensive transcending. But because, meanwhile, more than a million and a half people world-wide had enlivened the collective consciousness through regular transcending, the next big step in the development of consciousness of humanity had, according to Maharishi, become possible. And, evidently, this trial of the techniques of consciousness from the science of yoga, long misinterpreted, had been successful in those many six-months courses. So now these new sidhi techniques, which would surpass even the effects of TM, would become available to humanity. Maharishi had opened a new door. Every meditator could learn the TM-Sidhi Program after a minimum of practicing TM for one year. The only requirement was a six-week TM-Sidhi prep-course.

As soon as Jochen raved about a beautiful spa in southern Germany, I was on fire. Lindenberg in Allgau, with its beautiful hotel right next to Waldsee, would be the next surprising place in my eventful life. Nobody would have to waste any time persuading me. I'd already noticed the enormous energy and spiritual power in the hotels where I'd worked as the manager. It was more than obvious that I'd want to get these new techniques for the development of consciousness. My favorite thing would have been to become a TM teacher first; that was really my only heart's desire. But now, word was that people should learn the sidhis first, before taking the TM teacher training course. Maharishi had said it himself: "The sidhis are more important for the development of the consciousness of the individual and for the whole world."

After three months, I'd earned enough money to take the TM-Sidhi prep course. For my boss, the world ended, when, after my vertical take-off, I wanted to quit. But money was not my major attraction. I wanted to grow and, with that, do something good for the world. What could be more attractive? I was young and not tied down, and another exciting inward adventure beckoned me.

I took the story of how I'd found the job and how easily everything fell into place for granted. I was glad about this act of providence and my success, and enjoyed all of it gratefully and innocently.

Endless Luck

The forest hotel in Lindenberg kept Jochen's promise, situated in untouched nature, right next to a peaceful forest lake, I moved into my new quarters for the next six weeks. Every week new participants showed up while others had already completed their six-week prep course and were leaving our meditative domicile. The techniques we'd learn after the prep course for the TM-Sidhis course depended on a rested nervous system, one that was already accustomed to the deep silence of meditation; otherwise, these new techniques would not bring the desired results.

The air was once again full of intoxicating rumors: People who'd mastered the sidhis could levitate, read others' thoughts, be clairvoyant, see celestial beings, know everything without having to learn, and could develop healing powers—our euphoria and expectations knew no bounds. Even so, every one of us asked ourselves, "Could this be real? Could something like that really function here and now in our materialistic and hectic world?"

Here, for the first time in my life, I was part of a long "rounding program." I meditated many times each day, and in between meditations I did a breathing technique and yoga exercises—all of it embedded in a clearly structured schedule so that the nervous system could get the rest it needed to release deep stresses and nervous tensions. And this had its results. Apparently, my two years in Maharishi's presence had prepared me, and I took off like a rocket. I only had to close my eyes for a short time before I almost exploded with ecstasy. Sometimes I had the feeling that my body could hardly bear it, but I got used to it quickly. So that was it: the inner bliss of which the wise had spoken throughout history, this condition of bottomless and never-ending joy. Before that, if anyone spoke that of bliss, I always thought it was an exaggeration and I took it as an obsolete, kitschy expression. But now, I noticed that this word did come closest to express what I was fortunate to experience here, even though there really were no words that could describe it. For what people usually call bliss is only a poor reflection of this overwhelming experience. You really have to experience it for yourself in order to know it.

It was never boring because this inner bliss contained the most various facets, always new, always creating happiness in a new way. Sometimes it was soft and quiet, interwoven within everything and illuminating it, presenting itself to me as peace, sacred and unending peace. It was accompanied by such a reverence, such a grateful astonishment, that all I wanted to do was to bow down before the greatness of the Creator and all there was here on Earth. Often this bliss was everything but gentle. Powerfully, it pulsed this new energy through all my cells. It was so strong that sometimes the boundaries of my physical body seemed to vanish.

These inner experiences were crystal clear within themselves and needed no explanation. But after a few days, it was impossible to miss that outside of meditation a broad smile was often on my face also. When I looked in the mirror while shaving every morning, my skin seemed to glow—as within, so without!

At the end of the long meditations, we read Vedic scriptures, in which the rishis had transmitted their inner experiences and insights thousands of years ago in the form of verses and hymns. We could not yet understand much of the content of these recitations but what Maharishi had intended to accomplish with them did happen: a new level of Being opened for us. I saw a white light during these readings that, like a subtle liquid, flowed through my body. More and more of us had the shining eyes and radiant faces that I'd already seen around Maharishi's course participants.

How glorious it must be always to be able to live like this! Finally, it was now clear to me that I wanted to be enlightened in this life time, to be a blessing for my environment—and for me. Back on the SCI course, enlightenment had been something incredibly exalted for me, something to be venerated, something far away for an ordinary mortal being like me and my friends, and only thinkable, at most, in the distant future. After all, we lived in a different time, in a completely different culture than the enlightened rishis at the flowering of Vedic civilization. But maybe didn't a glorious fate beckon us, even here in the West, greater than I could imagine back then?

Those were my thoughts in my youthful innocence and enthusiasm, carried by the eminent good fortune of my inner life.

Nature Supports Me

The forest lake was beautiful as a dream. Clear yet dark, the trees were reflected in the still water. At dawn, before the meditation program, I went either with a friend or by myself to get refreshed in its cold moorland waters. During the lunch break we went two-by-two with a trusted friend along the narrow path that went around the lake. The silence of nature mirrored the peace within us.

This time I went with Herbert, a nice guy, talkative, enthusiastic, and a good fifteen years older than I. As usual, I was radiant down to my toenails; my inner happiness was clearly visible. Out of the clear blue, he turned towards me and said, "Lothar, I have a feeling that you really have to be a TM teacher. And I also have the feeling that I should help you with it. Is there something I can do for you?"

How could he have known that becoming a TM teacher was my most burning desire? Naturally, I needed a lot of money to make this dream come true. After all, the TM teacher training course included eight months in a hotel, plus food and tuition. I'd used up most of the cash I had left from the city map job for the prep course. With some hesitation, I presented him with my tight financial situation—after all, I hardly knew him. That didn't seem to bother him in the least. "Two days from now, my course here is over, and then I'm going home. You know I have a carpet shop in Lindau at Lake Constance. I'd love to give you a loan guarantee for whatever you need for that course."

"But I need twenty thousand!"

"No problem; I'll call the president of the bank tomorrow,

and you can come down on Sunday. Then I'll call him into my shop, and we'll take care of everything. My carpet shop is right on the waterfront promenade. You won't have any trouble finding it.

All this seemed to be the most natural thing in the world for me. This was divine providence for sure.

At the beginning of the SCI course, when my group lodged in that filthy hotel, Maharishi had already given us to understand that the highest knowledge came with a price and that, often, some obstacle would show up when something especially precious in terms of spiritual knowledge was in the offing. That was an inner test to see if one was ready and had earned it. In many spiritual traditions in the East and in the West, this was used in a deliberate way to test a prospective student to see if he was serious in his intention. Only after he'd passed this acid test would he be allowed to pursue this path.

But now I was experiencing the most pleasant flipside of this. It was also an ancient experience that doors would open in the most unbelievable ways when someone wanted the highest knowledge, and it was the right time for it. It seemed that all of nature was waiting to take such a person under her wing and to remove all obstacles from his path. We called it "nature support" when the powers of the universe, whatever they might be, removed a rock from our path and made things connect with one another in the most wonderful ways. To have good luck no longer seemed to be pure chance. We all had experienced in this context that, through the rediscovery of the natural, effortless access to the transcendent, this could be cultivated by anyone.

After this had become clear to me, I also saw that even

just the first part—financing the TM-Sidhi prep course—had been like a miracle. Everything had fallen into place just so, as if it were meant to be.

This kind of divine intervention pervaded my life since that time like golden thread, and I was grateful to be here in Lindenberg, and thanked my Creator from the bottom of my heart. And things were about to get even better.

It was not customary to interrupt a course because then the nervous system would be exposed to influences that would destroy the subtle levels that had just been won. But I would soon be back, and, moreover, it was for a just cause. So, I informed my course leader, and then I was on my way to Lake Constance; it would be just half an hour of hitchhiking; my effervescent good luck was with me as part of my luggage.

Sunday morning was the decisive day. Herbert was waiting for me in his shop, but of me there was no trace. How could I have found my way there? I only knew the name of the town and that his shop was within view of the lake. What to do? In Lindenberg, I would have been meditating with my group during this time. Well, I could also do that here. Untroubled, I sat down on a bench. With the still and wide waters before me and sitting on the hard boards of the park bench, I closed my eyes, and, with my legs crossed, I began to meditate. Herbert was waiting for me patiently in his carpet shop. Suddenly, a stranger burst in on him, "You have got to see this: there's a guy sitting on a park bench down there—you've never seen the likes of it in your life—he's gonna lift off any second!"

Yes, I did sit there with a blissful smile on my face, which, presumably, was an unusual sight for passers-by. I had just turned twenty and was totally carefree! But for Herbert it was the cue—that could only be me! The innocent messenger had brought him to me without realizing anything, and I had to do nothing to make it happen.

After Herbert had brought me to his shop, I sat down in the same position on one of his many, comfortable piles of stacked-up carpets. Next to Herbert at the desk, the bank president was already sitting there in his best threads. They put their heads together and filled out the papers without any input from me. "We arranged for me to guarantee an advance for twenty thousand Deutsche Mark," said Herbert insistently.

At that same moment, something within me said clearly, "Forty thousand would be better," but, of course, I'd rather have bitten off my tongue than to say it out loud. But, as if Herbert had heard it, he interrupted himself, "Or would you rather have forty thousand?" And as a confirmation, he nodded and then answered himself, "Yes, I believe that would be better!"

I only had to nod without saying a word. The old contract was torn up without further comment, and the two of them filled out the second one for me. Finally, we all signed, and that was it.

Yay! That meant the road was free for all courses: the eight-week Sidhi course as well as the four months of the third phase of the TM-teacher training course, including my hotel room and food—all that in just one stroke. On top of that, I had some leeway so that, if necessary, I could take some for the start-up capital of a center after TM teacher training was completed. If I hadn't been sitting on cloud nine already, I'd sure be there now.

To this day, I'm grateful to Herbert for all this. How

could a person be so trusting and so generous, and all that to almost a stranger? I was moved and still am today.

Once again, unbelievable providence had come to help me without my having to do anything myself. Yes, in my opinion, it should always be like this; like this, life was fun!

Higher Powers

"Welcome to the TM-Sidhi course! Do you know how lucky you are?"

If anyone knew it, it was me! That I could sit here so relaxed and joyfully expectant was thanks to a mid-sized miracle. Once again, I was sitting in a lecture hall, this time in the Swabian Alps. From my room, I'd already enjoyed the view of the gentle yet rough landscapes of the Alps with their blue range of hills disappearing in the distance. And above all, eight glorious and auspicious weeks lay before me![5]

Mr. Ritterstaedt, the national leader of Germany, had come to teach us these longed-for techniques. He directed his introductory words to us in a rather formal way, as was appropriate for his age: "On this course you will receive techniques and knowledge that only a very few masters had access to in the last hundreds of years in India. To this day, they are kept secret and are transmitted only within the tradition of Vedic masters. Over several hundreds of years, however, the key to their perfect implementation was lost because these techniques work only when the student has mastered the effortless art of transcending."

Okay, so that was the deeper reason for the long prep courses!

"Maharishi has brought the implementation of this ancient and unbroken tradition of the Vedic masters back to light and has tested them to see if they would work on the six-months course for TM Teachers. And to his infinite joy,

---

[5] Because so many more people meditate now and so have enlivened the collective consciousness over may years, the TM Sidhi techniques can be learned in a markedly shorter time frame.

they did! He has let us know that through these practices the collective consciousness was enlivened to the extent that these techniques could now be made available to anyone. And you are some of the first who will learn them!"

A pregnant pause emphasized what we'd just heard. My suspense mounted. With me, about 45 other aspirants had come, and their eyes were glued on Mr. Ritterstaedt.

"The word 'sidhi' is Sanskrit for 'perfect ability'. It refers to skills that, here in the West, are normally thought of as supernatural because, in our culture, they don't belong to the normal human repertoire."

He reminded us of the unbelievable abilities of Indian yogis, and of Francis of Assisi and other medieval saints who could levitate. And then there was Theresa von Konnersreith, who went for decades without food. "Maharishi Patanjali wrote down the various stages of meditation, the ones you are practicing now, in his Yoga-Sutras a very long time ago. They were short sutras about yoga, together with all the steps with which an adept recognizes the eternal nature of his innermost Self."

He looked around: "But if these sidhis are to function properly, you need not only a nervous system already habituated to the more subtle levels of thinking and to transcending, but you also need the knowledge for how to use these spiritual techniques properly because, with the aid of the sidhis, you think from the level of pure consciousness—that is, the realm of the Absolute. If you practice this regularly, this ability also develops in every-day life. You think and act more and more from this subtle realm.[(G)] And with it, the abilities of full human potential that have always been part of every human being, and, Ladies and Gentlemen...", he smiled mischievously, "…should be available to every human being."

Aha, so that was the main difference between East and West! In the West, divinely gifted people are thought to be geniuses in various fields. If someone was clairvoyant or could heal with spiritual power, then this was simply held to be an extraordinary talent. But for thousands of years the East had used techniques to cultivate these brilliant talents systematically through consistent spiritual practices. With all the youthful enthusiasm that was already mine, Maharishi would not have been a great seer for me without the following explanation: "These abilities are merely a side effect of the sidhi techniques, even if wonderful experiences are waiting for you. The main thing is the further development of your human potential to higher states of consciousness and its organizing effects on the environment."

Fascinated, I listened to his further expositions: "With advancing spiritual development, you realize that everything in creation is part of the unbounded whole, your own Self. This great and unbounded Self is precisely what Socrates, Kant, and other philosophers have called 'Being'."

My thoughts took their own course: Hmm, that was true; almost always I experienced myself as separate from others and had the feeling that "I" ended with my skin. But, obviously, it was our essential nature to experience ourselves as boundless consciousness and to perceive that same unboundedness as the common source of all creation. And I remembered that in the peaceful days of my prep course in Lindenberg, and, especially during the week of silence with Maharishi in the endless silence in the hotel in Hertenstein, I had clearly perceived this unbounded all-encompassing field of silence beneath all the diversity of the external surface of things.

Mr. Ritterstaedt continued: "The practice of the sidhis is important for you personally and it is also important for the world. But, to attain the highest state of consciousness, there must be no attachment to these perfect abilities."

What a pity! I—a babe in the woods and a small light— would have wanted to keep them for myself a little, if, in fact, they became real.

As in the previous courses, bed-time was early. On the following morning, we'd begin with the first sidhi techniques. Little by little, we learned many spiritual practices that we performed effortlessly. We learned techniques to develop friendliness and compassion, as well as others to look within the body and heal it with spiritual power, and yet others to cultivate more subtle sensory perception; these abilities were regarded as supernatural as long as they were not part of the normal human repertoire. But for people with expanded consciousness and subtle sensory perception, they were the most normal abilities in the world, and a natural part of every-day experience. For us, these things would develop soon enough.

With these new techniques, my experience of the transcendent became unbelievably stronger. I had the feeling of being without thoughts for minutes while sitting in the unbounded inner vastness and being one with the universe, while my breath became completely still and my body was suffused with a sublime peace.

With these various aspects of the sidhis, I often, though not always, had clear experiences. I could feel distinctly how the body changed according to each of these techniques. My face took on a different expression according to the implementation of the sidhi being practiced. With the practice of the various sidhis, a gentle and pleasant energy began to flow and, once again, a spiritual realm I'd never seen before opened for me. I had never yet felt this so completely. It was as if a substance, to which I'd not previously had access, would nourish and maintain my body. I also felt a tingling sensation and an energy in various parts of my head. My whole brain felt as if it were being structured anew. And, presumably, that is what was happening.

It was always captivating to share our inner experiences with other course participants, when these were the topic of group discussions. We were all so well prepared with the long weeks of meditation earlier that almost all of us felt something extraordinary. Some felt the friendliness among the planets and the galaxies; some began to hear heavenly sounds, others could smell the scent of roses and sandalwood in more subtle and flowery ways than anything that had yet entered our noses here on earth. A new world of experiences with the most varied facets opened for us.

Regularly, one of the four course leaders that took care of us read Vedic texts while most of us had our eyes closed. Once, such a deep love and melting devotion to the Divine that became more and more intense until I seemed to dissolve in it completely took hold of me. The ecstasy that came with it was boundless and overwhelming. There was no desire left in me for anything else. I was completely one with myself and with the unbounded and I merged with the fullness of life. Quietly, I slipped into my room, surrounded and fulfilled with this otherworldly sweetness. My desire to speak was totally extinguished. This condition maintained itself for many hours and—to this day, I still cherish it in my heart as an incomparable treasure.

Not a few of us felt an unbelievably fine and sweet taste in our throats and mouths that we called *Soma*, just as it was described in the Soma Mandala of the Veda.

One thing was certain: While we had not attained any perfection in the command of the sidhis, we had landed in a magical realm that most of us had never yet entered. Here in Urach, I recalled again the statement of my TM teacher shortly before my initiation into meditation back in Koblenz: "Human beings normally only use three to ten percent of their mental potential. But through regular meditation the other areas can be accessed." This certainly must have been a hint of that! The new experiences showed extra clearly that we human beings carry far more within us than the abilities we've used in our daily lives up till now. These refined sensual perceptions are there, but for most people they are unnoticed and atrophied because they are not cultivated. And it became clear to us that even normal Westerners like us could, if we wanted to, use our brains completely differently and could experience a bliss and a deep silence in our daily lives that had been unknown till now.

But it didn't work every time. Some techniques brought clearer results than others. Yet even course participants who rarely had clear experiences did not doubt that these abilities were real after attending this course. If you wanted them, you had to develop them further through continuous practice.

On a video tape Maharishi explained this: "The experiences we have through the TM-Sidhi Program depend on the purity of the nervous system. There are two kinds of blockages that impede the free flow of consciousness, structural and biochemical. Through systematically refining and cleansing the physiology both are reduced, and then the abilities of the sidhis come by themselves."

Similarly, it was clear that the promised stronger fulfillment of desires began to develop. For example, in the morning, someone would wish for a certain dish for lunch—and what a miracle—exactly this was being served at noon. Or someone wanted to speak with someone else about a special topic—and, shortly afterwards, that person came towards him and started to talk about it on his own. Another one of us wanted to read a certain book—a few hours later someone approached him and said, "Man, I just devoured a fabulously great book; do you want to borrow it?" And who would have thought it—it was exactly the one that was wished for.

In the Yoga Sutras, their author, Maharishi Patanjali, described this cosmic lawfulness as *ritam bhara pragya*, literally translated as "the intelligence that knows the truth." Such a person's consciousness is so solidly grounded in the transcendent that he or she can have thought impulses without losing the eternal silence of the unbounded Absolute. It was exactly this that we'd been practicing for weeks with Patanjali's techniques that Maharishi Mahesh Yogi had brought to life for us. The Absolute, or pure Being, is the realm that lies at the basis of everything and that connects everything to everything else at its root. With the natural ability to think thoughts from this subtle level, we were anchored more solidly than is usual in the "World Wide Web" of the great cosmic computer; with the "search and order function" on this finest level of thought, the wise, organizing powers of nature were mobilized automatically. And in this way, we miraculously attracted whatever we had just thought of or whatever we needed just then. Patanjali knew that thoughts in the state of ritam bhara pragya—supported by the unbounded energy and all the possibilities of nature —became so powerful that they immediately manifested in the relative world. Obviously, we were experiencing the first, faint beginnings of this law of nature that gave us unimaginable wish fulfillment or amazing providence.

All our lives had improved dramatically in many areas. We had new, sometimes overwhelming, inner experiences. Many of us had, for the first time in our lives, a much deeper understanding of our own faith because all that we'd learned earlier in our Christian upbringing now had a much deeper meaning through our own practical experience, and even prayer was intensified enormously through the repeated experience of silence. We did not just believe; we had experiences that were so crystal clear and convincing that no one could have taken them away.

The most awe-inspiring thing was that each one of us, really each and every one of us who had experienced this exaltation and deep silence that suffused everything, felt with undeniable certainty that this quality of life really was life as it should be and that something decisive had been missing from the typical human life in our time, with its worries and sorrows and frequent dissatisfaction that we knew all too well. We knew that the vague longing that often motivates people and gives them the instinctive feeling that there must be something better and more beautiful than the life they know, that this longing made sense and was necessary because it allowed them to seek what we course participants had found here: a deep, inner happiness that accompanied life and that was completely independent of outward circumstances.

The course leaders often amazed us. They frequently had a surprisingly well-functioning intuition; they were there for us and always in an astonishingly good mood. At our meetings, they often made the whole group roar with laughter. They showered us with immense inspiration.

Obviously, the course leaders assumed, as did we, their spiritual charges, that soon there would be a world-wide breakthrough in consciousness. Our hearts were wide open, and good fortune surrounded us. In this environment among all the other course participants, everything seemed conceivable and easy. We really did have a handle on the Age of Enlightenment and we hoped the rest of it would come soon.

Fortunately, none of us having these thoughts could guess what sort of storm was brewing: harm from our fellow human beings for whom all these treasures were a book with seven seals.

Lift-Off

The suspense continued to mount because the high point of the sidhi course would be the "flying course;" that much had trickled down at that point in time. So, was there something to that old, ineradicable dream of humanity? Whatever the case, in the elevated mood of this group, there was a joyful anticipation of what was to come.

For the last two weeks of the sidhi course, we traveled from Urach back to Lindenberg to the forest lake. Immediately after our arrival, I sneaked a quick look into our future meditation hall. And I did indeed see there a lot of freshly covered big foam mattresses over the entire floor. With all my enthusiasm, a small doubt crept into me: could that really work, that "flying" thing?

On the following morning, we gathered in the lecture hall with our course-leader couple, Armin and Renate, at the front. He was dressed in a light-colored suit, and she, her hair long and blonde, wore a softly flowing dress. Aside from the fact that they were both downright beautiful people, they also seemed to be competing about which one of them was more radiant. Once again, I was seeing the phenomenon that I'd noticed in the hotels in France and in Switzerland. It wasn't just the eyes that shone, but even the skin seemed brighter, more translucent than that of other people.

Armin revealed to us: "This sidhi can only function perfectly with an impeccably pure nervous system, only when all stresses and physiological impurities are completely dissolved. The human body really does have the ability to levitate. But the precondition is that the qualities of pure consciousness have to suffuse and transform you to the extent that your cells lose their weight. The body then become lighter and lighter until it finally becomes weightless. We also know from the ancient Vedic tradition, where these techniques come from, that there is a preliminary stage of floating or levitating. The body does lift up into the air, but comes down again quickly, and it looks as if frogs are jumping."

Armin didn't let our grins deter him: "This sidhi is the most powerfully transformative one; it gets us used to unite two complete opposites because the body can only become weightless when consciousness remains completely grounded in silence while the body is active at the same time. As you all know, being able to maintain transcendental consciousness while you go about your outside tasks is a sign of Cosmic Consciousness. That is why higher states of consciousness develop more quickly through this joining of opposites during the flying technique."

Would my physiology be pure enough for this? I sure hoped so. But I was so confident and in good spirits that, relaxed as well as expectant, I just let things come to me. Finally, we got the instruction for the actual technique and sat down in the hall covered wall to wall with foam mattresses, and, with silence all around, we closed our eyes.

No one had prepared us for what happened now. And this innocence was in fact good for us. When I began with the technique of yogic flying, I didn't notice much of anything. But after a while, I felt my body gradually become lighter and even weightless. What a new, wonderful feeling to perceive the body to be so light and gossamer, almost free of earth's gravity! But then, at the same time, a powerful, spiritual energy began to build up, that flowed through me and extinguished all boundaries. Despite this, the silence of pure consciousness, in which I was already established, was maintained. Unmoved, I continued practicing my technique.

Suddenly, right in front of my mat there was a subdued, but distinct... thump... thump... thump.... Clearly, a body was plopping on the mat very close to me. It was happening, that had to be it. It worked! With my yogic directedness and introversion, it was gone more quickly than I could think. My eyes opened, and I saw—I almost didn't trust my own eyes—there was the first one who, cross-legged, was jumping around like a frog. Her eyes were wide open with joy, a devoted smile all over her face like Mary Magdalene in the most beautiful paintings. And to my utter amazement, I saw that it was our young course participant, the one who only had one leg!!! Thump...thump...thump....

I closed my eyes again and directed my attention inward, continuing to practice my sidhi. The energy within me became stronger and stronger; it shot through me and it straightened my spine bolt upright all by itself. As the energy shot upwards through it, my spine shook a few times back and forth on its own, and then, very suddenly, there was a jolt, and I was "pulled up" again and again, many times, until finally, I remained sitting on the mat, happy and dumbfounded at the same time.

Something else happened which none of us had counted on. We thought, naturally enough, that we'd become lighter and would float or hop decorously. So wrong! Little by little, more "frogs" became active. And things became outrageously active. Enough of the meditative tranquility. The energy that pulsed through us and that we could mysteriously activate with the help of this anciently transmitted technique was so powerful that it took everything with it that stood in the way. It especially targeted our own inner blockages—not yet resolved stresses, tensions, and traumas that had taken hold deeply in our nervous systems at some point in our lives and that reduced the free flow of physiological energy. And we seemed to carry a lot of that within us. We could feel how many pent-up emotions came to the surface and then, dissolving, left our bodily form. This process was always supported by a spiritual energy that catapulted power and bliss into our bodies. It was simply an unburdening of the gross body, and only very rarely did the relevant memory occur at the same time with this emotion. The energy that accompanied this process was indescribable. The body made movements, that you just couldn't do through your own will. Sometimes it twitched, twisted, and produced the strangest contortions or sounds. Despite all that, some of our group sat inward and unperturbed—or they did quiet little hops. We felt clearly how this powerful spiritual energy transformed our mind-body system. But one thing was crystal clear in a short time. Nobody levitated; we were all in the first phase—the frog phase!

Something that impressed me particularly was the fact that in the space of a minute or two the whole spectacle was over as soon as we stopped doing the technique. Now and then, a sound danced through the air, and then the group descended again into the deepest rest as if nothing had happened. But our bodies glowed with energy. We felt as if all channels were powerfully cleansed and made free. While lying down during the rest phase after the sidhis, the silence became powerful, and the experience of the transcendent became ever deeper. Often, I had the feeling that the unbounded silence made my body rigid and any impulse to move was extinguished.

Ever since the SCI course, in which Maharishi had described the different states of consciousness in depth, I had always imagined that Cosmic Consciousness, the state in which the inner unbounded and restful alertness even during activity and in deep sleep was maintained, would develop first and that then God Consciousness would unfold with its perceptions of heavenly realms. And then, last of all, like ducks in a row, Unity Conscious would be established, in which a person realizes the highest level of "I am that, thou art that, and all this is that"[10] as it is recorded in ancient Vedic scripture. On the TM-Sidhi course, however, I noticed that Maharishi's programs were designed in such a way that all these aspects could develop at the same time.

Back then, many of us felt increasingly and gently connected with everything else. Many of us saw it as a very concrete experience that is difficult to put into words. We got a quasi-taste. However, these experiences were not yet stable; for that, more practice was necessary, more cleansing and restructuring of the body-mind system.

Even so, an inner connectedness with everything, even with the external environment, was established clearly, because the magical "coincidences" in my life kept right on coming after the sidhi course.

I wanted to go home to visit my family. A lovely course participant was driving her car to Cologne. Of course, she was glad to have me for company. It was quite a distance on the freeway. The two of us together in the car enjoyed our silence as well as our lively conversation. Suddenly, for the first time on this long drive, there was a colossal traffic jam between Bad Camberg and Limburg, about 20 km from my home town—shortly before the exit where I wanted to get out and hitchhike the rest of the way. All lanes were blocked. Cars went slower and slower, and, finally our car stopped. My view drifted out of the window to the car next to us. The driver rolled down his window and said in the typical Nassau dialect, "Hey Lotha, whachoo doin' here?"

It was incredible. It was one of my friends from Balduinstein! He lived just a couple of houses down from mine. "Thomas, dude, I wanna get home, can you take me?"

"No problem, just get your butt over here!"

I thanked them both and, grabbing my bag from the trunk, I jumped into the other car, slamming the door—then laughter and joy. The traffic jam dissolved in no time flat and I was off in a private taxi directly to my front door.

Aha, another example of nature support, a little miracle! I really wouldn't have minded at all if life continued in that same way!

Not Far from the Goal

For a short time, I once again enjoyed my native soil and, still at home, I organized everything necessary and then drove north to the "Academy of Personal Development" in Blumenthal, a suburb of Bremen. We were 40 Germans, who would complete the last four months of their 12-months teacher training together.

Seen from the external structure, things went like the first part of the training: Mornings and evenings in silent meditation, and, during the day, we had countless video lectures about the most diverse topics to take notes on, to digest, to discuss, and to learn. In Phase I, we had learned how to give lectures and presentations; and, for presenting those, we also learned the connections to science. Now, these things went deeper, and we memorized all the steps that were necessary to initiate someone into meditation and give him or her all the explanations they needed to practice at home without making any mistakes.

The small German-speaking group was very pleasant. Naturally, we got to know one another deeply. With many of them, I am still in touch to this day and bonded through a deep trust. Again, there were new and exciting lectures on scientific research about what was happening during TM and what its effects were for the body and the spirit. And there were the parallels in chemistry, biology, medicine, and physics that brought to light all the mechanisms of human consciousness.

My own understanding of exactly what goes on in consciousness and in the body during meditation deepened. I could relate better to how old and unprocessed impressions were released from the nervous system. We called this process "unstressing."[(H)]

We also saw a few video lectures by Dr. Hans Selye, the famous father of research on stress, a man who'd dedicated his life to research the consequences of mental as well as physiological stress on living beings and who was honored world-wide with a total of 43 honorary Ph.D.'s. He coined the term "stress" and, later, the concepts of "eustress" for positive stressors and "distress" for negative ones. And he found something amazing, namely that the reaction of the body and the nervous system are identical, regardless of whether there is extreme joy or extreme sorrow. Too much is just simply too much, regardless of the subjective content of any overload.[6] In the second part of his life, Hans Selye learned TM and studied the research that had revealed what happens to the body during TM meditation. He spoke about it publicly: "I've researched the consequences of stress for my entire life. All reactions that occur in the body during TM are diametrically opposed to stress reactions."[(11)]

In Phase III, we again deepened our knowledge of the laws of nature and compared them with the mechanisms within human consciousness because, later, we'd have to answer to their satisfaction any questions other people might ask, so they could understand their individual experiences. We learned that the various advanced techniques that Maharishi taught on the basis of his tradition would help meditators not to get stuck in Cosmic Consciousness.[(I)]

During the morning and evening meditation programs, all that new knowledge would often circulate in my head.

---

[6] Newer insights in neurophysiology have expanded this view of the stereo-typical stress reaction. Thus, with eustress, for example, greater amounts of the "happiness hormone", serotonin are excreted, whereas these diminished with distress.

Even so, I still had many beautiful and clear experiences during my time in meditation and in the practice of the TM-Sidhi program. As one of the few who already practiced the Sidhi program back then, I got my own foam mattress in my tiny room so I could practice yogic flying there. I especially loved this technique because, with it, the gate to happiness opened wide. Like pushing a button, my access to the inner realm of energy, power, and happiness freed my head to take in yet more knowledge without strain.

During this training course, intense feelings of love and gratitude came, as well as great appreciation and profound gratitude for the great tradition of Vedic masters who, for thousands of years, had guarded this highest wisdom about how to make the experience of unboundedness available so effortlessly to every human being. On the level of the heart, this appreciation increased more and more during the course.

During the last weeks, we learned the steps to initiate people personally into TM in such a way that, like me five years earlier in Koblenz, they meditated perfectly the first time. We learned the long Sanskrit verses of the traditional ceremony of gratitude that, according to ancient custom, prepared both teacher and student for the initiation into the first meditation and touched their consciousness with the sounds of the Sanskrit syllables. We recited them, questioned each other—everyone totally enthusiastic about the longed-for goal. In just a few weeks, we would be TM teachers.

It was my burning desire to become a TM teacher. Never in my entire life had I so consistently and with every fiber of my being desired anything so much. But, at the same time, a wordless and exceedingly queasy feeling crept into my heart that something could still go wrong.

An Uneasy Feeling

Four weeks before graduation, having already passed almost all tests, my father called, "Lothar, there's a letter lying around here for weeks already; it's from the district recruiting office of the military, and there's a few other letters also. I think I better send them to you!"

Two days later, I had all the expected envelopes in my hand, opened them, and got a stomach ache. In front of me lay a draft notice from the *Bundeswehr* (the German military), as well as a serious warning to be in touch immediately. I instantly called the number at the bottom of the letter for the district recruiting office.

I got a cold shower: "We've been looking for you for months without success, so we've already classified you as a draft-dodger. There's no excuses left; you're being drafted as of now!"

I explained my situation to them and asked for a deferment: "…at least until I've got my TM teacher certificate in my pocket!"

"No way! There are no more deferments for you, not even for four weeks!"

No explanations from me were accepted. "What if I just don't show up 'til later?"

"Forget it; there's no way you can do that because we'll send the military police after you!"

Well, I was in a pickle. I didn't want—or could—leave in this decisive phase; I wanted to keep learning and finish everything. What a miserable concatenation of circumstances! Instead of being a TM teacher, I'd be a soldier—that couldn't be true! There was nothing I could do but comply. Phone calls weren't going to accomplish anything anyway. I quit the course, and the next day I drove to Neuwied to the recruiting office.

"Young man, you have got yourself in a real mess here!"

He was nice, a mid-forties guy, meticulous, a bit stocky, and with a good-natured face. "My superiors insist that you be drafted in the next few days; they will not go for any deferral for you. Rules are rules."

Wow! Still, I laid out my situation in detail and my mental anguish at having to quit now so near my longed-for goal and wait for two years. He wrinkled his brow and thought about it. "Oh my God, please let him think of something." My quick prayer seemed like nothing next to my inner pleading in this moment.

"Well, there's really nothing that can be done here… unless…well, maybe if you're a conscientious objector?"

A ray of light on the horizon. Of course; that's the thing: conscientious objector—so much better. But it doesn't work that fast; how could that help me now?

I was part of the generation that could go to court to fight for conscientious objector status, but people rarely won. But the official told me that there was recently a change in the law, which was in process of being repealed, but as of now it was still in force. I just had to apply in writing. "Well, actually, I'm not allowed to do this, but let's just see here!" And the helpful angel assisted me in filling out the necessary forms!

A week later, the notice came from the government for conscientious objectors in Cologne. My status was accepted! There was also a civil service position for me in an old age home in Diez, to begin day after tomorrow. That was impossible! I called immediately and asked for a deferral.

"No, you have to start with us right away, we need you urgently, someone just dropped out. On top of that we have instructions from the government for conscientious objectors to start immediately."

So close to the goal, and the thing became contentious again. That was just not going to work! Distraught, I called the government office for conscientious objectors in Cologne directly and had some luck. I got to another clerk who had a sympathetic ear. "There is one way out: you find an alternative community service position for yourself, one that will agree to wait for four weeks. But, young man," and he raised his voice with a warning, "We'll obviously need this in writing!"

How was I going to magically pull a position out of my hat? I could think of absolutely nothing. So, I called the course office of the German TM organization and explained my dilemma. "Unfortunately, I can't finish the TM teacher training course! It's totally impossible to find an alternate position—and I've tried everything; I'm at the end of my rope!

And now finally, at last, the miracle I'd been fervently hoping for this whole time went into high gear. Dumbfounded, I learned that the central TM office employed conscientious objectors: "That's a super fit. Somebody just quit here; you can start immediately if you want."

"Yes, but I can only do it in four weeks!"

"No problem, we can work things out in the meantime!"

They sent the certification directly to the government, and the road was clear. Or so I thought. Once again, they asked for a return call.

"We'll monitor this thing closely. On the 3rd of March at

9:00 A.M., you will start your service! And then one of our officers will be there to check on you personally. If you aren't there punctually, we'll send the military police to come and get you."

That was exactly on the morning after the completion of the TM teacher training course! Impossible. I knew that the final exams usually went late into the night. But somehow, I was going to get this done.

On the next day, all of us drove to Switzerland for the last two weeks. More than 200 people from various countries, who had all finished their teacher training at the same time as we had, came together here. We all took the final exams, and on the last day, Maharishi personally made us TM teachers. The last instructions did indeed go deep into the night. In wise forethought, I'd already packed my bag. And as soon as it was over, I ordered a taxi, grabbed my stuff, finally sat in the car at 1:00 a.m.; in Lucerne, I jumped on the express train that was already moving, got out in Osnabrück, ran to the next taxi and rode—while urging the driver to speed— the distance to Schledehausen, past small villages and the wondrously beautiful curves of the foothills of the Wiehen Hills. At the end, the taxi drove up a hill just outside Schlede- hausen. There stood two long buildings that had once been a sanatorium in a splendid and green parkland. Quickly, I paid the driver, swiftly strode into the course office of the German center, and pulled out my wristwatch—it was exactly 9:00 a.m.

A gentleman with a briefcase already stood in the office, the head inspector of conscientious objectors for several counties; he'd come specially to check on me and was exactly as punctual as I was. Whew! Made it!

IV.

TEACHER OF TRANSCENDENTAL MEDITATION

A truth can only be effective when the receiver is ripe for it. It is thus not the fault of truth when human beings are still so full of ignorance.

Christian Morgenstern
German poet and writer
1871-1914

Course Office

Spiritually, I had already prepared myself for the typical work of a domestic worker up here in these beautiful surroundings: washing dishes, cleaning, maybe even gardening. So, imagine my amazement when I learned from Herbert, a warm-hearted guy in his mid-twenties, that they'd planned for me to be the head of the course office. "Mr. Ritterstaedt called a few days ago and asked about everything. And I read your name and informed him that you will come to us as a "conchie." He knows you and he arranged for this."

Well, wasn't that something! Mr. Ritterstaedt, the national leader of the German TM-Movement, who'd gotten to know me as the hotel director at the Prätschli and had been so charming with my parents and from whom I'd learned the sidhis not too long ago! So here our paths crossed again.

The TM organization had been recognized as a non-profit and could therefore employ conscientious objectors. All the work back then was done by volunteers: students on semester break, pensioners like Mr. Ritterstaedt, and others who were glad to be useful for something important, and in a pleasant atmosphere.

The course office was in a small one-story building annex. In several rooms, there were desks as well as many shelves for files. At first sight, I was already impressed by how professional and orderly everything was here.

To the extent I proved myself worthy, Mr. Ritterstaedt trusted me with more and more responsibility and, after just a few weeks, he gave me the oversight over four co-workers. Our assignment was to coordinate and oversee everything that had anything to do with nation-wide courses. And that was a lot of work. At that time in Germany, there were an average of 700-800 people on various TM courses simultaneously, and this came with quite a lot of correspondence and filing. We phoned co-workers and the teachers of the TM centers who wanted to know about any details, and we took care of around twelve locations that the Movement had rented back then for courses. There were SCI courses going on in local TM centers and sidhi prep courses, as well as the main courses in the academies (in Germany, these were venues for "rounding courses," i.e. courses in which participants did more than two "rounds" of meditation program per day). Through my work, I got to know many TM teachers on the phone and loved supporting them in word and in deed.

Miraculously, I was given a lot of freedom. Mr. Ritterstaedt only came by every three weeks to see that things were going well. Thank God, he was so impressed with my commitment that he didn't just let me do my thing, he also gave me assignments that were sometimes quite confidential—and I accepted them joyfully. Soon, we worked together as an efficient team. I took over the assignments in Schledehausen. Only rarely, when I had complex situations, did I call him for advice in beautiful Seelisberg, Switzerland—which had meanwhile become the international center of the TM Movement.

The women from the international course office who were responsible for the Movement world-wide came from Seelisberg for an inspection. I already knew some of them from my time in France and Switzerland, and they, too, were very satisfied with my work. It was fun, and it all went smoothly. The office was neat, and things were never boring. The phone conversation with people at the TM centers enlivened our work, and we always dealt with kind and inspiring people.

For me, this time was heaven on earth. I lived in beautiful surroundings in the middle of nature and no traffic. I had an assignment that was fulfilling and I enjoyed the luxury of long meditation programs mornings and evenings. And to top things off, most of the time there were about 50 or 60 people in both big buildings who were there for TM teacher training or the sidhis courses and who uplifted the atmosphere through their bliss and their enthusiasm.

This magnificence went on for exactly eight months.

Forced Transfer

In a good mood, I'd just opened the office and had jumped into the first task with my colleagues, when a little later I went to the entrance to get the mail and, unannounced, there stood two guys in black leather jackets—probably in their early forties. They smelled like whiskey and cigarettes. Some pretty rough-looking dudes.

"What can I do for you?"

"We want to speak to the boss!"

Because Mr. Ritterstaedt wasn't there, I introduced myself as his representative and asked what they wanted. "We're from the ZDF (*Zweites Deutsches Fernsehen* or Second German Television, a German public-service television broadcaster) and we want to make a film about conscientious objectors in this organization for our political magazine."

Whew. I had a bad feeling about these guys. "What's your intention with this film?"

"The TM Movement is controversial, and there are people who are asking themselves how come you are getting government assistance by employing conscientious objectors!"

The man hardly looked at me; he had dull and disagreeable eyes. My uneasiness grew. No way did I want to decide on my own whether to consent or to refuse.

I called Seelisberg immediately but could not speak to Mr. Ritterstaedt and, instead, got another close co-worker of Maharishi's who gave me the green light to refuse.

"I'm sorry, Gentlemen, I have a feeling that your intentions aren't good and that you wouldn't do an objective report. We are not available for any interviews and you do not have permission to film on these premises."

They let their masks drop. Their expressions became even darker and, frustrated, they became abusive. One of them even raised his finger and threatened me: "Don't think for a minute that you can get away with this! There will be repercussions, you can count on that. We've got connections, and within 24 hours all your conchies will be outta here!"

I only took them half-ways seriously, because the international TM organization was registered with *IMS Deutscher Verband e.V.* (a non-profit registration organization that no longer exists) and had been recognized as a non-profit for years in Germany. What could possibly happen? Everything was on the up and up. The applications were properly filed with the appropriate agencies and had been accepted. Plus, it was clear that everything that the TM organization did was beneficial for the common good. People became healthier and more stable spiritually and physically through this practice, and TM teachers were welcome in many prisons in Germany as honorary co-workers. They taught TM to the prisoners, which helped with their rehabilitation and they took these prisoners under their wing individually or in groups. In the drug scene, TM had been successful and it was in wide-spread usage as a withdrawal therapy. Meditation helped countless young people get off drugs, from marijuana and even from heroin and other narcotics. When drug addicts began to meditate twice a day, most of them quit using after a few months of regular practice. There were several pilot studies about this phenomenon, and scientific studies in similar programs had been published in the professional literature.[12]

Even though the term "cult" had haunted the German media here and there, I looked at these threats with composure for now.

But that only lasted for 24 hours.

That very night, I got a call from a representative of the government agency for conscientious objectors. He was a nice guy who'd looked in on us every month or two to get an idea about how things were going with us conchies. "Mr. Pirc, I have to tell you that all the conchies on your premises will be transferred tomorrow. I'm really sorry, and, personally, I don't get it. All of you up there are the conchies I like best in my whole territory. It's the only place where the conchies feel totally great about their work place, and the usual problems and complaints that I have to deal with at other places have never been an issue with you. Also, in my whole time on this job, I've never got a call at night; or that anything had to be dealt with right away. As I said, I am so sorry, this thing is coming from on high with no reason given. My hands are tied. I'll call you back tomorrow morning and tell you where you're being transferred to."

I was in shock. My first impression of these guys from ZDF had unfortunately been right on!

The following morning, the official called again. Overnight, a new place had been organized for every conchie. The four of us packed our bags and drove to the Red Cross in Ammerland that same day. The team from ZDF obviously did have "great" connections and they had done their job.

Community Service at the Red Cross

Within our bad luck, we were lucky. Our group got a four-bedroom attic apartment in a big, red brick house at the Red Cross in Rasteede.

"You'll have rotating shifts here, always starting at 7:00 a.m. For a week, you'll drive an ambulance 24/7 and then you'll have 24 hours off; the following week it's the taxi for the sick (they exist in Germany) from 7:00 a.m. to 7:00 p.m." Each one of us got a Red Cross uniform: grey, sharply-creased pants and a dark grey jacket with the Red Cross emblem on it.

Next morning, right away, the inspector for the government showed up to make sure we'd taken up our duties properly.

We made ourselves comfortable in our apartment and got some foam mattresses and set up our own "flying room." At 5:00 a.m., our alarm clock rattled and, undaunted, we got up to do our TM-Sidhi program together. Just before 6:00 a.m., we started the flying technique, and then added a rest period before we grabbed a bit of breakfast to give us the strength for the exhausting day ahead. Often, the whole house shook from our wild hops. And that was the wake-up call for the full-time staff who slept one floor beneath us during their time on call.

After some time, one of them asked, "Say, what in the world are you doing so early in the morning? Moving furniture or something?"

As the only TM teacher in our crew, I shot back with an answer, "We can't explain this to you on the fly. We're practicing a special meditation technique and we'd love to give you an intro lecture. Best thing would be if you also brought your wives!"

I'd meanwhile finished my twelve-months TM teacher training course and I used every opportunity to tell people about the blessings of Transcendental Meditation. No sooner said than done. A few days later, twelve people were really sitting at our place: six staff members and their wives. We laid it on thick and told them everything about TM and the sidhis and, naturally, we also mentioned yogic flying while they, fascinated, listened to the details. It was a beautiful evening, and we had a lot of fun.

Three weeks later, the boss came back from vacation and found a letter on his desk from the government agency for conscientious objectors. In it, he was advised in beautiful "bureaucratish" that he had four new conchies at his workplace who he should watch carefully because they were some weird birds. He was instructed to report on their activities. What should an employer do about such information? Well, he first asked his regular staff what was up with us. By way of answer, he heard the whole nine yards. That we could "fly," that we'd given them an intro lecture about TM, and that I talked to people about TM on the job—while wearing a Red Cross uniform! But, other than that, he was told that we did our work especially well, that we were nice, and that they really liked every one of us. Despite this update, he thought the whole thing was highly dubious; in any case, he did not want to be responsible for these "birds" all by himself. Besides, he had to report back. What does an employer do when he feels insecure? He calls the appropriate inspector and asks for a visit.

So, the regional government representative for conscientious objectors in this area came by and asked me for a private interview so he could form his own opinion. He didn't have to wait long, I grabbed the opportunity with both hands and gave him an introductory lecture on TM. He was totally in to it.

"I'll have to tell my wife about this; this is exactly what she needs." He was impressed with what we were doing and found it remarkably good. He had no objections, but, at the end, he did have a request: "Please Mr. Pirc, promise me that you won't do any more lectures in your Red Cross uniform!"

I promised, and I kept my promise...

...but only during work hours.

My enthusiasm for TM now required a new outlet. So I rented a lecture hall in a hotel and I distributed posters advertising the talks. About twelve people showed up, and—wearing my own suit—I laid out the positive effects of this technique on spirituality, health, social conduct, and world peace. The audience followed along well, especially four older women in the first row, who nodded energetically the whole time, which gave me wings. They listened attentively, nodded, smiled, nodded, and then smiled some more. Well, finally, my first TM initiations were on the horizon. For sure, the four of them would joyfully want to learn TM. And I would, equally joyfully, teach them the art of meditation. That my first instruction would go to these great women was an extra bonus!

After providing the information, I answered questions from the audience and then asked all those who were really interested to stay. Those who wanted to leave things with just the intro were excused to go home. Just as I'd expected, the four older women stayed. To my utmost amazement, one of them said, "We don't want to learn to meditate, but we'd like to talk to you a bit later!"

It was one big question mark, but I went with it.

So, I first turned to the fifth women, a confident blonde in her mid-thirties, and she invited me to give the second preparatory lecture at her house—she'd invite a couple of her friends, and we made a convenient date. Silent and patient, the four older women waited till she had gone, and only then did they introduce themselves in turn and let me know: "Your introductory lecture was really good! All four of us are TM teachers in this area, and we came so we can get to know you."

Whoa! Was I ever surprised. I really hadn't expected that! During my time in Rasteede, we subsequently met for several lively and deep conversations about God and the world.

Soon after and as promised, I repeated my talk for the young woman in a posh house in the suburbs and, in the end, I could initiate my first five people into Transcendental Meditation. I remember to this day that, after a short time, all five of them were impressed with the positive effects in their lives.

After six months with the Red Cross, my friends and I had finished so many hours of over-time that we could finish our conchie service four months ahead of schedule. Thus, we ended our interlude as paramedics in Ammerland.

Finally, an Active TM-Teacher

After completing the civil service assignment, it was my biggest wish to work as a meditation teacher. And again, I was lucky. In Darmstadt, they were looking for a full-time TM-teacher. Beautiful new and bright rooms above a pastry shop in a pedestrian area had been available, and enthusiastic and well-situated meditators had rented them. With fiery zeal I started there, giving intro lectures with great joy at the teacher training center itself, but also at companies, clubs, and associations. And I loved initiating people from all walks of life and all social classes and professions. From my own experience and through all I'd seen meanwhile, I knew that deeply-held stresses in their souls would dissolve little-by-little and their very own unique personalities would be liberated. They would be able to live with fewer inhibitions and fear, and with a stronger will toward the positive; they'd be less edgy, and they'd laugh more and be happier, and they would have more strength for external problems. Because of their evening meditation, they would be able to enjoy their evenings with new energy instead of being tired after work. What a beautiful and fulfilling profession I had chosen!

I now experienced what I had already observed at the beginning of my time as a meditator with other TM teachers. I was beaming when I came back out of the initiation room. The greatness of the tradition of enlightened masters who'd given us this knowledge touched my heart each time. I felt very clear and often downright humble, as the souls of the new meditators opened and they, frequently for the first time as adults, experienced this depth and boundless silence consciously within their own awareness. I became very silent myself and felt completely connected with them—this activity was for me the most uplifting thing I could imagine. From many of them, I heard these words afterwards: "I know this experience from my childhood, but I haven't had it for many years. The last time maybe when I was a little boy (or girl)!"

How beautiful it was to be able to put into their hands the key to their own innermost domain—the key to their most silent essential core that reveals itself on its own, like a treasure believed to have been long lost, when our incessant mental activity comes to rest in meditation.

I held well-attended center evenings with various themes and with full hands gave away the knowledge that I'd received in the last few years. I could even lead Phase I of the TM teacher training course back then, to my knowledge the only part-time course of this kind that interested parties could complete after their professional activities. We met two evenings per week and once a month for a weekend course. The participants appreciated all the new knowledge and I was happy to be able to pass on my newly acquired knowledge and to deepen it yet again.

In addition, I led a SCI course and organized a TM sidhi course for meditators, as these courses now could be largely completed at the TM centers. We all grew together as a friendly group, celebrated seasonal holidays, and meditated as a group. It was an easy and glorious awareness of life. I felt free and unburdened.

Gradually, however, a shadow fell on this wonderful time. Despite my great commitment, I did not earn enough to pay back my bank loan for the months-long TM teacher training. The interest rate was so high in that time that despite regular payments, I could not pay it off. Back then, the basic TM course cost was 140 DM of which the teacher could only keep part for himself. Another part of it stayed in the TM Center for rent and other expenses and a further part went to the German and the international organizations for management and expansion.

My enthusiasm before the TM-Sidhi and the TM teacher training courses had been so great that I—enlivened by my intensely exhilarating experiences with the sidhis— once again made assumptions about other people. And so with trust, I'd taken it for granted that people would stand in line to learn this fantastic technique, and that through this I would be easily able to pay back the principle and the interest for the loan Herbert had guaranteed. Unfortunately, I had misjudged the situation completely. I did teach TM to a few people every week, but it wasn't enough to pay off the loan in addition to my modest living expenses. After a year of Darmstadt, it dawned on me that, for better or worse, I'd have to take another job to pay off the mountain of debt that weighed me down.

And so, with a heavy heart, I reduced my teaching load that was so fulfilling to a few hours per week and worked the main profession I'd learned as a textile merchant. It was unbelievably boring and exhausting. And despite a ten-hour day, I realized after barely a year that in this job as well it would take many years to pay off the loan because of those high interest rates.

So I gave notice and instead looked for some with excellent earning potential. Wasting no time, I applied as an independent sales rep for rare books and began to sell expensive books, biographies about the most important personalities of world history, to good clients for a well-known book club. My customers could purchase the 24 volumes, heavy tomes with gold embossing and gilt edges, little by little over four years. I arranged for appointments on the phone to meet and get the club members enthused in their own homes about these dark purple books and then finalize a contract and its term limit.

It turned out not to be as simple as I'd thought to sell a book series for 2,400 DM, even after I'd gained the necessary technical expertise. At the beginning, I went along with the most successful salesman and he taught me some sales techniques. But it wasn't my thing to palm off books to folks with aggressive sales pitches. I took the parts I liked from him. But I omitted putting pressure on people because it made me feel bad.

I did it my own way, and by the third month I was the second-best salesman among 120 colleagues in all of Germany. On average, I earned 8,000 DM per month in commissions. Even so, I lived pretty frugally.

However, nothing had prepared me for what was to come.

First Death

An intense impulse I couldn't shake urged me to drive home for a visit. For several weeks, I'd not seen my parents. We ate together at the kitchen table, had a harmonious evening, and talked as we had in the good old times. I soaked up the gentle love and care of my mother, who had, as always, a big heart for everyone. Even my father was very cheerful; he was proud and happy about my good earnings in those days—and he wanted to know every small detail about it. Relaxed and peaceful we finally went to bed.

During the night, my father suddenly called with an agitated and fearful voice: "Lothar, Lothar, come down, something happened to Mom!"

I rushed into my parents' bedroom. There she lay on her bed and was obviously in terrible pain. She whimpered and moaned, but she wasn't conscious. I knew immediately that this was serious, very serious. For years, my mother had complained about headaches and everyone in the family knew that she took pain pills more and more often to bear this relentless pain. Modern medicine was powerless in finding the cause of these headaches, so she just swallowed more of those round white pills that made the pain more bearable for a short while.

My father was so upset about her condition that he was almost paralyzed. So, I called an ambulance and, immediately afterwards, the village priest, asking him to come to the hospital for the last rites. After just ten minutes, the doctor and the ambulance were there and drove with us to Diez. And there she lay, her head on a thick, white pillow of the hospital bed, her face distorted with pain. Several times in the last few years she had said that her "watch had almost wound down." But no one took her seriously. She was only fifty and seemed alright, aside from her chronic and severe headaches and high blood pressure. And, naturally we hoped against all hope she would recover, although we all knew better.

The door opened. A team of doctors sent us from the room in order to examine the sick woman. Their unanimous diagnosis when they came back out was this: "She doesn't have a chance; it's the end!" And we were allowed back into her room.

Her breath became more and more faint and intermittently came in gasps; she could no longer speak or perceive anything. My father and I sat by her, incapable of saying anything, each one alone with her and with his grief. I quietly held her hand, meditated and sent her loving thoughts to make the great journey that lay before her easier.

Only a few minutes later the priest came to give her the last rites. While he gave her the last anointment, he spoke to her, loud and firm, calling her by name. And then the first miracle happened. My strictly devout mother, who had been totally unresponsive, reacted visibly. The death agony eased and she listened to him.

But then the doctor on duty came back, looked into the room, and said, "All of you have to come out, it's only going to be a few minutes!" And then we again stood outside the door.

When he let us back in after one or two minutes, she was completely changed. She must have had a severe cerebral hemorrhage, half of her face had become dark purple. But she had an otherworldly and blissful smile on her face. I was deeply awed and relieved because it gave me the certainty that wherever she was now, she was alright. Even after three days, shortly before the burial, this smile was still unchanged, so that all the relatives who saw her for the last time in her coffin were deeply moved by the blissful look on her face.

I was immensely grateful to the inner voice that called me home so I could be with her in these last minutes and could see her blissful smile.

But shortly afterwards, grief set in—a never-yet-felt despair about this forever good-bye. It raged in my gut, shook me, and made me speechless and empty. The loss hit all of us to the bone. My father loved my mother very much. She was the harmonizing center of his life and of our small world. It was inconceivable that she, who had always been the loving focus of our family, had so early and unexpectedly left us.

My father and I were deeply shaken. The swing of transience and loss had thrown a dark shadow on my life that had always been so happy. Even meditation could not completely drive this deep sorrow away. It would be a long time before I didn't miss my mother so painfully and this wound was healed.

My father was inconsolable for months. So, I stayed at my parents' home in this difficult time and helped him with his needs while also pursuing the sale of rare books. Despite everything, this stroke of fate had its good side. This togetherness brought my father and me closer. After many years of estrangement, the old familiarity and love of my childhood came back.

Soon after, the CEO and the regional leader who'd trained me came from Stuttgart to Frankfurt to the Intercontinental Hotel expressly to meet me there. They were most pleased with my success and offered me a good career—with the super premiums I could have made 20,000 DM per month. I declined.

No money on earth could replace the joy I felt when I followed my dream and initiated people into TM or spread the Vedic knowledge.

A little later, I could pay off the last of my debt at the bank through sales and through my strict frugality. At the time, I sent a magnificent bouquet to Herbert in Lindau on Lake Constance for his generosity and his trust. In my heart, I'm grateful to him to this day.

Government Contacts at the Rhine River

Once again, a happy coincidence came to fulfill my great dream to become a full-time TM teacher. At a TM teacher conference in Urach, I got to know Charlotte more closely. She was an unbelievably charismatic and warm-hearted psychologist. She could give excellently well-founded presentations and express herself with unequaled eloquence. Many TM teachers and meditators admired her. And, of all people, it was Charlotte who was looking for a TM teacher who could contact politicians in Bonn. For this position, the TM teacher could move into a villa, right next to the Rhine in Cologne-Rodenkirchen, into a villa that the German TM organization had rented. I didn't hesitate for long. To work with Charlotte and learn from her was a tremendous opportunity.

A little later I looked up addresses, made appointments, and invited politicians to our prestigious villa. Charlotte and I soon worked together as an excellent team and, full of enthusiasm that our illustrious guests could not help but notice, we presented the benefits of Transcendental Meditation for the various areas of concern of modern society.

For the government officials from the Ministry of Health, we explained the positive effects on public health and laid out for them what savings for the whole society would be possible if health insurance companies were to offer recompense for meditation as a therapeutic measure. We showed them graphs and several scientific studies that indicated impressive improvements in health, such as the lasting reduction of long-term sleep disorders within a few weeks of practice,[13] the quantifiable reduction of bronchial asthma after only three months,[14] and the systematic reduction of high blood pressure—the number one killer of all industrialized nations—and that this reduction occurred with a decrease of blood pressure reducing medications at the same time.[15]

Meditation instead of blood-pressure pills? The whole time these politicians were with us, they listened with fascination to our expositions. They asked many questions, and it wasn't hard to see that they were impressed with our presentation.

We introduced a high-ranking representative of the Ministry of the Interior, who'd come at the request of the Minister, to the results of the American prison studies. Two hundred and sixty prisoners had learned TM and practiced regularly in various maximum-security prisons, including the infamous San Quentin. After they'd been released, the frequency of their recidivism had been monitored by governmental agencies over five years. The surprising result: The convicts practicing TM committed significantly fewer crimes after their release and were 40% less likely to return to prison than their non-meditating fellow inmates. In addition to the better social reintegration of these convicts and the positive effects on their personal lives, the financial benefits for the government were nothing to sneeze at. The therapy of silence showed demonstrably better results than the much more expensive government-financed programs for education, the promotion of talent, and the psychotherapeutic rehabilitation programs.[16] According to the researchers, the government saved $20,000 per person per year—in other words, five million annually, even with the small sample of 250 offenders tested. What would the savings be if this were done in all the prisons of a country?

The results of research on the Maharishi Effect should also be mentioned; it showed that crime rates, hospital admission rates, and traffic accident rates were all dramatically reduced if 1% in any city practiced TM.[6, 7] This too is not only an enormous improvement of the quality of life for citizens but also a significant potential savings for the state.

The politicians we'd invited were more than interested; they were impressed and promised to discuss these results with their superiors in their various ministries. Every time, Charlotte and I were sure that with such well-documented numerical data, steps would be taken to integrate TM in the German rehabilitation programs or the health-care system in the foreseeable future. But, every time, our disappointment was equally certain. All that impetus eventually ran dry. None of our guests were committed enough to this old, and yet new, knowledge for it to be implemented somewhere in his or her sphere of influence or at least tested with a small pilot project. It was just too new, too different, and they were in no position to give it a chance. It was one thing to listen to the research results, to understand the underlying principles, to recognize the authenticity of the scientific studies, and to vividly imagine the advantages but it was quite another thing to advocate it when the TM experts were no longer present. Who would have wanted to introduce such an unusual proposal in the circle of government colleagues and possibly become a laughing-stock? After all, every politician ultimately wants only one thing: to be re-elected. So, for the time being, our enthusiasm fizzled out. I was sad for all those whom this knowledge could have helped to live happier and healthier lives with a more fearless and relaxed psyche—and above all, outside of prison walls!

In Love

What a beautiful smile! Such a pretty and open face! Once or twice a month, a slender young girl with dark blonde, long hair came to Rodenkirchen to take care of the garden. I found her to be pretty, gentle, and exceedingly attractive—I began to look forward to the day she'd come. I was hooked! In all my years, women had never interested me—not even the radiant women in Switzerland and France—no more so than the many young women that I'd gotten to know and to value in the past eventful years.

She seemed to be drawn to me also. So I gathered all my courage and invited her for a friendly walk in the woods. We rattled off in my bright green Renault R-14 and talked; the attraction seemed mutual.

A few more walks followed. But I was shy and didn't dare to get closer in any intimate way. She seemed disappointed, but I just couldn't jump over my own shadow. She remained friendly and relaxed, but I seemed to have chosen the perfect way to successfully scare her away with my indecisive demeanor. She withdrew. I suffered inner conflicts; on the one hand, I wanted to let things to take their own sweet time, but on the other hand, I wanted the relationship to deepen. A few days later, she went to Arosa for a TM course.

Head over heels, I went after her. On the spur of the moment, and in hopes that a relationship could develop between us, I registered for a course in the immediate vicinity to hers. However, just outside Arosa, my car ended our friendship. On the way across the pass, I had probably asked too much of it. In front of my windshield, a thick, white cloud of smoke rose suddenly and under the hood things boiled like crazy. And it was just before midnight!

A little later that night, a friendly driver took pity on me and, looking at the mess, he enlightened me: "You'd better wait till your motor cools off, then you can risk driving the last four or five kilometers without the coolant."

No sooner said than done. However, the summer night was warm, and so it took almost two hours before my over-exerted friend was once again cool and willing. As if sitting on red-hot coal, I crept forward to Arosa. I was almost there when the car started steaming again. All kinds of warning signs lit up the dashboard and white clouds obstructed my view. What to do? At the edge of town, I parked that unfaithful dude and went the rest of the way to the hotel on foot.

It was 2:00 a.m. All the lights were off and reception was closed, obviously. I was dog tired, but where could I sleep? Looking for a way, I saw my salvation—a window directly next to reception was open and inviting. "Wonderful," I thought, "I'll just climb in there, lie down on a sofa in reception till the hotel opens in the morning and I can move to my room." It was pitch-dark, and, full of hope, I swung my legs over the window sill quietly, so as not to disturb anyone, and landed softly and lightly. As soon as my feet touched the bed, a deep, full voice yelled in Swiss German, "A burglar, oh my God, a burglar!"

Standing straight up in front of me was a deeply shaken man in his pajamas. He was gasping with agitation. I was quick to calm him down and told him that I was a course participant, also mentioning my pig-headed car and the tedious cooling-off maneuvers. But it got even more unpleasant and embarrassing for me: I had landed with both feet exactly on the director of the hotel! After he got over his initial shock, he showed his more gentlemanly side. Ready to help, he gave me a blanket and sheets for my room and, in the morning, he even found an auto-repair shop for me. Thank you!

For two weeks, I enjoyed a wonderful course, but, alas, in a different hotel than my flame. And I suffered profoundly from unfulfilled love. Wherever I was, and, naturally, especially while meditating, I thought about her loveliness, grieved that my tender love for her was out of the question, and imagined that she would want a real boyfriend and all that went with it. I was torn here and there by my desire to calmly let things take their own course and my longing for her. Trapped in my dilemma, I did nothing but languished in my misery and indecisiveness from a distance.

At the end of the two weeks, all the TM teachers went to Seelisberg, where we met with Maharishi and could ask him questions without any constraints. Maharishi talked about the coming Age of Enlightenment and asked us how every TM teacher could multiply himself a hundred-fold because that was what we'd have to do to realize this new age of peace and loving togetherness. With my whole heart, I fervently wanted nothing more than for this quality of life that I experienced around Maharishi and many other meditators to be real for all the people of this planet. But at the same time, I had felt more than clearly with all my activities in Germany that my Master's golden vision of the future obviously could not be implemented as quickly as I and many others had believed early on.

Unless, yes, unless something truly dramatic happened that would open people's eyes to the fact that they were created for more than just eating, drinking, sleeping, working, and having kids. An unusual idea took shape in my head and my finger went up: "Maharishi, I've been doing my sidhi program blissfully for two years now and I am grateful for the many positive improvements in my life. But I'm still doing the same small hops. If we could really fly, as we've told everyone, then we'd be more plausible, and more people would follow us. How long will it be before we can really fly?"

Maharishi looked at me gently and benevolently. "Keep on doing as you have been doing, then you'll be able to fly to Mount Shiva, the Himalayas or wherever you like". Mount Shiva was the name he gave to the majestic mountain across from Seelisberg on the other side of Lake Lucerne.

Yes, Maharishi, but why isn't it working already?" Patience has never been one of my virtues. Amused, the audience laughed out loud, but Maharishi confirmed with a gesture that he was serious.

He went into silence for several seconds and then looked at me seriously and with appreciation. "For that to happen, two things are necessary. We can only stay up in the air when consciousness is 100% pure. If it's only 99% pure, that's not enough. The mind can change quickly, but the body needs more time. To be able to fly, all the components have to be transformed and that takes its time. Have you heard how some people make dog and cat sounds during the flying program?" Exhilarated laughter all around. We all knew exactly what he meant.

"Those are the *samskaras*, old impressions or imprints, and they have to be released from the nervous system so that consciousness is 100% pure. But there are ways to help the nervous system free itself from these early impressions. I'm currently working day and night to bring out *Ayurveda*. This science of life will help you to eliminate the toxins and blockages from your nervous systems—without that, it's not so easy to gain enlightenment."

Ayurveda—I was hearing this Sanskrit word for the first time—without a hint as to what a huge role it would play for me and my life in the yet distant future.

"The second thing is this: We are dependent on the collective consciousness of the world. People today are constantly violating natural law and thereby stress is accumulating in world consciousness. This stress influences each one of us and weighs us down. When we practice TM or the TM-Sidhis program in a group, that's like a collective washing machine that frees world consciousness from this burden. To master the sidhis completely, we need more people to better deal with the stress of the collective consciousness. The groups we now have aren't yet big enough for that."

In addition to everything Maharishi had explained, something else, something quiet and unexpected happened. Through his attention, my broken heart mended and my inner anxiety vanished. The waves of my grief calmed down, and I once again felt calm and mellow. When I noticed this, my inner voice said immediately, "Now I'm free, but I have to be careful that I don't enliven this pain again. This freshness and this clarity are a gift from Maharishi and I have to take care that I don't fall back down."

And that was indeed how it came. I drove back to Cologne-Rodenkirchen, never again to awaken this longing, and I rested, free and happy as before.

V.

CLOISTER YEARS

*If a man's eye is on the Eternal, his intellect will grow
and his opinions and actions will acquire a beauty
that no amount of education or advantage
of others can compete with.*

Ralph Waldo Emerson
1803-1882
American philosopher and writer

Among Men

"To raise world consciousness more quickly and to accelerate the enlightenment of every one of you, I'll create a group for women and one for men, so they can practice an intensive TM-Sidhi Program together."

This is what Maharishi gave us to think about a few days ago in Switzerland, and I had taken this new opportunity to heart.

Broadcasts via phone with this new information went to all TM Centers, so that everyone who wanted to be part of such a group could apply. The requirement was that you had to commit to two or three years and you couldn't have any other responsibilities, such as family, outstanding debt, or other obligations to take care of. Well, I had nothing of the kind. I cleared up everything that could have stood in the way and I was prepared mentally. As I was putting the envelope with my written application into the mailbox, I heard my inner voice, "With this, a completely new and meaningful part of your life will begin and will bring big changes for you."

A few days later, the phone rang at our villa in Roden-kirchen. Reinhard, one of Maharishi's secretaries, was on the line: "Lothar, I got your application. Would it be possible for you to lead an international Phase Three TM teacher training course? But you'd have to come right away because you'd be replacing someone who's needed for an international project somewhere outside the country."

Whoa, things were going head over heels once again! "But I just applied for the new men's course!"

"That doesn't matter. When you finish the teacher training course then you can still join that group—no problem!"

Of course, I said, "yes." What would be better than leading a TM teacher-training course? I loved it, and I was free and unattached.

Elated, I drove to Arosa once again. The course was in a guest house directly next to the Hotel Prätschli. For meals, we went over to that elegant hotel that I'd managed some years earlier for a few months. Gradually, I felt at home here. I led the three-months course with Roger, a French-Canadian guy with a strong French accent, who loved telling weird and dry jokes. Our course participants were about thirty men from America, Iran, Lebanon, France—from all continents. It was instructive, intense, and as beautiful as always.

The special thing about it, as we soon learned, was that at that time Maharishi was establishing *Purusha*, the group he'd been telling us about, right next door at the Prätschli, with about 100 single men who'd come from Seelisberg by bus. The Sanskrit word *Purusha* signifies the original, eternal human being and emphasizes the fundamental nature of man, the divine essence, which through intensive meditation programs can be set free. This Purusha group was said to be an effective contribution for raising the collective consciousness of the whole world. And not only that. Maharishi also announced, "I will personally and actively monitor the experiences of the participants so that each one of you can attain a new level of consciousness."

A few weeks later, the whole group moved into an empty former monastery that the TM organization had rented in Germany. And indeed, when I'd finished leading the TM teacher training course, I followed the others back into my German homeland and into the cloister Marienberg in Boppard on the Rhine.

The monastery Marienberg in Boppard on the Rhine where, from 1982-1984, I meditated daily for many hours in a group of about 200 young men, studied the Vedas, and came into contact with Ayurveda for the first time

From the medieval center of town, I went up the hill on foot and soon stood in front of the baroque monastery that was first built in the 12th century but had been remodeled several times. Brightly whitewashed walls, three stories high with transom windows, rose before me.

The dark grey, slate-tiled, overhanging roof massively enclosed two rows of clerestory windows on the two upper floors. I went across the cobblestone courtyard that had been worn down through hundreds of years by many feet and through the heavy, double French doors in the center of the main building. About two hundred men had meanwhile been living and meditating here. I got a simple room with a bed, a desk, and a closet on the second floor with a view onto the romantic inner courtyard, whose flower beds flaunted summery touches of color.

"Lothar, you can just sign the admission forms and then

bring it down to the office!"

Reinhard, a tall guy with a pale face, blue eyes, and straight black hair was responsible for organization. I already knew him a little. He had completed his degree in education and had then become one of Maharishi's secretaries. Reinhard was not a man of many words but he had great organizational talent and a sharp intellect. As soon as I'd arrived, joyfully ready to spend the next two or three years of my life here, there was an unpleasant surprise. With my signature on the form, I would make a commitment for life. No one had mentioned this before, and I didn't like the taste of it at all. So, I went back to see Reinhard.

"What's this all about, Reinhard? It says here I have to make a life-time commitment. I don't want to do that. Later, I want to get married and have a family and kids!"

Reinhart took it lightly. "Well, now, just let it go! Go and meditate in your room and go within. But if you don't want to make that commitment, then you can't participate in this course, unfortunately."

So, okay, I meditated alone in my room and went within. But the answer was always the same. Even though I wanted to participate in this new program, a life-time commitment was not an option for me. That, I felt clearly. With regularity, the two Purusha course leaders, Joachim and Wolfgang, came by and tried to paint the program with tempting promises and pretty speeches but I did not vacillate or falter. Now and then, Reinhard came by also. "Lothar, there's nothing better in life than to evolve. What could be more important than gaining enlightenment?"

I was in total agreement with every fiber of my being. But for a whole life? No. That was out of the question for me. I knew a whole bunch of Purusha here and really longed to be with them for the extended group meditations. A few well-meaning friends suggested a possible way out of this thorny state of affairs: "Just sign the thing! And if you don't like it any more, then simply leave; that's how I did it!"

But that was not for me; either it was all above board and honest, or it was zilch. And so, a week after another went by. For two entire months, they let me hang there, and then the whole thing got to be too much. "Reinhard, either I can stay here and make a commitment for two to three years, or I'm leaving right now. Then, at least, I can go on initiating people into TM, or lead a TM Center or do some other sensible thing with my life!"

Then, suddenly, a door opened. Surprisingly, the rules had just been changed, and now it was possible to register for just a few years. How great it was, that I had waited it out. Now I could sign the thing with a good conscience and be on the program.

Monk for a Time

How wonderful! Finally, I was allowed into the big meditation hall where, with others, I could close my eyes for a better part of the day. I enjoyed it to the fullest. This was a whole 'nother thing compared to closing my eyes alone twice a day, day in and day out!

In the hours outside of meditation, we studied Vedic knowledge in work groups, watched video tapes, or listened to lectures on various subjects. Some of us kept up our contacts to the local TM centers and supported them from here in Boppard. Our well-regulated schedule gave our nervous systems the necessary rest to open up and enliven the subtle realms in the depths of our consciousness. Only rarely did we leave the premises. So as to make the best possible spiritual progress and to create a harmonizing effect on our environment, we stayed among ourselves and did not get distracted. And once a day, we went down the long and winding path for a walk behind the garden walls of the monastery's park.

This time was not only characterized by beautiful and deepened experiences within ourselves, but also by unbelievably great comradery. Because of the cost, we no longer had the staff that in our earlier courses had taken over the housework for us, and so we were all responsible ourselves for the good condition of the facility. In teams, we took turns daily to take care of a certain assignment to keep things in order. Here, I once again met Frank, who'd taken me under his wing so amicably back in Seelisberg. He was a trained chef and the only one who had a permanent job here. Under his professional guidance and perfection, we learned to create tasty meals. We laughed and joked around, and the tintinnabulation of many languages animated the air. In groups of ten, we scrubbed the vegetables, cleaned the kitchen, set the tables elegantly, served the others, cleared the tables, or cleaned the common rooms. Without exception, everyone participated, and there was no hierarchy in these daily tasks. We were not just a community of meditators; we also became good and close friends with everyone.

As he had promised, Maharishi came often, and, sometimes he stayed for weeks. He discussed our experiences with us and gave us new instructions. As always, he was cheerful and full of humor—it was a great time! In the many hours of the daily meditation program, an enormous power condensed and suffused the monastery walls with liveliness and at the same time with silence, enriching all of us deeply.

Maharishi in the time when he frequently visited our Purusha group, commenting on our experiences of pure consciousness and sharing with us extensive new dimensions of Vedic knowledge

In the afternoon hours, we began to study Ayurveda, the knowledge of life, that had spread from the Himalayas to India, Tibet, and Thailand, and whose stores of knowledge influenced many medical systems —as far away as Greece and China. We collected all the papers of the ancient transmissions that were available in English translation and studied them intensively. We learned from these classical texts that this healing system, that comprised all aspects of life, had originally been perceived by rishis, or seers, in deep meditation an unbelievably long time ago, when people began to get sick. Earlier, during the full flowering of Vedic culture in India, sickness was unknown. The profound understanding of Ayurveda, of the mechanisms of consciousness, body, and soul, was designed to create a state of perfect balance that would not only help to prevent sickness, but, ultimately, would also pave the way to enlightenment. This was so because Ayurveda created health from the level of *atma*, the innermost transcendental core of the personality, which is designated in the Vedic texts as the *domain that never becomes ill.*

Inspired by all this new knowledge, we soon began to use the Ayurvedic principles of balance in our daily diet.

In groups, we also studied the major parts of the Vedic literature, such as the Rig Veda, the Puranas, the Smritis, and the Upanishads, as well as the famous Mahabharata and the Ramayana. Some of our work-groups compared the principles of modern science with the testimonies of the various Vedic scriptures. The fascinating consonance between the modern natural sciences and the thousands-of-years-old realizations of the rishis that we were formulating broadened all of our horizons.

In his meetings with us, Maharishi proved again and

again that he really was a shining example of consciousness. He commented on every one of our experiences and put them into the context of the structure of creation, and he elucidated the texts of the Vedas in which each of these experiences was described and explained. In this way, we all researched human consciousness together. The theory was always tied to the practice of meditation, and both these aspects enriched one another. The descriptions increased our trust in these fascinating realms of consciousness and deepened our experiences even more. All of it held great attraction for us because it was so amazingly alive. We never learned dry psychological connections, but experienced much of it within ourselves at the same time and we were often suffused with the bliss that came with these experiences.

After several months, things got a little busier in our monastery. Germany's administrative center for the TM Movement moved from Schledehausen to our place in Boppard. And, at Reinhard's request, I once again slipped into my old shoes, managing the center and keeping up the contact with the German TM Training Centers. For this, we outfitted three rooms as offices on the ground floor of a neighboring building. I had three or four co-workers; but with urgent jobs all the German Purushas would lend a hand for a few hours, for example, if we had to call all the German TM Centers within just a few days for some special project or had to send out letters with important bulletins to all the centers. Each Purusha had his own buddy so that we could help and support one another when necessary. My buddy was Norbert, a blond beanpole who was a good head taller than me. Not only did we work well together at the central office, we also loved horsing around with each other.

Maharishi, in his boundless creativity and his desire to improve the lot of mankind, always thought of something new. So he placed full-page ads in *Stern, Der Spiegel*, and other publications, ads offering the German government solutions to their problems through our programs. For weeks on end, he worked to improve the texts with the help of a group of us and some scientists. In painstakingly meticulous detail, they compared the central statements of quantum physics with the functions of human consciousness. Finally, Norbert and I placed the ads that, admittedly, were fairly challenging for a layman. After they'd appeared for a few weeks, these publications refused to accept further ads. What was up with that? It's a free country and we couldn't place the ads? But, as we were to learn, our country was not as free as we'd thought until now. Curious about the reasons behind this, we asked a friend, who held a management position in one of those publications, to find out what was going on there. The answer to the puzzle: The ads were no longer accepted because of the opposition of the tobacco industry. Their CEOs had threatened, "If you continue to run these ads, we're pulling ours!"

Was that industry afraid of losing customers? A whole lot of studies had shown that TM lowered the consumption of alcohol and cigarettes.[17] Or was there something else behind all this? To us, at any rate, it was clear: Influence and money rule the world! And the magazine publishers bowed down to both!

The Extended Maharishi Effect

Maharishi, however, seemed not to know any frustration. In a stressed-out world like ours, he seemed to expect a hostile climate. Undaunted, he came up with ever new ideas. If it didn't work out one way, maybe there was another way. For his next maneuver, he concentrated on implementing the group dynamics of consciousness in a big way. For that, he wanted to create a huge and permanent group of practitioners of the sidhis, who would ease the stress of the collective consciousness and bring more harmony to life in Germany.[7]

But how could a comparatively small group have such a big effect? The first studies of the 1% cities in America had demonstrated that a positive tipping point could be reached when one of every hundred people practiced TM. Those were the results before the TM-Sidhi program was introduced. The more accurate analyses of these advanced techniques had meanwhile brought to light the existence of a far greater effect.

Years earlier, a group of neurophysiologists had already used a giant computer that not only measured the brainwaves of experimental subjects like a normal EEG device, but this metallic monster also measured the coherence of the brain waves of various derivation sites of the cerebral cortex and presented them as graphs on a printout. Most people have quite a muddle upstairs, which is apparent because the brain-waves, the electrical impulses of our grey cells, are a tangled mess. But this stops immediately when a person begins

---

[7] Of course, he called similar activities to life in many other countries at the same time.

Transcendental Meditation. The researchers were fascinated. Even in someone's first meditation, alpha waves are present not only in the frontal cortex of the brain, as is usual when a person is relaxed and closes the eyes, but the brain suddenly produced these deeper wave patterns consistent with wakeful rest in all other regions of the brain. Most surprisingly, the alpha waves that were detected showed a high correlation in frequency (density) and amplitude (height) between very different connection points of the cerebral cortex.

In addition to this, the researchers observed yet a further development: With regular practice of TM, this remarkably orderly image began to occur concurrently with all other kinds of brain waves. And not only that, researchers observed yet another occurrence. While this coherent brainwave activity was, at first, only observable during meditation, with longer practice, it increasingly remained present throughout the day. The brain functioned in a more orderly way, even during activity. This explained all the improvements at a whole new level that the extant scientific studies had already shown: more creativity, more stress tolerance, and even a higher IQ, as well as better health.

That much, I'd already known. But when I saw images of brainwave activity that had been recorded during the TM-Sidhi Program for the first time, I was totally thrilled because, especially during yogic flying, there was virtually only coherence in all areas of the cerebral cortex and just about no disorderly activity at all. So, not only were the subjective experiences during the sidhis much, much stronger, but regarding brainwaves, one could also see that these advanced techniques intensified the effects of the basic technique of TM many times!

And Maharishi knew that this enormous coherence within individuals during the TM-Sidhi Program could be made many times more intense if these spiritual techniques were practiced in a large group in the same place. Quite obviously, it is the case that different brains influence each other, enter into a connection with each other, and this too could be seen in EEG graphs.[18]

The effects of such a big group certainly exceeded what we had at first imagined. In the Vedic texts Maharishi Patanjali had formulated it clearly ages ago, "In the vicinity of Yoga (coherent atmosphere) hostile tendencies are eliminated."[19]

This seer knew that such a state of consciousness has balancing effects and even creates peace.[J] Just like Patanjali, our Maharishi also held that with this spiritual approach it was possible to guarantee the invincibility of nations—no longer needing to wage harrowing wars with uncertain outcomes.[K]

To test the validity of this assumption, the effect of the TM-Sidhi group programs were examined in field studies soon after. Various groups of "yogic flyers" went into crisis regions where there was active combat. The size of the groups was always equal to the square root of 1% of the affected population. And indeed whenever these critical numbers were achieved, the conflicts diminished.

This also opened a totally new perspective for us as TM teachers. In previous years, even the possibility of the simple *Maharishi Effect* had been impressive. This effect comes into play when individuals practice TM in their own homes and when their numbers equals 1% of that city's population. But now, a much simpler solution in terms of numbers had come into play: If the much more powerful coherence-creating

TM-Sidhi Program was practiced by many people at the same time and in the same place, then individual effects of coherence would intensify through a resonance effect. The whole is more than the sum of the parts—the life-supporting influence multiplies many times over.

Researchers called this newly discovered field effect of consciousness on the fate of whole cities or nations the *Extended Maharishi Effect*. The noteworthy aspect of its mathematical lawfulness was this: the bigger the group of the population to be balanced, the smaller, relatively speaking, the percentage of necessary coherence-creating individuals had to be. To create the Extended Maharishi Effect for Germany, with its 80 million inhabitants, and using the square root of 1%, only 900 people who practiced the TM-Sidhi Program, including yogic flying twice daily in a group at the same place, were needed to create the influence of the desired coherence effect.

Maharishi therefore suggested the establishment of such a coherence-creating group of 900 people in Germany. So, we prepared a campaign for the five biggest cities in Germany. My friend the airline captain, Karl, soon flew four people all over the country in our small propeller plane: Mrs. Eickhoff, who managed a big meditation academy in Bremen-Blumenthal, where she also helped countless young people to get off drugs, Mr. Ritterstaedt, our national leader, Wolfgang, one of Maharishi's secretaries—and me. Mrs. Eickhoff, Mr. Ritterstaedt and I spoke to big groups of meditators in those cities to motivate them to learn the sidhis—for their own good and to exert a positive influence on our homeland. After my long time behind monastery walls, I felt like a fish thrown back into the water at those events: I loved seeing those many people beaming at us from the audience and getting them excited about this new possibility.

Just through that effort, many hundreds of people attended the TM-Sidhi courses. Many of them were motivated by the idea of not only helping themselves, but also their country and the world. The spark of a positive future for humanity had set them on fire! However, almost all of them were so tied down by their families and their profession that they could not do their programs at the same place in Germany. So, we organized group programs in those cities in which, at least evenings and on weekends, somewhere between sixty and a hundred people came together in the service of their city, acting as a "washing machine" for the collective consciousness of their country.

Every evening we called Maharishi to keep him current about the progress of our efforts. I felt lucky to work for this great vision—as far as I was concerned, this could go on for all eternity.

Of course, Maharishi had the whole world in his sight at the same time. In many countries of our Earth people learned the TM-Sidhi Program and thus enlivened the silent field that connects all people. To allow the blessing of consciousness to spread as effectively as possible around the whole world with the help of this Extended Maharishi Effect, Maharishi launched a brilliant plan: In every time zone of the world the TM-Sidhi Program would be practiced at the same time, namely in the early evening so that most people could easily arrange it after work. In this way, many people in bigger or smaller groups practiced the sidhis in each of the 24 hours of a day in their own time zone—even those who remained at home would meditate at the same time whenever possible. Already since the end of the 1970s, an unbroken wave of silence and peace from the unified consciousness of thousands of people moves around our planet every day and slowly and surely helps to uplift the consciousness of all peoples.

And I was rock solid in my conviction: on this invisible basis of growing consciousness, more and more people would understand the healing and coherence-creating power of silence and use it for themselves. Just as Maharishi had predicted, big, permanent coherence-creating groups would later be established and sustained by governments. And through the enlivenment of the evermore subtle organizing power of natural law in the collective consciousness, countless people—each in their own way—will be on their way to solve the big and still existing problems of our planet with their growing insight and creativity.[8]

---

[8] In fact, Maharishi's predictions are meanwhile coming to pass: forty years later TM and the TM Sidhi Program have been implemented in schools, universities, military establishments, prisons, and in government fire departments, etc. in various parts of the world for the betterment of the quality of life of individuals and their whole countries (compare Chapter XIV, Maharishi's Worldwide Programs Today, p. xxx)

Inside and Outside

In Boppard we lived quietly and withdrawn, as is proper for monks. But one day, there was suddenly some loud and blaring folk music on our monastery grounds. Surprised, we looked out the windows and saw a colorfully mixture of men, women, and children in our inner courtyard; they'd brought their musical instruments and were striking up a joyful melody and dancing wildly. They were following an old tradition to have an annual procession in honor of a saint who was said to have freed the city from the plague. It was just before the evening meditation. Our windows opened and many Purushas looked out curiously. Some of them went into the inner courtyard and, leaning on the wall, watched casually. The mood was exuberant. But what we didn't know was that for a long time the tradition had been to dance with one of the monks. A woman, probably in her fifties, separated from the dancing group, smiled mischievously and danced toward our group. She was a typically hefty German housewife, dressed-up in a red and black traditional *dirndl.* Her heavy breasts heaved. Suddenly, she swerved towards me: "Well, my boy, let's get it on!"

She grabbed me, pressed me to her glorious bosom, and waltzed with my small person for an entire, eternally long song straight through the inner courtyard—much to the delight of my Purusha friends. My brother monks giggled and laughed and enjoyed my pain and my wooden dance moves. They had a field day! As soon as the song was over and with my face almost purple, I fled back to the saving grace of the wall, where the others teased me mercilessly. For days after, they made fun of me—I must have been a funny sight indeed.

From our windows, we saw the children of the small medieval town come by the monastery on their way to school and back home. But one day, they no longer came. We wondered about it. Soon after one of the Purushas went into town to the dentist and came back with an unbelievable explanation. Allegedly, the priest had spoken from the pulpit and had advised the members of his congregation not to let their kids come past our place. It was dangerous; we would eat small kids!

Well, we didn't know what the preacher actually said, but at least it did have the effect that the congregation began to believe our group capable of evil things. Mind you, the year was 1983! And we lived in "enlightened" Germany during a time when one should have been able to assume that superstition no longer bore its most terrible fruits! On the other hand, wasn't the last alleged witch indicted and convicted at the beginning of the 19th century? We shook our heads and were stunned. That the priest had allegedly preached this was one thing; but the townspeople still believed it! From that point on, the students had to make a detour of a good five minutes just to avoid us cannibals. We were speechless!

Of course, the theories and the claims of the TM Movement did turn upside down a few things that humanity had accepted as true for the last millennia. There was only one way out. They ridiculed them because they didn't understand them. And they began to fight us. Just about nobody took the time to read the statistical data of the scientific studies in the original. Instead, the term "cult" haunted the land more and more often. And increasing headwinds came from the churches that we could feel even behind our monastery walls. And, of course, none of us had even the remotest idea that these events would become a bigger problem. We felt sorry for the priest, for his little sheep, and above all, for the children, because we assumed that obviously, they experienced the bliss and the serenity that we'd all been gifted with through our TM practices only in rare moments of their own lives. The good would prevail! Surely, the knowledge about the functions and the mechanisms of human consciousness would shortly become common knowledge, and most people would use the boundless potential of their own awareness soon in the not-too-distant future and in targeted fashion. But before that would come to pass, who could have guessed that our optimism would be abused for decades?

Now and then, we went on wonderful boat rides on the Rhine with Maharishi. One or more boats would be chartered and tied to one another. On the biggest ship, Maharishi would give a speech that people could watch on TV on the other steamers. Sometimes scientists were part of the group also, who then explained their discoveries to us. Maharishi was not the only one who loved these outings. For us Purushas, too, the warm summer nights with the sinking evening sun were memorable.

On one of these trips Maharishi conceived a new, magnificent idea. Our group at Boppard was not big enough for a relaxation effect for all of Germany. Maharishi would have liked to have 800 people, but where could we get them and put them all together in one place? Why not live on a big hotel boat and be independent of the locality?

One evening we all sat together in our lecture hall on the ground floor, formerly the church. Outside, trains rattled by; the train tracks came past us directly in front of the monastery.

"That put us in a traveling mood! Pack your toothbrushes

and a small carry-on; we're going to the boat!"

We didn't have the slightest clue where we'd be going. Our flexibility was once again in demand. All the way to Bonn we went on Father Rhine and from there a few busses took us to Holland, to the academy Laag Soeren. We arrived at night. The academy was hardly occupied so there was room for all of us.

At the next group meeting on the following afternoon, Maharishi took up the relevant topic right at the start. "Who wants to do some research about buying a cruise ship for us?"

Before I even realized it, my hand was up and I was engaged. "Please come back every fifteen minutes and tell us what you've found out!"

What amazing luck; I could complete an assignment for Maharishi directly—my absolute dream! With swinging steps, I went out, straight to the nearest phone to get the information. Maharishi, meanwhile, had begun the afternoon lecture for the others.

By chance, Hartmut, a little older than me, was outside in the hall and took me down a peg, "Dude, Lothar, don't get too excited! This is just one of a thousand projects that Maharishi gives to various people so they can evolve—and nothing ever comes of them!"

Unperturbed, I dove into the assignment full of vim and vigor and was blissed out and highly motivated to find a shipshape boat. I called various shipping companies. As we were in the Netherlands, we were exactly in the right place. Every fifteen to twenty minutes, when I had an offer, I peeked into the lecture hall, as per orders and, with my eager face and my information I provided a highly welcome pause. Everyone looked amused. It was great fun for me.

Finally, a couple of ship owners invited us to a viewing of their boats. Hans-Peter, a fun-loving dentist from Switzerland, Wolfgang, Maharishi's secretary, and I went on an excursion to a small harbor in the Netherlands and enjoyed this diversion from our contemplative monks' life in full measure. Four days later, we all went back to Boppard. But I, undaunted, continued to do research. The first few shipping company owners arrived at the monastery Marienberg to present their offers and negotiate with us directly.

Wolfgang, Maharishi's secretary, took me aside at some point: "Lothar, I think you better stop. Otherwise you'll drive the whole market nuts."

But I could not be stopped. I prepared a two-by-two-meter graph with fifteen of the best offers on which everything was visible: year of construction, seating capacity, beds, and the needed crew, etc. Occasionally, Maharishi asked Wolfgang, "Any news of the bright boy with the boats?" This, of course, put an even bigger fire under me.

When everyone, except Maharishi and his secretaries, had gone to bed one night, the topic of discussion turned to this matter. I, too, was sleeping like a log and clueless while the fate of this initiative was being decided. Maharishi called for the graph and had his secretaries explain the offers to him. After he'd looked at them at length, he finally said, "I think it's too expensive!"

That was the end of my project just as Hartmut had predicted! Good-bye—and I had been so sure! Although nothing had been accomplished on the outside, those were exceptional days for me. Through Maharishi's attention, I felt even more blissful and enlivened than I normally did. It was impressive how much more energy and bliss I felt, and how much the attention of such an enlightened being could uplift my own consciousness.

Inspired by this experience, the desire took shape in me to work directly for Maharishi more often.

The Birth of the Phantom

Knock, knock, knock. Dazed and slow, I came out of deep sleep. Again, there was the knocking, loud and resounding, down at the big wooden door in the inner courtyard. A quick look at the clock: Darn! It was shortly after 2:00 a.m. Then there were quick, muffled footsteps in the hallway and someone knocked at my door.

"Lothar, get up! Dr. Reusch is here and wants to talk to you!" In the middle of the night? Well, that had to be something urgent!

Dr. Christoph Reusch was a good friend of mine. I'd known him since the days when I was just beginning to meditate. When I went to visit my father on the weekend, I almost always made a detour to his place, often stayed the night and then enjoyed family life with his wife and their three small, lively children. Christoph was a judge and, recently, he vigorously defended TM against the defamation from the state and the church. After initial goodwill, the German government had, surprisingly for us, called a big press conference about "the problems regarding the so-called 'youth cults". This was the start of their warnings that TM was a dangerous cult—on hand of extant "documentation of reports of experiences" which, according to a statement by a government representative, allegedly "proved" the negative effects of TM "conclusively."

After Maharishi had inspired all TM teachers world-wide to speak in public about the imminent age of enlightenment in which humanity would engage its consciousness in a way never yet seen to prevent problems and in which wars would be a strange relic of the past, a resistance by church and state had risen. Obviously, Maharishi had struck a hornets' nest with the terminology that was customary in Vedic circles.

Inspired by the vision of a better future, TM teachers had gone out to spread this new knowledge everywhere, and not just privately among persons but often in public places, to win them over for the implementation of this new weapon of silent human consciousness—and with initial success. But, in the meantime, it was no longer a group that attracted a few other-worldly seekers. A huge movement that could no longer be ignored had taken shape, which made the whole thing suspect for many: at its head, there was an Indian guru with long hair, a beard, and white robes. Many from all age groups and walks of life had joined him, and he spoke—and this was for sure the most threatening of all—about the "World Government of the Age of Enlightenment." By that he didn't mean that meditators would take over governments world-wide but, instead, that every human being could, from the silent level of his own consciousness, co-direct the fate of his own country. However, these Vedic concepts took so much explaining it was difficult to lay them out in just a few sentences.

Understandably, alarms went off everywhere. That Maharishi's programs could withstand every critical investigation was of no concern to most critics. People did what most had done for thousands of years—they let their inner fears and boundaries rule them and they judged the whole thing lock, stock and barrel without even taking a closer look.

Especially in Germany, a country multiple times traumatized in its recent history and full of deep-seated fears of any kind of "Führer" figure, who people seemed to follow willingly, was a thorn in the side of some government officials.

TM meditators were now stigmatized as members of a youth cult.

After TM had been proven successful with prisoners and drug addicts in other countries, a few relevant government offices in Germany had been open to implementing these programs. Six international scientific studies with a total of 2,000 drug addicts were already available and showed the tremendous effectiveness that TM had for these young people. [20] Based on these, the Federal Workers' Welfare Association in Mühlheim an der Ruhr offered TM to drug addicts. A study with 76 addicts showed that, after nine months 70% were completely drug-free[21]—a result the members of significantly more complex and expensive drug-prevention programs could only dream of. Many drug addicts quit using hashish and even heroin after a few weeks or months. Here are two examples: *"When I was on drugs, I was looking for something in life that I didn't have. Now I no longer have any need for drugs because I found out what life is and how I want to live it"* and *"After TM, life finally became satisfying. I no longer needed drugs. Drugs just quit by themselves. I didn't try to quit—after a while I just noticed that I wasn't using anymore."*[22, 23]

The successes in American prisons were available back then and were documented in four studies.[24] Several motivated TM teachers subsequently taught TM to people in German prisons, and their potential aggressiveness diminished while their satisfaction with life and their motivation increased. These positive changes could not be overlooked and they were appreciated.

All that was over now within just a few months. In official locations in all counties, the German government distributed free pamphlets which warned about new movements. The conchie positions, which had earlier been approved for the non-profit TM organization were canceled and all official promotion of TM programs ceased. People just didn't understand that this was an effective technique to heal people from within through deep rest. It smelled like a religion when seen superficially—and it seemed clear to many that this had to be eradicated. The result in the ensuing years was that reprisals were taken against meditating individuals. Mothers lost their children in court custody cases against their and their children's will; fathers only had to mention that the mother practiced TM, and the judge knew immediately in whose favor to decide. Some public high school teachers lost their teaching certificates as soon as it became known that they meditated. On the other hand, many teachers and officials were not harassed at all but the state and the churches mobilized against the TM Movement itself.

Christoph, too, had not been spared. As a hopeful candidate for the Christian Democratic Union (CDU), he had not kept it a secret from his constituency that he was a meditator. He also never hid the fact that he thought this to be a good thing, and that he found the efforts to lower criminality through consciousness programs, as well as all the other innovations connected with the practice of TM, to be highly interesting for sociopolitical reasons. No one had objected. But when the vilification by the state and the church took on more and more destructive forms and public opinion shifted, his party suggested that he withdraw his candidacy for the next election so as not to hurt the CDU. Christoph was an energetic fighter and not the sort of man who could be forced into anything that was against his personal convictions.

After thinking about it deeply, he quit his promising career in politics. But on top of all the other prejudices he already knew about, this suggestion from his party was the straw that broke the camel's back. He convinced the German TM Movement that it wasn't a good idea to waste time on individual court cases, as they'd done until then, but to grab the evil by the roots and defend itself against the Federal Ministry of Family Affairs. And he prevailed. Not long afterwards, the German branch of the International TM Movement, a registered association, filed a complaint against the German government to make an end to the unjustified defamation campaigns and personal slander.

And now, unannounced, he stood in front of me in the middle of the night with his typically precise haircut and laconic face that told of decisiveness and, at the same time of humor. "Hello, Christoph! What's up?" I had just splashed a handful of cold water on my face, had slipped from my PJs into my suit and now stood in front of the door to my office. Christoph's steel blue and alert eyes were fixed on me; he pointed to a couple of plastic laundry baskets filled with papers: "Lothar, I need your help!" I opened the office and, once inside, his words came like a geyser: "Imagine, tonight Mr. Ritterstaed called me and said, 'Dr. Reusch, something unbelievable has happened!'"

The background was that our national leader had received a distraught call from Angela*, a 26-year-old secretary. She and her older brother had started TM some years earlier, and, now and then, they went to a meditation course. Innocently, they had told their parents about it, and many long conversations had followed. Angela worked in her profession, and her brother, after finishing his course work in chemistry, was writing his dissertation. Even so, they worried their parents exceedingly. This new thing was a source of various fears for them. Above all, they were afraid that their son and daughter might become psychologically sick because of it. Conversations didn't calm the parents any more than had the extant scientific studies that both young people had presented to them. The parents had only one thing in mind; they wanted to make their children stop this disastrous practice. When they were not successful, the togetherness of parent and child, which had been so trusting and harmonious, went south and stress entered the picture. After some time, the parents seemingly gave up. They no longer expressed their fears and seemed to have swept the whole thing under the rug. But an underlying dissatisfaction remained.

Angela lived with her husband a few kilometers from her parents' house, and, on this Saturday, she had spontaneously come for a visit. But today, this strange and incomprehensible tension was again palpable. After their good-byes, father and mother remained seated in the sunny garden and Angela left through the house. Suddenly, she saw a bunch of keys on the hall stand. Following an impulse, she grabbed the keys and went into the basement. There stood a little steel filing cabinet that the father kept tightly locked. She opened it and saw many papers and folders. Right on top there was an official letter from the Ministry for Family Affairs to her father whose first lines caught her eyes immediately: "Dear Mr___, many thanks for your commitment to resolving the situation about Transcendental Meditation. We thank you for your selfless cooperation and your research to get to the bottom of the machinations of this cult.... Many thanks for the teamwork, Sincerely Yours___". Angela hardly trusted her eyes. Never in her life would she have got the idea that her own father, sales manager for a large concern, could be involved in something like that behind her back. As if under duress, she opened the first folder, and things got even worse. The correspondence revealed that her father had obviously frequented the Ministry for Family Affairs in this matter. And here's what made the whole thing even more unbearable for her: The Ministry was only a stone's throw from her own work place! Dumbfounded, she stared at the papers. Her father was the head of an interest group for parents of meditating young people, a group that fought actively against this new "virus" that had infected their children. Abruptly, the cause of the unpleasant and subliminal tension that had held sway over her family became clear. She looked further and discovered that the parents of a good friend were also members. They had all done everything up front and in a friendly way—and now from behind, such a breach of trust! Shocked by this hypocrisy, she reacted impulsively: "Now I want to know what's going on here!" She didn't hesitate for long, grabbed the file folders and some disorganized papers, put them all into two laundry baskets, and took them home with her to study them in peace and bring them back the next day. But when she looked at the folders in the early evening, she was deeply stunned at the extent of what her father had done behind her back for years.

Dismayed she had then called Mr. Ritterstaedt, who, in turn, informed Christoph. Spontaneous as he was, Christoph said immediately, "These things have to go back as soon as possible—but first, we'll take a look!"

A brief return call from Mr. Ritterstaedt to Angela, and she was ready to take the three-hour drive. But her phone rang again. Her father was on the line. "Do you know anything about the missing files from the cabinet in the basement?"

"Yes, I took them!"

"Bring them back right now! I have to take them to Bensheim tomorrow morning and I'll fry in hell if those folders are missing!"

When Angela refused to hand over the documents immediately, he threatened angrily: "I'll report you, you can't do that, some of them are secret state papers! If you don't move right now, I'll call the police!"

Trembling, she hefted the laundry baskets full of this highly explosive information into her car for the second time and got on the way to Christoph's place just a few minutes before two policemen rang her doorbell to force the return of the folders. Unsuccessful, they'd had to leave.

Late in the evening, Angela arrived at Christoph's in Westerwald, gave him the hot goods, and then went home right away. After a brief look, it was clear to Christoph that, in his position as a judge, he should not have anything to do with this explosive and ill-gotten material. So, he loaded the baskets into his car, drove just under an hour through the night, bringing them to me in the National TM Center in Boppard.

And now he was sitting in front of me: "Lothar, this stuff is too hot for me. Look at it, but I can't have anything to do with it! Copy what you think important!" And then he was gone.

So, I woke a few co-workers, and, together, we went to work on this mammoth task to get to the bottom of this unexpected find in just a few hours. Obviously, we wanted to give those papers back next morning so as not to bring trouble to Angela and her father.

It didn't take us long to realize that an abyss was opening in front of us. Among the papers there were the original documents of the "documentation of the report of experiences," the very ones that the government had been plugging. It was financed—who would have guessed—by the Government Ministry for Youth, Family, and Health. And it was abundantly clear that this collection was intent from the get-go to put this new method for the development of personality in a bad light. Even if you had no wish to assume evil intent on the part of the government representatives, they didn't exactly choose their research team carelessly. This was one mistake with fateful consequences, and not just for the TM Movement. For a leader, they chose, of all people, Alex Schratte,* an active member of the association *Militant Young Christians*. This club was an aggressively missionary commune, located in Bensheim, whose aim was to fight "cults" with all determination. Alex Schratte had said flat out in several anti-cult public talks, "The activities of the TM Movement are worse than what Hitler did in the Third Reich."[25] This absurd statement throws a defining light on the serious bias of this observer and seriously undermines the legitimacy of this so-called "expert." So much for objectivity.

The machinations began with the dubious selection of test subjects of the so-called Bensheimer Study. For questioning, they purposely chose only the parents of young people, parents who were feeling anxious about this alien— to them—meditation practice and about their offsprings' enthusiastic dedication to it. These parents had taken it upon themselves to contact the *Institute for Youth and Society*. This was the cover name for the association of *Militant Young*

Christians that offered consultations in case of questions about beliefs and cults. So, they quickly ran a "scientific" study to support the alleged damages that TM occasioned, a study that no university in Germany would have accepted as a doctoral dissertation, or even a civil service examination, because of the biased choice of test subjects and the lack of any control group.

We looked through folder after folder. Aghast, I stared at the list of questions that had been used to interview the parents. The biased formulation of the questions was bursting with insinuations. They asked about "extreme vegetarianism" of meditating young people, about their style of dress, changes in physiognomy (!), attitudes toward money, even whether they came to the evening meal on time, or communicated less with their parents. And—we could hardly believe it—they assessed whether these people "believed" in the Maharishi Effect, which was, of course, seen as proof that they were not quite right in their heads and had lost any ability to think for themselves. (Meanwhile, there are fifty scientific studies that demonstrate this effect and most of them were published in prestigious scientific journals.) My stomach contracted. As if paralyzed, I looked at this vicious mixture of bias and deliberate underhandedness.

Of course, the "research team" had neglected to question other parents or even a few of the ten thousand people who had benefitted from TM—that would effectively have ruined the preferred results. Equally hair-raising was the fact that these researchers, according to their own admission, had seen the more than 100 published scientific studies about the changes brought about by TM. But—and how could it be otherwise—they swept these findings, which presented an objective view and should rightfully belong to any scientific discussion, under the rug.

Angela and her older brother turned out to be two of the "problem cases." Evidently, people like her father had been interviewed. He, according to Angela, was a man who had his own, highly personal problems with the normal release of offspring from the parental home and believed he "knew better" what would be best for his children. On top of that, these parents were interviewed behind the backs of their grown children and without knowing that their data would become part of a "study" and—as would be the norm for any balanced study—without the researcher having obtained the personal assessment of the young people for contrast.

And then we stumbled across a list that once again took our breath away: with those prejudged and sentenced "children" they were listing, believe it or not, eleven young people with an average age of 24.5! Every single one of them had completed a professional education or was studying at a university, and all of them were busy with their lives, even if they closed their eyes twice a day. It was a total mockery! And here, unexpectedly, we held in our hands, the distorted, "impressive evidence," the phantom with which the public had been deliberately misled for years.

And to complete the picture, we also found a whole bunch of official letters from high-ranking government officials, which, through their correspondence with representatives of churches, gave us some insight into how they had come up with a sneaky plan for how to best finish off the TM Movement.

What they were cooking up behind the curtains was a kick in the teeth of the German civil law, widely recognized as one of the most liberal and progressive in the world. Here, however, neither the lawful freedom of opinion nor ideological minorities was being protected. Instead, the sad reality of the 20th century was that the state, unnoticed by the public, had rewarded fanatical Christians with tax money to help the Church rid itself of a presumed competitor.

I was shocked. But then it dawned on me what a colossal find had fallen into our hands. We had highly explosive evidence of the background of the anti-cult campaigns that were meanwhile at the height of their game. With that evidence, we could show the press and the public that tax money of the German government had gone to an ideologically one-sided splinter group to create and cement prejudices with the most slippery of methods, and further, that the state and the church were engineering that conspiracy behind closed doors. As great as this evidence was, I was creeped out by the thought because—as was clear to me—this would cause quite a stir, and there would be consequences. I felt out of my depths in deciding on my own what was to be done about all this.

That's why I woke up Reinhard, Maharishi's personal secretary and brought him up to snuff. He was immediately wide awake, "For God's sakes, Lothar, get rid of that stuff as fast as possible! Maharishi is in house; I'm personally responsible for his safety. And if these top politicians who are party to this and who are doing this dishonest stuff find out that we have the evidence in our possession, then they might sic the national security services on us. Who knows, what else they might do to get this incriminating stuff back. See to it immediately that you get rid of the stuff. We're not thieves; we're honorable people!"

I really got queasy now because it hit me like a ton of bricks that he was right. If it became known that we were cognizant about these conspiracies and about what sort of wrong and put-up game this was they were playing on us, all hell could break loose. Maybe some of the complicit high-ranking officials would have to hang up their hats! And so, I had only one controlling thought; I for sure wanted nothing more to do with this stuff and wanted to get rid of these explosive documents as fast as possible.

So, we missed an enormous chance to reveal this swindle through which the public had been so radically misled.

Already fearing that the police could be after us, my friend Norbert and I drove to the freeway while it was still pitch dark. There we gave those secret papers to a reliable courier and were relieved to be rid of this burdensome filth.

That same night, the two baskets with its unholy cargo got back to Angela, who then promptly gave them back to her father next morning, and he then withdrew the accusation of theft.

The Last Straw

Under the guise of science, church and state brazenly used results obtained through bias on eleven (!) young people for their own purposes: they vilified Transcendental Meditation as well as an increasingly growing number of other organizations over the years, organizations that often had no complaint against them except for not following mainstream opinion and were only wanting to make life better for people using methods that did not have the blessings of official churches.

For decades, church and state in homey collusion made TM meditators run through unimaginable gauntlets. And they'd always cite the small and biased "study" of the Bensheim Institute, in which the state appropriated as its own the terminology of religious institutions: the concept of "youth-" or "psycho cults" soon became a term of abuse and invective.

Of course, the public were not informed that Alex Schratte belonged to the work group Militant Young Christians. Nor were they told that Mr. Schratte had designed his "Documentation of Experiences" as a half-done critical evaluation on his own, and as being insufficient from a scientific point of view. All that drowned in the hullabaloo of the subsequent witch hunt.

The ensuing attacks from the press, radio, and TV on the so-called youth cults in general almost always singled out Transcendental Meditation and, calling it by name, these attacks were a dark chapter for human tolerance and freedom of expression in our open-minded country. These attacks were fomented by so-called "sect preachers" who were installed and well-paid by the churches and who were not ashamed to trample all over one of the most important commandments "Thou shalt not bear false witness against thy neighbor" to spread lies and smears among the public with vehemence and at great expense. Throughout Germany, they offered presentations, conventions, and evening lectures to the public about the "problem of youth religions" and all too willingly "informed" journalists. It was a cheap and transparent way to nip unwanted competition in the bud. They copied one another; conjectures and distortions were the order of the day. On the other hand, the many positive experiences, as well as the objective research about the effects of TM, were systematically killed off through silence. Hardly any of the journalists and politicians took the time to study the sound research studies or to verify unqualified statements and check their truthfulness. The mob pounced on us: at least 5,000 vituperative articles appeared in these years, articles that rehashed the statements of church and state, pounding them into the public mind.

My friend Christoph, who followed all this with a mind trained in jurisprudence, once again explained, "You know, the approach of the Ministry for Youth, Family, and Health is downright fiendish because the information pamphlets that they send out can be divided into fundamentally two sections. In the first part, the public one, they recount some real reprehensible or criminal cases in detail that are attributable to some pseudo-religious splinter group or one motivated by some weird worldview. And it's crystal clear that these crimes were usually committed by individual evil-doers or psychopaths."

Then he really got cooking. "There you find a collection

of true or exaggerated cases of prostitution on the part of a cult leader, child abuse, the creation of dependencies, unfair financial conduct, financial exploitation, murder, manslaughter, other criminal machinations, occultism and witchcraft, mass-suicides—all that is mixed together in the general section, and, of course, it doesn't say who was responsible for any specific act. And here it is: after that comes the "special section." There all the groups are listed by name that have recently been stigmatized as youth cults or psycho groups. Of course, there's no mention that for most of these groups there's nothing, not one thing from the general section that applies to them." He took a breath: "And with this treacherous association, the whole evil brew of the general section is dumped on each one of these groups in ways they can't defend against. TM, too, is always neatly thrown into the same pot with all this other filth, even though we have nothing whatsoever to do with the unspeakable accusations in the general section."

Stoked by all that, the reprisals against meditators increased progressively. If a TM teacher held a public lecture, then in eight out of ten cases, a local churchman showed up, sat somewhere anonymously, and at the end, incited the audience to hateful abuse. They spread their poison only from the outside; they avoided TM Centers like the devil avoids holy water. All this went so far that many meditators no longer dared to mention to their colleagues at work that they practiced TM in their free time. In our "free country" you'd be immediately labeled as a brainless dreamer; sometimes you had to accept professional disadvantages and even vilification from coworkers.

This was a well-known and endlessly repeated pattern

in human history. Wasn't the great philosopher Socrates, "the master of all masters," as he was called later, given a cup of hemlock because of his critique of established myths, which allegedly spoiled the young people and taught them to worship foreign gods? He had dared to question calcified ideas and was teaching new ones. He paid for it with his life, yet he accepted the judgment instigated by his adversaries with stoic calm, which only increased his posthumous fame.

Didn't Galileo Galilei, the great physicist and astronomer, have to recant his truer knowledge that the earth is a sphere rotating around the sun to save his life because his astronomical observations revealed Christian doctrine to be false? It took 450 years before the Catholic Church finally and officially admitted its embarrassing error.

Have we learned nothing in the past 2,500 years? It is sad but true that church and state officials, as well as the average person, still ostracize and fight against anything that doesn't fit into their habitual but outdated ideas. Oh, well, presumably we should be thankful as meditators that, these days we only have to deal with public character assassination and we are not burned at the stake or sent to prison.

Many people who stood in the limelight of the public sphere —prime ministers, supreme court justices, and even a German federal chancellor—had learned TM a few years earlier and valued it highly. But because of the hype around cults, even they could no longer advocate for the rehabilitation of TM because, like many others, they would inevitably be denigrated and ridiculed, or they might even have to step down from their responsible positions overnight. Those who had initially stood up for TM and had spoken well of it, after related unpleasant experiences, asked to no longer be connected to us in public, although many of them continued to practice in the privacy of their rooms undaunted.

The witch hunt had taken on such monstrous forms that, slowly but surely, there were neutral warning voices who came forward and began to protest them. Respected university professors, serious politicians, as well as religious scholars explained, sometimes even in the press, that in its proceedings against youth cults in general, and TM in particular, the German government had not only taken sides in a conflict about worldviews masterminded by a church-affiliated sect official, but had also completely overshot the mark. But all the interviews, articles, and specialist publications generated by these neutral voices evaporated like a drop of water on a hot stove—and nothing changed.

But at some point, there was a last straw even for mild-mannered meditators. In solidarity with 63 members of the Union of Physicians Practicing TM, as well as about ten TM teachers, all of them seasoned scientists, judges, and educators, the International Association of Meditators, German Division, sued the German government in 1980 to cause it to cease and desist from its defamatory statements and to rectify previous ones.

But who would undertake the necessary background research for the government? Not too surprisingly, Alex Schratte came forward and zealously offered his assistance. Recall his accomplishments with the "documentation" that had been so distorted by fundamentalist Christians and that had set the "inquisition" in motion. The self-same fanatic who gave frequent public lectures and compared Maharishi, a gentle, wise man who taught people the benefits of silence, with Hitler and his crimes, now received not only a letter of thanks from the general secretary of the CDU (Christian Democratic Union) and the Federal Minister for Youth, Family, and Health but also the honorable task to assist as a co-worker with this process. From their department, he received access to all the documents and was asked for his opinion and recommendations. It is not hard to guess, who really did lead this litigation on the part of the government. It is unbelievable how much a government institution allowed itself to be misused as the toy of a Christian fanatical persecutor of cults.

On the side of TM, however, there was also much activity. For years, Christoph had donated most of his free time to do the groundwork for the attorney hired by the TM organization. He first set the record straight that Transcendental Meditation was a method, the most thoroughly researched, to be effective against the wide-spread sicknesses of civilization caused by stress, that its practice was completely neutral regarding any worldview, and that it had nothing to do with cults or religion. Christoph gathered information and documentation for the lawyer. He collected counterarguments and research results as well as reports of neutral university professors, that showed the far-fetched assertions of the Ministry to be utterly absurd. As a brilliant speaker and attorney, he formulated briefs behind the scenes, making the proper outcome of this action an affair of the heart for him.

But it wasn't exactly a cakewalk for him. Word had spread like wild fire among meditators that here was a competent attorney who represented TM. He constantly got calls from people who'd been abused because of the anti-cult campaign and who needed legal advice, or, simply, a sympathetic ear. Dr. Reusch this, Dr. Reusch that—a significant part of all the underhandedness that was dealt to TM teachers and meditators from now on flooded his private line and desk. On top of that, he had to read many thousands of sometimes brutal disparagements in the papers to demonstrate the extent of this cult hysteria in court. You'd have to be a saint not to slowly but surely let that brew of perverse opinions and viciousness get under your skin. Unfortunately, Christoph was not a saint.

Whenever I was at his house in Westerwald for a weekend visit, I could see this at first hand. He'd lay out the latest events in the persecution of TM as well as the progress of the court case, and I could feel the tremendous pressure he was under. Sometimes he just sat there, his face resting on his hands and then pulling his hair. To get it all off his chest now and then, it did him good to vent his spleen by telling me all about the intrigues of church and state, as well as all the dirt in the press that he had to deal with day in and day out. He poured out his tortured heart to me: "Lothar, sometimes I have such a rage in my belly for these filthy pigs! I would just love to punch these idiots in the nose!"

Now and then, he just had to blow off some steam to rid himself of the garbage he had to deal with every day.

A Horrendous Court Case

When evidence was being recorded at the administrative court in Cologne, the government failed in putting forward any facts to support the alleged physical damage caused by the practice of TM. To strengthen their case, the only expert they'd brought along was Alex Schratte, the bigoted, preprogrammed cult chaser. Nevertheless, the judges rejected the suit brought by the TM organization as unfounded. Obviously, the court had been so indoctrinated with vilification by the church and state, as well as the media in the preceding years, that an objective and just decision was just about unthinkable.

Equally as frustrated, but still hopeful, the TM organization subsequently filed an appeal with the Administrative Tribunal in Munster.

"Lothar, it's me." Christoph's familiar voice came over the phone. "You won't believe what just happened!"

"OK, shoot!"

"Several judges from the Senate tried to get an amicable agreement between the parties before the actual decision in our appeal. In this hearing, the presiding judge asked the representative of the Family Ministry flat out: 'Except for your blanket accusations, do you have anything concrete to present against the TM organization?' Because after five years of litigation the government still couldn't show a single instance that would prove the accusation brought against TM."

"Well, that's great!"

"Yeah, it would be! But the representatives of the people rejected the amicable agreement lock, stock, and barrel anyway. And you won't believe their incredible reasoning." He quoted: "It is the case that the problems with TM are not entirely grievous, but we are under extraordinary pressure from the representatives of the German government, and for this reason we cannot agree to any settlement.[26] That makes you wanna tear out your hair! They couldn't make it any clearer: cheap propaganda wins against facts!"

After that, the high court in Munster let the case rest for four years due to a docket overload. Then it carefully checked the opinion of experts and other documentary evidence for months. Christoph had obtained several positive opinions of ranking university professors who, as independent experts, did away with those constantly repeated pre-judgments.

Again, and again during my sporadic visits, he kept me up to date: "Lothar, if only you knew what's going on behind the curtains! I just heard about something monstrous that proves the unbelievable prejudice of the Family Ministry. Imagine, as preparation for the case, the government commissioned Professor Kehrer, a religious studies expert at the University of Tübingen, to do a preliminary study on the overall problems with youth cults. However, the piece of writing he submitted had an unexpected twist. Instead of putting the groups studied into a negative light as desired, his opinion was positively in favor of these new age communities." Christoph looked at me triumphantly. "Well, but what do you think they'd do with such an inconvenient document that is diametrically opposed to the original?" and he answered his own rhetorical question, "Not hard to guess—they let it vanish into a drawer without further ado and then pretended that this document never existed!"

Finally, there was an unusually thorough two-day hearing in which the presiding judge of the Supreme Court decreed that the Senate would only entertain one question: whether

TM could hypothetically lead to any psychological damages, as the Ministry had proclaimed for years. The judges had, meanwhile, rejected all other accusations as obviously unfounded.

The court had called on two respected heads of university clinics, Professor Scharfetter from Zurich and Professor Kolinski from Geneva as neutral expert witnesses. They witnessed the entire proceedings and stated unequivocally: "The actual causes of any endogenous psychosis are unknown. For that reason, no causal connection can be made between any incidence of such psychiatric disturbance and the simultaneous practice of TM. The occurrence of psychosis can sometimes be observed with incisive life events such as engagement, marriage, pregnancy, divorce, as well as military draft—and TM."

Later, and in a completely twisted way, this unambiguous and exonerating expert opinion would come back to haunt us.

At the end of these two days, the verdict, eagerly awaited on all sides, came down. Subsequently and in a state of complete euphoria, Christoph called me and virtually bubbled over: "Lothar, thank God! Things couldn't have gone better for us today. The government wasn't just ordered to cease and desist from all negative statements about TM in the future, but they are no longer allowed to send out any information packets that are directed against TM. And that isn't all! In addition, they have to officially retract any accusations they've made against TM. This is unprecedented in the Germany's legal history: Never has any government agency been court-ordered to make a formal apology. And they have to inform the public of the tenor of this judgment through the press service of the Government Agency for Youth, Family, and Health.[27] And the best thing is this: The Ministry is not allowed to appeal! Man, I am psyched; we did it!"

A great sigh of relief went through all the ranks of meditators. Truth and justice had won the day. The craziness of the last few years would be over! We'd been rehabilitated and, from our side, we'd be happy to forgive and forget. Finally, finally we could bear ourselves as was only right: happy and forward looking.

Our ecstatic hallelujah would be silenced soon enough. Some things just aren't meant to be.

Despite everything, the Ministry filed a complaint not-withstanding the court-ordered inadmissibility of any appeal. And the Federal Administrative Court allowed the appeal based on an especially pedantic reason. This case sought grounds to question whether the government was authorized to warn the public of dangers that could possibly come from associations supporting certain world-views, such as the TM organization and its members.

Christoph was totally flabbergasted. Next time I went to see him, he was having a cow. "Just this minute the court in Munster finally affirmed that we have nothing to do with these groups and so-called cults and now we're being thrown into the same pot again. Can't they comprehend that TM doesn't have members and it's not connected to any worldview? Every meditator can believe anything they want and use the technique individually for themselves."

So, there we were again; the accusations came sneaking in through the back door.

Three and a half years later, the verdict we'd been waiting for with bated breath came down. And this was the clincher:

"The highest court let it be known in its final statement that, "For the public, the compendium of negative associations with the concept of youth cults contains the notion of unlawful pseudo-religions and destructive practices of various sorts including punishable acts such as sexual assault, fraud, and any malfeasance against sexual self-determination. The over-all impression remains an abhorrence of the endangerment of young people." Well, cool; we couldn't have said it better ourselves. It was all exactly this garbage that had been dumped on us for years and for no reason whatsoever! Even so, there still was no reason to celebrate because it went on, "The plaintive had to condone this because, based on the hearings of evidence, the practice of TM or even the engagement in the TM Movement could, as a "life-event" trigger psychoses. A trigger element could be any occasion that engages the whole person: an engagement, a marriage, childbirth, military service, and TM."[28]

Christoph's whole world collapsed: "This really takes the cake! Because, with this spurious justification, the high court has not only granted a revision of the federal ministry, but it has also shot down the entire case of defamation of character of the TM organization at the same time through legal connections. It was mind-boggling. Because of this, the Ministry of Youth, Family, and Health could once again assert all the stuff that the court in Munster judged to be false after a thorough investigation of the facts."

Stunned, I could only agree with him. This opinion of the court was far-fetched in the extreme and completely untenable because the two expert professors, who the court had called in for the hearing, had stated repeatedly, unanimously, and most emphatically for the record: absolutely no causal relationship can be established. And exactly for this reason the wording in the judgment that TM could "trigger" psychoses was fundamentally wrong.

And now, it was finally officially decreed: The practice of TM, like marriage, divorce, and the draft, etc. could constitute a life event that could trigger a psychosis in predisposed individuals. The misquoted professors, who had been commissioned by the court, protested against the false interpretation of their testimony in both judgments. Dr. Scharfetter, head of the research division the of psychiatric university clinic in Zurich, wrote in a letter to Christoph that he had clearly stated to the court "that a causal connection between TM and psychosis could not be affirmed." And Dr. Klosinski seconded that opinion: "As the head of the psychiatric youth clinic of the University of Bern, I must point out that many of our psychotic young people come from Christian religious sects that are more or less accepted by the public and that are not classified as 'dangerous'. I would refrain from prematurely regarding this movement as triggering psychosis." And, resigned, he concluded, "For me this judgment of the high court is not verifiable."[29]

Even the rapporteur of the Administrative Court of Munster, with whom Christoph spoke on the phone after this perverse judgment, could not understand it: "If this decision were correct, then the state would in the future have to warn that military service and marriage trigger psychosis!"

Now what? The TM organization filed an appeal to this appellate judgment with the government. But the highest German court outdid itself: It refused to accept this complaint for the outrageous reason that the designation as a youth cult by the government was not defamatory. Just think about that!

Well, yes, if someone is presumed to have committed sexual coercion, dubious financial conduct, criminal offence, or fraud, then, as the high court itself had stated, then, to follow their logic, nobody's honor is the slightest bit cheapened. What the hell? After a brief and hopeful blossoming of fairness and justice, we were once again in the modern version of the dark ages.

Who knows if the judges were the slaves of the prevalent *zeitgeist* or were influenced behind the scenes? It was abundantly clear that they didn't have the courage to come to a decision based on the abundant facts in favor of TM. Obviously, even academic studies and an intelligent mind did not protect anyone from "howling with the wolves."

And so, things stood as they were. The duty of the government to maintain neutrality vis-a vis worldviews remained a beautifully worded phrase in the long-suffering pages of the Constitution. And the Christian commandment not to bear false witness proved once again to be pure theory, thwarted, ironically, by the Christian churches.

Because of his training in law and his activities as a judge, my friend Christoph had had the greatest trust in the German judicial system up till now and had always been proud of advocating for justice through his work.

For years, he had advocated with utter conviction for the rehabilitation of TM because, for him, there was no doubt that in the end justice would win. He could never get over this absurd result of the proceedings, after we'd already won the case in every point, and the German government should have made a statutory declaration in our favor. His faith in the German jurisdiction was and remained deeply shaken through this scandalous miscarriage of justice.

Don't Let it into Your Heart

For the fanatical representatives of the big religious communities, the verdicts of the court were grist for their mill. Despite the untenable nature of all their accusations, as the latest hearing of the facts had determined, their defamation campaign went into full swing with slurs on radio and TV, instigated directly or indirectly, and spurred on by representatives of the church who had the upper hand for now. As mentioned in the previous section, they brazenly omitted the following inconvenient part of the adjudication: "as well as an engagement, a marriage, childbirth, military induction," and presented only the "sanitized" fragment that TM allegedly triggered psychoses; this would haunt the German media for decades.

With extreme vehemence, they implied that the TM Movement had lost the case and that this made it crystal clear, as endorsed by the court, that TM was a dangerous cult that people should be warned about. As soon as any scheduled project, such as the purchase of a house, the rental of a hotel for courses, or just a friendly interview on the radio about the positive effects of TM became known, the church folks made their political influence count big time. The preachers misused their worship services, and, from the pulpit, put fear and terror into the citizens of the region with the most absurd fantasies about the alleged danger these meditators represented. Everywhere, they were in the right place at the right time to pound into people's brains—people who on their own might have been to improving their lives through meditation—that it would be detrimental to their salvation. And, even in the 20th century, the reporters of all newspapers, magazines, TV stations, and even most politicians followed them like pious little sheep. Of course, those directly affected, the people who were practicing TM who would have had something positive to say from their own experience, were not being taken seriously and were dismissed as cult members nobody needed to listen to.

Representatives of the German government didn't think it beneath them to warn other governments in many countries about the allegedly deleterious effects of Transcendental Meditation on the psyche and the mind. Not content with this, they urged them to actively suppress the spread of TM. Often, these countries succumbed to the powerful German influence. But, by no means always. When German parliamentarians tried to motivate people in Sweden, they would not accept this unexamined preconception. Instead, and because of this suggestion, the Swedish National Ministry of Health did a large-scale study and sent a questionnaire to the 182 psychiatric institutes in the country.

Dr. Ottoson, the scientific advisor to the Swedish National Ministry of Health, compared the data from psychiatric patients with those of the total Swedish population. Five percent of the six and a half million Swedes had been treated in psychiatric hospitals. On the other hand, and completely surprising was that, of the 35,000 TM meditators in Sweden, the frequency of admissions was miniscule, just one in 3,500, and was thus 175 times under the average for the total population.[30] TM obviously was not just harmless for mental health, but proved itself to be an exceedingly powerful protective agent for mental balance!

When, after the publication of these results, TM teachers approached various German government offices, the results were—zip—the same way these statistics had been unable to keep the appellate court from returning a verdict exactly contrary to the facts. It had been shown that the false statements made for years lacked all basis in fact but the unfounded accusations and vilifications went on unabashedly.

Understandably, these situations slowly but surely got under the skin of many meditators and TM teachers. Whenever they were successful somewhere and this became public, the clergymen of various denominations showed up, destroyed the project and pigeon-holed the organizers as second-class citizens with whom any contact should best be avoided. But in the same measure as this upset most meditators, Maharishi handled it calmly.

At Boppard in 1983, I was actively involved in preparing a big promising project with a few other Purushas. Maharishi had persistently inspired us in those days to build up a big group in Germany. We would have needed about eight hundred appropriately trained people to create a palpable Extended Maharishi Effect on the collective consciousness of Germany. For this purpose, the TM organization wanted to acquire a big apartment-hotel complex that had been standing empty for years in Wachendorf, a dreamy town embedded in the pristine environment of the northern Black Forest.

During that summer, a few hundred meditators were already in that hotel for a world peace assembly, not only to further elevate their own positive attitude towards life, but also to have the uplifting feeling of being able to provide an invaluable service to their homeland. That was exactly the great thing about this approach; to the extent that they evolved personally, the life-supporting influence on the environment became greater also. About five hundred people had already promised to attend vacation courses in the future or, whenever possible, to even relocate their homes to participate in this groundbreaking field study. Our enthusiasm was huge. If it worked out, our beautiful country would fare better; through the organizing power of silence there would be unexpected improvements in many areas of private and public life, as had clearly been shown to be the case in pilot projects in other countries.

The negotiations in the purchase of the complex were ongoing; we were all in high spirits.

But, once again, there was something we hadn't reckoned with. When this project was heard through the grapevine, a member of the Bundestag raised an objection and church officials immediately became busy beavers. The municipal council and the public got incited systematically by church officials and the local preachers who all showed up in no time. Three-foot high defamatory slogans appeared on the hotel walls that were dreadfully reminiscent of the dark ages and the Third Reich: "Gurus get out!" "Screw Gurus!" Children on the streets chanted defamatory verses after meditators: "If you see a yogi fly, shoot him down and let him lie!" or "If a guru's dead on the ground, thank the Wachendorfers all around!" There was a bomb threat and aggressive cacophonies of car horns in front of the hotel. Children were brutally beaten up on the street and cursed only because their parents were meditators. A series of hostile newspaper articles appeared, while the county commissioner suddenly even tried to legally prohibit the continuation of the vacation courses by threatening a penalty payment via an interim injunction through the courts.

This went too far, however, and was rejected by the administrative court due to the untenable nature of the claims.

When I spoke to Mr. Ritterstaedt about this, he told me, "Well, Lothar, this is not the first time by a long shot! Believe it or not, but a while back, in Rothenburg ob der Tauber, we already had the purchase agreement in our pocket for a senior group home of the town standing empty. So, when the persecution by the church began, it was exactly like here in Wachendorf. The mood changed, and there were negative newspaper articles. The public and the city council, which had earlier been sympathetic, believed the church people implicitly and then became scared."

"And then?"

"Well, because the city couldn't back off from the contract that was already signed, they did what was legally still possible. The town's representatives subsequently exercised their right of first refusal and they quickly sold the home, as the city had no use for it—who'd have guessed—to the Protestant Church."

I remembered that, back then in Boppard, the church folks stirred up a ruckus among the people "as if the Apocalypse were imminent," as a journalist of the Rein papers put it aptly.

A terrible disappointment took hold of me. First the high spirits for being able to do something great and decisive for Germany and then—for the umpteenth time—the unfair cold shower of this concentrated negativity.

This defeat in creating a coherence group was even more disappointing because a comparable project in England with about four hundred meditators had reduced the crime rate in the district of Merseyside by 40% for decades. In 1987

Merseyside had had the third highest crime rate in all of England, but, five years later, it had the lowest of all rural communities. This sea-change clearly followed when the necessary number of meditators was reached—a unique phenomenon in the whole country; in all the other forty-two districts in England, the crime rate climbed unabated during that same time. Extrapolations from the crime data of the police, broken down into robbery, car theft, and total crime, showed that the English meditators saved around 2,500 million Euros through their silent service during the period of investigation.[31]

Despite all this concentrated animosity, I didn't doubt that in the future, when the knowledge about the mechanisms of consciousness would prevail, such groups would even be organized and supported with the help of the government—as surely as policemen and soldiers are employed for the protection of the population today.

Back in the Monastery Marienberg, I shared my sorrow about missing this chance in my homeland with Maharishi, telling him about the ways we'd been plastered with insults and abuse. But the great Master always kept his balance. He helped me again to gain a bird's eye view and observe things from a higher perspective. "Lothar, our existence is not on paper, our existence is based in pure consciousness."

Of course—how could I have lost sight of that? It was good to hear it again. What a relief to be reminded of the fact that outside events are only temporary fluctuations! The weight and the frustration began to fall away from me.

And Maharishi continued, "What does the elephant care when he comes into the market place and a few dogs start barking?"

That's how sure he was that the elephant, this invincible consciousness, would prevail; he rested so deeply within himself that none of that got him upset in the least. "We must be careful never to let negativity get into your heart."

And his profound silence, the greatness of his being, and the infinite love that he radiated transferred itself to me and my agitated mood. Within a few minutes, I felt relaxed and uplifted.

The mere presence of such a Master, and the harmony that emanated from him, transferred itself to me in a physically perceptible way, reorganizing my cells and letting them become calm and soft again.

And once again I bathed gratefully in the blessing of Maharishi, the great seer.

Traveling with Maharishi

Weeks and months of meditative seclusion alternated with exciting projects for Germany and the world. For me this combination was ideal. On the one hand, there were deep inner insights; on the other, I could satisfy my drive for action while also doing something good and meaningful.

But lately I was becoming restless. Something was about to change, something unknown. I felt it distinctly: something new was in the offing. This is a surprising side-effect of opening ourselves so deeply into subtle realms of consciousness as we had been for several hours each day. A kind of transparent feel for what was to come opened and developed on its own, along with the confidence that these impulses from within were right. It was as if you were increasingly in tune with the plans of nature and of creation.

As the leader of the German TM organization in charge of the coordination of more than a hundred German TM centers, and answerable for expansion, as well as for the audio and video library, I carried a lot of responsibility. We were a well-functioning team of six or seven members of Purusha, and with much joy and excitement, we implemented Maharishi's inspirations. But I was driven by the question: how would it be possible to transfer these tasks to someone else? Despite all doubts in my mind, the premonition remained. Under the pressure of this urge, I micro-managed all the office tasks and projects for hours each day and for several weeks. I had each co-worker prepare a detailed job description. A co-worker, Jürgen, shaking his head, offered the following commentary: "What for? But, hey, if you insist!" And so, he and the others acquiesced to their fate.

Maharishi was once again staying with us at Boppard. As often, we were sitting in the big monastery chapel, studying intently, discussing things, laughing—and, from the near-by railroad tracks, we could hear the rattling of a train. Suddenly, Maharishi smiled, "This noise puts us in a traveling mood! Go to your rooms, please, and pack your things; early tomorrow morning, we're flying to Greece for a brief stay. After spending some years behind thick monastery walls, it'll be good to have a change. But those of you who have some responsibility here, you must stay, and I want to talk to you."

My heart was in shock: "Only those who don't have any responsibility can go?" Oh man, that was not good news for us!

More than two hundred men left the lecture hall full of joyous anticipation. About thirty people remained. Almost all of them could delegate their responsibility somehow and could go along. Near the end, it was our group's turn. Maharishi looked at me. He knew my job and felt that, of course, I absolutely wanted to come along. Despite this, he said: "Better keep it under your wing!"

That's what I'd been afraid of. So, everything would remain under my supervision. Dejected, the six of us put our hands together in the Indian greeting. I said for all of us, "Yes, Maharishi." But our hearts bled as we slowly left the hall. At the dark wooden door, about thirty meters away, we turned around to face him. And, suddenly, he smiled full of love and enticed us with a movement of his index finger to beckon us toward the front. Clearly, because of the pain in our souls, he'd had yet another insight. "You can come along by early tomorrow morning if you can find some fully qualified married couples to replace you."

Hallelujah—of course, we could. Everything for a transfer of responsibility was already prepared!

In no time at all, we were on the phones in our offices. And the unbelievable thing happened. We found a few nice married couples who had experience with those tasks and were flexible enough to jump in under these conditions. They were here in just a few hours. All night, I systematically instructed them in their new assignments, packed my bags in haste the next morning—and just made it, jumping on the bus, as the driver had already started the engine. There I sat with all my other friends, expectant, infinitely relieved, though missing a night of sleep.

Whew, that certainly went well!

A vacation trip? Maharishi had never yet done that with us. But welcome to sun and beach! The worldly desires of 250 inward guys were suddenly alive and kicking.

Late in the evening, we moved into our bungalows in a vacation park on the island of Kos. Siri and I shared a double room. Here we learned that in a far-off part of this establishment there was also a group of women who were part of the excursion. They were Mother Divine of the TM Movement, who, like us practiced an extended meditation program and normally lived secluded in a Swiss academy.

The following morning, the wide, blue Mediterranean Sea stretched before us enticingly. There was a lot of sun and some sexy, tanned, bikini-clad beauties. After our extended yoga and meditation program and after we'd enjoyed the exceedingly tasty Greek cuisine, we gravitated, like the relaxed vacationers we were, in swimming trunks and with towels in hand, to the beach. Our gaze strayed to the neighboring island, and not far behind it, maybe five kilometers, there lay gigantic grey ships. Were they warships? One of our group ran to get some binoculars. And, indeed, Turkish battleships were bobbing up and down; silent and prophesying war, there they lay.

A light dawned on us! We were luxuriating in the belief that we were taking a harmless vacation. But now it became clear to us that Maharishi was after totally different goals.

We did some research and learned that, just then, there were severe tensions between Greece and Turkey, and the battleships had shown up only two or three days earlier. So, Maharishi had obviously already seen this within himself. As usual, he didn't talk much about it so as not to worry anyone. But he had immediately taken counter-measures and had mobilized the harmonizing power of silence to avert the worst—unnoticed and unrecognized. And indeed, after a few weeks these threatening warships vanished from the sea as the situation had de-escalated. Our Purusha group stayed put, pursuing its peace-creating meditation program.

But I got a totally different assignment. After a few days, Wolfgang, one of Maharishi's secretaries, stuck his head through our door: "Maharishi wants take along a small group of Purushas whom he knows personally. Lothar, you in?"

What a question! As per instructions, I brought only a carry-on; the thing would only be for a few days. My roommate, Siri, promised to watch the rest of my bags in the meantime. With four other Purushas, a few scientists and close co-workers, I could fly to Cyprus with Maharishi. There we looked for a convenient hotel complex for a large world peace assembly in which several thousand people who, meditating together, would create the impetus for peace in the Middle East and the world. Was the danger perhaps not yet past? In any case, Maharishi once again had a new project that he attended to personally. Every evening our group met with him in his hotel room. We reported our activities and, completely relaxed and private, we had him all to ourselves. What a gift!

After we figured out, crisscrossing Cyprus, that there was no possibility to house so many people in one place and on such short notice, our area of responsibility was unceremoniously moved to Italy.

On the first evening, I could just sit in Maharishi's hotel room in Pescara and experience firsthand how many projects he worked on while in touch with countless people. And as always, I soaked up his enormous radiance of silence that filled us even when he was extremely active.

In Italy, our group negotiated intensely for weeks with many hotel managers. But even with the greatest effort, we could not come up with anything suitable.

When Maharishi had traveled elsewhere, we occasionally gave him reports on the telephone about how things stood. And again and again, we were amazed about how often he knew about the details from his side that we were just about to report to him. Once again, we got a hint of what a Vedic master, one whose consciousness was fully developed, was capable of.

At the same time, I enjoyed the terrific holiday feeling. In full measure I loved the freedom outside of the monastery walls. And I acquired a taste for it.

7,000 in Snow and Ice

After the sunny excursion in the Mediterranean and back in the Monastery Marienberg, we experienced a few days of assiduous activity, although we were only there for a few days before traveling on—to the United States. After a flight across the Atlantic, we all met again in Washington, D.C., spread across several hotels in which Purushas from other continents had arrived as well. About five hundred men from all parts of the world met daily in a gigantic ball room with our indefatigable Maharishi, often from early morning to late at night around 3:00 a.m. These mammoth meetings were interrupted only to eat, to mediate, and, briefly, to sleep. The reason: Something extraordinary was being prepared. A world peace assembly of an unprecedented size would demonstrate conclusively that it was possible by just uplifting the collective consciousness to get a grip on the pressing problems of mankind on our globe.

All other efforts on the political, social and military level had failed up to now. In the last 3,000 years, a total of 8,000 peace agreements had been made, which, on average, had failed after only nine years. Even the well-meant engagement of the UN and of NATO could not change things.

After world peace assemblies had been organized in many countries, in which as many as two thousand people on vacation practiced the TM-Sidhi Program together, there were scientifically evaluated studies from Holland, England, India, Puerto Rico, and the U.S. that all confirmed the Extended Maharishi Effect.[32]

But now, on Maharishi's recommendation and for the first

time in the history of mankind, this effect on the whole globe would be expanded, if only for a limited time, as a demonstration project. Maharishi deliberately called this assembly "A Taste of Utopia" because, with this demonstration, he wanted to give the world a foretaste of what he thought possible for the whole world if such a large group practiced their sidhis day-in and day-out somewhere on Earth.

Would the Extended Maharishi Effect with its formula of the square root of one percent of the world's population really be enough to effect a global improvement? And would it be measurable? Would it be possible to show that only 7,000 experts would create positive trends and a worldwide relaxation effect? That was the hypothesis that would be tested with this large-scale demonstration project. And this time, it would not be happening quietly and unrecognized in the background as it had until now. Those responsible wanted that as many people as possible would be informed of this effect produced by our consciousness—and would know of it ahead of time, before the demonstration had even begun.

This projected world peace assembly would take place in the middle of America, in Fairfield, a small town in Iowa, the location of Maharishi International University (MIU). By 1973, Parsons College had lost its accreditation, gone bankrupt, and closed, and in 1974 the TM organization had acquired the campus to move its own university there from Santa Barbara, California. Every day, before the beginning of classes and in the afternoon after their end, the MIU students meditated together regardless of their individual majors. In addition, the study of individual subjects was planned in the light of the interdisciplinary field of the *Science of Creative Intelligence*, courses which Maharishi and the professors had developed. Because of this, the students did not just become specialists in their own chosen fields, but, at the same time, they learned new knowledge in its relationship with other areas of life and fields of expertise, as well as how to connect this knowledge to their own lives to understand it better.

The results were unusual from the beginning. After the regional accreditation commission had come to examine the university, a friend, Michael was there studying physics. He told me with a mischievous grin, "Imagine, those high falutin' gentlemen came past our bulletin board which had a $20.00 bill pinned to it. When they asked about it, the prof showing them around looked at the note next to it and said, "Oh that's been there for two weeks. Somebody found the money and is looking for the person who's lost it! Can you imagine their jaws dropping? They'd never seen anything like it!"

The commission was so impressed by the course offerings, and the studiousness, orderliness, and positive charisma of students and teachers, that they accredited MIU after thorough inspection. In the entire history of America, this was the shortest time in which a university had gained official acceptance. And so that's where the world peace assembly would take place during the Christmas vacation. I was happily looking forward to finally see this university with my own eyes, after I'd heard so much about it.

But first we were in Washington, while hundreds of dedicated American meditators worked with us on the logistical tour de force to mobilize seven thousand people in the space of four weeks and to house and feed them.

That whole time, Maharishi improved on every detail. He wanted whole-page ads in the biggest newspapers all over the world, so that the world could not miss this historically unique and huge field test. But how could you sum up the background for this unusual and unprecedented event in one page? As I'd already seen in Boppard, Maharishi wanted all the theoretical background for the effect on collective consciousness to be in that ad: complicated connections from quantum field theory, as well as the scientifically proven presentation of the Extended Maharishi Effect that would give the whole world a positive boost for coherence and peace. With all that struggle for the perfect wording with an advisory panel of top-ranking academics, there was a pleasant side-effect: All of us, who were attentively following this almost all day and night, took part in a deepening of our knowledge of the most subtle laws of nature.

Finally, after four weeks in D.C., we got it done. We moved to Fairfield. Once again, we were assigned two to a guestroom in dorms of students who'd gone home for Christmas vacation, or with host families, who had made room for us, and in hundreds of mobile homes that had been brought in just for this assembly—all in the middle of ice and snow and with temperatures down to minus 40 degrees Celsius. And, how fantastic! Seven thousand people had come from all parts of the globe and at their own cost. They paid a course fee to make this initiative, supported by euphoria and huge input from all sides, financially possible. This whole effort bordered on the miraculous. Even the workers of the building firm that had built the gigantic meditation hall in the space of four weeks, a building that would normally take four months to build, told us with amazement what incredible coincidences occurred when some obstacle manifested itself so that everything could be done on time. Thousands of foam mattresses were brought in for our field test, ten thousand kilos of food had to be chosen, ordered, prepared, and served—and all that happened with volunteers whose main career was in some totally different field, and who'd never done anything like this.

A group of scientists, sociologists, and psychologists had also been drafted. They were gathering data from independent and recognized data banks in all parts of the world that went back six months before the beginning of the assembly so that later they could be compared with the data collected after the Taste of Utopia experiment.

Meanwhile, we met in small groups throughout the day and shared our experiences in meditation that had been given wings by the gigantic size of the group. The air fairly vibrated with all our optimism. Fired up and elated like bouncing rubber balls, we waited for the glorious results of the activity of us half-enlightened folks. In the evenings, all participants came together in the newly-built meditation hall. Here we presented not only special experiences in meditation, but we also learned about the changes in world consciousness through news reports from all over the world—all that, often in Maharishi's presence. It was huge what was happening here, and it exceeded our most audacious expectations. In the short time of three weeks around the turn of the year from 1983-84, trouble spots all over the world calmed down. Countries that had remained in hostile silence and had broken contact with each other took up friendly relationships; a whole series of wars came to an end. Even from the troubled Mid-East there was positive news. And in far-removed corners of the world, the crime rate dropped and the stock markets went up. Under the eyes of the world-wide public and reported in their own news magazines—I was not surprised—the predicted change in trends had come to be. In these three weeks, 7,000 souls could get a foretaste of the positive future of our planet and could experience firsthand how light and suffused with bliss life would be! The assembly was true to its name. Here in snow and ice we really did get a foretaste of utopia.

7,000 practitioners of Transcendental Meditation and the TM-Sidhi Program at the peace demonstration project Taste of Utopia Assembly, 1984

Seven months later, the research team published this unparalleled turnaround indicated from the data collected in many countries. War-like actions had reversed themselves measurably. Trouble spots had calmed down and heads of state had handled their national problems more constructively. There were fewer plane crashes world-wide. In countries from which relevant data was available, the traffic accident rate, as well as the crime rate, had fallen. The world-wide socio-economic growth had increased, more patents had been registered, and there were fewer infectious diseases. As soon as the meditators were back in their homelands and back on their jobs, the unfortunate conditions that existed before the assembly came back, as the data of the six weeks following the assembly showed.[33] The big deal once again was the statistical significance of the sociological studies: it was 99.9% certain that the sigh of relief of the globe, even in far-away countries, could not be due to chance.

The "utopia" of the Vedic technologies of consciousness had been documented and was doable with the smallest input of means. A small peace-creating group of seven to eight thousand people could decisively improve catastrophic situations if, yes, *if* humanity had the maturity and was free enough from any prejudgment to implement it. After these positive results, I was consumed by only one burning question: Which government on this beautiful blue planet would be the first one to have the openness and the courage to leave the well-worn paths and put such an army of the future into action?

VI.

African Interlude

If you listen to the depths of your heart and
measure the height of the horizon,
you will hear a single melody,
and in this melody
stars and stones tune in equally.

Khalil Gibran

1883-1938

Lebanese-American

painter, philosopher, and poet

Suddenly, the Sun

After the Taste of Utopia adventure, most participants had spread out to all corners of the world. But, responding to Maharishi's wishes, about five hundred people had stayed behind in Fairfield; the national leaders of various countries, almost all Purushas, and a couple of dozen of Mother Divine. We felt enlivened by the numbers that had documented the changes in world consciousness daily, and we now held in our hands concrete data that could be presented everywhere. They showed incontrovertibly that the Vedic principles, known for thousands of years, could bring about peace and prosperity through the coherence of consciousness and that this was no mere pipe-dream.

Maharishi was highly satisfied with these concrete data. For his entire life, he'd done nothing but tirelessly employ ever new solutions for the problems of modern life, and he was once again a step ahead of the game. We Purushas were to participate in the *Global March* in teams of four and spread out into various countries of the globe for eight weeks, introducing our programs and, based on the new data, inspire representatives of governments to institute a permanent group of 7,000 in their respective countries.

Inspired, we met in the gigantic round meditation hall with a domed roof painted gold. It could accommodate 2,000 people; the Americans lovingly called it "the Golden Dome." There, we began to discuss amongst ourselves who would go to which country. Suddenly, the whole world opened before us!

I hesitated between India and Thailand, when, unexpectedly, Reinhard appeared before me. "Lothar, come up to the front, Nandkishore wants to talk to you!"

I was taken aback. Brahmachari Nandkishore, one of Maharishi most trusted associates, wanted to talk to me? Far in the front, he sat on stage, an Indian with shoulder-length somewhat wavy, deep black hair, a long beard, and a narrow nose slightly curved downward at the tip. Beside him sat a couple of gentlemen I didn't know. As we were walking, Reinhard brought me up to date: "You know, Maharishi was in Kenya a year ago for quite a while. He spoke with their president, made a lot of contacts, and many hundreds of Kenyans had learned TM during Maharishi's visit." As we arrived at the front, Reinhard pointed to a small, dark-skinned Indian: "May I introduce Mr. Singh*? He owns twelve schools in which he wants to introduce TM."

At Reinhard's words, Mr. Singh gave me a friendly nod. With his noble and, at the same time, gently loving face, I liked him immediately. "In Kenya, a lot is already prepared for. Maharishi has great hopes for this country. And so, he doesn't want to send just four, but ten especially experienced Purushas. They should be able to give good presentations and have a skillful touch in their handling of government officials. We'd be happy if you took on that task and put together a team."

Well, wasn't that a surprise! So, it was to be Kenya! Of course, my friend Norbert, with whom I'd worked with well at the German center in Boppard and with whom I'd always shared a lot of laughter, would be part of the team. I also chose the others. When our team was complete, we met with Nandkishore one more time for our final instructions. "Maharishi wants you to continue to do your long meditation and TM-Sidhi program regularly mornings and evenings and that you behave in accord with the laws of that country. Do not ever pay anyone any bribes to achieve certain things. And you won't be allowed to exchange any money on the street because you can go to prison for that!" And then there was a special gift from our Master who always knew exactly what was running through our heads. "Maharishi also wants you to know that, during the week, you have to concentrate on your projects. But on weekends you can go on safaris and get to know the land and the people." My goodness, we'd really be going to Africa with all the trimmings!

A few days later, we left Iowa for a quick visit home to Europe and a brief stay at the Monastery Marienberg to exchange our winter gear for summer clothes. And soon, we were sitting on the plane and off to completely new horizons.

I was highly motivated and inspired by the extraordinary trust Maharishi had given us. Still on the plane, I whipped out my little notebook and began to structure the new assignment. My brothers-in-arms meanwhile began to plan safaris with fiery gusto.

Arriving in Nairobi, the capital city, we were welcomed by a radiant blue sky without even the smallest cloud. At 1,600 meters above sea level, the tropical climate was mild and the pleasant warmth made us happy. We drove directly to the national office that was also the local TM Center. Soon we arrived in a magnificent mansion from British colonial times in the middle of the neighborhood of diplomats. The garden, adorned with flower-borders and with a lush green lawn, was an unexpected welcome—and this blaze of color in the middle of January lifted out spirits. As we stepped through the doorway of this beautiful former embassy building, we were pleasantly surprised. The rooms were orderly and dignified, so that we could invite any diplomat or government representative without embarrassment!

Five hundred meters away we found our lodgings in a modest rental, a townhouse with just five rooms. So, we'd have to share a room for quite a while! This didn't kindle any enthusiasm in most of us, so little, in fact, that ten individualists got all tangled up in lengthy discussions. Some grumbled and wanted to get their own place somewhere nearby. But, finally, we got it together and moved into our rooms in trusting twosomes. A few days later, ten Indian Purushas, who also were to participate in the Global March in Kenya, moved into an identical neighboring building. When we visited our new neighbors for the first time, we were nothing short of stunned: They all slept together in the biggest room and the rest of the house stood empty! Cultural differences indeed clearly evident!

As soon as we were done with our morning meditations, we went over to the magnificent TM Center and enjoyed the unexpected luxury that awaited us there. After having lived in cold Germany under simple conditions, we suddenly lived in luxury. The house servant prepared us the most delicious breakfast according to our wishes with sun-ripened, fresh, juicy papayas and pineapples whose sweetness put us into ecstasy. During the day, too, he prepared our meals. Maids did the dishes and cleaned. Even our laundry was taken care of. No wonder that we all thought that, with Kenya we'd won a great prize.

On the first morning, we already sat comfortably on the terrace for our strategic planning. We enjoyed the view of the carpets of flowers in strong and glowing colors in the beautifully designed gardens and we allowed our pale winter faces to be tickled by the rays of the sun. In my group, some of the guys just wanted to enjoy the warmth and relax. But that wasn't my thing. Inspired by Maharishi's trust and convinced that I'd be able to realize a model project for the world here in Kenya, I plunged into the activities I'd chosen for myself with fiery enthusiasm.

School Children on the Upswing

Right on the first morning, I called Mr. Singh, the owner of twelve schools whom I'd met at the end of the Taste of Utopia Assembly in the U.S. In Kenya back then, there was free education only for the first four grades, for children from six to ten years old. Only the best ten percent of the country's students could attend state schools after that; for all others, parents had to come up with tuition for private institutions.

Four married couples had accompanied Maharishi on his visit to Kenya a year earlier. They subsequently remained there, had already done excellent preliminary work, and had trained teachers from various schools in an eight-months course. So, there were about a dozen local TM teachers ready and motivated, but still completely inexperienced. We Germans wanted to get the school projects going, and the local TM teachers would then, later, continue to keep them up on their own. At least, that was the plan. Mr. Singh was completely convinced that his students would profit from being initiated into TM. However, the respective directors of the schools would have to carry out the whole project by themselves; he just supplied the contacts and gave us his recommendation.

That same day, for the first time, I drove to the Shari Moyo Muslim Harambe Secondary School for children in the fifth grade or higher. Arriving in the slums of Nairobi, I was immediately shocked. Outside, on the unpaved street covered with red dust, plastic bags were lying everywhere, with other trash in piles. The school building was a massive, square block with two floors and plastered badly. Broken window panes greeted me, and, inside, it looked even worse. In my first tour of the place, I saw the extent of the students' vandalism. Doors hung from their hinges or were kicked in. Everywhere there were broken furniture, smashed, dirty toilet bowls; and in every classroom and hall, there were broken windows. Obviously, nothing was being replaced or repaired. It was an overwhelming expression of the apathy of the teachers and the owner, who were both powerless against the frustration and the mounting aggression of the students.

The principal of the school was a short and stocky Kenyan who had hopelessness written all over his face. "My doctor told me that I absolutely had to close the school. The stress of this job will kill me. If I don't do it, he only gives me another year because of my high blood pressure." With just a few words, he gave expression to his greatest conflict: "But if I do that, these children, who already don't have much hope in their lives, would be out on the street without an education because I can't find anyone who'd be ready to continue this work responsibly." He wrinkled his deep brow anxiously. "I just can't close this school! On the other hand, this unrestrained violence is doing me in."

First off, I presented him with our approach and introduced him to the scientific studies about the implementation of the TM technique in schools in the U.S. and other countries. These showed that the achievement and the grades of students improved[34] and that even IQ increased measurably in the space of a few months.[35] Reading, linguistic expression, and mathematical aptitude had been compared with specific before-and-after tests that documented significant improvements through TM.[36]

Brainwaves during the practice of TM showed a higher

synchronicity as the expression of greater coherence in the functioning of the central nervous system in all areas of the brain, instead of the usual jumble.[37] The logical consequence of this, also substantiated in numerous tests, was increasing creativity and the ability to concentrate,[38, 39] as well as the reduction of anxiety and a growing self-awareness.[40] Researchers had also compared scholastic achievement with TM compared to a Chinese meditation technique as well as with regular naps students took after lunch. The positive changes through TM were far greater in all areas to these two other methods.[41]

The principal immediately wanted to grasp the "life preserver" that had been offered, but I applied the brakes a little. I convinced him that—if he really wanted to lead his school to success—he should first experience the blessings of this meditation for himself and evaluate it. No sooner said than done. Even after a week of TM practice, his blood pressure fell markedly. He was more than happy that he could sleep better at night, and we took the next step together. A little later, I repeated the presentation to a big circle of the teaching staff—except for one teacher, twenty-five educators began to enliven the deep silence within them. I wanted the teachers to know from their own experience exactly what would be given to their students because it would succeed under those difficult circumstances only if they were fully behind this project. "I want that you test TM regularly for yourselves. Only when you are satisfied and know that it's a good thing, will we begin to teach the students this technique."

After nine weeks, the time had come to ask them all to write down their experiences. Even though the children had not yet learned to meditate, the teachers noticed big differences in the behavior of their students simply because they were more relaxed themselves. The lessons were more harmonious than before as they no longer felt they had to return the aggressiveness of their students directly; the teachers had gained greater authority, as they had rested within themselves. They'd made up their minds and it was "game on!".

And now I was standing in classrooms with lots of little faces in front of me, expectant, bored, or resistant. They sat there in their school uniforms, the girls in navy blue, pleated skirts and white blouses; the boys in navy pants and white shirts. Here and there, some of them wore a matching sweater with the embroidered yellow school emblem. Quite strikingly, two twelve-year-olds sat next to an eighteen-year-old, which astonished me. "The older ones had to either work at home and therefore could not come to school for long periods of time, or the parents could not afford the tuition for a few years. Some also were held back a few times," the homeroom teacher explained.

For me, it was a real challenge because I had to present the effectiveness and the advantages of TM in a lively language suitable for children, which was completely new for me, and I also had to capture different age groups at the same time. But finally I was successful. For the initiations, I called in some reinforcements, Gisela and Johannes, a married couple who'd already been living in Kenya for a year.

Kenya is in large parts hot and dry as well as plagued by months-long droughts that almost made the grass on the surface of the soil vanish. Malnutrition and death in the nomadic peoples and their livestock are part of daily life. When Johannes, Gisela, and I initiated 550 students in the

span of a few days, class after class, the whole region was unexpectedly drenched with downpours. The rain pelted on the
roofs and against window panes and splashed and sloshed
in the streets of the city—it was not the rainy season, and it
happened only in this place in Kenya where so many people
recently had begun to meditate together. For me, there was
a connection. Didn't the wise men in the full flowering of
Vedic culture pass down the knowledge that the climate and
the weather would mirror the collective consciousness of the
people? In an age in which many people enjoyed a higher
state of consciousness, it should be sunny during the day and
rainy at night—an expression of the inner coherence of the
inhabitants. There was even a study on this subject.[42] I was
sure that exactly this was happening here, right in front of
my nose, and it brought a satisfied smile on my face.

Despite the bleak conditions at the school, this was a
happy time for me. Just the positive changes in the faces of
the children were reward enough for me. In just a few days,
their eyes began to shine; resignation and dullness yielded
to hope and joy. I loved seeing it! When, in the afternoon
after school was out, I was on the way to other activities and
I would see "my" students somewhere on the street, I would
recognize them even without their school uniforms because
their faces showed that they had begun to make systematic
use of the treasure within them. Here they walked around, the
poorest of the poor who had experienced so much hardship
in their lives, but they looked radiant from within, relaxed,
and more beautiful and harmonious than most of the rich,
well-nourished children in expensive school uniforms.

But it was to get even better. For months, I was sitting
in a different classroom almost every morning shortly before

eight to accompany the morning meditation and to stabilize the successes that had been achieved. Opondo, a recently graduated TM teacher, was always by my side.

The teachers meditated at home. In the classrooms, however, each class president sat in the front and led the meditation by himself. The students sat relatively quietly, eyes closed, their faces soft and relaxed. Now and then, a student peeked curiously out of the corner of his eye to see what was going on all around. At the end of ten minutes, the class president rang a little bell softly to signal the end of the meditation. After two more minutes, he rang it a little louder: the students could open their eyes again. And the exuberant, lively noise began again. The children jumped up; the regular lesson could begin. Before the end of the school day, the whole process was repeated with the afternoon meditation.

Students and teachers of Shauri Moyo Muslim Harambee Secondary School. One of about 10 schools in which our team introduced Transcendental Meditation for the teachers and students in Kenya in 1984 with great success.

After a few weeks, the school day had completely changed. The noise level was less; after long years of resentment and hostility, teachers and students once again took joy in the lessons. The destructiveness diminished. Everything was on the best path. And I loved my students and the whole school. But it could be even better! So, after a few months, I called for a fundraiser for urgently needed repairs and acquisitions. The Kenyans very obviously loved Harambe and the collection of donations started. Little by little, I got the support of many parents as well as meditators. And, finally, I could even win over the Honorable Mr. Soba, the Minister of Communications, to sponsor our Harambe. He had become a staunch meditator and, understandably enough, with him as the magnet, the collection of donations became even easier.

Finally, close to three hundred people, all full of expectation, came together for a ceremony in the garden of our national TM Center. The owner of the school, Mr. Singh, had come for the occasion, and so had the principal, the teachers, and the representatives of the parents who watched with pride as the students performed dances, songs, and recited poetry. The high point came when I presented a check of several thousand dollars to the Minister in the presence of the press and our Purusha friends, a check that we then gave to the principal of the school, who was moved to tears.

Soon after, the broken window panes at the school were replaced, the leaking roof was repaired; the broken tables and chairs were replaced with new ones, and an orderliness outside that had not been seen in years also came about.

1984 in Kenya: the Honorable Mr. Soba, Minister of
Communications of Kenya (standing 3rd from left) presents the
principal (4th from left) with the sum of several thousand dollars for
repairs and purchases of his school at the fundraising ceremony
organized by me (2ⁿᵈ from left), in front of several hundred
meditating students and parents.

At the same time, class participation increased and
achievements grew. In a few months, the violence that had
been the order of the day and that had so frightened the
younger students as well as the teachers, simply vanished from
the scene. Our students, who because of their lack of discipline had always been last in any kind of competition, won
second prize in the handball competition of all the secondary
schools in Nairobi; in other words, the upswing could no
longer be missed.

These successes were a clear sign. With a good conscience,
I could now hand over the Shauri Moyo Muslim Harambee
Secondary School to Opondo, the local TM teacher who,
with lively gestures and his radiant eyes, could tell wonderful
stories. To make sure that everything was okay, I now only
went to supervise "my" students and teachers, people who

had won over my heart, every two or three weeks.

In similar ways, we soon completed two other projects, one of which was in an even worse slum. Here the furniture was not just battered, but frustrated young people had even burned the tables and chairs in their classrooms. Their inner brokenness and the resentment in their lives was just too great; they had to break fresh ground by force. When Gisela, Johannes, and I initiated hundreds of children into meditation, the blessings from above came soon enough. In the first few days already, strong and continuous rain made the whole region fertile. And a few weeks later, the positive changes in both of the new schools were as good as those in the first one had been, and I, overjoyed, could observe how these new students relaxed deeply, became more harmonized and happier in their everyday lives, while also learning better and achieving more. Everything went exceedingly well, and, once again, the work was pure joy for me!

Unsuspecting, I came to the school in the slums one morning seven months later and was scared to death. In front of each classroom there stood a grim-faced soldier with a machine gun in firing position. What was that all about? The principal explained quickly: "Every six months we have exams. The results of these tests decide who will graduate to the next grade and who will be left behind. And because this always leads to riots, we must protect the teachers. The students attack them with knives or start fighting."

Heavens alive, he seemed to think this was completely normal!

But this time, the soldiers stood in the hallways all morning without any action. Without incident, the exams went well. When the results came in later, everyone, the principal, the teachers, and the students, too, were totally surprised. In every other year in this school an average of seventy percent of the students did not graduate to the next grade. And now, after only seven months of implementing two ten-minute meditations per school day, it was exactly the other way around. For the first time since the existence of the school, seventy percent of the children had passed the exams!

When I heard this, my face became radiant and so did my heart. I was so thankful to be part of this and experience all of it first-hand!

Sassy Monkeys and Scarlet Heads

In Kenya, we Purusha all felt super rich suddenly, at least for our circumstances, because the money that had always been tight in Germany now unfolded in this sunny land with unexpected purchasing power. Since the dissemination of TM, together with the activities of the TM Movement in all the world's countries, devoured untold sums of money and everything had to be covered somehow through private means, every Purusha was responsible for his own cost of living. So we regularly looked for donors who would support this good thing every month with a smaller or bigger bank transfer that was normally just enough for our living expenses plus a meager sum of pocket money. But here it was equal to a royal honorarium!

In contrast to our situation, our African TM teacher colleagues got their food and lodging, as well as a small salary, from the TM organization. Maharishi saw that the entire African continent would be dependent on aid from rich countries for a long time to come. For the TM activities in poor countries, the money obtained in industrialized countries through TM seminars and courses was used to make it possible for people in developing countries to unfold their spiritual potential and stand on their own two feet sooner.

Evidently, the money we had available seemed just about infinite to our African TM teacher colleagues. When we all sat talking comfortably together in the garden one evening, one fellow, Naituli, suddenly burst out with, "That is really unjust! My countrymen have to work hard for that little bit of money here. And you just push a plastic card into the wall and can get as much money as you want. That's really not fair!"

We Purushas needed quite a while to wipe the bewilderment off our faces and explain lovingly what was up with this "unfairness." Of course, we did understand him. With the much greater purchasing power of our small income, we were indulging in unaccustomed luxury. We enjoyed visiting restaurants and other creature comforts, and, on weekends allowed ourselves frequent excursions into the near and far surroundings, getting to know the beauty and the uniqueness of Kenya, and loving them. For us, who'd had spent most of our time behind monastery walls, this was pure freedom. We reveled in it in full measure while never missing our extended meditation programs. But our African friends also profited from the "money out of the wall." Now and again we invited Kenyan TM teacher colleagues with whom we worked together on various projects to eat at the classy Hilton. In homey togetherness, we filled our stomachs with the best cuisine. Our native guests, however, always missed their beloved staple food, *ugalli*, the traditional starchy (for us Purushas, tasteless), tough cornmeal.

"Guys, let's do a safari! Right in front of the city gates, south of Nairobi, is the 120 km square national park!"

Bodo's suggestion was accepted enthusiastically after a brief exchange of opinions. And so, five young men joyfully explored their new home in a rented Land Rover on one of the first weekends after getting here. The view of the landscape stretching far to the horizon with the graceful black trunks of the acacias and their sprawling crowns silhouetted against the deep blue of the sky are unforgettable for me to this day. For weeks, already, or even months, there'd not been a single drop of rain. Cracks up to ten centimeters wide cut across the clay-colored, dusty soil everywhere. Overwhelmed by the immeasurable vastness and the breathtaking silence, I marveled at zebras, lions, leopards, buffalo, rhinoceroses and giraffes in the wild for the first time in my life. In the silence of the steppe, I felt one with the animals. A deep love for these creatures, who could live here in the wild according to their own nature, filled me. I felt the unique character and the idiosyncrasies of each single kind of animal clearly. And my heart opened with gratitude that I could be here and take it all in so intensely.

Many weekends I spent with various Purusha friends in the unending vastness of Kenya, sometimes in luxurious safari lodges, where at a first-class breakfast we could watch elephants bathe in a waterfall, or in simple tents amid open nature. We drove around in the old Volkswagen bus with the top down. Often, we looked out, standing on the seats, and enjoyed the endless horizon as well and, equally, the cool wind. Now and then, on the dusty roads a car would come toward us, recognizable from afar because of the big, yellowish cloud of dust it raised behind it. And when it had passed us, we were covered every time with that ochre-colored dust fine as powdered sugar.

After just a few weeks, we were drawn to Lake Naivasha, a lake surrounded by extinct volcanos just seventy kilometers north-west of Nairobi. There, we crowded into a narrow, brown wooden boat from whose hull the bleached-out lacquer was peeling off. It held six people and took us across the clear, dark blue water to the national park on the island in the middle of the lake. Just as the boatman was about to land, massive dark grey, shiny hippos broke the water's surface next to our rocking boat. The guide had the greatest respect for them; with extreme care, he maneuvered around them. All too easily, they could have capsized our boat, but, thank God, they didn't feel like it that day.

Safely on land, we roamed over the pristine island and were thrilled when we suddenly saw antelopes, Thomson gazelles, gnus, and zebras up close, or when, near enough to almost touch, we saw rhinos lazing around on the shore. It was blazing hot and beautiful. In high spirits, we pulled off our shirts and roamed all over the uninhabited island. After two hours, we went back across the open lake to our safari lodge right on the water for our evening meditation. Only after we got there, we greenhorns noticed that we'd made some unwelcome acquaintance with the tropical sun. We had the worst sunburns of our lives. And, two mornings later, we had an important date at the Ministry of Education! We'd be looking quite horrible.

On Sunday morning, we drove to another part of this huge lake. When the sun came up and covered everything with gentle light, we held our breaths. Tens of thousands of flamingos stood before us on their skinny legs. A sea of pink spread before our astonished eyes. Walking on the shore, we discovered other kinds of birds, ibises, African fish eagles, goliath herons, marabou storks, pelicans, and black cormorants. It was as lovely as a dream!

On Monday morning, we sat in front of the Minister of Education and three directors in their darkly paneled office: we three Germans, dressed to the nines in suits and ties, and arriving for this important presentation as red as tomatoes! We were somewhat embarrassed; the statesmen, on the other hand, took it with typical Kenyan ease and just were happy that we treasured their country so much!

A few weeks later—now always prepared with a thick layer of protective sun-screen—we explored the gigantic national park Amboseli, which was exquisitely situated at the foot of Mount Kilimanjaro, near the neighboring country of Tanzania. Late in the evening, our guide led us to our resting place surrounded by protective, meters-high palisades. The four of us slept on hard metal beds in a simple wooden hut with a bare concrete floor. When darkness came, I innocently turned on a light. Oh horror—in the shortest time, our mosquito nets were covered by gigantic black spiders and insects. None of us dared to leave the protective mosquito nets around our beds. In the middle of the night, however, I did have to go out. So as not to wake my friends, I quietly stepped out the door. Pitch black darkness surrounded me. When I relieved myself a few meters away from the hut, I heard undefinable sounds close to me. Slowly my eyes got used to the pitch-black darkness and—my breath stopped with shock—three meters away, the outline of a massive elephant towered in the night. Cool as a cucumber, he combed through the garbage cans for something edible. I was back in the hut faster than I could think and, alarmed, woke the others. Breathless we listened, as the elephant rumbled around and, soon after, made a deafening sound right next to our wall. We were frightened and petrified. This full-grown elephant could have smashed our simple wooden hut with a strong and well-aimed kick. A half our later, we heard the excited screams of men in Swahili, the loud pounding of sticks and the muffled but heavy vibration of the floor. The answer to the puzzle next morning was this: the game keepers had driven a whole herd of elephants out of our fenced-in resting place.

During most of the endless hours of these safaris, we were surrounded by incomparable nature, animals that came singly or in groups over the prairie, along with much, much silence. One day we stopped near a watering hole. We just sat there and silently looked through the open window of our VW bus. Again and again, various groups of animals showed up to refresh themselves with the standing water. Once five or six elephants stayed a little while and then, trotted away ponderously, only to be replaced a bit later by a group of zebras. When these had strolled off, a herd of gnus showed up after a little while. And so it went for a long time. We saw giraffes spread their legs wide, bending their long necks down and then vanishing with their majestic gait. Never did I see so many different kinds of animals quench their thirst at the same time but as if connected through a mysterious form of communication, they only showed up in groups, always of the same species. More than an hour we sat there almost immobile, taking everything in. Fewer and fewer thoughts went through me and finally let me submerge myself in the unboundedness of my inner self and my surroundings. So, here I sat, outside in this unending steppe with the wide horizon, far from any civilization, felt the infinite silence and deep peace that pervaded everything and that is so often hidden from our busy perceptions.

Now and then we also experienced exciting adventures. On another safari, Lüder sneaked from our parked jeep toward a herd of elephants. He absolutely wanted to catch a baby elephant with his camera. Closer and closer he dared to go and again and again snapped his camera. The elephant mother stood like a protective, unmoved colossus near him completely relaxed. Suddenly, she lifted her trunk and trumpeted into the air announcing calamity and started moving toward him with heavy steps. We got scared and started the motor. "Lüder, dude, come on, this is deadly dangerous!" But, running backwards, he had to take a few more shots.

Calling loudly and waving our arms, we slowly started to drive with the trotting elephant mother close behind us. At the very last second, Lüder jumped into the vehicle with the furious and wildly trumpeting elephant mother directly behind him. We counted every second till the Jeep got rolling and the pachyderm gave up the chase.

Another time we wanted "pure Africa" and sleep at night outside in the savanna, taking in the sounds of the steppe near all the animals. The tourist guide was completely surprised and shocked at this request. With all his speaking skill, he tried to dissuade us. But, what the heck, we were young men and knew no fear. In no way did we want to miss this special adventure. The guide gave us to understand that this would be too dangerous even for him. He thought we'd completely gone off the rocker. Even so, he declared himself ready to pitch a tent with us and gather firewood—enough to keep the wild animals away from us for a whole night. Then he literally ran off. We stayed, six intrepid young men, in three yellow and blue nylon tents.

With the speed of wind, the velvety darkness descended upon us. With it came the sounds and the shadows of night. We took turns guarding the fire that we had to keep going at all cost because, as soon as it got smaller, hungry hyenas dared to come as close as ten or fifteen meters away. The most diverse animal voices sounded all around us from countless throats and became exceedingly loud. They screeched, chattered, crackled, and squeaked, and, sometimes, you could hear a roar whose unfamiliarity sent terrified shivers racing across our backs. We didn't dare to let the protective fire die down and took turns, dead-tired as we were, to watch for an hour while the others slept if they could. At dawn, dead-tired, I sank down on my air mattress and crawled into my sleeping bag.

As quickly as it gets dark near the equator, it also becomes light and searing hot in the morning. After a short sleep, I was awake again. What was rustling in my tent? I was startled as I saw the troublemakers: skinny, small, grey-brown monkeys uninhibitedly working on our food stocks. We had stored the provisions for several days in my tent, fruit, bread, nuts—all stockpiled neatly in paper bags tucked within plastic sacks. Still half-asleep, I screamed as loud as I could, "Hey, monkeys are stealing our food!," waking my sleeping friends as well as startling the monkeys, who scampered off holding one of our bags with our precious provisions in each of their hands. Not to be outdone, we ran after them, maybe fifty meters, only to be left standing without having achieved anything, under the first convenient tree the monkeys had fled up, un-perturbed and in which to enjoy themselves with their stolen goods. But, in their hasty flight, they'd lost about half of the bags and scattered the contents all over the ground, which we finally gathered up, laughing. And so, we all finally had breakfast in cozy and pleasurable harmony, the monkeys up in their tree, and we bipeds underneath!

A little later, our tourist guide came back. He, too, looked tired and confessed with a crooked grin, "Man, oh, man, guys, I was so worried all night! I've never seen it before that tourists wanted to tent in the wild savanna overnight.

You guys are really completely nuts!" And he seemed deeply relieved to see us all unharmed. And, admittedly, we really were also!

Known throughout the Land

On weekdays in the early mornings, I was on the way to one of the schools under my care. After 11 a.m., I most often had appointments with agencies, firms, and various ministries, or in prisons. In the first weeks, I had to search for the appropriate numbers and addresses in telephone books; even so, I was successful in getting dates for presentations in many places through these cold calls. In this, too, Mr. Singh was of immeasurable help. He generously made his impressive house in a wonderfully landscaped park available for visits from influential personalities. In his oversized living room with its tasteful Indian furnishings, fifteen people could sit comfortably on sofas decorated with hand-carved wooden components. His Indian cook was a genius. He brought snacks, pakoras, the delicious fried Indian vegetables, and other delicacies to the table in never-ending abundance and we were served by the most delightful, helpful souls.

I taught the basic TM courses to ever-increasing numbers of people, and continued to take care of my students afterwards. In these months in Kenya, I felt Maharishi's attention and love focused on me in these situations. I felt his boundless consciousness across all countries and oceans, often even more intensely than I'd felt it in Boppard, where he was physically present.

Our group of Purushas and the programs we offered spread among the Kenyans, and so did our successes. People, who had just learned TM a little while ago, recommended us. Others, who'd promised themselves advantages for introducing Transcendental Meditation in their institutions or firms, contacted us directly. Again and again, I presented our research in new places in English, explaining the blessings that came through the practice of the TM technique for the individual and society. All the while, I felt that I was uplifted in a very special way as soon as I began to speak about Vedic knowledge. I submerged myself in the field of consciousness of my Master, into that of his Master, Guru Dev, as well as the chain of all the masters that had lived and passed on this knowledge about the unfolding of the greatness of life since time immemorial.

A special coherence and peace took hold of me. Often it even deepened to the extent that I had the feeling of no longer choosing my own words, but watching, like an indifferent observer, the words come from my mouth without my having anything to do with it. When I spoke with high-ranking politicians or university professors, then, in this condition, I was often completely surprised and, at the same time, fascinated at what came from me and with what power and authority it was expressed. I felt connected to everything and could draw from an infinite source without having to strain at all. Just through passing on this elevated knowledge to my various listeners, I began, here in Kenya's heat, to experience Cosmic Consciousness, the state of maintaining transcendence while engaged in outer activities. It was a magnificent state in which I gained energy instead of losing it.

After a good two months, four more German Purushas, who'd completed the Global March Project in Uganda, joined our team to help us with all the many TM initiations in Kenya. One fellow, Andreas, tall and slim, was always dressed to the nines and was excellent at writing letters. The two of us soon became a well-coordinated team, often working with contacts to the government, giving presentations together, and we complemented one another magnificently.

After a few weeks Norbert, Lüder, and Clemens had moved further inland to Nakuru on Naivasha Lake. There and in Kisumu on Lake Victoria, many hundreds of school children learned to meditate under their direction.

"Dude, Lothar," one morning early, Norbert was on the telephone, totally beside himself with joy, "You won't believe it, but what's happening here is exactly the same as what happened with you guys! Since we've been initiating the students here into TM, it's been pouring buckets over the entire region!"

Of course, that wasn't the only effect. They, too, saw the same far-reaching changes for the better with students and teachers, just as we had here in Nairobi.

After a few months, Norbert and Lüder moved to Mombasa, and, on our last phone conversation, they raved about the amazing beaches of the Indian Ocean. When Norbert then called soon after, I thought he'd be reporting excitedly about his latest safari. But I was wrong. He had organized a big TV program with the "Voice of Kenya" in Mombasa. "It would be so cool if you could come here and, present the educational offer of Maharishi International University about the Science of Creative Intelligence with Lüder and me. We'll have a whole hour program, and it's aired all over the country. Show up in two days. But be prepared: it's awfully hot here, hot and humid!"

The adventuresome bus ride of almost 500 kilometers was arduous and interesting at the same time. The unbelievable size of the steppe with its meager African vegetation was an experience all by itself. In the un-air-conditioned bus, my lively, local, fellow passengers transported cages with chattering chickens and geese and even slaughtered animals still dripping with blood. About every half hour a small hamlet came into view on the side of the road with simple mud or corrugated metal huts. Hand-painted signs alleged these to be hotels and restaurants where passengers could get soft drinks or tea. But despite the refreshments, all of us on the bus were sweating from all our pores, and the odors from people and animals became just about unbearable during the long, arduous trip.

The long road often had huge pot holes so that the colorfully dressed passengers were regularly shaken or tossed up into the air. We moved at about 80 km/hr on the asphalt road that was just wide enough for one bus to be driving on it. When another bus came racing straight at us, I saw, with my eyes open wide, how both vehicles drove directly at each other without breaking. The first time this happened, my breath stopped with shock. But during the trip, I soon saw the rule: the driver with stronger nerves stayed on the pavement, even if a little close to the left edge. The one with weaker nerves, on the other hand, jerked the steering wheel at the very last moment to swerve away, and then rattled for a couple of hundred meters on the bumpy edge of the road over the dried-out soil. Indeed, the drivers were so well-versed in this driving style that head-on accidents were relatively rare, whereas it happened with regularity that the yielding vehicle sustained a broken axle or other damage because of this shaky maneuver. Just on this trip, I saw two busses that were left to stand there; the passengers stood or sat around the broken vehicle resigned to their fate. The casual commentary of our bus driver: "Well, they'll have to wait a few hours till the replacement bus comes. It often happens that those folks become the victims of wild animals."

Oh, my God!

The humid heat kept increasing more and more as we got closer to the coast. Mombasa was like another world. Big, white, sand beaches with luxury hotels by Western standards stood in contrast to the oppressed slums with crowded alleys, trash, and corrugated metal houses.

Extremely glad to have escaped the crowd and the stink in the bus, I looked forward to a refreshing bath at the TM Center. After getting there, I was first off surprised about the local standards of the apartments in the inner city. The electricity, and with it the air conditioning, had gone off several hours earlier, and running water was only available for a few hours each day. Instead, there were a few buckets filled with water in the bathroom, ready for a bit of refreshment, but I was told to use it sparingly.

Next morning, we went to the TV studio. For such an important occasion I was dressed formally, but extremely inappropriately for the climate. In a three-piece suit with a notched-up tie, beads of sweat rolled down my forehead after just a few minutes under the glaring spot lights. The back of my freshly ironed shirt was soaking wet in no time. Despite that, it was fun to answer the intelligent questions of the well-prepared moderator. We had time for one hour to present the functioning and the effects of TM on physical and mental health, to report on the positive experiences of the school day, to introduce the project for the establishment of a university we'd planned and, at the same time, to elucidate a few research results in detail. As the high point, we offered ten scholarships to Maharishi International University in Iowa, U.S.A., for young Kenyans who could get in touch with us after the program. The response to the presentation was so good that those responsible at the headquarters in Nairobi decided to rebroadcast the show.

Back then, in Kenya there was only one TV station and nothing had prepared me for the consequences of this show. With my white skin, blond hair, and blue eyes, I was immediately recognizable. Wherever I now walked down the streets, small, cheeky boys dared to show up, grinning and giggling and, holding their hands in front of their mouths, but still loudly audible, yelling "Maharishi" at me, or retreating on their skinny legs to a safe distance despite my friendly "hello".

We got a lot of calls and invitations to give presentations from schools, parents, official entities, and from students who wanted to study at MIU in the U.S. The response was magnificent and increased our fame even with politicians all over the land.

Back in Nairobi, I got an invitation from Mr. Sandhal*, an Indian I'd not met before, for an official reception with many ambassadors and ministers. Mr. Sandhal was one of the wealthiest businessmen in all of Kenya; his oversized mansion in a well-kept garden was surrounded by police. On site, I learned the reason for this. For this official celebration, half of the Cabinet had been invited to welcome the ambassador from Tanzania. He was eagerly anticipated because Kenya and Tanzania had broken off diplomatic relations many years ago and only recently had reconnected, in fact during the Taste of Utopia Assembly with 7,000 meditators.

Inside the house, I was astonished at the magnificently luxurious interior design. Servants in posh uniforms and white gloves swarmed all over and served pakoras, deep-fried vegetables dipped in spiced garbanzo paste as well as chapatis, Indian flatbread, and countless other typically Indian delicacies—all on exquisitely decorated platters.

When I stepped into the room, my gaze fell on an African standing about thirty meters away, with an unbelievably noble face and white hair, who held me spellbound. We looked at one another, and a spark jumped between us. We went toward one another and introduced ourselves. He was the guest of honor, Mr. Alatanga*, the ambassador from Tanzania. In the same moment, I felt that we'd captured one another's heart, that I'd meet this most extraordinary person frequently, and that he would bring me luck. Here in Kenya, I always introduced myself as "Lothar" without using my last name. "I come from the Maharishi Research University and, here in Kenya, am introducing scientifically tested solutions for problems in education and health that rest on the consciousness-based techniques of Transcendental Meditation."

He was tremendously warm-hearted, and his lively eyes sparkled with interest. He listened intently and asked intelligent questions so that, finally, I told him that we could offer this to his country as well. Mr. Alatanga gave me his business card and asked me to call his office in the following week to agree on a meeting date. Mr. Sandhal, the man of the house, joined us toward the end of our conversation and confessed to my amazement: "Gentlemen, you know, I learned this meditation at the beginning of the sixties from Maharishi Mahesh Yogi himself, and I am still practicing. It helps me a lot!" After that, he made the rounds with me and introduced me as a very special guest to many dignitaries.

Finally, he asked me, "Come, Lothar, would you be so kind as to give an introductory lecture to my closest friends here?" He led me with four gentlemen into a smaller room, where I did just that with zest and joy, as anyone could easily have guessed.

I felt once again that nature was carrying me on her wings because, at this cocktail party, I got to know many ministers. Some of them I had already been trying to reach for weeks, but had only got as far as some outer offices; this evening, I could make dates with all of them for presentations in the following few weeks. All around, it was a magnificent evening. I got to know many interesting people and, late at night, I went home completely delighted and uplifted.

The icing on the cake of that evening was that those four friends of Mr. Sandhal came together to our TM center in the beautiful embassy building and allowed me to initiate them into the practice of TM.

And the ambassador also came for an individual appointment. Slowly his dark, highly polished state coach with the green, black and blue striped Tanzanian flag drove up. His driver got out and carried several gigantic and splendidly arranged flower bouquets into our center together with several equally impressive baskets filled with the choicest exotic fruits. This was unparalleled in my entire TM teacher career. To the right and the left of the table with the picture of Maharishi's Master, Guru Dev, I put an extra tray on which to arrange the entire splendor and began the traditional Sanskrit ceremony surrounded by the most glorious scents.

When Mr. Alatanga was writing down his experiences on the questionnaire after his first meditation, he had not just experienced pure consciousness, silence without thoughts, but also moments of intense bliss. He looked up at me with a heart-felt smile and then, profoundly moved, this great soul said, "I have been waiting for this day my entire life!"

That this noble person, far older than me and extraordinarily successful in his life, clearly expressed this tremendous appreciation of TM so clearly even on the first day, moved me deeply also and strengthened once again the feeling of gratitude for being able to pass on the art of transcending.

Again and again, I caught myself during this time waiting for the expected adverse reaction, the slanderous vilification of the success of TM we'd experienced so thoroughly in Germany, and the difficulties connected with this. But the exact opposite happened. Little by little, most the government officials of this country learned Transcendental Meditation and, with African openness and cordiality, as well as full of appreciation, they recommended us and the meditation to others.

The Indian Bride

On my way to school and in the immediate vicinity of downtown, a sign, "Birmingham Secondary School and Business College"* caught my eye and the idea hit me like lightening that I should talk to them. Had I known what waited for me there, I'd certainly have made a beeline in a different direction with my self-assured steps. Unburdened by events to come, I asked to see the proprietor of the school, and, a little later I sat across from two Sikh brothers who owned it jointly. I gave then the usual presentation for educational systems, while they nodded their heads in agreement until, at the end, I gave them the advice to try out Transcendental Meditation for themselves, before introducing the program in their school.

Sure enough, both appeared at our TM Center a little later with their wives and kids in tow. In accord with Indian culture, I only initiated the men of this group to meditate; to initiate the women, I asked Anju, an Indian TM teacher to step in.

From then on, this tight-knit group of nine often showed up on Sundays in their VW bus. We discussed their experiences in meditation, and they were most interested in Vedic knowledge, which I naturally gave with open hands to this receptive family. Mr. Singh's* daughter was about twenty years old. She was extremely shy and always looked down, but occasionally gave me a quick glance, which made me realize that she was not indifferent to me. The other family members obviously also took a liking to me. The more often they came, the more frequently one or the other of them asked to speak to him or her alone. Then they began to suggest point blank that I could become a member of their family and marry their daughter. They were already dreaming about my expanding their school and opening a series of them in India. I, on the other hand, didn't take them up on it and suffered their hints without commenting. But soon it couldn't be ignored any longer, and my TM colleagues had fun telling slightly off-color jokes at my expense.

At some point, the two families invited Anju, her husband, and me to their shared home. Suspecting nothing, I joyfully anticipated an excellent Indian meal and a nice, thought-provoking evening. As a gift to my hosts, I brought a framed and lovingly wrapped portrait of Maharishi and a book. When I tried to give it to my hosts, they declined with a friendly smile: "Lothar, you can give it to our daughter yourself!"

Gosh, how embarrassing! It was intended for the whole family. I had nothing, nothing whatsoever, in mind with this delicate girl! But they wouldn't have any of it, so that there was nothing I could do but give it to that beauty with velvety eyes and ebony black and braided hair. But that wasn't the end of it.

The two brothers and the mother of the girl—always nicely one after the other—got me alone into a separate room and again asked point blank, "What do you think, would you like to become a member of our family and marry our daughter Rohini*?"

Oh, jeez—how awkward! I had no clue about how to worm my way out of that situation politely. On top of all that, this obviously absurd idea did begin to take hold in my head as a vague possibility. And so, albeit I'd never exchanged so much as a word with her, I had begun to look at this bashful Indian bride more closely, and I began to appreciate how beautiful she was.

Finally, we sat down at a long table that was set for

twenty. The head of the household indicated that I should sit at the head of the table. There I sat enthroned on a wide and especially elegant armchair, realizing to my dismay that a video camera on a tripod was focused on me and ready. When I asked about it, the head of the household told me, "We have a big family, some of them live in London and some of them live in Gujarat, and all of them have to agree to this wedding."

I was totally shocked. Here I was expecting a normal supper, intent on implementing TM in the school of the two brothers, but they were set on palming off their daughter to be my wife. Unable to say anything directly, I didn't know how to get out of this mess and couldn't bluntly tell them "No." I was in a tight spot and had no idea what to do about it. In my distress, I talked about what was closest to me. In front of the camera, I explained the Unified Field of Natural Law, talked about enlightenment and scientific research on the effects of TM, and reeled off on my most treasured expertise to them. In the space of two minutes, I was in my element and all the nervousness and cringe-worthiness of the situation that I'd just felt so keenly was erased. How could I have guessed that I was jumping from the frying pan into the fire?

Anju and her husband Sushil naturally had nothing better to do than report everything hot off the press to the rest of the gang. The whole story spread like wildfire among the German and Indian Purushas, all the married couples, and our African TM teacher colleagues. I, the bridegroom against my will, was the subject of discussion and, as could be expected, the others began to tease me mercilessly in all kinds of ways. How could this have happened, that I, as the spokesman of our Purusha group, could slide into this thing?

My friends tried to help and explained to Mr. Singh at

their earliest opportunity that I was Purusha and so belonged to a group of unmarried men whom Maharishi personally employed and guided spiritually. Nevertheless, the prospective father of the bride could not be stopped, "It's all good, Lothar, I've got word from our relatives in England and in India. You've made a good impression on them, and they all agree that you should marry Rohini. Just give me your father's and Maharishi's phone numbers. I'll arrange everything!"

It was incomprehensible; I slipped even deeper into this strange trap! It was literally shortly before midnight, and I could finally defend myself, "I don't have to ask either Maharishi or my father—this is entirely my own thing, and I can decide it for myself. I'll think about it for a couple of days!"

And that is what I did. As promised, I went deeply within myself. She was pretty for sure, and who knows, maybe this was exactly what my fate had organized for me? Had nature, Divine Intelligence, give me a clear indicator and, on a silver platter, served up the future delights of wedded bliss with a beautiful and gentle Indian girl at my side? Well, maybe, just maybe, should I give this crazy thing a chance and get to know her personally?

Thought became action: I gathered up all my courage and, in all innocence, called Mr. Singh. After a short introductory speech, I presented him with "I'd like to invite Rohini for lunch at the Hilton so I can get to know her better." I'd stuck my fist straight into a hornet's nest. Loud and angry, the horror-stricken father chewed me out: "That is the height of insolence! You have insulted my entire family and dragged it into the mud. That is totally out of the question!"

After he'd calmed down a little, he did add as a kind of

closure, "I'll have to talk to my brother about this since he's the oldest one in our family and makes all the decisions. I'll tell him about this. Call back in an hour!"

With my heart beating in my throat, I called back an hour later, only to get my hair washed once again, this time by Mr. Singh Senior himself. He ranted and raged on the phone, and screamed, his voice breaking while rejecting my indecent offer lock, stock, and barrel. And even that was not enough. He called Anju and Sushil, complaining bitterly about me and how I could be so low and shameless as to invite his daughter. But they understood both cultures and tried as much as possible to explain. To me, they made it clear that in Indian culture something like that would be completely unthinkable and indecent, and that an unmarried woman who goes out by herself with a man would lose her reputation, and, after that, could not easily be married off. On the other hand, they explained to the enraged family that from my side nothing untoward was intended and that my behavior was entirely normal in my culture.

Even so, there was total silence between me and that family for three months. But one fine Sunday morning the whole united clan came back to the TM Center as if nothing had happened, and the game began anew: the secret and shy glances of the daughter, the comments and vague suggestions of family members, and, don't forget, the merciless teasing on the part of my Purusha buddies.

Finally, the brothers came up with a very special proposition. They wanted to sell their school and their college to the TM Movement and, with the money, build a group of 7,000 in India, and, with this, create world peace. Again, and again, they brought up this wild idea, until, at some point,

I called Maharishi's secretaries in Europe and relayed their proposal and their (most probably not entirely selfless) ideas about the price. The finance committee of the international organization wanted to see some numbers before making a counter-offer: yearly sales and profits, necessary investments, and so on. As soon as I passed on these suggestions, I once again seemed to have stepped on the feet of the entire clan. "We've never done that! Never, ever have we shown those numbers to anyone. No, that's totally out of the question!"

They were being unbelievably difficult, but after a lot of ifs, ands, and buts, they decided with a heavy heart to show those sensitive numbers. I gave the information to the guys in Vlodrop to evaluate. When I got the counter-offer a few weeks later, it was only a quarter of the amount that the brothers had proposed.

Not expecting anything good, I took that thorny path. I went into the school by myself, where the two brothers waited for me with high hopes on the top floor. As soon as I mentioned the price to them, they contorted their faces. Loud and excited they abused me. "If you weren't a friend of the family, we'd kill you right here and now and throw you out the window!"

They completely lost their tempers. They screamed louder and louder and egged each other on into more and more rage. In the middle of evil curses, they grabbed me by my tie and my collar a few times. Utterly brow-beaten and taken off guard by their angry outbursts, I saw to it to get down those life-saving stairs as fast as possible!

And that was it. I never saw the brothers again, or my lovely and shy Indian bride.

VII.

BACK TO EUROPE

*We should not flee from the vita activa
into the vita contemplativa,
nor the other way around;
instead, be on the way, alternating in both,
be at home in both
partake of both.*

Hermann Hesse
1877-1962
German writer, poet,
and, in his free time, artist

A Sudden End

Within a year, our Purusha teams had gradually initiated about 3,000 school children in various places in Kenya, including the teaching staffs and the principals. Radiating bliss, we'd tell each other about the positive changes that we'd observed first hand whenever we met anywhere. Of course, we all knew the research about the improvements in academic performance in various fields. But to experience this quick and significant turnaround among the poorest of the poor first-hand day after day was another thing altogether. It inspired us to the extent that all of us began to dream of a rosy future in which this blessing would benefit countless children. Wouldn't it be great if children all over the world could look forward to school joyfully, would be cared for lovingly, and could unfold their consciousness and tap into new and meaningful knowledge with great enthusiasm?

As fabulously as it went with the schools, the construction of the university Maharishi wanted, and with it the 7,000 group which really was the main purpose of the entire "Global March," turned out to be difficult. After the documented positive results for the whole planet of the "Taste of Utopia" assembly, we wanted to win over a government for permanently financing such a big group, no matter where. The expenses incurred by any government would pay off in no time. They would only be a fraction of what they would save through reducing costs in healthcare, with fewer traffic accidents, less criminality, droughts, and natural catastrophes in their own countries. Nor should we forget the socio-economic upswing that the power of silence would have brought with it, as well as the relief for the heads of state who would have been less influenced by the stress in the collective consciousness of the population and would thus have been able to make better decisions for the land and the people. As simple as all this sounded, and as solid and airtight the extant pilot projects were, the implementation turned out to be difficult. This beautiful, new approach demanded the abandonment of patterns of thought and behavior that had been entrenched for thousands of years, and activated all kinds of reservations on the part of decision makers.

The first hurdle in Nairobi was the chief of police himself. After several different presentations of TM teachers and colleagues, he completely understood our purpose and had judged the drastic reduction of criminality correctly. The twisted conclusion he drew from all this followed his own unique logic. "Gentlemen, it is completely clear that this is a good thing. But you must understand that I cannot support the creation of such a group. I would make myself and most my colleagues with the police unemployed. I am sorry!"

Many high-level politicians and officials from different ministries found the implementation of a 7,000 group in their country a noble objective that they wanted to support with all their might. Maharishi himself had already promised them a year earlier that his organization would build a university if the government would donate the necessary land for it. The ministers of various departments had promised him to support this effort—but nothing ever came of it. When we took up this project a year later with renewed momentum, politicians vigorously supported our acquisition of land. At least, that's how it looked to innocent non-Kenyans. Various government agencies pursued investigations of where the land would best be located. There were any number of promising discussions but things went forward at a snail's pace. And again and again, it all petered out. After many months of wrangling, the reason for their behavior dawned on me. According to an unwritten law in African countries, things only played themselves out when the key people could rake in a whopping bribe, otherwise, the thing would be waylaid forever. But this was not a path we could or would go. One of the first instructions Maharishi had given us, even before we traveled to the U.S. on our way here, was that out of principle we would never under any circumstances pay a bribe, even if it was business as usual in the country we were visiting.

So even after a year, there was still no progress in terms of a university despite all the demonstrable successes in the schools and the many presentations in the ministries of Kenya. Maharishi had let the secretary of state to the president know that he would recall his people for other important projects if things didn't move forward. That is what he finally did little by little.

One fine morning, my phone rang. To my surprise Felix, a Swiss man who laughed and was just about always in a good mood and who'd become one of Maharishi's closest co-workers during our absence, was at the other end, "Hello, Lothar, there's big news. All of us moved from the Marien Monastery at Boppard into a new building in Vlodrop in the Netherlands just across the border from Germany. The Movement bought that building, and Maharishi wants that all of you should come back right away to help build the Maharishi European Research University there and build the European administration center."

This information started a whirlwind of activities. We began—more or less happy—to "take down our tents."

When Charles Otieno, the national leader of our organization in Kenya, learned about this, he tried to keep at least me and my friend Andreas in the country for longer.

But Maharishi had other plans for us and knew precisely, and without being in touch with us per telephone, what was going on here. "The lives of my young men are too precious to waster there!"

And that was that. The Master once again put us through a massive flexibility training, in which, with his wise guidance, we were catapulted from one moment to another, from one situation to another.

In the space of just a few days, we booked our flight tickets, and now, in the middle of an icy cold January, we stood in Vlodrop in front of the massive dark-red brick, neo-gothic building complex with its pointed roofs over the corner towers. This former Franciscan monastery would now be our new home. Many Purusha groups had ended their "Global March" in other countries earlier; most of those were meanwhile already busy with another big project in the Philippines under Maharishi's guidance. Because our projects in Kenya had promised much, our team had spent a whole year there. It was great to meet these old friends with a big hello, to hug them, and hear about their experiences in all parts of the world!

Fascinated, I listened to Alain, a small, dark-haired Frenchman who, with his team, had created a magnificent prison project in Senegal quite a while back. "First we informed top politicians and initiated them into TM, and only then we taught the people within the penitentiary, first the director, then the personnel, and only then the prisoners."

Interesting—so this step-by-step procedure had proven

itself in other places as well.

"If anyone in these poor countries is released from prison, then, on average, he's back in four months because he can't survive staying on the straight and narrow."

After a year in Kenya, I could imagine this vividly!

In the last few years, Alain's team had initiated into TM a total of 11,000 prisoners, as well as 900 enforcement officers and prison directors in 31 of the 34 penitentiaries in Senegal. Infraction of rules had gone down drastically, medical expenses in the penitentiaries had been reduced by 70%, and best of all, recidivism was reduced dramatically as well! Earlier, 90% of the perpetrators released had come back to the prison all too soon, but after initiating them into TM it was only 8%.[43]

"The percentage of recidivism has gone down to such an extent that most penitentiaries in the country have already closed simply because they were standing empty for the lack of prisoners."

Too good to be true? Alain and his team had documented everything well. Back in Vlodrop, he had begun to put a whole book together with the impressive data, supplemented with photographs, as well as countless letters of recommendation and narratives by ministers, prison directors, guards, and inmates.[44]

At about the same time, with similar projects in the US, 3,000 inmates had learned TM, and there too had similarly noteworthy results.[45] These were by no means no longer small pilot studies; they were hard and repeatable realities. If only those responsible in all countries had the openness to implement all this!

It was magnificent to enjoy much-extended meditation

programs after such a long time and feel the coherence effect of such a big group in Vlodrop, this new, remote environment. The experiences of infinite silence without thoughts, with just expanded consciousness, once again became noticeably clearer and sustained. The gentle flow of energy during the whole day was a pleasure. All around, life was great. Despite this, something gnawed at me, first quietly, and then more and more clearly.

The financial means of the TM organization must have been somewhat exhausted through the purchase of this monastery complex with at least two hundred rooms, arranged in a square with two courtyards and surrounded by a huge park and a small, hidden lake. In any case, the circumstances allowed no other conclusion; we at first lived in almost unfurnished rooms. Each of us just had a mattress on the floor and a rickety clothes closet of laminated particleboard, as well as an old chair. In that time, the orange crates we'd snagged in the kitchen and stacked on top of one another and draped with sheets served as bookshelves. In addition, in those first weeks we lived two to a room, and on top of all that it was the heart of winter. It was cool inside of this monumental brick building but it was icy cold outside on our daily short walks. The building needed help in all nooks and crannies. We painted, we repaired, and we cleaned. After the warmth and the luxury and comforts in Kenya, I found things a bit difficult.

For years I had restricted my outer freedom to gain a greater inner freedom. But it wasn't easy to submit once again to the tight schedule I'd been used to before. It was clear to me that this was necessary to create the effects of such a big group on the collective consciousness. Even so, I longed for freedom now and again, for sun and for activities as well as the outer, satisfying successes that I'd enjoyed so much in Kenya. And again and again, the thought came up: I want out of here, out of this wonderful routine. I want a new project!

With about 200 participants of the Purusha Group in front of Maharishi Vedic University, a former Franciscan monastery, in Vlodrop, Netherlands, 1985 (1st row, 2nd from right)

Panchakarma and Ayurveda Conferences

Thank God, nature understood me. Had my desires attracted new circumstances? Or had I just noticed within me that something would change? One thing was sure: something completely new would come into my life.

Here in Vlodrop, in addition to our long meditation programs, we devoted ourselves intensively to Ayurveda once again. Whereas we had already been delving deeply into Ayurveda since 1982—studying its theoretical basis and ancient texts at a time when it was virtually unknown in the West—Maharishi now began to work on enlivening this ancient, comprehensive healing system for the whole world. And all of us, here in its center, were into it.

Behind the scenes, Maharishi had begun to gather Indian experts since the 70s to bring Ayurveda back to its original form and greatness. In 1984, a one-year course in Ayurveda for Western medical experts was offered in various parts of the world. Maharishi organized big conferences for hundreds of vaidyas, the traditional Indian Ayurvedic experts, and continued these activities here in Vlodrop, in our newly acquired old monastery.

He had us organize a symposium in the grand, one-thousand-square-meter church that formed the central axis of the two square buildings. Thirty or forty herbalists from all parts of the world met under his guidance. Dabbing colorful spots on the attentive participants, the sun's light shone through the colorful glass of the gothic windows framed with opulent carvings with which the Franciscan monks had decorated their church almost a hundred years ago. To this conference, each one of these herbalists had brought healing plants from their own countries, herbs that were now laid out on an incredibly long row of tables.

A leading expert in *Dravyaguna*, the Ayurvedic science of healing herbs, Dr. Balraj Maharishi, the representative of the government of the Indian state of Andra Pradesh, had also accepted Maharishi's invitation. He became a significant supporter and promoted holistic Ayurveda with an all-embracing commitment. He looked noble in his kurta (the traditional white silk shirt with a stand-up collar and decorated with fine embroidery) and his dhoti (white, wrapped trousers that reach beneath the knees) of Indian men. This man was surrounded by an aura of authority and dignity that I have rarely seen. His reputation preceded him: he was known to "talk" with plants and knew 6,000 of these healing herbs together with all their applications. Serenely, he went from table to table and told the amazed assembled experts what the stems, leaves, roots, seeds, and blossoms of plants from all parts of the world, plants he'd never seen, were good for and how best to use them—all based on the appearance of the plants and his mysterious communication with them. And he was correct every time. It is easily understandable how amazed and impressed the guests were. It was rumored that he was enlightened. In any case, he was a wise man with special abilities.

Opening new worlds for us, some of the vaidyas who had come gave highly interesting lectures to us Purushas about the healing effects and the practical uses of Ayurvedic therapies.

We learned that the body regularly accumulates *ama*—metabolic accretions or environmental poisons, which, absent any treatment, will clog the body as sticky, difficult to excrete waste material. Ama blocks micro-channels, hinders their functioning, and forms a significant basis for the development of various illnesses.

Some of us worked under the direction of Dr. Gogte, an older vaidya, who, together with his wife, led an Ayurvedic hospital in India. We were to establish the first small panchakarma clinic here in Vlodrop as a model for Europe. Dr. Gogte had treated his patients with classic Ayurvedic cleansing methods, known as *panchakarma* for his entire life. *Pancha* means "five." This refers to the five different big groups of cleansing therapies that Ayurveda uses in successive steps to dissolve metabolic waste deposits, flush them from the cells, and excrete them through the intestinal tract.

We prepared rooms for the panchakarma clinic and constructed big wooden treatment tables according to the Indian model. Over several weeks, the Indian physicians meticulously trained several Purushas as technicians, teaching them how to produce the complex medicinal oils exactly according to the instructions of the classical texts and then perform their various applications. In brief, a completely new wind of great industriousness blew through our free time outside of meditation. All Purushas could serve as Western lab rats—to our complete delight—and so, one by one, we experienced the first panchakarma cures in our lives. We consumed ghee, butter that had been clarified through prolonged simmering and freed of hard to digest proteins, and after several days went to an appointed day for cleansing, in which the toxins that had earlier been dissolved and released from the cells were now removed from the intestines. We enjoyed the wonderful oil massages, *abhyangas*, that were applied with light or strong massage strokes by two fully synchronized technicians. These massages, by the way, also synchronized the left and the right hemisphere of the brain. We indulged in deep relaxation with the slow flow of oil on the forehead, *shirodhara*, which deepened our meditations even more; we allowed the cells of our bodies to warm up in herbal steam baths, and after all these procedures, we felt free of waste products and super relaxed. Never, had I experienced such a gentle, pure, and beautiful feeling in all the cells of my body. Who could have guessed that Maharishi would have something like that up his sleeve for us?

Maharishi organized big conferences of Western and Indian physicians who compared the insights of Ayurveda with those of modern medicine under the high vaults of the monastery's church. Eastern and Western knowledge inspired each other in this way. To find common ground, a whole group of experts dedicated themselves to the task of studying the ancient texts in the original, to find common features. Further, Maharishi motivated Western doctors to systematically perform scientific research on the various forms of therapy. He wanted to show that these ancient therapies were not only highly effective, but also, and especially with chronic illnesses, that they were better by far than the therapeutic successes of conventional medicine, without the frequently harmful side effects of the chemically produced medicines currently in use.

Introducing Ayurveda to Europe

During this time, my task was to assist Reinhart in taking care of important guests. I welcomed Indian experts of Ayurveda at the airport, made sure that there was nothing they needed, and that they were comfortable staying with us. For ministers of health and high-ranking politicians from India and Sri Lanka, I organized tours in the surrounding area and gave them an overview of the world-wide movement Maharishi had built. Above all, I gave them an understanding Maharishi's main concern: to put Ayurveda back together in its wholeness, as the rishis of the advanced Vedic culture within themselves had cognized it to be but which over long periods of time had been fractured into isolated parts. Over many years, Maharishi succeeded in winning over high-ranking representatives not only of classical Ayurveda, but also of newer traditions—from families who had been the caretakers of healthcare procedures that had been carefully guarded over many generations. They were concerned that their valuable traditional knowledge might be lost in modern times. Now, with great esteem and gratitude for Maharishi, they passed on their share of knowledge to re-establish Ayurveda in its wholeness. This included various techniques for the development of consciousness, techniques that had always been an integral part of Ayurvedic therapies, but that had been neglected gradually in India during the last hundreds of years. So, I elucidated in wall charts on the Unified Field that showed several modern quantum physicists knew that all matter manifests from an all-encompassing pure consciousness. Since all matter originally comes from this field of consciousness, it follows logically that spiritual and physical disorders could be healed if they were rendered coherent once again at this level.

In this way, Maharishi brought Veda back into Ayurveda. He recreated the exceptional knowledge about herbal medicine, nutrition, daily routine, and methods of detoxification that had survived for thousands of years in East, transforming it into a truly holistic medicine based on pure consciousness. While studying the first written records of this orally transmitted holistic knowledge, we found references to consciousness in many places. Maharishi Charaka, who was the first to write down this ancient knowledge 2,500 years ago, again and again noted that the fundamental reason for disorders and illnesses is *Pragya aparadha*, the mistake of the intellect. Pragya aparadha always occurs when someone identifies so much with the external aspects of life as to be overshadowed by them to the extent that he or she is no longer aware of his or her own unboundedness. One forgets that one is part of the cosmic whole and is connected to everything at its basis. All Ayurvedic procedures ultimately serve to lead a person back to one's own inner nature and to help one to avoid errors intuitively and so—as it is described in the ancient tradition—pave the way to enlightenment.

In the spring of 1986, and as per Maharishi's wishes, a small group of Purushas, primarily scientists and physicians, drove to the yearly main conference of the WHO in Geneva. There, we contacted ministers, secretaries of state, and directors of health ministries from many countries of the world. We invited them to the presentations and banquets that we had organized, and in which we presented the advantages of Ayurveda as a holistic healthcare system.

Dr. Triguna had come from India as the leading expert of

Ayurvedic pulse diagnosis. He was an advisor to the Indian government, director of the National Academy of Ayurveda, as well as chairman for decades of the "All India Ayurvedic Congress," the Indian association of vaidyas and Ayurvedic physicians with a total of more than 350,000 members. The most important personalities as well the poorest of the poor consulted him. He was the personal physician of the Indian president, he treated the most eminent persons of the Indian subcontinent and, at the same time, ministered to more than four hundred poor patients at his clinic in Delhi—for free. He had immediately recognized the greatness of Maharishi's endeavors and came joyfully to do his part in the dissemination of this great healing system. He gave the representatives of the government, to whom we had spoken, a taste of his brilliant pulse diagnosis in a hotel suite rented especially for this purpose, where he made his diagnosis simply by placing three of his fingers on the wrist pulse —most of the "patients" were so impressed afterwards that they were more than open to other aspects of Ayurveda.

Dr. Triguna's presence touched me deeply. He radiated a humble authority and such dignified charisma that no one could doubt his competence. One of my assignments was to speak to the ministers of health of the most diverse countries, make them aware of our offers, coordinate appointments with Dr. Triguna for their consultations with him, and then accompany them. Through this, I was present at many sessions and was amazed again and again about the accuracy of his pulse diagnosis and the certainty of his recommendations. Many representatives of government were so fascinated by Dr. Triguna and our presentations that, in the coming years, they invited speakers from Maharishi European Research

University (MERU) to their countries at universities and at physicians' conferences. This, in turn, brought about the expeditious dissemination of Ayurveda all over the world.

In many cities of Europe, we organized press conferences in which we presented the greatness of this healing system that included all aspects of life. The journalists we'd invited could afterwards receive a personal pulse diagnosis from one of the vaidyas, which conjured up amazement in their facial expressions and impressed them deeply. Everywhere in Europe, there appeared countless positive articles which helped to make Ayurveda known on our continent.

Dr. Michael Jensen and Dr. George Janssen, Danish and Dutch physicians respectively, both members of Purusha for years, joined forces under Maharishi's personal guidance. In solidarity with expert vaidyas, they eagerly took on the mammoth task of developing courses for Western physicians and therapists. In doing so, they were in regular communications with our American doctors who on the other side of the Big Pond were dedicated to the same task.

Maharishi worked on it day and night. The course of instruction was systematized, and hundreds of charts and graphics, as well as abstracts of important Ayurvedic principles, were prepared for physicians. For this, Maharishi did not use the extant and accessible English translations, but, instead, translated the classical and original Ayurvedic texts anew, with the help of Sanskrit scholars. Frequently, he presented regular lectures about specific concepts and principles. He could evidently see—as did the rishis eons ago—the subtlest layers of creation and describe them in detail. He integrated and honored the knowledge from the family traditions of the vaidyas. In that way, he crystalized the original, deep meaning of the primary knowledge in the most minute detail and countless steps in collaboration with many experts.

The Ayurvedic faculty of MERU worked out twenty different therapeutic concepts of Ayurveda and included them in these courses. Ayurveda, as it was taught at MERU thereafter, included much that is no longer available in its wholeness in contemporary India, even in the years-long and exceptionally thorough Ayurvedic training at the universities there. Thus, we soon called it *Maharishi Ayurveda* so as to make known that we were offering a revived, holistic Ayurveda that once again corresponded to the original knowledge of the great seers, the maharishis of the Himalayas.

Now, all we had to do was to organize and implement these courses and make them known. In the team of the two doctors, George and Michael, I was once again in my element because everything had to be coordinated, and dozens of details had to be thought about and managed. About eighty physicians from all over Europe took the first four-week intensive course in Maharishi Ayurveda. At the same time, an equal number of technicians learned how to administer Ayurvedic treatments so that they could implement panchakarma therapies in their homelands. Several freshly trained doctors subsequently opened small and big Ayurvedic treatment centers in various European countries. From Vlodrop, we assisted them as necessary with advice in word and in deed.

During that year, I helped to organize a whole series of advanced courses. Again, and again I was overjoyed at the amazing response of our course participants who reported their impressive achievements in healing their patients.

And in this way, a wave of enthusiasm for Ayurveda spread in many Western countries for the first time.

Going AWOL

Like me, Andreas, with whom I'd worked so successfully with government contacts in Kenya, had got a whiff of freedom in far-away Africa. Because I was pleasantly busy with my Ayurveda assignments, the situation had come together for me in the most wonderful ways. But Andreas was increasingly feeling his oats during the long meditation programs behind monastery walls. He most definitely wanted to get some successful projects going again somewhere in the world, preferably together with me. He found open ears: I, too, wanted some outside activities. I would have loved to introduce TM and Maharishi Ayurveda to some government and to have seen to it that both were integrated into the healthcare system. But I did arrange for myself a short getaway!

At the airport in Amsterdam, I was supposed to get a couple of lithographs we'd been expecting urgently. Immediately, my inner eye saw the images of a splendid motorbike tour across the country. So, I planned to use this trip to go "AWOL" from Purusha—something I'd never done—to let a bit of fresh air blow into my face outside of monastery walls. I made arrangements to borrow a motorbike, a helmet, and some biking duds from Peter, one of our volunteer helpers. I packed all of it into a plastic bag and lowered the contraband carefully from my window into the courtyard. A little later, a blonde German Purusha, perfectly styled in suit and tie, could be seen stepping out of the main entrance, and, with an innocent expression on his face, saunter unseen around the corner to retrieve the bag in the garden, and then serenely exit through the main gate. The motorbike Peter was lending me stood in a garage just opposite. There, unseen, I changed clothes, put on the helmet with a tinted visor, started the rumbling machine, and then with an ever-so-slight grin, passed dozens of clueless Purusha friends who came toward me on their after-lunch walk. On the highway, the headwind blew into my face. In full measure, I enjoyed these two hours of high-speed adventure and the smooth rumble of the motorbike.

At the airport the lithographs however had not yet arrived. So, I would get them on the following morning. Conveniently, I could spend the night at the Amsterdam TM Center. In the evening, I parked my motorized co-conspirator in front of the entrance, hooked the chinstrap of the helmet into the mounting bracket on the side under the seat and locked the cylinder of the bolt. However, when I went out to get going in the morning, somebody had helped himself to the helmet: only the chinstrap of my helmet hung on the hook. I had to get a new helmet! I got on the bike and rode here and there through the narrow alleys of Amsterdam looking for a store—without wearing a helmet, of course. Suddenly, a police motorbike came towards me and, in the rearview mirror I saw that the cop was turning his bike and had already turned on his blue light. He was after me. And it was completely clear that he was going to get me because of my unprotected skull; I ignored him. He drove faster; I did too. I whizzed around tight corners and through narrow alleys; he was hot on my tail. I couldn't shake him. I was afraid of a whopping fine when finally, finally a desperately needed savior came into view. Breathless and shaking, I stopped in front of a motorbike store. I was about to vanish into it unseen when the cop stopped me and demanded a fine for illegally riding without a helmet.

"Look here, somebody stole my helmet, and I've just been driving around to buy a new one!" I held the evidence under his nose, the sad-looking, cut-off remnant of my chinstrap.

He looked at me very doubtfully. After that wild chase, he just didn't quite trust me.

"OK! But I'm waiting right here and I'll cancel the fine only if you immediately buy a helmet."

I saw the cop really keep his eye on me until I left the store with my new acquisition. Phew, that went well this time! I again went to the Amsterdam airport, and, this time, I was successful.

Late in the afternoon, I stepped through the massive and beautifully carved entrance portals of the monastery in Vlodrop, dressed again to the nines with a harmless-looking plastic bag under my arm, as I had transformed myself back into a well-behaved Purusha.

Brahmachari Nandkishore, Maharishi's closest co-worker during that time, traveled for weeks here and there all over Europe. He visited TM Centers and academies. At big assemblies, he gave talks about Maharishis most recent plans and endeavors, answered questions, and inspired meditators to new ventures. Due to time constraints in his extensive travels, he had left out four countries: Portugal, Turkey, Greece, and Cyprus. As soon as Andreas got wind of this, he smelled a big opportunity. It just wouldn't do to deprive these countries of this blessing. Straight as an arrow, he reached out to one of Maharishi's Indian secretaries and with all his power of persuasion, he proposed suggesting to Maharishi that both of us were ready to take on this assignment. As soon as Maharishi had said "yes" to this, we got everything ready to go. We went off to Greece. As soon as we'd begun with our tasks in

Athens, Reinhard caught us on the phone, "I just talked with Maharishi and mentioned you. He remembered that you're both Purushas. And he doesn't want you to travel around outside. You have to come back immediately."

For Andreas, whose best-laid plans had presented him with a new adventure in the freedom outside, this was a heavy blow.

"For me, that's totally out of the question. I'm staying here!"

I wasn't keen on leaving either. But I would have controlled myself and, following Maharishi's wishes, would have decamped and gone back. So, with Andreas taking the lead, we really got into it and laid it on thick with Reinhart with all we had: "Man, Reinhard, this won't work. We already have appointments in the president's palace in Cyprus. Can't we at least follow up on those?"

So, Reinhard once again turned to Maharishi, praised our proven abilities with government contacts in glowing terms and, finally, the liberating okay came. "Tell them they should stay there and build up a university for 7,000 students to create world peace. Cyprus is ideally situated close to the constantly smoldering Middle Eastern conflicts. From Cyprus, a permanent peace could spread to the whole Middle East."

Relieved and with much joy we finished up our appointments in Greece before we landed in the south of Cyprus, on the Greek half of this beautiful island in the Mediterranean Sea.

VIII.

Cyprus

Every individual has the infinite potential of creativity.
The genius of man is hidden in the silence
of his consciousness—
the silent condition of his mind
from which all thought springs.

Maharishi Mahesh Yogi

Nicosia

Full of positive expectation and eagerness for action, several excited and well-situated mediators were waiting for us at our arrival in Nicosia, the capital city of southern Cyprus. Secretary of State, Alexis Pavlidis*, and Antonis Papadimitriou*, the top lawyer in the country, both had the best connections and had also prepared a full schedule for us before we even got there. One presentation followed on the heels of another. We had appointments in the presidential palace in Nicosia, a gigantic, two-story sandstone-colored building with white, round arches. We met with the ministers of health and education. We spoke in college where our presentations were very well received and they would love to cooperate with us. Well-meaning friends organized numerous public lectures for us, as well as meetings with meditators. We were welcomed with open arms everywhere. Our presentations and lectures were received with enthusiasm. From these, new meetings and new activities developed. Andreas and I were in our element. We had great support of nature; many things fell into place as if by themselves and everyone wanted to have Maharishi's programs. It all went like clockwork. Here another one of Maharishi's insightful slogans verified itself, "If you favor natural law, natural law favors you!"

When we arrived, we were fortunate to have lodgings with George Hadgiorgio who'd been hosting group meditations regularly in his living room for several years. With typical Cypriot generosity and hospitality, he and his beautiful wife, Susie, invited Andreas and me into his tiny house in the countryside. There, the two of us shared the children's room, while their two sweet children slept with grandma in the house next door. And, oh, how I enjoyed the kids, the relaxed coziness, and Susie's delicious Greek cooking!

After a few weeks, we rented a spacious, 120 square-meter four-room apartment in the center of Nicosia. The meditators supported us with all they had. It was a wonderfully beautiful give and take, and so, a small TM Center came into being in a short time, including two cozy rooms for Andreas and me. George Hadgiorgio, who'd meanwhile become a close friend, used every free hour after his job at the American embassy to drive us around in his rattling, old red Mini. He basked happily in our success and the strong revival of the TM Movement on his island. Every week, we taught the basic TM course. People were pleasantly surprised at the relaxation and the positive changes that TM brought into their lives. In no time at all, word got around. We were invited everywhere, gave informative lectures, and new meditators brought their friends. In short, it was an active and lively center that expanded in many directions.

We also gave lectures about Maharishi Ayurveda. Soon, we asked one of the vaidyas in Vlodrop to come and give consultations to our friends on this sunny island. The meditators were visibly pleased about this additional new offer. Impressed with the recommendations of the vaidya, they sent their friends and relatives. More than a hundred consultations took place in our small TM Center.

Andreas and I organized the first TM-Sidhi course in the country. It was a pure pleasure for us to take care of the people who absorbed all that newness with such warmness and openness. Every weekend, about twenty course participants came and received sidhi techniques to deepen their experiences at home. After a few weeks, they got the most powerful sidhi, the flying technique. From now on, many of them came to the center regularly to practice this technique with us, which created brain-wave coherence like none other and so achieved an especially powerful coherence effect for themselves and for the "Island of Aphrodite."

A Sweet Secret

Alexis Pavlidid was Secretary of State in the Ministry of Finance. He and his wife had been meditating for years. He was also the head of a family-planning center and he had arranged a talk for us. About fifty people had come and, in the middle of the audience, I saw her! She was sitting in the fourth row with her dark, shoulder-length, curly hair. Her pleasant face revealed respect and interest. And in that same moment, I knew: "There'll be something with her!" But as quickly as this intuition had come, it was gone. After the presentation, she came up to us and said, "My name is Vivian*; I'm a siddha* and I live here in Nicosia. I saw your announcement in the papers and I'm curious about what you're doing here. Can I join your group meditations? And what else are you doing around here?"

So many questions; so many answers.

From then on, she came to the center often. She helped and supported us and came to our seminars. We talked and spent time together occasionally. Now and then on a Sunday, I took her with me for an outing in the mountains. As with the girl in Germany, soon I was burning with desire for her but I was also shy. On top of that, I was a Purusha—you could say a kind of modern-day monk—a situation that restrained me as well. Vivian lived only a few meters from the Center and, during the day, she pursued her profession. In the first weeks, her mother was visiting and living with her. After her mother left, our conversations became deeper and longer. Then came the first walks under the full moon and, very, very carefully my first full relationship took shape. After

303

a few weeks, the time had come. I stayed the night with her and, for the first time in my life, submerged myself in the great mystery of attraction and joy that men and women could give one another since time immemorial. As much as this new intimacy made me happy and fulfilled me, I also clearly wanted to keep it secret from the active meditators at the center and from Andreas. Presumably, however, they were on to it anyway. Sometimes their faces expressed an understood but never spoken assent. But they thoughtfully played along with this little game of hide-and-seek. In any case, I kept this tender flame of love to myself and Vivian respected this. When, one morning I was taking the short way back to the center at the crack of dawn to protect my sweet secret, I impulsively bought some fresh buns that were still steaming deliciously. And with that, I had coincidentally developed a functional tactic. From then on, Andreas could enjoy the luxury of fresh buns every morning, albeit with some astonishment at my getting up so early.

Here in Cyprus, which grew ever closer to my heart, I also indulged in my hobby during my free time. On a rented motorbike, I let the wind blow in my face, and, in the bright sunshine of the Mediterranean, I rode—sometimes with Vivian, sometimes without her—into the deep forests of the cool mountains, far away from the noise of the cities and into the untouched nature of the island.

The Little Monk

The Cypriots who learned Transcendental Meditation at our place felt exhilarated by the positive changes in their lives that came with the regular descent into the finer levels of thinking and the regular experience of deep silence. With Panos Panadakis,* this enthusiasm came in huge waves immediately after his initiation. "I just want to meditate and become enlightened and that's why I want to go to the Netherlands and join Purusha."

All well and good, but it just doesn't work that fast. Andreas and I talked to him: "The nervous system needs some time to get used to long meditation programs. You have to let it happen slowly! First off, a whole lot of stress and tension that's accumulated in the nervous system has to be released. If you meditate a lot and a for long periods too early on, then it's possible that you stir up too much stress. And then you won't feel so good or you'll react a bit too emotionally to your environment. Let it happen gradually! We can't give you a recommendation just yet. But we'd love to later, when the time is right!"

But that did not sit well with a spiritual hot-head like our Panos. He wanted it now and that meant immediately! Again and again, he assailed us. We consoled him every time. And so it went for many weeks. First, he burst in on us every day; later he came once a week. He was inspired, his bright eyes were sparkling, and he wanted more. We loved him but we also had to hold him back.

One fine day, he stopped coming. One, two, three weeks went by. Where was he? Well, he'd show up eventually since he was so enthusiastic.

A few days later, I was looking out of the big window of our lecture hall and down on the busy street. Cars honked and hustled by one another in the typical southern way—it was all as usual. And yet, something was strange. Directly in front of our entrance, there stood a few wildly gesticulating and somehow excited and overwrought Cypriots. A few moments later, our doorbell rang. And these same men crowded in, rough and unruly, "Where's our brother; where did you hide him?"

Heavens alive—it was Panos Pandadkis' two brothers and an uncle! The oldest brother pulled a dangerous-looking knife out of his pocket with a threatening gesture. "If you don't cough him up right now, there will be big trouble!"

Their aggressive looks and their loud and sharp voices were clearly threatening that I was afraid for my safety. When Andreas and I tried to make it clear to them that we hadn't seen him for weeks, they didn't believe a word of it. Even so, they eventually left with loud cursing.

For days, they took turns positioning themselves on the street, across from our entrance, threatening and suspicious figures who were extremely worried about the welfare of the youngest member of their family.

Meanwhile, Andreas and I transformed ourselves into private detectives. We inquired about Panos with all our meditators and told them to look for him; we called everybody to see if we could find him anywhere. Finally, and totally frazzled, we called Vlodrop to find out if maybe a young Greek had shown up there, wanting to join Purusha come hell or high water. No, we were dead wrong; he wasn't there. We asked to be notified immediately in case he'd show up, while we were pulling out all stops to find Panos Panadakis; the furious brothers were equally busy.

Police detectives showed up and interrogated us because the Panos family had set them on our tracks in case we'd sent the young man to the Netherlands. We saw bored detectives change shifts as they "staked out the joint" in front of our TM Center. A few days later, I saw a man on the sidewalk who focused on our center with a telescope. When I pulled back the curtains, he made it disappear behind a newspaper with oxymoronic showmanship to make it seem subtle. But Andreas and I felt so innocent that we took it all lightly and even joked about it.

Then a series of articles about the disappearance of Panos Panadakis appeared in various papers. And every one of them mentioned that he was last seen at our center. There were some unpleasant commentaries, stoked by the Greek Orthodox priests of Nicosia, who spread this rumor unperturbed, even in their church communities. But we had already gone through the fires of purgatory of slander and insults in Germany. Amused rather than exasperated, we discovered under the warm Mediterranean sun, that the clergy here weren't any warmer than they were back home. Panos, meanwhile, had a warrant out for him. His picture was prominently displayed all over Nicosia. But nothing helped. The search remained unsuccessful all around. Our golden boy seemed to have been swallowed by the ground. After some weeks, the scene calmed down and our center once again blossomed and thrived undisturbed.

After six months, the mystery was finally solved. Panos called his family on the phone. We were relieved but we were also rolling on the floor with laughter when we got the news. He had fled up high into the mountains and entered into a reclusive Greek Orthodox monastery! What a grotesque joke! He'd been living there this whole time as a monk, praying and having found the kind of inward journey that he'd been searching for so passionately. Even in our dreams, we couldn't have guessed this!

We were relieved and yet also somewhat irritated. No apology for their behavior toward us came from the brothers or uncle, no sign of contrition from the priests about the false accusations, and—this seemed most familiar—not a single retraction from any of the papers!

A Miraculous Healing

Andreas and I were extremely busy and successful. Leading politicians learned TM at our center, as well as several ambassadors, the owners of big businesses, and a few executives at big institutions, as well as special representatives of the General Secretary of the UN. It appeared the General Secretary's main task was to negotiate between northern Turkish Cypriots and southern Greek Cypriots, who had been enemies of each other for many decades. He didn't just learn to meditate himself, but because he considered what we were doing for the country really great, we were invited to numerous dinners and banquets. Subsequently, important personalities of the country brought others with them, and all of them heard with great interest about the possibilities this age-old Vedic technique could make available to them.

We organized a presentation about Maharishi Ayurveda and Transcendental Meditation for the Minister of Health, all the department heads of the Ministry of Health, as well as all the executive directors of all the hospitals. When we had everyone's commitment, we got a fellow Purusha, Dr. George Janssen—the Dutch physician who'd played a key role in the development of Maharishi Ayurveda—to come from Vlodrop to our presentation. Afterwards, the directors and executives were so keenly interested in Maharishi Ayurveda and TM that they wanted to integrate both into the entire health-care system of southern Cyprus. They asked us to write down the concrete steps though which the programs we offered could best be implemented.

The previous Minister of Education, a highly-educated man, had the task during this time, as the advisor to the

President and of Parliament, to build the first university in Cyprus. He was especially captivated by the idea of creating an educational system that included the development of the potential of consciousness. The studies already extant and the successes of Maharishi International University in the US were essential for him. The Minister was effusive. "I have offers from other partners. But this university will be built in partnership with you. I'll advise and help you in its development step by step!"

Andreas and I had already been on the island for ten months and were busy with the further development of the offers of cooperation from the Ministries of Health and of Education. Then came an unexpected invitation from Maharishi himself. He invited all of us Purushas, as well as other guests from all parts of the world, to be with him for four weeks in India for the *Guru Purnima* festivities—a celebration in honor of the spiritual masters, the gurus, on the first full moon of July.

So, we hugged and kissed our new friends good-bye, and temporarily gave our blossoming center into the care of George Hadiorgio, who wanted to become a TM teacher and then we once again we were off on an airplane.

In Noida, a southeast suburb of New Delhi, Maharishi was in process of having a huge facility built in a park; it included many incredibly long buildings, up to three floors high and beautifully decorated with Indo-Islamic round arches. The work on these buildings was still a long way from being completed. And the number of finished rooms was clearly smaller than the number of the Purushas who'd been invited. I moved into a room with two others. The still-fresh cement floor was dusty.

Later, when I looked into the main kitchen, I saw a horde of flies feasting on the food. I lost my appetite to the extent that I ate almost nothing on these premises. As a result, I took one of those constantly honking tuk-tuks, the bright yellow, three-wheeled taxis open on the sides, to the Ashoka Hotel in Delhi every third day to fill up my hungry stomach with a more cultivated meal. For more than that, I had neither the time nor the money.

In contrast to the unpleasant physical arrangements, the nightly talks and lectures with Maharishi were like heavenly dreams for me. He sat in a round garden pavilion in the middle of a big lawn. In front of him sat more than 1,500 people in tight rows of chairs, people who were enjoying the balmy Indian summer nights, and especially Maharishi's presence, under the moonlight. Besides us Purushas, there were about two hundred physicians from all over the world who were here for a five-week advanced training in ayurvedic pulse diagnosis. There were also hundreds of other participants who were either taking the course in pulse diagnosis or a weeklong introductory course in *jyotish*, or Vedic astrology. At night, all of them drove to various hotels in Delhi. Every morning, they came back on busses, attended their lectures and together practiced the TM-Sidhi program in two big halls.

On several occasions, Swami Vishnudevananda Saraswati, the then-reigning Shankaracharya of Jyotir Math[9] came also. He sat next to Maharishi in the garden pavilion and conversed with Maharishi before our very eyes and ears. Here, I experienced Maharishi in his homeland for the first time in conversation with this other spiritually great man

---

[9] A Shankaracharya is the equivalent of the Pope in our culture; he is, however, chosen according to his state of consciousness.

of the Indian sub-continent. The respect and the deference they conferred on each other impressed me deeply. The Shankaracharya radiated extraordinary peace and dignity. But I, personally, felt that the spiritual power and clarity of Maharishi was much greater.

My starved body became increasingly troublesome. Despite the hearty meals I ate, though with much time in between, I became weaker and weaker. My immune system hit rock bottom, and I caught a bad middle-ear infection. Days later, when I had to bury the idea that this continuously pounding pain in my ear would go away on its own, I once again drove to Delhi—this time to find a doctor. The doctor's office in a windowless room in a backstreet alley did not exactly inspire trust. Everything was extremely primitive and, for our spoiled European standards, also downright filthy. But I didn't have a choice. The Indian ear doctor wasted no time. Skillfully, he drew some liquid into a syringe to put into my tortured ear. "Don't worry! This is a very effective remedy. It'll pull out all the puss and it only has to remain in your ear for a few minutes—that's how strong it is!"

Obediently, I laid my head in a 90-degree angle on the side of the examination chair. Comfortable it was not. As soon as that stuff landed in my right ear, it stung hard and made a sound like that of bursting bubbles in my head. And then the electricity went off! The light went out, and with it, the obsequious doctor vanished also. I heard only the click of the door. The ventilations system had gone out as well, and the room, already stuffy, got hotter and hotter. I sat alone in the pitch-black room and felt as if acid were eating away my ear. But there was nothing I could do; I sat tight on that chair with my head to the side and that stuff in my ear. It felt cruelly horrible. The pain in my ear became almost unbearable, and, after an agonizing, slow-moving thirty minutes, the electricity came back, and with it, the doctor. Quickly he removed the liquid from my infected ear, and I crept away only half conscious.

After this "healing" I became terribly sick. I got a high fever and was soon completely debilitated with hunger and disease, lying on my cot in Noida more dead than alive. I just wanted to go back to my beloved Cyprus and as fast as possible. I was planning to book my return trip on the very next day.

But, just as I was ready to leave for Delhi, Dr. Geoffrey Clements came towards me. He was an English physicist who played an important role in Maharishi's team of scientists and was responsible for Maharishi's Movement in all of Europe. "Maharishi asked me to tell you and Andreas that you should stay here. He wants to speak to both of you personally and to George Janssen before you fly back to Cyprus."

What a great honor! But for me, in my condition, it was also a gigantic effort to stay here longer. My tortured body just wanted to rest. But my soul, that so loved and venerated Maharishi, was overjoyed with this precious opportunity. Unfortunately, Andreas had already left two day earlier.

So, with Dr. Jannsen, I slowly dragged myself to Maharishi's little house after the evening lecture at 11:00 p.m. We waited on the ground floor for our appointment. Time crawled. A whole slew of people were ahead of us. And I was weak, unspeakably weak. Around 2:00 a.m., Maharishi's Indian secretary finally came downstairs and asked everyone who'd not had their turn to come back the following evening. That process repeated itself for the following two nights. I became weaker and weaker. Late in the evening I crept to Maharishi's house, but could no longer sit, and, instead, just lay stretched out flat on the ground.

I just couldn't anymore. On the third day and with my last strength, I went to Delhi on a tuk-tuk because I personally had to get the ticket for the trip back at the airline office. When the usual evening wait started, I informed the secretary about my desolate state of health and said, "Regardless of what happens tonight, tomorrow morning early I'm flying to Cyprus."

We waited patiently—I once again prostrate on the ground. For days, I'd not really eaten. The infection raged in my body, and I was so sick that I could not even meditate properly. If I did it anyway, I kind of hung out on the surface of my spirit without a trace of more subtle levels of consciousness and certainly no experience of clear transcending. But Maharishi had taught us that it would make sense to meditate even if we were sick, since this increased amount of rest would activate our natural ability to heal ourselves.

Towards three in the morning, the secretary came again and repeated his little speech: "So, everyone should just go and get some rest. Come back tomorrow." Then he turned towards George Janssen and me, "But you two can come upstairs now."

I dragged myself up the stairs and directly into Maharishi's suite. Here it was pleasantly cool. The whole room was perfumed from the fresh jasmine of the flower garlands that lay on the table. Maharishi was not there. Even so, his presence filled the room with a gentle sweetness and silence and a crystal-clear wakefulness that penetrated the deepest layers of my cells. George and I sat down on a couple of empty arm chairs in the first row, directly in front of Maharishi's sofa that was covered with a cloth of white silk.

We began to meditate. And here, in his aura, separated from him only by a door, my consciousness was suddenly once again completely clear despite my illness. I had a heavenly and bliss-filled meditation. In the space of twenty minutes, my body felt light and healthy. The fever and the dejection due to the illness, as well as the raging pain in my ear, were miraculously gone and never came back!

Yogic Flying for an Audience

Suddenly, the door opened. Nandkishore came into the room and, at the same time the intercom on the little table came on. It crackled a little, and then we heard Maharishi's gentle voice, "Jai Guru Dev." As always, Maharishi had begun by giving respect to his guru. "What's new in Cyprus?"

He listened to us attentively as George reported, "Maharishi, the Minister of Health has asked Andreas and Lothar to work out a detailed draft of a resolution to integrate Ayurveda and the TM programs into the healthcare system nationwide. Do you want to hear it?"

He read Maharishi the draft the two of us had put together and Maharishi found it to be very good. Then I continued, "Maharishi, the former Minister of Education wants to support us in building a university. However, he wants us to proceed cautiously because he'd heard that our activities in Cyprus have caught the attention of the archbishop. The church is concerned that so many people and so many well-known personalities are involved in this and wants to prevent its proliferation. So as not to endanger the success of building this university, the former Minister first wants the contracts to be signed, sealed, and delivered before going public."

At the other end, there was a little pause before we once again heard Maharishi's voice, "That man is very wise! Follow his advice."

But he wasn't yet done. When we were already thinking that the conversation was over, Maharishi added one more sentence, "Lothar, when you get back to Cyprus, immediately organize big public demonstrations of yogic flying in the five biggest cities and invite the press! It would be best if you call your friends in Cyprus right away so they can start with the preparations."

Nandkishore spoke up, "It's not possible to get through to Cyprus. We've tried it many times in the past. The connections are so bad that you can't get through."

Maharishi was unfazed. "Yes, but Lothar just has to try it once and he'll get through!"

Brahmachari Nandkishore handed me a telephone. I dialed the long number—and was immediately connected to George Hadgiorgio on the other end. He was completely beside himself that I was talking to him while Maharishi was in the background. Maharishi only had to focus his attention on it and even the phone connection to Cyprus worked like a charm!

Once back in Cyprus, Andreas and I tackled this new challenge with enthusiasm. Quickly, we'd prepared flying demonstrations in Nicosia, Limassol, and Paphos, as well as two other cities. Longish articles appeared in six daily papers that called attention to this first-time ever event: two young men claim that they can lift into the air with the power of their consciousness and that with this method they can achieve world peace.

People came in droves to the first demonstration in the large ballroom of the Hilton in Nicosia. Ever more people showed up. The hotel manager finally had to open the folding doors to the next hall. And even after that one had filled up, bunches of people stood in front of the jam-packed hall to catch a glimpse through the open door. Our friend, Alexis Pavlidis, the Secretary of State, was also present. Suddenly he recognized a few men from the secret police. What was up with that? Slightly disconcerted, he spoke with them and found out, "The archbishop insists that these two tourists be expelled from the country. Their tourist visas do not entitle them to stage such public events."

Aha, so the archbishop was getting to be a bit queasy. And his excuse to get rid of us was presumably not so easily dismissed. To protect Andreas and me, Alexis implored us, "You should immediately cancel this performance so you don't get into hot water. I can't do anything else for you!" Andreas might well have acquiesced, but with me, the guy was knocking on the wrong door. We can't snub 400 guests and cancel everything! In the front rows, there are people from the UN that we've invited and other important people including the entire media. No way; we're gonna pull this thing off come whatever!" Moreover, Maharishi had personally suggested this flying demonstration. Just for that reason alone there was no stopping it for me. Alexis spoke for us with the secret police. "You don't have to worry. I know these people well. They'll do nothing wrong here; I'll stand by them!"

They nodded. But they stayed.

The eyes of the curious, excited onlookers were all focused toward the front. Andreas and I, standing—and as always wearing suits and ties—held a brief presentation about TM and the advanced techniques, the TM-Sidhis. We projected slides onto the wall, slides that showed brainwaves during yogic flying. We explained to our audience that it wasn't about flying *per se*, not about what they'd be seeing in a few minutes from the outside, but, instead it was about the enormous coherence that is always produced within. To illustrate, we showed an impressive slide of an encephalogram. Even a lay person could recognize at first sight how, during the practice of TM, the brainwaves begin to move in unity with one another—physicians called it brain-wave coherence.

On the same slide, they could also see that—as soon as practice of the flying sidhi began—this coherence immediately intensified and spread to all areas of the brain and the entire frequency range of the brainwaves.[46] This unique brainwave pattern evinces the integration of all functions of the cerebral cortex and resulted, when practiced regularly, in a coherent functioning of the various sense perceptions as well as the most diverse activities in daily life.

To our audience, all this was completely new. To demonstrate to them that brain functions made coherent in this way really did contribute to world peace, we described the results of the two relevant scientific research studies that were already extant. One of them, the Taste of Utopia Assembly of 1983 in the U.S.A., resulted in an attenuation of crises world-wide; the other study, a comparable world-peace conference a year later in The Hague, the capital city of the Netherlands, had already been well-documented also.[47]

In addition, we explained to our listeners that the practice of the flying sidhi technique, passed down through the ages, can make the body completely weightless, but in these modern times, only a preliminary state is possible. The body lifts into the air, but also falls back down quickly. After this introductory talk, we quickly changed into some casual yoga pants behind the stage. And then we both sat cross-legged on the foam mattresses our Cypriot friends had prepared for us.

For just a few minutes we closed out eyes to practice TM. We could feel the concentrated attention of all the people in the room. The media were focused on us, as were many cameras in the audience. It was so quiet in the room that you could hear a pin drop. Then we began with Patanjali's spiritual technique for yogic flying, and—hop, hop, hop... the audience saw us in the air briefly and fall back onto the mat with a dull thud before the next hop lifted us into the air again. I had one of the strongest flying experiences of my entire life. That whole time, I saw a blinding white light in front of my closed eyes. An immense energy shot through my body that was lifting me into the air again and again. It was pure bliss. I felt Maharishi's blessing in this event that he'd initiated and I was just vibrating consciousness that was at the same time calm and alive. I felt at one with everything. Everything was within me, the room, the audience, the secret service agents, the whole universe. What a heavenly state!! I hopped in gigantic leaps, a seeming lump of flesh and blood that was in reality pure, unbounded energy.

Next morning, on the front page of several newspapers, there appeared extremely positive reports with pictures. Our message was correctly understood and spread by the media! How great was that! Nevertheless, Alexis advised us not to offer any further demonstrations. But I could not be stopped. The conference halls in a five-star hotel in Limassol and in Paphos had already been booked. And the advertising was in process.

That night in Limassol, in the first row, there sat two instantly recognizable policemen—holding handcuffs. I didn't take it seriously; that's how uplifted I felt about everything. In the last minutes of our presentation, the audience asked many questions indicating interest, and we answered calmly. When the room had emptied, the policemen came toward us. "Can you give us some identifications? What kind of visa are you on? You must know that you are not allowed to hold any public events! We have orders to deport you!"

Cyprus • *Cyprus Mail*

Nicosia 10 September 1986 (English)

Meditating on the prospects for world peace

THE Maharishi Mahesh Yogi's Programme to create World Peace has been put together to try to eliminate the basis of terrorism and war wihtout loss of life.

The Maharishi's programme was inaugurated for the whole world on July 21 this year in New Delhi, India. The inauguration included a demonstration of 'Yogic Flying', the mechanics to create coherence (a much-used word here) in world consciousness, the basis of world peace. But in answer to my question to Lothar Pirc and Ted Pizenis, who themselves gave a demonstration of this 'flying' technique at the Apollonia Hotel in Limassol on Friday evening, as to whether anyone had got past the first stage of 'Yogic Flying'

to the second stage of actual levitation and staying there, or to the third and final stage of 'flying', the answer was no....

Theoretically, a yogic flyer has very orderly brain waves and fluid co-ordination between mind and body. Consciousness and matter become completely integrated and all this 'coherence' can, it seems, spread peace around the world if enough meditators gather together at the same place and time. This was told to newsmen at the New Delhi demonstration by Dr. John S. Hagelin, a noted U.S. scientist.

The phenomenon produced by the TM-Sidhi procedure of 'flying' gives the experience of bliss and generates coherence between consciousness and matter in the body. EEG studies have shown

that during this phenomenon, when the body lifts up in the air, matter and consciousness are completely integrated. This integration takes place at the level of the unified field of natural law, which has the character of infinite correlation. The impulse of coherence from this level instantly reconstructs the discordant tendencies in nature to become coherent.

Coherence in world consciousness can be produced only by creating coherence in individual brain physiology. This is achieved through the Maharishi Technology of the Unified Field (Transcendental Meditation, its advanced techniques and the TM-Sidhi programme.

Scientific research has apparently shown that 7,000 individuals (the square root of one per cent of the world's population) practicing the Maharishi Technology of the Unified Field together in one place create a powerful influence of coherence in the whole world consciousness, producing an upsurge of positive trends and tendencies in life everywhere.

Lothar Pirc is a lecturer in this technology, and Ted Pizanis BSCI, MBA is the Cyprus Representative of International Programmes, and after completing their course of demonstrations at the Golden Bay Hotel in Larnaca yesterday and at the Hilton Hotel, Nicosia tonight, they hope to have aroused enough interest to start courses in TM here in Cyprus.

■ Yogic flying by Lothar Pirc at the Apollonia

Helen Stylianou

One of seven newspaper articles from Cyprus, which in 1986 reported on our public events and our offer to create peace in the Mediterranean with the help of Vedic Technologies of Consciousness. In the same period, several thousand newspaper articles about the Maharishi Effect appeared in all parts of the world.

Fortunately for us, another friend, George Psychis, helped us out of the pickle this time. He'd organized the flying demonstration and was ready to drive us home. He'd worked for the police a while back and was still friends with both these officers. Peacefully, the five of us went to drink beer and lemonade. George talked at them in Greek about how much TM had helped him in his life—and with that, this prickly situation was finished.

I should have let it be. But I felt so inspired by Maharishi and Vedic knowledge that I just wanted to keep going! Ahead of the demonstration in Paphos, I called the chief of police whom I'd initiated into TM and who'd lowered his blood pressure because of it. "Can you do anything so we can go ahead with this demonstration without getting in trouble?"

"I'd love to help you because this is really a good thing, but my hands are tied!"

And so, the whole rigmarole was repeated in Paphos. At the end of the demonstration, two new policemen showed up, and to save us, I couldn't think of anything better than to assert with finality, "Your superior is informed about what we're doing here. It would be better for you if you let us be, otherwise, you could be in trouble later!" And I'd acted with such confidence that they retreated somewhat unsettled.

But now I understood that it was irrevocably over. We let the subsequent presentations go.

There was strong resistance anyway. Roused by our confident assertions about the coming Age of Enlightenment and our unbelievable claim that human beings could overcome gravity through the power of consciousness, the Greek Orthodox priests wanted to get rid of us once and for all. One of the most powerful ministers of the Cypriot government, who was known as being under the archbishop's sway behind closed doors, used all his contacts to get us expelled from the country. On the other side, Alexis tried in his function as Secretary of State to protect us. Caught in the conflict of which one of the powers to agree with in this tug of war, the people in charge of the immigration service called both camps to the negotiation table.

We came to a gentleman's agreement. We could remain in the country but could no longer do any public TM activities.

We did think we were okay from then on. But as soon as we left our meditation center in the following weeks, one or two men were tailing us. Andreas and I, in our youthful light-heartedness didn't take it seriously, and we even joked about it, "Hey, Lothar, do you see that dude that's so obviously inconspicuous behind his newspaper watching us?" Or, "Look behind you carefully, there another one sneaking after us, oh so discretely!"

Grinning broadly, we took the partly clumsy efforts of the secret police to shadow us with humor. But it was clear that if we could no longer be active here; the Cyprian interlude was coming to an end.

Everything had started out so promising. But then Maharishi started his test phase with the flying demonstrations he had initiated. This pattern was not unfamiliar to us. Again and again, at the apparent culmination or shortly before some breakthrough, he made his students organize something impossible which then brought the initial project that they had built carefully and with great effort to come crashing to the ground. As one might expect, this challenged our trust in the Master considerably.

We looked for a reason in this behavior, which was so

frustrating for us. Eventually, we thought we'd found it. Presumably, he was testing whether the collective consciousness of the people in any country was developed enough to be able to integrate this new knowledge without opposition. If this were not the case, then, in the end nothing would have come of the project anyway. And his co-workers would have wasted a lot of time and would have suffered from the resulting counteractions.

At the same time, he trained his closest disciples not to be attached to external successes, but instead—as it is written in ancient texts as one of the signs of enlightenment—be able to unite incompatible opposites without being upset by them.

Andreas did not want to go back to Purusha. He remained in Cyprus as a tourist and, together with a Greek TM teacher, led the center unobtrusively. But that was out of the question for me. So, I said good-bye with a heavy heart to my Cypriot friends that had become so dear to me. All of us had tears in our eyes at the farewell. This community had grown together so affectionately in the last months that separation was difficult. And what was even much worse: I said good-bye to my beloved Vivian—and we both felt that it was final: I knew that this relationship had no future because other assignments were waiting for me. We held each other in our arms and assured each other of our love and we both cried at the parting. As difficult as it was, my decision was firm: back to Vlodrop, I'd be a Purusha once again.

IX.

Monastery Life Once More

The deepest insights
are gained only through the highest
concentration of spirit.
Words do not reach down to this final depth,
only intuitive enlightenment will
bring about understanding.

Confucius

551-479 BCE

Chinese Master and Philosopher

Caught

"Hey, bro, you should really get your horoscope done!"

As soon as I'd arrived in Vlodrop, Norbert, grinning, slapped me on the shoulder. "Maharishi has dug up something new again. For months, we've been studying planets, houses, and the significance of constellations. We're learning the foundations of jyotish—Vedic astrology!"

Well, he'd come to the wrong address with that one: "Forget it, dude! I don't want to know anything about it, it's all hocus-pocus anyway." Ayurveda—great, but this really went too far for me!

Norbert wouldn't let it go. "Dude, don't be so stubborn! You should at least try it! I'm gonna go to our jyotish teacher; he'll do your horoscope. Then you'll see that there's something to it."

His enthusiasm was over the top, and so, a few days later, I sat in front of Herbert, one of our Purushas, a lawyer by trade; he'd been studying astrology for twenty years. With his gentle blue eyes, he looked at the printout full of numbers and graphics that he'd put together with his computer program according to the information I gave him about my place of birth and time; I didn't understand any of it.

Calmly, but firmly, he then began to report my character traits, my childhood, my nature, and special events.

"When you were ten, you had abdominal surgery. Did they maybe take out your appendix?"

How could this be? He was dead right!

"And here, when you were exactly twelve years old, they took out your tonsils…"

I was stunned; that too was right!

"And when you were six, you had a serious head injury—maybe an accident?"

Well I had him there; he was wrong. "No, I didn't have any such thing!"

"Well, maybe you should ask your parents. That had to be the case; I can read it clearly!"

Well, maybe it would all crash with that one thing! But he had one more surprise ready for me. "Well, Lothar, when you were in Cyprus you had a relationship with a woman!"

Taken by surprise, I turned blood red and stuttered, "Well, but it was purely platonic!"

"Naw, uh-uh, let it go, Lothar, you can't pull one over on me. Your Mars and your Venus activated each other, and so there had to be more. There was nothing you could do about it."

Oh, my God, he'd caught me.

A little later, I asked my father. And indeed, as soon as he said it, I recalled that indeed I knew that a bicycle had run me over when I was six, and I'd sustained a bad head injury! And that's why, all through my childhood and youth, I had such serious headaches that only went away after I began meditating. I knew that and had just forgotten it during the jyotish session.

Through this new confirmation, I was won over. Just like other Purushas, I was bowled over with jyotish fever. I crammed and studied the characteristics of the planets, the twelve signs of the zodiac, as well as the twelve houses that delineated certain spheres of life.

Herbert also had some amazing background information for us: "During the time of the full flowering of Indian culture, enlightened Vedic mathematicians had already determined the orbits of the planets of our solar system with high-level precision. They even built big, ingenious observatories with which they could observe the course of the heavenly bodies up to and including Saturn with great precision and could calculate them over thousands of years. And not only that, at the same time they knew the influences of the planets to the smallest detail. Everyone knows that the moon creates high and low tides, that it can cause mood swings and sleep disturbances. In that same way, the big planets of our solar system influence life on earth incessantly and in very subtle ways. But most people don't notice, as the planets run through their orbits so slowly that their influence is elucidated only through exact, systematic observation—or through inner knowledge. At the same time, the heavenly bodies reflect the life situations of every single human being perfectly. That is why their positions give information about the course of events." And he closed: "The cosmic connections are so fine and are interwoven with one another with such intelligence, that you can always read the whole in any part."

I was most astonished to hear that western astrology does not use the actual position of the heavenly bodies. Instead, it uses an image of the constellations as they looked in the sky in the year 500 years BCE. In contrast, Vedic astrology refers to the real astronomical sequence of the constellations against the fixed stars that the sun—as seen from the earth—traverses in a year. That is why, meanwhile, the zodiac signs, which indicate the position of the sun at the time of birth, as well as the ascendant signs—which, at the moment of birth, are rising on the eastern horizon—are completely different from the ones indicated in Western horoscopes for more than two thirds of the population.

We learned yet another big difference between the

eastern and western approach: contrary to the astrology of the western world, jyotish counts the constellations along the moon's orbit to be of equal importance as those along the sun's orbit. *Nakshatra*—the position of the moon at the time of birth in one of the 27 constellations as the moon traverses its approximately 27-day movement around the Earth— plays a very big role. First, it provides information about the life task and the character of a person. Secondly, the *Dasha* system, or time periods characteristic of Vedic astrology, is based on the moon's orbit, which is responsible for the enormous exactness of jyotish predictions. Depending on the position of the moon at the time of birth, a sequence of changing phases follows. And from these, one can read accurately the personal themes of a person's life, as well as events and learning processes.

We learned the foundations of jyotish: the characteristics of the planets, as well as the nature of their influence on various aspects of life, the connection to the Ayurvedic understanding of illnesses and personality types, and so much more. The methodology and the logic, as well as the mathematical calculations and their interpretation, mesmerized us more and more. In short, a new world opened for us once again. Through it, we recognized that the big tendencies in the life of every individual are not merely coincidental, as it may appear when seen superficially. Suddenly, I could also accept the peculiarities of my fellow human beings much better because I understood on a significantly deeper level than before that family members, friends, as well as all other people who crossed my path, had to be exactly as they were.

It was fascinating to study in detail and interpret the *Janma Kundali*, the graphic representation of the personalities, of other Purushas as well as my own. We studied it almost night and day in our time outside of meditation, sometimes studying seriously, other times joking around about the peculiarities of others. Almost without noticing, we quickly and thoroughly deepened our basic understanding of jyotish in this way.

Maharishi also gave lectures for us on this subject and expanded our newly acquired but still somewhat shallow knowledge into spiritual dimensions. "Jyotish translates to light, inner light, but also the light of knowledge. When the jyotishi deals with the subtle relationships between the individual and the cosmos and, at the same time, has access to the realm of the unbounded, the transcendent; then an inner vision develops in him spontaneously. He then does not just read the constellations and the meaning of the big stars from *kundali*, he also delves so deeply into each person—while resting within his own inner silence—that within him an inner knowledge of their life opens. This is the state which is called the inner light. With this, the study and the application of jyotish is also a means to develop more subtle capabilities and enable enlightenment."

Indeed, these were the deepest connections that were of such burning interest to all of us!

And he addressed another highly fascinating point: "These influences from the cosmos bring back karma, the mirror images of our own actions from the past; positive or negative karma, according to the position of the planets. Nevertheless, everyone has free will because, within the framework of his possibilities, he can always decide how he will deal with events and challenges that come towards him—and if, through his reaction to them, he accumulates new positive or new negative karma. Each person progresses to an ever-higher development of his consciousness. In this, the experience of unbounded inner silence plays a big role because it is the most positive, harmonizing experience that a person can have. It balances not only the meditator but also the entire cosmos. That is why the practice of regular transcending creates a lot of positive karma. Moreover, a meditator lives more and more in accordance with all the laws of nature, and it is easy for him to accumulate new, positive karma spontaneously."

These insights suddenly gave our enthusiasm for jyotish a wider and totally new dimension. And the queasy feeling that human beings could possibly only be the rather helpless play toys of the stars and that they didn't really have free will evaporated. With his words, our hearts opened. What could be more exciting than to see shallow knowledge suddenly expand into this more encompassing dimension that our Master shared so generously with us on the basis of his un-fathomable inner knowledge?

Despite all these exciting new things, I did suffer badly in the first weeks and months due to the separation from Vivian that I'd imposed on myself. I thought about her often and I longed for her passionately. Even so, I did not waver in my decision. Still, I felt so close to her and my friends in Cyprus that I wanted to do something good for them. George Hadgiorgio and Vivian both had the intense desire to become TM teachers. And I wanted to help them pave the way to it. The European price for TM teacher training was impossible for them. So, I found out that in the surrounding countries of the Middle East there were a few other meditators who wanted to become TM teachers. I made calls, organized, negotiated, and got so into this task I'd given myself that, at one point, Reinhard got perturbed enough to ask, "Tell me, why are you into this so much?"

Smiling like a fox, I didn't let him see my cards. But I didn't rest until, finally, a small teacher training course for the aspiring teachers from those countries took place in Seelisberg—for a far lower price than graduates from richer countries had to pay.

Like a reward for this, my luck did not desert me back then. Reinhard and George Janssen helped me on their own to secure one of the rare spots for my second panchakarma cure. It didn't just clean out my body, but it also brought my troubled soul a good bit more balance. The longer meditation program did the rest and, gradually, time healed my wounds and I once again felt centered.

Wrong Exit

I realized my love for Vivian, though slowly fading, had opened a door within me that could not be closed. I began to yearn for a partner and wanted ever more clearly to be married and have my own children.

One of my richly diverse tasks in Vlodrop was to take care of guests. One day, I had to go to The Hague because Vishnu Anand Gaur, the first Indian astrologer who Maharishi had invited to the Netherlands to make jyotish known to the Western world, wanted a visa to the U.S. Within an instant, the large, seventy-year-old man in white robes conquered my heart with his resounding laugh. And I would not let the one-time opportunity of this trip go to waste. I could trust him because he was an authority with decades of experience. I carried the print-out of my horoscope in my pocket in hopeful preparation. We conversed freely through his interpreter. On the way back, I gathered all my courage and asked him carefully if he could look at my horoscope and if I could ask a few questions about it. He nodded. I gave him the paper and he bowed his head over the triangles, parallelograms, and numbers of my print-out. As soon as he'd glanced at it, his whole body vibrated with joy on the passenger seat. He pounded his thighs with a full-throated laugh. "I know what you want to ask about. You want to get married!" He nailed it! The question that burned in my soul was about a certain young girl. On a trip to Switzerland not long ago, I'd fallen for a beautiful twenty-one-year-old "Mother Divine" and was dreaming of a future with her.

Full of anticipation, I waited for his next words, and he

continued, "But you'll have to wait a little while. Here's still the clear influence of Saturn. It shows that nature still wants certain things to ripen within you. You'll only meet your future wife next year.

Darn it! So long! I really had no desire for waiting! Resoundingly and amused, he laughed, "You've been trying for some time to find a wife. But there have always been obstacles."

I asked him about the attributes of this future wife in the hope that he'd describe the young Mother Divine for me. Vishnu Anand Gaur again looked at the horoscope and asked the interpreter to tell him the exact time. He looked at the position of the sun, and obviously began to calculate something in his head. He was compiling a *Prashna*, a horoscope devised at the actual position of the planets at the time the question was being asked. "Your future wife is very educated. She has enjoyed an unusually broad academic training and has a good public reputation, especially in your Movement. She is a TM teacher, but she's not working as a TM teacher."

Gosh darn, that didn't fit at all!

And he continued, "She looks good, can express herself well, and she has a good character—your marriage will be evolutionary and will endure...and oh, yeah, she'll be thirty-six years old!"

"Can't she be twenty-one years old?" I asked in anticipations, and then I heard the typical and charming negation of Indians who do not like to say a direct "no." "Yes, that could be—but she will be thirty-six years old!"

While that was not what I wanted to hear, my curiosity was not yet satisfied. And so I asked about my second heart-felt desire, "Will I at some point work directly with

Maharishi? For me, that had been one of the major reasons for joining Purusha."

A short pause on his part. He fixed his gaze on the paper. "Yes, I see that really clearly. It will begin in 1990 in July and will continue for exactly one year. In this time, you'll have daily contact with him. After that, you'll take on ever more responsibility and later, too, you'll be in direct contact with Maharishi."

I was grateful from the depths of my heart. What rosy prospects for my immediate future!

Despite this and still shocked that probably nothing would come of my dream girl, I looked briefly at the signs rushing by on the highway. Oh, my God, I had passed my exit and had driven way too far! How embarrassing! But who could concentrate on the outside world when significant details of your own future are being spread out in front of you." At the next exit I turned—and was silent and sunk within myself for the rest of the way, digesting what I'd just heard.

After months of intensive preparation, several experienced jyotishis traveled on behalf of Maharishi to many countries on the planet. They helped interested people not only to understand their lives better but they also more importantly helped them to recognize future obstacles and, when possible, to avoid them.

The wise men of Vedic culture are not satisfied just making predictions based on the positions of the planets. If they recognize an upcoming danger, they want to prevent it. Closely connected with jyotish, there are therefore also the *yagyas*, or Vedic technologies that are carried out in India since time immemorial to deal with existing—or even better—forthcoming imbalances. They are used to avoid difficult life situations of the seeker or, at least, to diminish them, even before its point in time has come. Yagyas also promote favorable influences, those that bring good luck or support for the success of a venture. In about the same way that a panchakarma treatment removes impurities from the whole organism and thus creates the basis for better health, yagyas systematically create a higher coherence that helps to remove obstacles in life through systematically enlivening natural law on a spiritual level.

For the practical implementation of such yagyas, pundits are systematically trained from childhood on. They practice and repeat the traditional recitations, as well as certain hand movements and actions that go with them, over many years until they become part of their flesh and blood. There are many different yagyas that are specifically aimed at neutralizing as much as possible any negative influences as they are recognized in the horoscope.

And here, too, Maharishi worked on the renewal and the deepening of old Vedic tradition. Since the mid-eighties, he has built pundit schools in India. In them, thousands of young students from Vedic families were trained over six to eight years in the Vedas while, at the same time, they practiced Transcendental Meditation and the TM-Sidhis. Maharishi knew that yagyas could only unfold their full potential if the pundits rested deeply within their own being. Their nervous systems should be so accustomed to the experience of the Absolute that this boundless silence penetrates all the actions of the yagyas in order to activate the organizing power of nature that is at home in pure consciousness.

Gems are yet another method used in jyotish. For eons,

the power of pure gemstones has been known. Through the organizing power of their molecular lattice, for the wearer of the gem they can balance any unfortunate influences from constellations or build up his or her strengths, based upon the constellations that are read in the horoscope. For years, Maharishi met with Indian jyotishis again and again to standardize the prescription of these effective gemstones, based on Vedic scriptures, on the experience of the jyotishis he'd invited, and on his own inner vision, and to correct any errors in the oral tradition. A good jyotish consultation therefore included a recommendation of certain gemstones for balancing or for strengthening. And so, even here, in the West, people could increasingly be seen wearing pearls, coral, sapphires, rubies, and other precious stones for this purpose. These precious stones are to be worn in rings or pendants in a precisely defined setting to provide the optimally support-ing effect.

The next time I had a reading, the jyotishi recommended, "You should wear a yellow sapphire all your life, and if possible also a pearl, as well as a red coral. But the most important gemstone for you is a yellow sapphire."

Suddenly, I remembered that even in my childhood I must have sensed something like this. Even as a small boy, I pressed my nose flat against the windows of jewelry shops and gazed, full of fascination, at the yellow-gold, glittering gemstones. Already back then, how I wanted one! But even now, I could not yet afford it. Still, I was sure that, one day, not far in the future, I would be wearing such a precious stone.

Expansion

In the following year, I worked actively on the spreading of Ayurveda in Europe—as I had before my year-long side trip to Cyprus. I took over the biggest part of the organization of vaidya tours and training courses for physicians and technicians. I helped to prepare for our participation in the coming WHO's annual general meeting and accompanied once again a group of scientists on their journey to Geneva. Here, I spoke to the delegates from all over the world and invited them to our presentations and banquets. I made appointments and accompanied the scientists, as I had done almost two years ago for Dr. Triguna's pulse diagnosis and consultation. I was elated to be part of these activities that served the spiritual and physical health of so many.

Reinhard coordinated the TM Movement for all of Europe from Vlodrop —and I was constantly in midst of it. For most of the time as his assistant, I had a list of forty or fifty projects that I worked through. Part of those were Purusha internal concerns, the leadership of a world-peace assembly in Vlodrop, as well as monitoring the final exams for TM teacher training courses. In between, I took care of honored guests who were visiting Maharishi. All this was part of the most diverse, never-ending number of assignments and projects that Maharishi's overflowing creativity brought into action to improve more and more aspects of life for the people on this planet.

Brahmachari Nandkishore, Maharishi's personal representative and closest confidante, planned a tour through the biggest German cities. And before I even realized it, I had a new mammoth assignment. I knew all the heads of the centers and a large part of the active meditators personally for many years, or at least through intensive contacts on the phone. Their photographs had passed through my hands as they applied to various courses and I knew how many TM initiations any one of many TM teachers had made and in what cities. Happy with this new assignment, in which I'd see many of them again, I prepared meetings in small and big cities in Germany. I phoned and organized. Soon, we sat in packed halls throughout Germany and kicked off new projects.

During our activities, June 17, the Day of German Unity, took place. Every year on this day, German TM teachers presented a big "yogic flying celebration" in Bonn, the capital of West Germany; Germany was then still divided. At least once a year, the German TM Movement wanted to bring together a group of 800 yogic flyers, the number needed for the Extended Maharishi Effect for Germany. What a remarkable feat for all those volunteer helpers to motivate so many people, as well as arranging all that went with it! They organized enrollments and mealtimes, low-cost housing, a small mountain range of foam mattresses, the settlement of finances—in short, everything connected to such a big, communal practice of the TM-Sidhi Program for a few days.

Nandkishore was invited to speak. Those were marvelous summer days with bright blue skies. In the gigantic white tent that held a thousand people, a stage had been built for the speakers. In front of it, there were rows upon rows of chairs. In a second tent, there lay 400 freshly covered foam mattresses. Mornings and evenings, there was an extended sidhi program, powerful and beautiful because of the number of participants. During the day, the stage was used for talks about Vedic branches of learning and their practical application. There was news from the TM Movement; there were musical performances, and humorous skits. It was a celebration with all the trimmings, elevated by the magnificent feeling of unity and a terrific atmosphere.

Nandkishore inspired the people who had come from all over Germany for this event, and he answered questions. Later, the two of us sat in the front row and enjoyed the various performances of our German friends.

Dr. Karin Christ, a decidedly likeable brunette physician with sparkling brown eyes presented a lively lecture to the assembly about Maharishi Ayurveda. She had recently returned from the Netherlands and from the first European advanced training course for physicians. She was opening the first Maharishi Ayurveda Health Center in Germany in the former sanatorium on the land of the meditation academy in Schledehausen, where I'd done the first part of my civil service. In glowing terms, she described the positive effects of panchakarma and invited the audience to test the healing effects of this Ayurvedic cleansing therapy for themselves. Her presentation was so clear and refreshing that a spontaneous wish surfaced in me, "I would love to work with her!"

The diversified program pulled us further into its spell. When necessary, I did simultaneous interpretation of the content of what was being said for our "Nandi". We let ourselves be enchanted by an opera chorus of thirty singers from the Hamburg Sidhaland, a housing project in which about 150 meditators lived together in an apartment complex and so had made it possible to practice their TM-Sidhi Program together. The powerful music, as well as the joy of the singers, went into my heart and was a welcome change.

Following this, there was a sketch by four people from Schledehausen. There, about 150 meditators were working and living with their families in the countryside and enjoying their TM-Sidhi Program as a group. What was I seeing there? Wasn't that the young doctor from a while back? She had boldly tied up her hair into Pippi-Longstocking braids with thick and glowing red bows. With a bright red pair of glasses on her nose, she was pulling off high-spirited jokes up there. "She'd be right for you!" was the sudden thought that flashed through me before I once again landed on the floor of reality. I knew her. More than ten years back, she'd made a positive impression on me in an advanced course for TM teachers. With her lively joyfulness, her quick-wickedness, and her charm, I wasn't the only one she'd beguiled. And now she looked mischievous with her bright eyes. Her humor and her laughter were catching, but—how could it be otherwise—she was already taken, married for years. Oh, well.

I enjoyed the subsequent lectures and, as I did every evening, I drove back to the hotel for the daily briefing with Nandkishore, where he also had individual appointments and meetings with small groups.

Inspired by this successful tour, Brahmachari Nankishore created an expansion team of four Purushas who would keep going the activities that he'd initiated. Part of the group was my friend for years, Norbert, as well as Hans, Helmut, and my own humble self. And so, I was once again on the job with body and soul of spreading Maharishi's knowledge in Germany.

Cruising all over Europe

Soon after, Brahmachari Nandkishore inspired a handful of Germans to start the *Corporate Development Programme* (CDP) for Europe. Through the implementation of TM in the work environment, these special courses offered to corporations had already improved the satisfaction and the health of employees in dozens of Japanese and American companies while also furthering the success of these same enterprises.

It was exactly what was being sought for so urgently. Aside from the professional qualifications of a person, in recent years economists had been making note of the so-called *soft skills*, for example, being able to use common sense, to deal effectively with other people, and to demonstrate a positive, flexible attitude. As the prerequisite of the professional success of the individual, as well as the profitability of the companies, having employees with soft skills was vital for teamwork, perseverance, and success. It had become increasingly clear to the corporate world, meanwhile, that the negative consequences of stress took away not only the joy of life but were also responsible for around 70% of all illnesses. The stress-related reduction of earning power in German companies amounted to several hundred billion Euros annually. Just the costs of loss of production incurred through illnesses were about 40 billion Euros annually. Economists estimated that the costs sustained through alcohol in the workplace to be another 40 billion. Added to this were the losses caused by employee use of sleep aids and other drugs in the blood and similar issues.[48] Nandkishore's idea to offer an effective program to companies had obviously been more than timely.

Four active Germans subsequently formed a limited

partnership, with me as the representative of the international organization and the fifth partner; all of us with great enthusiasm. In collaboration with successful businesses coaches, we structured a systematic training for TM teachers who wanted to specialize in these new programs for companies. We worked with exceptional dedication on the development of a special portfolio with a subtle, modern design in blues and greys, instead of the usual pastel colors with a lot of gold and scrolls that Maharishi loved so much and that were used in almost all publications of our Movement. We were glad to have something more relatable in our hands, something that would correspond to the taste of our future clients. We developed programs for the education and the subsequent care of all the employees of these companies, as well as for the scientific documentation of successes.

Even the first scientific study with forty-five meditating employees already showed the impressive worth of our endeavor. Compared to a carefully selected control group in the same firm, the fears and worries in the workplace were reduced for meditators. They consumed less alcohol, fewer drugs, were more satisfied with their work, and their physical health improved. They slept better and were less tired; their efficiency and productivity went up. And what was especially great: their feeling of togetherness in the workplace, as well as in their private relationships, improved.[49]

As an illustration, we made use of a video in our CDP presentations that had been filmed at *Sumitomo Heavy Industries*, a Japanese machine manufacturing company. After a large number of the 1,500 employees had learned TM, the testimonies of the managers clearly expressed the positive change in their personal lives, as wells as in the work atmosphere within this huge corporation. The recurrent laughter of the audience of this mostly serious film was in response to the manager of one of the departments. In his best English, he reported the many improvements in his own life. As the crowning glory of his results, he added, full of enthusiasm and with his eyebrows raised high, "In the past, I always had problems with my bowel movements; but since I've been meditating, I can go to the toilet every day!" Vigorous nodding and a huge radiance on his round face emphasized his statement as if it were the biggest success of the century. Even after I'd shown this film many times, I still had to join the cheerful laughter of the various audiences every time; it was just too funny!

Also impressive were two large-scale official studies on 800 employees of Sumitomo Heavy Industries, performed by physicians of the research institution of the Japanese Ministry of Labor and a second medical research institute. Half of the employees had learned TM, while the rest served as the control group. The physicians evaluated a great amount of data obtained from these employees about sleep disturbances, obesity, eating and sports habits, as well as the consumption of cigarettes, alcohol, and coffee—even the use of vitamins, sleeping pills, medicines for the reduction of blood pressure, and the number of sick days taken.

The evaluation after five months of practice confirmed the results of the American study completely: with meditating employees, psychosomatic disturbances and digestion complaints were reduced significantly. Their emotional stability had increased, they showed less depression, anxiety, and aggressive, as well as neurotic tendencies. Irregularities in daily life also were reduced. They could fall asleep faster and stay asleep through the night; they smoked less. Everything in the control group—except for one variable remained as it had been.[50, 51]

Those responsible in the Japanese Ministry of Labor were so impressed with these results that they publicized them everywhere in Japan.

After we had integrated all this into the CDP training course, I was free to once again indulge in my love for travel: I went to Switzerland, Croatia, Serbia, and Spain, and led a good dozen of international advanced courses for TM teachers with as many as seventy highly motivated participants, who subsequently could implement Corporate Development Programs for companies in their own countries.

In between times, I coordinated something new from Vlodrop. Maharishi had invited especially experienced Indian Ayurveda experts to give consultations all over Europe. Wonderful! Now, I could once again call TM academies and centers in many countries. These, in turn, informed their meditators that these vaidyas could, with Ayurvedic consultations, help them to come to grips with health problems and, at the same time, remove the obstacles that stood in the way of their enlightenment.

One day, I picked up Dr. Raju, a small, rotund, and almost always beaming Indian vaidya at the airport. Dr. Raju wore the traditional dress of the vaidyas. On top of his dhoti and the white silk kurta, he wore a carefully folded white shawl, decorated with a red or green border of embroideries glistening with gold and whose long ends hung down far in front. Since his fourth year of life, he had learned an especially exact form of pulse diagnosis from his grandfather; it came from his family tradition in a long line of vaidyas, and was a form that was not taught even at Indian Ayurvedic universities. In addition, he had for many years been a student of Dr. Balaraj Maharishi, the famous expert on healing herbs who'd already been in Vlodrop once before. Dr. Raju was the Secretary General of the *All India Ayurvedic Graduates Association*, as well as a long-time advisor of the Indian Government Ministry for Health and Family Welfare. Together with his parents and his siblings, he practiced in Hyderabad, South India. The healing art of these vaidyas was so impressive that patients came from far away and began to stand in line at four in the morning to secure a place for an appointment.

I accompanied Dr. Raju's tours all over Europe so I could take all the weight of organizing off his shoulders. During his consultations, I usually sat next to him and one of the European doctors, who accompanied him.

He was such a virtuoso in pulse diagnosis that his patients—myself included—were constantly amazed. That he could read mental and physical disturbances in the pulse was amazing enough already. But he could also report on earlier complaints as well as what the causes and the course of any illness were. So, I was astonished when, in the pulse of mothers, he could detail the complaints of their infants and small children; he knew everything about the complications at the birth of a child or could say exactly which illnesses were due to genetic inheritance from the mother's or the father's ancestry. Again and again, those seeking advice confirmed the accuracy of his diagnoses with profound respect. Dr. Raju had a cheerful word for every patient, inexhaustible patience, as well as all the time in the world for each single person, something that made me, as the organizer of the tours, regularly break into a cold-sweat! After all, it was my task to make sure that the appointments of the next patients were at least approximately kept.

These patients trusted him, followed his recommendations for their daily lives, and took the recommended Maharishi Ayurvedic herbal compounds for the restoration of their health. The more work Dr. Raju had, the more patients he saw, the happier he became. His energy was inexhaustible. Not a single time did I see him tired or in a bad mood. What a doctor! He was relaxed and always smiling about each and everything. His happiness was overflowing. Merely to be working in his presence was uplifting. During these tours, a deep friendship developed as well as a high esteem that connects us to this day.

And with all this, Nature spun her wise threads. Quietly and unrecognized, it prepared me for my future assignment in life without my even seeing any of it.

Nightly Phone Calls

As much as all these activities fulfilled me, the desire to get married became ever clearer in my awareness. I told the boys on my team about it. But all they did was to tease me, as they didn't take me especially seriously. At some point, one of the Purushas offered to give me a reading from I Ching, the age-old oracle system of ancient China. While, earlier in my life, I'd rejected anything like that lock, stock, and barrel, my near future meanwhile interested me so intensely that I was totally open to it. And what did the oracle say about my most urgent issue? "The servant wants to leave, but the master won't let him go just yet!" Heavens alive, in spirit that was precisely the same thing that the cheerful jyotishi had said: The time isn't ripe yet! And so, I submissively surrendered to my long meditation program and my various tasks.

A few weeks later, on a sunny Friday in September, Norbert, Helmut, and I went traveling. This time, we drove to Schledehausen, three hours away, to work out activities for expansion with the German National TM Center and to create a lecture tour about Maharishi Ayurveda.

While our newest acquisition, a rather outdated, and therefore half-way affordable for Purusha, grey-blue BMW was rolling down the grey ribbon of the autobahn ever closer to our goal, I mused—for the umpteenth time—about my heart's desire. And this time, I felt an answer rise from within: "If you really want to, you will meet the woman of your life this weekend." And then the impulse vanished into the background of my awareness.

Dr. Hans Schäffler and Dr. Karin Christ had been running a Maharishi Ayurveda health center for a year and a half in a large building on the property of the Meditation Academy in Schledehausen, surrounded by beautiful parks and a wide expanse of ancient trees. Their patients came from far away for consultations with the doctors and for panchakarma treatments.

As soon as we'd unloaded our belongings, we met for the first work conference with both doctors and their marketing assistant, Christine. The six of us sat in Karin's comfortable living room in a small residential area nearby where many meditating families had bought properties. There we devised our first plans. Karin's small children were already asleep in their rooms upstairs. Growling clearly, my hungry stomach made itself heard—we had skipped dinner to keep the appointment punctually. While the others continued the meeting, Karin and I prepared a small supper in the kitchen. We talked with ease. I enjoyed her relaxed manner and felt great in her spick and span kitchen. And, by the way, I learned that she'd been divorced for a good year.

All that Saturday we developed further joint activities in the health center. In the evening, we once again sat in a comfortable circle together, this time at Christine and her husband's place. After a delicious supper in the romantic kitchen of the lovingly renovated farmhouse, we moved to the living room with its cast iron heater. Karin and I sat cross-legged on the sofa, and our knees touched as though accidentally—all evening long. I was curious and relaxed; I liked her. Well, let's see what will come of it.

Of course, it was once again all about Ayurveda activities. But we joked and laughed a lot. And I once again noticed a phenomenon that always amazed me. I felt a deep heartfelt closeness to these people whom I hardly knew as if we'd known one another for a long time. What was the explanation for this oddity that was so delightful among all meditators? It was as if a reflection of the experience of pure consciousness, into which we immersed ourselves in every meditation, was maintained all day and created this gentle closeness even among strangers. Wherever it came from, I enjoyed it in full measure. When Helmut and Norbert urged our departure shortly before ten, reminding us of the early bedtime of Purushas, I was so totally not in the mood for it. Even after their subliminal insistence I didn't react as usual. "Naw, I don't feel like it!" Brief sideways glance: "Karin, can you take me to the academy in your car later?"

"Of course!"

The two of them departed a bit grudgingly. At some point, even Hans drove home and the four of us that remained were drawn outside for a romantic midnight walk under the starry skies after another hour.

On the drive back in Karin's VW Golf, we talked animatedly. When I got out, we exchanged our star signs. And I was now psyched: "I can't sleep yet; I'm gonna take a nice walk. Do you feel like coming along?"

In the bright moonlight the two of us wandered around on broad forest paths, told each other about God and the world, and, finally, I dared cautiously forward, "So, tell me, do you have a steady boyfriend?"

"No, I don't."

"How about an unsteady one?"

The slightly annoyed answer came like shot from a pistol: "Absolutely not that kind!"

So, slowly and carefully, I took her into my arms, was deeply touched by her unbelievable tenderness that, during the day, she'd hidden so well under her zippy humor. We stood there like that for a long time motionless, each enjoying the closeness of the other, and I gave her the first gentle kiss. Hand in hand, we wandered back, a deep peace and intimate connectedness had taken hold of both of our hearts.

Without having to talk about it, it was clear to us both that this new intimacy had to be kept secret from Norbert and Helmut. At the next lunch together, Karin was bubbling over with charm and wit and gave all her attention to my friends—giving me not even a glance. Suddenly, a fortunate coincidence came to our aid. In the heavily frequented meditation academy, the rooms became scarce: two of us Purushas had to double up. And with my most lamb-like, pious face and directly in front of my friends, I asked Karin, who was taken totally by surprise, "Karin, you have a big house in town. I'd be willing to move into town, if it's all the same to you."

And my little repartee expert crinkled her nose with the sweet freckles, as if she had to think about it a bit: "Well," she said slowly, "That might just work . . . when do you want to come?"

And so, we could get closer in peace and quiet in the next days, and completely unnoticed, while during the day I took part in the meetings with my Purusha friends at the German National TM Center. In the evenings, I horsed around with Karin's six-year old Aurel and the three-year old Elisa all over the house and was enchanted by these two blondies with their clear, blue children's eyes. Curious and freshly in love, I did a horoscope on my first tiny computer in Karin's living room from the time of our first kiss at night in the forest. Venus was in the first house and the rest seemed to look very sensible. We were looking towards a sunny future!

Back in Vlodrop, Brahmachari Nandkishore was waiting for me for a private talk. Hans, the fourth member of our expansion team had complained to him about my constant urge to be active. While the other Purushas were calmly dedicated to the meditation program, which, after all, was the major task of our men's group, I let hardly any chance to plunge into various activities go by. Nandkishore had already spoken with Norbert and Helmut. They saw it as less objectionable than Hans did, but they had to honor the truth and had to agree with his opinion somewhat. Now Nankishore stepped up to read me the riot act. Since he liked me and my activities, he tried with a theatrically strict voice, while steadfastly trying to suppress his grin, to remind me of the priorities of life on Purusha: "We do not always go out, out, out, out, out—all the time! You should be meditating more."

Norbert and Helmut were waiting in front of the door in anticipation, and I reported everything hot off the press. Immediately, that sentence got rubbed in my face with regularity. We were all entertained by the fun of it, but Hans made a slightly sour face because we didn't take his complaint seriously enough.

Since I looked after so many different tasks, I had my own phone in my room. And now, every night before falling asleep, I called Schledehausen. It was soon clear that something serious was going on between Karin and me. Because of Nankishore's intervention, my business trips were put on ice for a while. With the excuse of visiting my father, I nevertheless sneaked out for a few free days and we made dates for one of her child-free weekends in the Taunus region. There we had a gloriously intimate weekend in a small hotel at the edge of the forest and came up with our first plans during our walks.

A few weeks later, my sweetheart came to Vlodrop with Dr. Schäffler for the weekend to talk about further expansion activities. We were close enough to touch, yet we needed to hide our togetherness. It was difficult for us both. She slept in the hotel; I slept in my Purusha cell. All we could do was the usual nightly phone call and a short walk during the day—in clear view of all the others. This should not and could not go on like this.

Like shot from a gun, I went to see Reinhard and confessed: "Reinhard, I want to ask you to release me from all my Purusha positions; I have a steady girlfriend. I don't feel right about carrying Purusha responsibilities while I'm in a courtship.

Reinhard didn't want to know anything about that. He just didn't believe my serious affirmations that I would soon want to leave Purusha. It just went beyond his ability to imagine. He thought it was just a whim. But I didn't feel good about having a secret relationship—which could possibly be a bad example for other Purushas. For the time being, I complied but kept indulging in my new after-dark hobby of nightly phone calls.

Even when friends, who were clued-in, told Reinhard at the beginning of December that I wanted to leave Purusha, he thought it was one of my usual jokes. And when I invited Norbert, Helmut, and him for a farewell celebration with cake in nearby Düsseldorf, Reinhard still didn't want to believe it. Only when he saw my car packed to capacity with my few belongings at the big entry gates, did he seem to get it. "You really mean it, right?"

I nodded grinning, then hugged at least thirty Purusha friends assembled in the courtyard for the good-byes. I pounded them on the back for the last time, like men do when they are close. With them I'd shared wonderful, deeply inspiring and fulfilling years of my life. After that, I enjoyed the last hour in a café with my closest friends—and then I was off into a completely new life!

X.

COMMUTER BETWEEN TWO WORLDS

*Only when the spirit understands the superficial
and the hidden, can it go beyond its
limitations and discover
the bliss that is not bound to time.*

Jiddu Krishanmurti
1885-1986
Indian Philosopher, Author, Theosophist
and Spiritual Teacher

First Year as the Father of a Family

Once again, I had good fortune in my life. This time, enough for two. Good friends from Switzerland, Flücki, an ex-Puru-sha and a well-paid dentist, and his friend Rudi, a real estate agent, invited me and my sweetheart to their summer house in Florida. Karin let the kids stay with their father for two weeks. And so, the two of us, newly in love, set off for a premature honeymoon in mid-December in warm Miami. We spent the first night in a cheap hotel. The next day, we enjoyed the beach and the sun, and, in the early evening, we drove to pick up Flücki and his girlfriend at the airport. We looked for them in the waiting area of the arrivals section. When Flücki and his girlfriend showed up behind a stacked-high baggage cart, he waved at us in the best of moods, "Hey, you two, we've got so much baggage, we'll take a taxi—we'll see you at the Holiday Inn!" And they were gone.

Somewhat befuddled about this super high-speed greeting and farewell, Karin and I, only minutes later, also got a taxi to follow them. "Holiday Inn please!"

"Which one?" asked the taxi driver solicitously, "There's twelve Holiday Inns in Miami."

We didn't have the slightest clue to which one our friends had vanished. Flabbergasted, we got back out of the taxi. After we got over the first shock, I asked Karin to make herself comfortable in a corner of the airport. On the phone, I tried to learn from the central computer of the hotel chain in which of the twelve hotels my friends had registered. Nothing doing; the central computer was down. And the friendly American voice on the other end of the line couldn't help further. Unfortunately, we also didn't know the address of their house on the west coast 500 kilometers away and the useful invention of the cell phone was still in the distant future. What to do? Our cash supply for this vacation wasn't exactly abundant; that's why we'd planned to spend the night in a cheap room again before going further. But now, I spontaneously suggested just to drive to any Holiday Inn to start a new search on the main computer that would meanwhile have been fixed.

After getting there, I first made sure that the two of them hadn't by chance arrived at this hotel. They hadn't. So, Karin and I took a bite in the restaurant opposite reception while I asked for the state of things every half hour. But the central computer was being stubborn about not coming back to life. Not even on the following morning. Thanks to meditation, Karin and I stayed relaxed despite our dangerous financial meltdown due to this night. Finally, the computer functioned again—but Flücki was nowhere to be found. After this last negative news, I stepped onto the tiny balcony of our room that looked down on a big, green, inner courtyard of this gigantic 500-room complex, just as my neighbor was getting a bit of fresh air at the same time. I looked to the side and couldn't trust my eyes—unbelievable, just unbelievable! Just two meters away from me, there stood the long-lost Flücki! The computer couldn't find him because they'd registered under his girlfriend's name. I could hardly believe it. As if invisible threads had been pulled, and without any input from us, nature not only led us into the same hotel and into neighboring rooms, but had also made sure that we stepped onto the balconies of our rooms in the same second. This could not be just by chance! All glory to regular transcending together with all the wonders and the nature support that comes with it!

A pleasant side effect was that Karin's trust in me and my intuition rose significantly. What a remarkable kickoff for our first successful vacation!

Back in Schledehausen I gradually reduced my hours-long meditation and TM-Sidhi Program that I'd practiced for years and adapted it to my more active life. Thank God, I immediately had a super great connection to Aurel and Elisa. I played and cuddled with them, and often gave little Elisa her daily Ayurvedic oil massage, cleaned up their rooms with them in the evenings, or read them a good night story. So, I quickly felt closely bonded with them. A few weeks later, when Karin went to a one-week advanced course for physicians in Switzerland, I could play ersatz dad. Karin, still slightly in doubt due to my long career as a single man, called from Seelisberg, asking how we were all doing together.

But I could assure her with a good conscience. "I'm sleeping with them at night in the big double bed, Aurel to my right, Elisa to my left, and I'm enjoying it."

And I really did!

In the same week, I visited my father in Balduinstein with my new little son and daughter. He, too, enjoyed them visibly and was very kind to them. He also made no comments about my having fallen for a woman with two children. On the contrary, he seemed to be happy that I'd finally be settled. Despite this, I was a little anxious when Karin was coming to get the three of us in Balduinstein; there was no way to know how he'd react. But I had worried about nothing. She came, she saw, and she conquered. In nothing flat, she had captured the heart of my father who was not always welcoming. As soon as she'd arrived, she was sitting with him in the kitchen, talking and laughing easily as if they had been part of the family forever.

It was unbelievable how much fun Karin and I had together. We laughed all the time about this and that. Her easy ways were exhilarating for me and I thought she was totally sweet. Above all, she enchanted me with her gentle and mild vibe when I held her in my arms. Despite all that love, this phase in my life was undeniably mixed. I had the principled notion to be on financially solid ground before I formalized my connection with Karin through marriage. Moreover, I didn't want to take any old job. I wanted to continue working full-time for Vedic knowledge, didn't want to wear myself out, wanted to find time for meditation and, at the same time, make enough money so as not to be dependent on Karin.

So, I took a small loan, had letterhead printed, got a new computer, a fax machine, and a copier on credit, and got my own phone in my freshly furnished office in the attic of Karin's house.

I organized basic TM courses in the immediate surroundings of my new domicile and in more distant neighborhoods as well. I spoke with the CEOs of various firms about the Corporate Development Program—with moderate success. Several times, I could work with Bernhard in Munich, the same Bernhard, who'd shaken Maharishi's hand in Leysin and who'd become a TM teacher like me. On each of several long weekends, we initiated about a hundred employees of a big sales company within the framework of their sales training, and I made good money with it every time.

To my great joy, one day Reinhard called from Vlodrop and asked me to continue to lead the European advanced CDP courses for TM teachers. And so, now and then, I drove to Turkey and a few countries in the Balkans for ten days at a time. I enjoyed it a lot and was glad that, through leading these courses, I stayed connected to in the international TM Movement, and was making money.

Even with all that, I still could not support a family, but at least I was supporting myself and paying the rent for my office. It all worked out somehow, but it wasn't up to my ideal financial expectations.

At that same time, Karin and Hans, as the medical leaders of the Ayurveda Health Center in Schledehausen got an attractive offer from a Mr. Jäger*, who was just then negotiating his take-over of a spa clinic in Bad Bergzabern. He won over the two physicians for his idea of running this health center as a Maharishi Ayurveda clinic, with him as the major responsible party. The health center in Schledehausen had a flaw: despite all efforts at renovation, the standard of accommodations in the rather old building were relatively simple. As panchakarma treatments are enormously labor intensive, there are correspondingly high treatment costs. Despite the clean, lovingly arranged, and affordable rooms and the guest lounges, the lack of elegance did not correspond well with the high treatment costs. An oft-repeated statement of patients after their stay was this: "It was wonderful; I'm definitely coming back. But, unfortunately, I can't send my friends to this place."

The health clinic in Bad Bergzabern in southern Germany seemed better suited to the purpose. As a down payment, Mr. Jäger demanded money, a lot of money. Karin had already paid DM 150,000 for this huge project, in part with help from the bank. The preparations were going full blast.

The first time I drove to Bad Bergzabern with the two of them and met Mr. Jäger for the first time, I got the sneaking feeling that with such a big decision, I'd better get Maharishi's advice. Karin thought this idea somewhat strange. But I got my way; the following day, I laid out the details to Reinhard on the phone and, a few days later, I got Maharishi's commentary through Reinhard. It was affirmative, but closed with the words, "…but tell them that they should be careful with the finances!"

Knowing from experience that Maharishi saw things that were closed to others, this set off all the alarms within me. I impressed Hans and Karin with the fact that such a statement from Maharishi should not be taken lightly and made myself not exactly popular with the two of them. I was just barely able to keep them from throwing another DM 150,000 after him and taking on further debt.

Not long after, the whole thing tanked. Mr. Jäger had already frittered away the first DM 150,000. Had Maharishi not warned us, the financial problem would have been even greater for all of us. As it was, it was hard enough to pay of that horrendous sum over many years.

Financially back then, things went pretty much up and down. Added to that was the fact that Karin's mother was not exactly pleased with me as a candidate for a son-in-law. I was not an academic, which in her eyes was almost equal to a mortal sin. On top of that, I'd not pursued a "proper" profession in the last few years—and, maybe worst of all, I was as poor as a church mouse. For a concerned mother from a good family, it was a pretty disturbing combination. And she had no intention to keep her evaluation of my person a secret. Karin and I suffered it patiently and made the best of the situation when she came to visit. Of course, it could all have been better.

A good year after we'd learned to love one another, we celebrated our wedding on a sunny warm September day, selected as an ideal jyotish date. We'd had to wait for this for a couple of months, but what wouldn't you do for a kick-off promising the best luck? After all, the relationship was supposed to last for a whole lifetime. Because of this wait time, the wedding celebration fell exactly into the time frame that Vishnu Anand Gaur, the jyotish pundit, had told me on our travels in the Netherlands in which all the obstacles for a relationship would be removed. All his other predictions also hit the nail on the head: Karin had an especially high-level education: two different completed courses of study. She really was a TM teacher, though she did not work as such, had a great reputation in TM circles and was—though professionally independent and autonomous—closely connect to Maharishi's Movement. And—was it even conceivable? —she was exactly 36 years old when I met her. I found that all the other positive statements about her looks and her character were also exactly accurate.

I'd really wanted a small and modest wedding. But nothing doing. Karin was well-known in the whole country and I, too, had a lot of friends all over Germany. A hundred people had signed on. But due to the typical spontaneity and nonchalance of people who are a little too relaxed because of their meditation, we suddenly had to serve 180 guests in the big dining hall of the academy. Gisela, the head of the academy, and Karin's co-workers at the clinic responded as one. Unasked, they vanished into the kitchen and helped to feed even those who'd not registered. It was a wonderful give and take. Friends delighted us with a violin quartet and classical music; others performed skits. Yet others spoiled us with wedding ceremonies from India and Thailand; we danced and laughed. It was a sparkling and vivacious beginning for a happy relationship and a fabulous party with colleagues, friends, and relatives that went far past midnight with fireworks and joyful guests under a starry sky.

Ecclesiastical Intrigues

Our comfortable house amid small gardens in a side street in Schledehausen, where many kids could romp around in no danger became my starting point for small and big trips. In the surrounding areas, I diligently offered the basic TM courses and was quite successful. In just one doctor's office, I taught twenty-two people Transcendental Meditation and took care of the meditating patients as well as their doctor regularly. The success was resounding. When, a few months later, I asked this family doctor, a roundish woman in her mid-fifties, how "my students" were doing, she answered, "I really can't tell you exactly, Mr. Pirc. Since they've been meditating, their health situation has apparently improved so much that they rarely come to my office. I haven't seen some of them in months. I don't seem to be needed now."

Soon after, I'd rented a hall in a hotel in Bad Hersfeld and had the students hang posters and put out flyers in various shops. I advertised on the radio, organized an article in the papers, and placed small ads throughout the region for four informational lectures. In short, I'd plunged into some expense when—one day before the first presentation—an employee of the hotel I'd booked told me on answering machine, "Sorry, Mr. Pirc, unfortunately we made a booking error. The hall is already taken."

How could that be? We'd signed a contract. I called back immediately to clear up the situation. When she repeated the same statement over the phone, I asked to be connected to her boss. She merely said, "Just a moment, please!" And then I heard her talk quietly to her boss in the background.

"It's the guy, you know, who rented the lecture hall. He's

referring to the written contract and he wants to talk to you!"

And by way of answer, there came the brash voice of the hotel owner. "Oh, that's the guy from the cult; the preacher asked us not to rent him the hall. Get rid of him and tell him there's nothing we can do!"

When she then wanted to talk to me again, I said straight out, "I could hear what your boss said and I want to speak to him directly!"

She handed him the receiver, "…he heard everything and insists on talking to you personally!"

Now I explained to the hotel owner, "We have made a contract! I have already sent out all the announcements and have placed the ads. You can't do this; I'd bear significant financial loss!"

In those days, I had no financial cushion; the expenses already incurred were a big strain on my already stretched budget. When he didn't want to give in, I, in my need, shot my last bullet: "If you insist on this, I will unfortunately have no alternative but to sue you for damages!"

He was completely unmoved. "Go right ahead! The preacher has already assured me that if it came to this the church will pay for the resulting damage."

I could hardly grasp it; so that's where the pressure came from! Unbelievable! I was firmly resolved not to just take it and, for the first time in my life, I went to court.

"Oh my God, Lothar, what has happened? You're as white as a sheet!" My wife's compassionate welcome was a comfort to my wounded soul when, after the hair-raising process, I stepped into the hallway of our home with my brown briefcase under my arm. I was shocked by the mendacity of those people in the courtroom, as well as the devious machinations of the church. My attorney had prepared well. Stunned, I listened to the bottomless lies and distortions of the hotel owner before the court as, ice cold and without blushing, he insisted that he'd accepted another customer and that he'd never, ever spoken with a churchman about this matter. Contrary to any sense of justice, the fact that a contract had been agreed to played no role whatsoever. Similarly, the prejudiced and demeaning attitude of the judge, who, after the lies of the hotel owner, gave me the opportunity for a counterargument with the words, "And what does the gentleman from the cult have to say about this?"

After I once again summarized the facts, I had to listen defenseless as the judge ruled in favor of the opposition as if I'd only imagined all of it.

This miscarriage of justice deeply shook my belief in the trustworthiness of the German legal system. If even with such a small and clear case an equitable judgment could no longer function because of inappropriate prejudice, how would it look with big and complex adjudications?

Because of this absurd "administration of justice," I was stuck—innocent as I was—with the attorney and court costs, in addition to the costs incurred for preparations in Bad Hersfeld that led to nothing.

But much worse than all this was the fact that I was aghast for days about the abysmal malice and cowardice of people, the intrigues of the church, as well as the injustice I'd experienced. How filthy and unpleasant all this had been! In my diverse sojourns in other countries, I'd almost forgotten it but now I'd very obviously come back to my homeland, with its ongoing cult hysteria.

A few years later, I learned from a newspaper interview

that what had happened to me in Bad Hersfeld absolutely had a method to it. Dr. Martin Kriele, Professor of Political Science and Public Law, as well as a judge at the Constitutional Tribunal of Nordrhein-Westfalen, one of the leading experts of constitutional law in Germany, took issue with a newsletter of the ecclesiastical council of the *Evangelische Kirche Deutschland* [Protestant Church of Germany]. In it, Church "cult commissioners" were explicitly encouraged to fully exploit "in good spirits" the full scope of "freedom of opinion" to go after cults without fear that they would incur any personal risk—because the church would cover any possible attorney and court costs. When I read this, my breath stopped. It was exactly this underhanded game they'd played with me!

The church newsletter even explained the legal situation to inform the cult commissioners how far they could go in individual cases. It literally said, freedom of opinion "is far-reaching and even allows pointed and trenchantly rendered statements." Concrete, factual claims "are illegal if they are demonstrably about untrue factual claims." For Professor Kriele, this was the naked demand "not to shrink back from false factual claims if the opponent cannot prove your lie. For example, one can appeal to anonymous 'drop-outs' or any random personal enemies of the opponent with the formula, 'it is being reported,' and even cause lies to be spread anonymously in the media because the media can then appeal to their protection of whistle blowers and thus any clarification is impossible."

Thank God, I did not yet have a clue that I would have to experience this sort of calculated malice personally one day. In any case, Professor Kriele summarized this purely unbelievable writing with the words, "This newsletter can only be understood as a challenge to cult commissioners to go to the outer limits of what is allowed in their defamation campaigns and take the risk without any apprehension that this boundary could be crossed."[52]

In my case, this outer boundary had been crossed very substantially and, incited by the preacher, any number of false witness against 'thy neighbor' had been spoken!

A New Being

After I'd convinced my newly-wed wife that, besides Aurel and Elisa, I also wanted our own kids, everything went very quickly. My dear Karin had high hopes. Soon, her tummy became increasingly round. The nausea that had tortured Karin in her previous two pregnancies did not happen this time because of a helpful Maharishi Ayurveda herbal remedy. She was doing well all around. I love children, and this baby in her belly was something heavenly for me. In the fifth month, we had the first ultra-sound done and, presumably like most parents, we were deeply moved by the unclear black and white images of this growing being and with the pulsing movements of its tiny heart. We rejoiced boundlessly about this culmination of our love.

I was happy about our small and now growing family. I admired Karin, her empathy with her patients and co-workers, her organizational talent, and her conscientiousness. And I supported her wherever I could. Before her medical education, she had completed her degree in psychology, and so understood a lot about the special features of children's psyches. I saw that, with her knowledge and intuition, she was a super, loving, and engaged mother. Thank God, we could afford household help so that we could spend many hours with the children when Karin wasn't working. We laughed a lot and I knew I had been very fortunate to have this humorous, creative partner and her children. On weekends, we did excursions with Aurel and Elisa, met with other families, and enjoyed our new "foursomeness." The only downer was Karin's sleep disturbances that she'd had for years already and that bothered her so much that she was exhausted and irritable, sometimes even towards me. Aurel went through a phase of rejection and anger attacks, maybe a fit of belated jealousy towards me, that evaporated after a few weeks due to Karin's targeted attention.

It was a beautiful feeling to now be responsible for others, even though I wanted to do more financially for my loved ones. Anyway, I enjoyed getting big and small things together that the nest-building for a new arrival entails. I was touched when I could feel the hands and feet of our child through Karin's taut belly and often waited patiently for the fleeting movements of the limbs under the abdomen. What a joy! I experienced in amazement how nature in her unbounded intelligence allowed a child to develop and grow. And I sensed the soft breath of a very special person around us and felt clearly the character of the small being that was preparing its arrival, though I could not put it into words.

One beautiful Sunday morning in February at five a.m., the time had come.

"Come, Lothar, get up, it's happening!"

A little later I drove my round-as-a-ball sweetheart up the hill into the private birth clinic in Schledehausen. The morning sky was covered with thick, grey clouds. It was raining and stormy. In the delivery room, we distributed many candles. Karin was relaxed and meditated between contractions. Both mother and mid-wife were beaming with confidence and optimism. After two hours, the mid-wife asked Karin to stand to accelerate the birth. She stood behind her, to support her and to the surprise of us all, the baby slipped out with the first strong, second-stage contraction—directly into my spread-out hands. Not a drop of blood was on her, just a thin white and waxy layer covered the smooth, small body. And then the thick wintery cloud layer ripped apart. The heavens opened and the radiant sun bathed the face of the newborn in bright light. My little daughter opened her eyes, looked at me—and smiled!

A wave of unbounded bliss spread through me. I would never forget this precious moment!

The mid-wife was nonplussed. "I've never seen anything like it! I've always thought that newborns couldn't smile yet!"

Only for a few minutes the birthing room was bright with the sun; then the grey cloud cover remained for the rest of the day. Later, we moved into our room in the birth clinic. The three of us lay in the gigantic double bed. Our little one lay on top of me, belly to belly, where she was making soft little sounds and snoring a bit. And I felt her, sensed the joy of her spirit, grasped the wholeness of her personality and merged with her, this complete, small, great being.

3,000 in Yugoslavia

With Lilian, a completely new element came into our family. This tiny being united us all even more strongly with one another. She was the little star of our family with whom our bigger kids also loved to cuddle and play. I loved laying her over my shoulder in my office as I felt her heavenly, sweet vibration while she slept peacefully, completely untouched by any outer activity.

The phone rang; Reinhard's voice was on the other end. "Lothar, can you get free with your family? Maharishi wants to hold a big world peace conference in Yugoslavia and we're already in the middle of preparations. Can you take over leading that course together with Beat and his wife?"

What a question! Karin could come along too since the course fell within the spring vacation and our big kids spent the Easter vacation with their dad anyway. Lilian had just turned six weeks old and would come with us.

This world-peace conference was—as so often—planned by Maharishi with very short notice. He had insisted that as many people as possible should come, at best 7,000 once again.

"Why on Earth here, in Yugoslavia, this multi-national state?" The closer we got to our destination, the more often Karin asked me this question because, when we thought we were only an hour's drive away from our destination of Poreč, the road, only moderately paved, ran through poor towns and up and down hills for hours or snaked along the charming Croatian Riviera in tight curves. Karin's question seemed justified to me: "Couldn't we have chosen something more central for the course participants?"

"Right, but Maharishi's decisions aren't always immediately transparent. He'll have his reasons!"

Toward six o'clock in the evening, we finally arrived, hours later than we'd thought. It was already beginning to get dark, and we moved into our room on the third floor of the big hotel. I went directly back down on the elevator to find out how I could participate. I knew that at least 3,000 people had signed up and I anticipated moderating presentations and lectures with joy—and to participate in the magnificently relaxing meditation program in this big group.

But as soon as I was at the administrative office, the first complaints of the course participants whizzed at me. The rooms were too cold—some of participants lived in summer vacation rooms that couldn't be heated, and the blankets were thin. The food was not up to their expectations—they'd hired Yugoslavian hotel cooks who were hopelessly overburdened to produce delicious vegetarian and fresh food for so many people at the same time. The foam mattresses for the TM-Sidhi Program had not yet arrived—presumably they were held up by the same bumpy roads. Much had indeed only been prepared in the last two weeks. Within half an hour it was clear to me that I'd be putting on my rubber boots to save what could be saved. Corporations who want to organize meetings of this size begin a year ahead of time with their preparations, and they have a staff of employees trained for the purpose. We, on the other hand only had untrained volunteers, but they were into it with heart and soul. I negotiated with chefs, with disturbed course participants, with parents of sick children; I took complaints, organized, and coordinated our own people behind the scenes from six in the morning till one at night. There was hardly any time left over to meditate. In between times, I, the totally relaxed and elegant TM teacher in a suit and tie, sat on the big stage in front of a host of faces that had increasingly become calm and radiant. It was a hard job but it was also fun because after three or four days things ran rather well. But my night shifts remained.

Dr. Triguna was staying in Vlodrop then and Maharishi asked him to give Ayurveda consultations to our course participants. He came for three days. That meant an unplanned extra job to be reckoned with. Speakers from various countries had already held several talks about Ayurveda during the afternoon time for lectures. The available lists of people interested in meeting with Dr. Triguna were crammed full. What to do? Without further ado and with the help of the national leaders of various countries, I sorted out the people who, from a medical point of view, needed such personal consultations most urgently. In no time at all, a few physicians among the course participants could be found who had to be present at such consultations according to the law and who were needed for additional consultations—and, indeed, they wanted to be part of it for their own further education. Dr. Triguna did pulse diagnoses all day long from early morning till late at night, one after the other. Though he was already in his seventies, he gave everyone, even in this extreme engagement, his full attention while radiating unperturbable peace, as well as deep bliss and wisdom, just as I'd already experienced with him in the past. I took care of him, the doctors, and the participants, and I consoled those who were disappointed because they could not be seen due to time constraints. When Dr. Triguna left, I took a deep breath. I suspect that he, too, was relieved, although he'd been a tower of strength who'd done what he could tirelessly. Maharishi had once again done a flexibility training for all concerned, and I thought we'd made a good show.

All of us were sitting in a gigantic lecture hall, a tennis center in Yugoslavia, crowded with chairs. In front, on the stage, a scientist described in detail the effects of a series of seven different world peace assemblies in the years of 1983 to 1985 on the conflicts in the Middle East, a center of constant crises, and not only in this decade. "The duration of the world peace assemblies studied in many parts of the world ranges between one and eight weeks. First off, the researchers calculated, according to the formula of the square root of 1%, which assemblies were big enough—relative to the distance from Lebanon—to be able to create a harmonizing effect there. For, as you all know, the number of participating meditators on vacation changes from week to week—and, obviously, that had to be considered. All told, the research group collected data over 821 days, but only 93 days of that could have produced the Extended Maharishi Effect in purely mathematical terms due to the size of the group and its distance." And he added, "The further assessment was done by an independent professional analyst in a double-blind procedure. In other words, he knew neither the purpose of the study nor the dates of the assembly. For each of these days, he evaluated eight different news sources of newspapers and radio broadcasts with a standardized 16-point scale."

Well and good, but what was the outcome? Even for us, who were familiar with the group dynamics of consciousness and the theoretical background of the Extended Maharishi Effect, the results that he laid out before us were sensational. "When the number of participants had exceeded the threshold for the Extended Maharishi Effect, there were, compared to other days, 71% fewer war related deaths and, additionally, 68% fewer wounded soldiers in the area. Parallel to this, the intensity of the conflicts was reduced by 48%, while the co-operation of enemy parties increased by 66%." The scientist looked around, "At the same time what was especially impressive was the fact that the positive effects, calculated with the Global Peace Index, happened on the same day without any time lag as soon as the size of the group was large enough for the Extended Maharishi Effect."[53]

That such an unusual study would naturally bring a lot of nay-sayers into the picture was crystal clear. Even given this point of view, we were glad to hear that the researchers—as is customary in any serious study—had carefully eliminated all imaginable other variables such as season, temperatures, and religious and national holidays so that no other factors could distort the results. Even when the temperatures rose, which in the controls, immediately caused an increase in the number of conflicts, the Extended Maharishi Effect was undiminished and reduced violent clashes. The analysis of the days that directly preceded and followed the assemblies, in contrast, showed the abrupt change with the beginning and the end of the periods of sufficient group numbers every time.

Karin, an accredited psychologist, was familiar with statistics and was totally beside herself. "Lothar, these results are a blockbuster! The significances, that is, the statistical probabilities that these could have been due to error, are between 10^{-7} and 10^{-20}! In my entire studies, I've never seen such totally solid results in any scientific study!"

In plain language: the probability that all this had

happened by pure chance was at least one in a hundred million. In the result with highest significance, there were 20 zeroes behind the "1." That's equal to the truly astronomical chance probability one of ten billion trillion. So far as Karin knew, there was, to date, no study in the fields of medicine, psychology, or sociology that brought in even close to such highly significant results as did this study in the Extended Maharishi Effect.

Admittedly, this knowledge about the connections between the field of pure consciousness of a group of people and the actions of their fellow-human beings was totally new—for laymen as well as for most scientists in the world. These studies were trailblazing and broke all habitual concepts in how we think. Despite this, I was optimistic: In time, they'd not only find acceptance in the field of science, something that had begun with the publication of a comparable study in the International Journal for Conflict Resolution, a leading scientific journal.[54] Scientific works in respected professional publications such as this one were peer-reviewed as a matter of principle; they were published only if they passed muster with a committee of top-level experts in the respective fields. As one can easily imagine, the research into the Extended Maharishi Effect initially called forth some wrinkled brows in the committee of the science journal. After many heated discussions over years, these studies were finally published because they corresponded to all the requirements of the scientific practice and method.

And so, not only was I certain that these new technologies of consciousness would soon be used for the benefit of humanity to lessen smoldering conflicts but also to avoid wars before they even began.

Indeed, this refers to handed-down Vedic knowledge, knowledge whose practical effects Maharishi Patanjali had got to the heart of with his famous Sanskrit expression more than two thousand years ago: *"heyam dukham anagatam"* [Avoid the danger that has not yet come]!"[55] And it was exactly this that Maharishi had sought with his world peace assembly in Yugoslavia that he'd put together with such lightning speed. However, our targeted positive influence subsided, however, with the conclusion of this world peace assembly in Poreč.

A good year afterwards, at the end of June 1991, Slovenia and shortly thereafter Croatia, proclaimed their independence, which was regarded as a breach of the constitution by some branches of the Yugoslavian government and was the beginning of the Balkan wars that broke out soon after. And only then did it dawn on us why Maharishi had designated Yugoslavia a year before the first acts of war as the place to send his troop of coherence creators.

The Prophecy Comes True

In May I once again drove with the doctor's team of Maharishi's European organization to the WHO main yearly assembly in Geneva—this time with Karin and our baby in tow. The leader of the team was Dr. Tony Nader, a Lebanese neuro-endocrinologist who had completed his degree with honors at the Massachusetts' Institute of Technology—one of the most prestigious universities on the east coast of the U.S. I had led part of Dr. Nader's TM teacher training course years earlier. Dr. George Janssen and Dr. Michael Jensen were part of the team that had been part of developing the courses for physicians. As in the years before, I made the appointments with the ministers and coordinated Dr. Triguna's activities.

Lilian was so calm and peaceful that we could take her to banquets in the evenings in her baby carriage. There, we became friends with Dr. Kupferschmid, who'd been the first advisor of the Ministry of Health in East Germany. Dr. Kupferschmid, an extraordinarily nice and open man in his mid-fifties, had been responsible for tropical medicine and the coordination of disaster response for the WHO for decades. He was one of the few citizens of East Germany who, even before the recent opening of the intra-German border, had been allowed to pass through the Iron Curtain due to his office and the trust placed in him. As a doctor and a government official, he was well-traveled throughout the world, and he was fascinated by anything new and thus also by Maharishi Ayurveda. We got along well and kept in contact even after the conference.

One beautiful summer day, I was working at home in

my office; the sun shone directly through the window in the roof. Karin sat at her desk in the next room. The phone rang. "Lothar, Lothar, come quickly; Maharishi is on the line!"

Karin, with the receiver in her hand, put her hand over the mouthpiece and whispered with conspiracy written all over her face, "The time has come!"

I knew exactly what she meant. I'd told her more than once that Vishnu Anand Gaur, the laughing jyotishi, predicted on the memorable trip across the Netherlands that, by this July, the year I'd been longing for would begin, the year in which I'd be working directly with Maharishi.

"Hi Lothar; it's Holger," said one of my best Purusha friends, who now was one of Maharishi's secretaries. "Maharishi is on the line in India. Some time back, you taught TM to the ambassador of Tanzania in Kenya. Do you know if he's still meditating?"

Immediately the image of this wonderful human being rose before me, the man who, back then in Kenya, had the super-huge flower bouquets and baskets of fruit brought with him for his initiation. I hesitated only briefly, "Yes, I think he does. In any case Mr. Alatanga sends me a Christmas card every year."

"Maharishi has a message for the president of Tanzania. Can you fly to Tanzania and ask the ambassador to give the content of the letter to his president personally?"

"Of course. I'd love to do it; when should I go?"

And now Maharishi got on the line, "Lothar, can you fly today?"

That was my Master as everyone knew him. He lived totally in the here and now. Every impulse had to be realized immediately. My longing to work for him was huge. I felt only dedication to anything he'd want. "Um, yes, I have dates for several appointments, lectures, and TM checking. But maybe Charlotte could take over. I'll try."

"Good, I'll call back in an hour!" and the receiver clicked off.

Together with Charlotte, I'd made government contacts many years ago in Cologne and I knew her husband well. Dr. Heiner Roeder was a marine biologist by profession. Both had worked full-time for the TM organization for two decades; they were among the most qualified TM teachers in Germany—highly intelligent, well-versed in all aspects of Vedic knowledge, and authentic, warm-hearted, and full of humor. They lived not too far away with their two children, and now and then, they accompanied me to see my CDP contacts.

Charlotte could take over all my appointments. So that was no problem. I made use of my time and immediately afterwards called the Tanzanian embassy in Kenya's capital city, Nairobi, and asked to speak to Mr. Alatanga. "I'm sorry, but he flew to Tanzania a few days ago. No, nobody around here knows exactly where he's staying; he's traveling somewhere in the country."

Well, that didn't exactly sound encouraging.

Half an hour later, I again heard Holger's voice on the phone: "Lothar, are things good to go? Drive directly to Bonn and get a visa. As soon as you have it, call me back, and you'll get further instructions."

What followed was probably the fastest suitcase-stuffing action of all time. A friend drove me to Bonn and to the embassy building of Tanzania, where an employee told me that getting a visa would take several weeks. After a couple of seconds of shock, I went for it: "I have a special assignment and I have to speak to the Tanzanian ambassador personally." Within thirty minutes, I had the necessary endorsement in my passport.

From the nearest phone booth, I called Vlodrop, as directed, and Maharishi surprised me, "A driver is already on his way. He'll bring you the letter and your airline ticket at the Frankfurt airport. Go to the embassy of Zambia and get another visa there!"

One kilometer further, at the embassy of Zambia, I repeated the same script. I had the visa in my hands within half an hour, which normally took weeks to get.

There were no direct flights to Tanzania. So, I took the night flight from Frankfurt to an hours-long layover in Nairobi, the capital city of Kenya, the country where I'd spent one year of my life. From the Jomo Kenyatta International Airport, I called the permanent Secretary of State of the president's office, Mr. Maamuni*. In most African countries, presidents have the unchecked power to put acquaintances and trusted people into key positions in the whole country. While the ministers regularly change, the permanent Secretaries of State often hold the same position for decades. The trust that the president has in this person is equally great, as is the influence they exert in politics.

Mr. Maamuni had learned TM six years ago and had supported me and my colleagues repeatedly in various projects. His receptionist was on the phone immediately. "I'm sorry, my boss is in an important meeting. I can't possibly disturb him, but I'll hand him a note."

I heard her steps recede and come pattering back; she said, "Lothar, he absolutely wants to meet you! His driver will come right away and pick you up at the airport and bring you back there afterwards."

When I stood in the imposing ante-chamber soon after, we recognized each other. Mr. Maamuni's executive secretary was the same one as six years ago, and she remembered that I was a TM teacher. She used the occasion for some relaxed talk while I was waiting for the Secretary of State who was still in his conference. "You know, Lothar, my boss has five different phones, and I've had the instruction for years that I am not allowed to put through any calls during his evening meditation. The only exception is the President. For him, the red phone on Mr. Maamuni's desk in his office is reserved, and he'll only pick that one up. Look here."

She eagerly showed me the open appointment calendar with the dates in which I could see around twenty entries for every day of the week, and she pointed her finger at the times of late afternoons. "Here I put in his meditation time three to four months in advance. He works a lot, mostly twelve to fourteen hours a day. He is always very healthy and full of energy and he knows how valuable his meditation is for that. And that's why I have the assignment to support him in that, so he can meditate regularly."

It didn't take long for the Secretary of State to invite me into his office. Over a cup of tea, we renewed our friendship and talked about his personal experiences in meditation as well as about the state of the TM Movement in Kenya.

Hot Line to Africa

From Nairobi, I flew one hour further to Tanzania, Kenya's the southern neighboring country. When I arrived at the airport in Dar Es Salaam, I had no idea where or how I could get a hold of Ambassador Alatanga, to whom I had to give the letter for the President. So, at random, I asked the taxi driver at the airport, "Please take me to the best hotel around!"

A little later, I checked into the Kilimanjaro Hotel, beautifully situated at the Indian Ocean and close to the government and embassy district.

I had just received the key to my room at the counter, when I turned to go, and who came towards me straight through the lobby? He hesitated only briefly, and then his noble face brightened with a radiant smile, "Lothar, is that really, you? Lothar, what are you doing here?"

Before me stood the Tanzanian Ambassador, Mr. Alatanga, and my heart immediately opened to him as it always had. I could hardly believe it. I had just arrived and already our paths crossed exactly here, in this minute, as if guided by an invisible hand.

"Maharishi sent me here to meet with you!"

"Maharishi sent you to meet with *me*? More amazement and more joyfulness were not possible for a human face to express.

I felt the huge gratitude that he still had for Maharishi and how honored he felt that Maharishi had thought of him.

"Yes, I'm supposed to give you a letter for the President."

"And what does it say?"

I had no idea; I was as clueless as he was. He accompanied me to my room so we could open the envelope together. In front of my door, we both were amazed once more. "Lothar, this can't be possible, my room is right next to yours—if that isn't some coincidence!"

There really did seem to be a lucky star guiding this undertaking. Once in the room, we leaned over the content of this letter in silent togetherness. Maharishi offered the president a chance to create heaven on earth for Tanzania and described briefly the program he'd developed to overcome poverty in the land. Mr. Alatanga had to take a deep breath. "That sounds promising. But let me first win over his advisers for supporting this before we go to the President!"

This was the beginning of all the "coincidences" that I'd be experiencing in Tanzania. Even back in Germany, Maharishi had told me, "Your assignment is to deliver the letter. After that, just stay in your hotel room, do your meditation program, and wait to see what happens!"

The next miracle did not make me wait long. On the second evening, I stood under a clear, starry sky at the hotel pool in a short line for the buffet and exchanged a little relaxed small talk with the African standing next to me. And imagine this—he turned out to be the Minister of Health. After a few words, he spontaneously asked me to join him at his table. A laidback conversation ensued, and, in a few sentences, I summarized the possible improvements in public health through the implementation of the TM programs and Maharishi Ayurveda. Interested, he invited me to his home for the next evening, so that there, in the small circle of his most important colleagues and friends, I could present everything in detail. My presentation was met with positive resonance among these experts, and with this a lot more gained momentum. As in years before in Kenya, one person passed me on to the next. In no time, I had my hands full. Daily, I had three to four explicit appointments with the most diverse politicians and academicians in their respective departments to inform them about our programs and their potential in the improvement of problems in the areas of responsibility in their ministries. All this unfolded almost on its own, without my having to do the slightest thing. I only had to follow the course of things calmly and let everything develop on its own.

Maharishi's evolutionary idea for Tanzania consisted of winning over foreign companies to lend their machines to Africans. The Tanzanians could then earn money with these and over time pay them off little-by-little until they finally owned them. In this way, they'd free themselves from the bondage of poverty, use the riches of their own land, and become self-sufficient. This concept, too, was to help people to become free and develop their own spiritual potential. But Maharishi was clear that people who lived in undignified circumstances in poverty and had to fight every day for their daily bread, would naturally have to first be satisfied and have their basic needs met for a decent meal, a roof over their heads, clothes on their backs, and a good education before seeking something higher.

After a short time and with the support of nature, as well as the assistance of Mr. Alatanga, many doors opened—and arrangements were made for me to speak to the city council of Dar Es Salaam.

Every night between two and three a.m., Maharishi called me personally in my hotel room. Most of the time, I'd been asleep for one or two short hours by then. In detail, I'd tell him what had happened that day, which politicians and decision-makers I'd met, and what the plans for the next day would be. As soon as I'd mentioned the name of anyone to him, he seemed to immediately know everything about him, his interests, as well as his weaknesses. He was the conductor who told me with whom I should meet on the following day and what I should say to that person. Almost daily, there were some things that initially seemed impossible to me—he broke my boundaries every day. Despite this, I was on fire with unbridled enthusiasm about the idea of giving the people of Africa their independence back, and I was also so filled with the boundless love, knowledge, and vision of my Master that I fully implemented all he told me to do.

In front of the assembled city council, I announced full of enthusiasm, "Maharishi wants Tanzania to be the first country in Africa that will create heaven on earth and show how a poor country could generate wealth from within itself." "Heaven on Earth"—that was one of Maharishi's favorite concepts in those days, with which he outlined the vision of the future that he saw coming for the world: peace, health, prosperity, and a higher state of consciousness for all its inhabitants. Sometimes, laughing, he summarized it with a play on words that he loved doing so much: "All good every-where and non-good nowhere."

I continued, "He is asking you to name three wishes that you want to see fulfilled for this purpose first."

A lively discussion rose from this. The parliamentarians had a hard time uniting about which economic sectors were most important to them for this advancement. That is why, in the following days and weeks, I was chauffeured in planes or company vehicles across the land so that, all together, we could gauge the successes of the most promising projects.

We'd been driving several hours through the seemingly endless sugar cane plantations; the straight, tall, green stalks of sugar cane stood on both sides of the road. Finally we reached the Sugar Development Company, the biggest sugar factory in Tanzania. The general manager, Mr. Sentwali* was an impressive, honest man with a methodical mind. When, that night I described his positive characteristics to Maharishi, he agreed with me completely and was glad to hear that Mr. Sentwali had already done an estimated profitability calculation for our project. Two days and nights, I spent in the guest house of the sugar factory and worked out the details of an expansion of sugar production with the general manager. One of the biggest problems of production was that most of the partially outdated machines were nonfunctional, simply because replacement parts could no longer be obtained. Subsequently, John, one of Maharishi's secretaries in Vlodrop, made every effort to find the needed replacement parts somewhere in the world. After a few days of intensive telephone research, he succeeded.

In the ruby mines of Tanzania, a similarly sad picture greeted me. Tanzania has the second-largest deposits of quality rubies in the world. But mining these precious stones with outdated machines made this crucially important business for an impoverished state so difficult that it could not bring in the profits that would have been possible under better circumstances.

With the project to fight poverty that Maharishi had created, his major focus was on the economic aspects. Transcendental Meditation was of secondary importance. Many decision makers I dealt with felt like highly evolved souls to me, and I admired them in their work. I valued their competence as much as their cordiality and I loved working with them. But also among them, I did see a handful of crooks who knew how to camouflage themselves. But I was such a thoroughbred TM teacher that here and there our meditation program was mentioned. I especially and naturally wanted to impart the blessings of meditation to those who'd become dear to my heart. When I told Maharishi about this, mentioning also that I'd already initiated some high-ranking representatives of the country into TM, Maharishi said to my great amazement: "Your time is too precious to teach meditation now. I'll send a couple of TM teachers who can initiate those interested!"

His remark stunned me. Didn't Maharishi give us to understand that there was no higher calling than to teach the ability to transcend? More than once he'd said, "The time of a TM teacher is more valuable than the time of a head of state because not even the angels in heaven have the ability to guide a human being on the path to transcendence."

But here he gave me a different focal point. And, indeed, I was so engaged a little later that I wouldn't have had any time for further basic TM courses.

Whenever a project had been taken up, had been thought through together, and the consensus aimed at had been reached, the respective directors asked me to compose a brief about the results of our discussions. More and more frequently, I dictated to the ladies of the secretarial services on the ground floor of the Hotel Kilimanjaro the respective agreements, suggestions, and offers. Busily, they pecked on their typewriters, made copies, stapled the documents together, and sent them by mail. I was most certainly their best customer during that time because I gave those four ladies so much work that they were busy for many hours per day with just this one project. I read the proposals to Maharishi during the night, and after a few days, he commented, "That's really excellent! Your standards are so good that in the future you no longer have to read the proposals to me!"

A deep feeling of bliss flowed through me. It was infinitely beautiful to be able to serve Maharishi directly and to feel his satisfaction with me. Once again, I felt a gigantic blessing rest on me.

If you had the chance to work with Maharishi, you had to know that, during a conversation, he often made long pauses. With the first phone conversation here in Tanzania, I had anxiously assumed that the connection had been broken and asked many times, "Maharishi, are you still there?"

This happened till I remembered again what Holger had confided in me years earlier: "If you ask Maharishi something and there's a long pause before he answers, then you just have to wait patiently!"

And now I did exactly that. I learned to close my eyes in these periods of silence and sink into the stillness with him. Full of reverence and gratitude, I lingered at his door of silent awareness until he began to speak again. It seemed to me as though Maharishi let the question sink into the Absolute, the condition of unbounded awareness, and observed how it would be answered from the level of this self-referral field. It was as if he realized what backgrounds, cosmic constellations, and karmic entanglements played a role, and how nature would find the optimal approach with the least effort for any situation.

The fascinating thing in our conversations was that when this intimacy, this connectedness to silence came about, there were then phases in which I no longer had to ask my questions out loud. They only went through me as faint ideas, and Maharishi answered my most subtle mental impulses. After the phase of silence, when Maharishi began to speak again, I would write down the points he would mention word-for-word, so that, later, I wouldn't miss anything. Maharishi's recommendations were so rich in detail that, in just a few weeks, they filled three thick ring binders.

It was always great to hear the voice of the Master in the middle of the night and to take his instructions and feel his loving attention for a half or a whole hour. But this also had its price because, after every phone conversation with Maharishi, a part of his energy transferred to me. I was then so exhilarated and full of energy that it mostly took two or three hours to get to sleep again. Sometimes I just didn't go to sleep at all, as I did my yoga asanas, breathing exercises, and morning meditation quite early so I could afterwards begin the activities of the day well-prepared at 9:00 a.m.

After a few days, I got up my courage and told him about my dilemma: "Maharishi, might it be possible for you maybe to call me earlier in the next few nights so I can get more sleep?" Amused, he chuckled into the receiver and agreed to my request.

I found it moving and considerate that he really did call earlier for a few days. But then it once again got to be 2:00 a.m. Don, one of Maharishi's long-term assistants, who most often put through the phone connection for me, whispered softly, "Lothar, please don't ask Maharishi again if he could call you earlier. He enjoys your daily reports a lot and, in the evening, he always says, 'Let's now get the good news from Lothar before we close the day!'"

And so, it stayed the way it was. My nightly sleep in all those weeks was mostly reduced to four or five hours. Despite this, I didn't seem tired, and during the day I had almost boundless energy and drive. I felt uplifted and could feel that the close contact with the consciousness of the Master in the middle of the night carried me on its wings throughout the day.

Coincidences in Tanzania

Maharishi intended the project for fighting poverty in Tanzania to be implemented throughout the land. According to his wishes, several university professors came from India; they were specialists in agriculture and forestry, Vedic agriculture, and soil evaluation. Maharishi's organic Vedic agriculture required higher standards than were required for conventional organic food. Sowing, fertilizing, and harvesting times of the plants are chosen according to precise seasonal influences, as well as the propitious moment chosen with the help of jyotish. Additionally, specially chosen and attuned Vedic sounds are used—from the time of germination of the seed to the growth of the leaves, the blossoms, and the fruits—to enliven the inner intelligence of the plants and thus elevate their nutritional value.

I introduced the professors to the respective ministries. They too drove all over Tanzania and took soil samples from various places to ascertain which plants would flourish best in which soils of the country. They talked shop with the directors of the various departments, exchanged experiences with one another, and matched concepts Maharishi had developed to the conditions of the land.

According to Maharishi's plan, fallow land was to be watered and transformed to fruitful farmland, since a good 80% of the population lived dependent on agriculture, though most were below the poverty level. In addition, Maharishi suggested the development of additional sources of income through enlivening the timber industry, as Tanzania had huge forests. For every tree felled, however, two new ones had to be planted immediately. For all this, functional machinery was needed as well as good infrastructure. The roads were developed adequately only in the coastal areas, but the further you went west, the worse they became. There, dirt roads were the only ones, and they were frequently so flooded during the rainy season that they became equally as impassable as the rail network in the interior, which was in any case only poorly developed. The rural population of Tanzania lived in large part without electricity or drinking water even though the three biggest lakes of Africa lie in Tanzania's territory, and several big rivers traverse the country.

From Vlodrop, Purusha conducted extensive and promising negotiations with representatives of the Caterpillar corporation, which seriously considered delivering road construction and other equipment necessary for completion on a larger scale, and as an advance towards the payment system created by Maharishi. Purusha called milk farms in Argentina to learn which breed of cattle could best live in which climates of Tanzania. The cows would be paid for gradually with the profits of future milk sales, so that, finally, they would belong to the farmers. They could then earn money with their own cows and, at the same time, improve the nutritional state of their families with that milk.

As I had back in Kenya, I now took the people of Tanzania into my heart. I loved the simple people on the street who, with their playfulness and their attitude, displayed an innocent and accepting outlook on life. The emaciated agricultural laborers in the villages moved me, for even these poor souls had a warmth and an innocence that seems mostly lost in the affluent West. But I also saw the poverty and the harshness in the faces of city-dwellers in the slums and was highly motivated to help improve the lives of all.

I was so uplifted by Maharishi's deep consciousness and by the greatness of my assignment, that I was "witnessing," as we called it, when I gave speeches in parliament or in various meetings, meaning at those moments I often experienced an expanded state of consciousness, where my own unbounded consciousness was a silent witness of my actions.

I was surprised myself with what power and conviction new ideas and inputs flowed from me without any contribution from me and with the audacity with which I presented myself to substantially older and more experienced parliamentarians while I, unbounded and imperturbable, rested within in deep inner peace. After learning to meditate in my youth, and especially after learning the TM-Sidhis, I was frequently amazed at the acts of providence of nature. But with Maharishi's constant guidance of my activity here in Tanzania the intensity of my support of nature eclipsed all my previous experiences. It was a feeling of being carried along by a great power, a feeling of invincibility. Things simply worked out in the external world and flowed without friction, while I wasted no time with long deliberation and the removal of unnecessary obstacles. That whole time, I flowed with Maharishi's impulses and was at one with everything that came from him in those intense days.

Meanwhile, almost six unforgettable weeks had passed. Every day things proved true that Maharishi had told me the night before. The projects had already taken very concrete form. On behalf of the politicians, Mr. Alatanga finally advised us to try our concept on almost 500,000 acres, which is about equal to the size of the biggest ranches in Texas, and based upon the success of that project to eradicate poverty, to extend it to the rest of Tanzania. I found this approach most reasonable and Maharishi agreed, after some hesitation.

Of course, during this time I kept in phone contact with my family in Germany and learned that Karin was gradually feeling exhausted back home. She nursed Lilian several times during the night, worked at the clinic during the day, and took care of three feisty kids, doing all that went with it. In addition, Dr. Kupferschmid, the first advisor of the Ministry of Health in East Germany with whom we'd become friends at the WHO event in Geneva, would come to see us in Schledehausen the following weekend. He and his wife wanted to learn TM during this long-planned visit. it was time to go home, at least for a while.

That night, I described this situation to Maharishi, and he didn't hesitate for a minute, "Lothar, you can book your flight back immediately, under one condition. Stay in the country for two more days to establish a company. The whole project has developed enough that it needs a legal operational framework."

The following morning, I prepared everything for that to happen.

During the last few weeks of my stay in Tanzania, the soccer world championship matches had begun and, as a great soccer fan, I had been watching the games in the hotel bar, when time allowed. This evening as well I watched the oversized screen, spellbound with many others and followed the game. During the intermissions, I got into a conversation with a couple of Europeans. One of them introduced himself as the CEO of a famous oil company. In answer to his question, I reported briefly on my project to these gentlemen, including the company we were about to create. The industrial magnate waved me aside with a laugh, "Forget it! What you're planning there is just about impossible! The wheels of progress turn slowly here. When you want to get something done in this country, you'll have to come up with a lot of bribery money. Without that, nothing gets done here. Even big, well-known companies with a lot of influence need at least six months to start a company."

That same night, I reported the unfortunate experiences of the oil magnate to Maharishi. But he remained completely untouched by it: "He's totally right in his descriptions, but you'll be able to do it within two days!" After that, I could hardly sleep from the excitement because I absolutely wanted to go back home, but I also wanted to satisfy Maharishi's assignment.

Early next morning, I guided my steps to the nearby office of the sugar company manager who I'd initiated into TM and with whom I felt connected in a real friendship. "Mr. Sentwali, you have to help me! I absolutely want to go home because my wife is totally exhausted; she's alone with three children and her career demands her time. On top of that, I have a really important date for an initiation that I can't put off. But Maharishi expects me to start a company before I go."

"That really is almost impossible. But I'll do what I can." To his secretary he only said, "I have an unexpected project and I'll be traveling in the next few hours."

And he was out the door with me and on the way to a friend's who was a notary public. I gave him the thirty pages of telefax I'd received overnight from Vlodrop on the subject, as well as the by-laws of the company to be created. He wagged his head, "Well that won't be easy. The biggest problem is getting the necessary permits for starting a company of foreigners from the government's central bank."

Quickly, we went to the office of the head of the Central Bank of Tanzania, with whom Mr. Sentwali obviously also had good connections. There, he praised our project we'd planned in the most glowing terms, and I outlined it more specifically for half an hour. Then the head of the bank asked me, "Please come back in two hours, and then we'll present your endeavor to the heads of the departments." No sooner said than done. Two hours later in the big conference room, the CEO of the Central Bank asked his assembled department heads to fill out the necessary, and lengthy, forms, which, normally—and obviously—is the job of the applicants. The department chiefs called their secretaries to do it, and soon ten or fifteen heads were busily bent over those forms. Another hour later, the head of the Central Bank came back into the room—this time with his secretary in tow—and she put stamp and seal on the filled-out forms.

As a last big step, I had to open an account at a normal bank for the new firm, which required quite an effort for a foreigner. And here, for the first time, the whole amazing endeavor began to stall: the official at the counter would not play along.

Mr. Sentwali's art of persuasion took top form. For the second time, he called in the notary public who, from his side, showed the papers and documentations with their stamps. Soon, even this last hurdle was overcome. And the notary public, who'd never experienced the establishment of a corporation with such breath-taking speed, gave me the final blessings: "I can take all further steps and do the registration with the commercial registry for you tomorrow. Please sign the power of attorney for me that I just now prepared!"

When I did, he smiled, "Well, now you can go home to your family!" We shook hands. Since the founding of the firm was all wrapped up, I invited Mr. Sentwali to dinner. He was most pleased about what we'd accomplished on this exciting day. We hugged as we said our good-byes.

Next morning for the last time, I brought a full dictating machine into the typing room of the Kilimanjaro. Until shortly before my flight, the secretaries typed letters and documents on their machines, which various politicians were waiting for.

Especially in the last two days, I felt as if I was in a movie. Everything just fell into place without friction and like clockwork. Maharishi's big idea to give the people of Tanzania back their dignity in the fight against poverty had taken on concrete form in the last hours. And it had done so as if it was the easiest thing in the world. I was exhilarated to have accomplished everything. Soon I'd come back and experience first-hand how all those minute preparations would take on living form—or so I thought.

This breath-taking tempo pursued me even into the car that was to take me to the airport. While riding in the car, I did the final lecture for the basic TM course for a cabinet minister. Unannounced and taking me by surprise, he'd knocked at my door four days ago at seven o'clock in the morning with flowers, fruits, and a handkerchief and urgently wanted to be initiated by me personally. Well, I'd be the last person who'd say no to a request like that!

If I had even the slightest doubt about Maharishi's spiritual abilities and his access to more subtle levels of consciousness, I would have lost that doubt completely in these last six weeks in Tanzania. Daily, it became clear that his consciousness was all-encompassing. He saw and knew everything. For him there were no boundaries in time or space, and his creativity knew no limits. His focused attention on a project was enough for things to fit together without friction like a puzzle, and it all looked like lucky coincidences. As an immediate participant, I could experience, as never before, what human consciousness is capable of when spirit and heart are evolved enough.

Negotiations in East Germany

Karin and I spent a most relaxing weekend with Dr. Kupfer-schmid and his wife. Mrs. Kupferschmid, also a physician, often accompanied her husband on business trips. When I showed her a picture of Maharishi during the first lecture, she exclaimed with surprise, "That's not possible! The picture of this man has been on my nightstand for years!"

Right away, she explained, "During our travels, my husband and I came past a big hotel in Switzerland, high above Lake Lucerne. Curious, we went into the foyer and looked around. I picked up a brochure and took it along, and there was this picture in it. I thought it was beautiful somehow, and at home, I cut it out, and since then, it's been framed next to my bed."

Her path had led her through Seelisberg and now, many years later, she sat here with her husband to learn exactly this meditation. God's ways are wondrous indeed!

In between times, the four of us sat on our terrace, ate, talked shop, went for walks, joked with one another, suggested we go on a first-name basis, and deepened even more the warm feelings that we'd already had for each other back in Geneva.

On Sunday morning Maharishi had someone call me and ask about our well-being, especially about Dr. Kupfer-schmid. After my brief report, he spontaneously invited the four of us to visit him in Vlodrop. In Vlodrop? I thought Maharishi was in India, where'd been for several years. So, he'd changed his residence during my time in Tanzania.

One and a half hours later, we all sat in the car: Karin,

Lilian, and I were in front in our dark-red BMW, which was getting a bit long in the tooth, and Gerd and Marianne clomped behind us in their small, white Trabi, the legendary car model which was manufactured back then in East Germany and was used by almost all its citizens.

As soon as we arrived in the big, familiar MERU building in Vlodrop, we were sent to Maharishi's suite.

Dr. Geoffrey Clements welcomed us at the door. I introduced him to Dr. Gerd and Dr. Marianne Kupferschmid. He smiled at us, "We all know you're coming. Beaming with happiness, Maharishi told us in the big assembly what great successes you've had in Tanzania. And how glad he is that you've brought along the former First Advisor of the Ministry of Health of East Germany and that you've initiated him and his wife into TM."

What a warm welcome! Geoffrey showed us the way into the small reception room with its off-white shimmering wall paper and the soft wool carpet of the same color. In front of Maharishi's sofa, over which, as always, a white silk cloth had been draped, there stood about ten or fifteen gold upholstered armchairs with softly curved arm rests of light wood; two or three people were already sitting there. We were about to sit down when Maharishi came into the room. And now something happened that I've experienced only this one time in my life. Maharishi went towards Dr. Kupferschmidt with his hand extended, took it and held it while beaming over his whole face: "It's great that you have come at last! I've been expecting for you for a long time! And then, Dr. Tony Nader has also told me all about you."

What a greeting! We sat down and, as if they were old friends, Maharishi gave a short introduction to Maharishi

Ayurveda to the couple and emphasized for them the deeper aspects of this holistic healthcare system. "Ayurveda understands and treats all aspects of life from their basis. From the subtle, unmanifest, yet unexpressed levels within consciousness, in which all unmanifest differences reside and from which all expressed, manifest, material aspects of body and soul emerge."

He explained further with an example that he'd liked using again and again, "The all-penetrating consciousness is like a seed, a tiny seed, which contains the building plan for the adult tree within itself and from which everything unfolds: first a small sprout, then the stem, the leaves, the blossoms, and the fruits, until, finally, it becomes a gigantic tree. The tiny, small seed contains all that, everything emerges from it. Exactly in this way, the unified field is the actual source of creation from which everything unfolds sequentially. Ayurveda thus begins with the root of all differences in the realm of pure consciousness. And the aim of Ayurveda is to enable the experience of bliss—and on that level, there are no illnesses."[(56)]

As he spoke, and we, attentive and relaxed, listened to his words, I saw a bright, white light around his person, a sight I'd become very familiar with in the past years. Silver white, it shone around his whole body—I was always deeply moved when I saw this, and it happened mostly in an atmosphere of gentle silence, as today.

Shortly afterwards, Maharishi sent us to rest at the hotel.

The day after, we went to Maharishi's suite as per our appointment. They had two rooms for official purposes: a small reception room, where we were the day before, as well as a bright, big lecture hall for about a hundred people; Maharishi's sofa stood a bit elevated on a platform, and in front of that there were comfortable upholstered chairs with arm rests. A little separate from that, there was his bedroom, a room for Brahmachari Nandkishore, and another one for his cook. More than that, Maharishi did not need—he not only knew no free time, but also no luxury or personal wealth. He lived only for his great mission.

When we came in, the big lecture hall was already packed. We were shown to the front row and, after a brief opening speech, Maharishi asked his new guest, "Do you feel you'd like to work for the dissemination of Maharishi Ayurveda?"

And Dr. Kupferschmid, smiling and urbane, "I've already thought about that because I've met so many nice doctors from your ranks, already in Geneva at the WHO. I would like to know more about Maharishi Ayurveda and would like to organize lectures for physicians in Berlin and in East Germany to motivate doctors to get trained in Maharishi Ayurveda."

Maharishi nodded, visibly impressed.

Dr. Kupferschmid continued enthusiastically, "I'd very much like to help, so that a Maharishi Ayurveda clinic can be created in East Germany. Since the opening of the German border, the government health spas are being privatized. I think that this is an ideal point in time to acquire a suitable property. If you could send someone who can make such decisions, I would be available for contacts."

Maharishi went within himself for a few seconds, then looked at Dr. Kupferschmid and said, smiling, "I'll send Lothar. He accomplishes things quickly!"

When the meeting was finished, Maharishi wanted to speak to me alone. And before I knew it, cosmic intelligence, who spoke through the Master, gave my life a completely unexpected turn. "Lothar, I'd like for you to stay with me now, just to be with me and to implement projects that I'll give you. Your wife can come on weekends with the kids, or whenever she has time." I was speechless. How much I'd wished for exactly this for so many, many years!"

While Dr. Kupferschmid prepared my tour through the East German provinces, Maharishi allowed me to partake of just about all his meetings and events in his suite. Never yet had I experienced so up close and personal and been witness to how many projects Maharishi worked on day and night and in how many countries in this world he guided and inspired people at the same time, while also holding any number of lectures for big groups here in Vlodrop.

As Dr. Kupferschmid knew most of the mayors and government representatives personally through his long years of professional activity, he soon had appointments for me all wrapped up. For almost two weeks I drove through the countryside of East Germany and inspected various houses and spa arrangements. On average, I sat in my car for twelve hours per day; I wanted to complete the assignment for Maharishi as well and as quickly as possible.

Dr. Kupferschmid had done a good job. First, I inspected Bad Heiligendamm, rich in tradition, on the coast of the Baltic Sea where spas were lined up like pearls on a string right next to one another at the beach and patients could look out on the rolling waters. The manager led me through the various and somewhat run-down houses of the spa facilities. The spa physicians showed me their rooms for bathing, explained their procedures, and I was impressed by their winsome friendliness. The people in West Germany seemed to be under constant stress and pressure, and money was the most important thing in life; many of them were hypercritical and often grumpy. In contrast, the people here in the East, who'd for decades had to make do with a lot less, were open, authentic, and warm-hearted, which made a positive impression on me.

I went on to Bad Saarow, the spa at Scharmützel Lake, and to many small and big spas across various East German provinces where I was welcomed warmly. I inspected one building after another and looked at a lot of different spa businesses. Everywhere, I saw the same picture: Everyone in all those establishments was most eager to sell. After there'd been many shortages under the East German government for years, managers were hopeful for crowds of investors from the West promising to improve conditions.

In between appointments, I kept Maharishi up to date about what amounted to big operations. For every call, I stood in a long line in front of a telephone booth and waited patiently for my turn. If the conversation sometimes was longer than planned, I ran out of coins and the conversation was cut off. I'd have to organize a new cache of change and dutifully stand in line again. That led to crazy situations in which I sometimes had to rush or even interrupt my revered Master: "Maharishi, we don't have a lot more time; I only have a buck!"

Finally, I landed in the corner where the Czech Republic, Bavaria, and Saxony meet in Bad Elster, a dreamy place with big parks and spa facilities. Here I had a date with Mr. Altmeier*, who had gotten back a big area with several building complexes after his property had been dispossessed by the East German government. In his establishments, officials of the Russian military had come for decades to recuperate and for healing treatments. When Mr. Altmeier led me through the facilities, the last few houses were being emptied. During the long tour, I told him about Maharishi's programs and his techniques for bringing about peace, and he immediately understood the scope of what we were offering. He was so impressed that he wanted to rent out the whole establishment for a very cheap rate per month and, on top of that, offered from his side to let the TM Movement take possession of it after twenty years. Now that ownership had been given back to him, he was pleased to do something so positive with it. When I reported all this to Dr. Kupferschmid that evening, he was amazed at this one-time offer.

On that same evening, I told Maharishi about it. He liked the project not only because of the advantageous financial terms, but, above all, because he'd now and then played with the idea of building a coherence-creating group at this border triangle, a group which would assure peace for Europe. I offered to take a few pictures of the facility and send them to him. But he declined, "You don't have to send me a picture; I know how things look there."

Well, what a surprise that was! Maharishi just about never spoke directly about his spiritual abilities. He never sought attention. On the contrary, he gave everyone the impression of a normal, simple human being, albeit an especially blissful one. Only when, within the framework of his lectures or explanations about the subtle connections and mechanisms of human consciousness could one not miss the competence and exactitude of all that he described and it became clear that he was speaking from experience.

Now, things moved fast. A few days later Maharishi sent Reinhard and Holger to Bad Elster, and we worked together on the draft of an agreement. When everything was resolved, the two left again. But I spent some nice time with Mr. Altmeier, before my faithful, dark-red friend took me back to Vlodrop over the terrible roads of East Germany.

Workgroup with the Master

In Vlodrop, Maharishi had a new assignment for me: "Find three German TM teachers who will come here to implement projects with you."

After a few phone conversations, I'd found them. Alois and the two Hartmuts were happy to come to Vlodrop and work near Maharishi.

A week later, another CDP course would begin with me as its leader. When I was getting ready to drive off, there was suddenly the message: "Maharishi wants to talk to you."

I double-timed it to his suite, since I also had to catch my flight. In the small reception room, Maharishi greeted me with the words, "Lothar, show me what you are actually teaching in these courses."

With complete peace of mind, he began to examine the charts that showed the scientific studies of our presentation kit. We were proud of our professional material that we had developed so thoughtfully. Maharishi, on the other hand, thought our plain color scheme in greys and pale blue needed some improvement, "Add a few gold lines here and there."

Hartmut dutifully got a ruler and a gold pen and tried to rescue what could be salvaged. Underneath the printed headlines, he drew proper golden lines. "Yes, that looks a little better…"

But Maharishi was somehow still not satisfied, "I think we should work over this course one more time and meet once again tomorrow." And I missed my flight.

A new day, a new try. This time I asked Brahmachari Nandkishore, who'd gotten that course going, to help. At the appointed time, we sat in the reception room of Maharishi's suite. Hopefully, things would move quickly today; after all, I had to get to the Düsseldorf airport on time. Maharishi, meanwhile, with complete peace of mind, discussed their projects with other people in the room. Slowly, but surely, Nandkishore became restless, and interrupted him, "Maharishi Lothar has to go."

Now, Maharishi had me explain the course structure and all its content to him. With conviction, I reported on the system, the sales techniques, and our thought-through pre-sentations. But his expression showed clearly that he didn't think too much of it: "I think we should thoroughly rework the course and for that we need more time."

Now Nandkishore got into it: "Maharishi, Lothar has given this course many times. It really is professional and participants have praised it in glowing terms."

Maharishi remained unmoved: "Can we cancel the course?"

Again please?

Nandkishore explained, "Maharishi, that won't work. The course has been advertised for a long time; 50 people have registered and they're already in Seelisberg."

Unimpressed, Maharishi began a discussion about whether it was even necessary to offer such courses for TM teachers. After some lengthy back and forth, Nandkishore finally succeeded in convincing him that, at least, this course had to be taught, since participants had come from all over Europe. So, it would go forward. I was relieved.

Meanwhile, I nervously sneaked a look at my wrist-watch a couple of times—if we didn't finish soon, I'd miss my second flight. But Maharishi still had all the time in the world, and he now brought up his second objection: "Lothar, you better stay here; you have more important assignments here. Someone else can lead that course."

Bravely, Nandkishore kept objecting: "That's not possible, Maharishi, we announced Lothar as the course leader. In any case, the second course leader is a total newbie. He has never yet taught this course. Really, Lothar has to go." Slowly but surely, I started sitting on a hot stove. Time passed, and now, by the time I'd get there—experienced or not—the TM teacher Jens, a professional economist, would be standing in front of an international course with participants from ten countries. Again, there was a prolonged pro and con, so long that I missed the second flight also—and, finally, Maharishi let me go.

I reached Seelisberg two days after the beginning of the course. Jens had done his thing well, nobody was upset about my being late, and it ended up to be a wonderful course, as always.

Here, too, the contact with Maharishi was not broken off. Per telephone, he asked about the progress in Bad Elster. When I wanted to discuss Tanzania with him, however, he only said, "We'll discuss that later."

At the end of the CDP course, Maharishi called the whole group and asked the participating CEOs and TM teachers for their evaluation.

"Maharishi, this course was the best course for us after TM teacher training."

"It's great that it includes practical sales techniques."

"The German material we have access to is really professional and should be translated into other languages. We joyfully anticipate exporting this."

Maharishi congratulated all for their participation in this course and encouraged them to introduce these new programs to many businesses in their respective countries. He closed with the words, "Lothar has trained soldiers, but didn't give them any bullets. He'll now come back to me in Vlodrop and work with me intensively for eight days to create new materials for presentations. But don't wait for it. Start working with what you have. Jai Guru Dev."

When I was picked up at the Düsseldorf airport, the driver conveyed to me: "In Vlodrop, you're to go directly to the suite and start with the work."

On that same day, Maharishi put together a work group. Day after day, we met in the big assembly hall: a married couple of professors from Maharishi International University, the British and Dutch national leaders, as well as a successful Dutch businessman, and our troop consisting of the two Hartmuts, Alois and me. Maharishi had his full attention on us. He wanted us to meet from 9:00 a.m. till late in the evenings, breaking only for meals and our meditation program.

Every morning, we did our two-hour yoga and meditation program. One day we had decided among ourselves to sleep somewhat late after we'd met with Maharishi till 3:00 a.m. Today, we'd just begin a little later. But, as I was getting ready in a relaxed way in the morning, someone knocked at my door just a couple of minutes after nine, and Maharishi's cook yelled, "Lothar, where are you guys, Maharishi is already asking for you!"

Nothing remained hidden from the Master.

In no time at all, I notified the others, and a few minutes later, we were all on the spot. Now and again, Maharishi just came ambling into our workroom without being announced and without one of his secretaries, and he looked at what we were doing and then left again. I'd experienced Maharishi this intimately and close only in the seventies when I was the manager in his hotel.

We discussed, formulated, and then, in the evening, often presented Maharishi with our progress. He frequently went into the smallest details. He could chop away at every single word, change around sentences, or substitute words until he felt it was right. He trained us to pay attention to every nuance when we spoke with course participants about the highest Vedic knowledge, or when we were creating texts about it. And by the way, his logic and his clarity left their traces in our thinking. Word plays, flashes of genius, boundless humor; often, we laughed heartily and long without impairing our efficiency in the slightest.

Maharishi's energy was boundless. He rested only for a few hours in the very early morning. Once, he had a small workgroup read him a text in his suite at three in the morning. All were highly attentive; there was an intimate and homey atmosphere in the room. Maharishi, whom I'd always seen sitting on his sofa wide awake or speaking, made himself comfortable that night on his sofa in a relaxed, almost horizontal position, and at some point, our little group heard faint snoring sounds. So as not to disturb the sleep of the Master, the speaker first lowered his voice and then fell completely silent. Maharishi's voice came softly from the sofa, "You can go ahead and keep reading."

His body was sleeping, but his mind was wide awake. He was once asked at a press conference if it was true that he only needed two hours of sleep. He answered mischievously: "Yes, that's true, but nobody except me knows what I'm doing in those two hours."

In all that time, Maharishi never said another word about Tanzania. Instead, he taxed me with the most diverse projects and again and again gave me other tasks.

Every time, when I wanted to direct the conversation to Tanzania in his presence, he suddenly changed the subject or turned to other people. It went that way for weeks. Karin reported to me now and again that somebody from Tanzania had called our house, wanting to talk to me. One or two ministers had called, as well as Mr. Sentwali, the CEO of the sugar factory whom I'd liked so much. My internal pressure increased. How, in heaven's name, should I act in view of all the promises made? Things could not keep going like this. But despite all tries I just couldn't get through to Maharishi on this subject.

Commuter Between Two Worlds

My family life was restricted to phone conversations and weekends during that time. Every fourteen days, I drove home and enjoyed my time as the father of the family. Anyone who worked in Maharishi's immediate vicinity focused on him and his projects day and night. I could not just simply vanish every other weekend without asking the Master.

"Maharishi, I'd like drive home on weekends that Karin can't come here. She needs my support with the kids."

He agreed. But I felt that he didn't exactly like it. "But check in with me every Saturday before you drive home and let me know when you'll be back."

And I did.

From then on, I sat in the small reception room every other Saturday at nine in the morning, at a time when Maharishi normally was not available for people. I received his parting words on the intercom and went to his suite first thing on Monday to complete the ritual, "Maharishi, I'm back."

These trips to my family were a big exception because they meant there would be an interruption in my focus and, with that, a disruption in the frictionless flow of activity around Maharishi where all threads came together. And though he surveyed all this with a scope I could only guess at, the Master let me have my way out of love even if he was a bit reluctant. Every time, I was conflicted because of this, but went anyway, because on the other side, I felt my responsibility to Karin and the children.

The weekends in between, which the big kids spent with their father, Karin and Lilian came to visit me. We spent the night in a hotel in the neighborhood and both my girls could be with me in Maharishi's suite during the day when our CDP workgroup met. As always, Lilian was most quiet and peaceful. She could spend hours on our laps or sitting on the floor playing with her fingers or small toys, schmoozing with us, or taking a little nap. The three of us loved these quiet days in which my beloved could recover from the strenuous week with patients and children while, at the same time, getting some insight into my world and getting to know my friends more closely.

Now and again, we could be present at special meetings to which Maharishi invited mostly larger groups for discussion of various themes in the conference room of his suite. It was always something special for me to be close to Maharishi. This time, however, it was almost even more beautiful and heart-felt because I could now share it with my wife and our sweet little daughter.

When one afternoon the bulk of the visitors had left the room, Joachim, a Purusha who I knew well from back in the old days, hauled the three of us to the front so I could introduce my wife and the baby to Maharishi. Lilian was approximately six months old and had just learned to sit. Quickly, Joachim put a light pink rose into my hand for her and her little stubby fingers immediately closed around the stem that had had its thorns removed. I went to the front and with my arms extended held our proper little daughter so she could give him the rose. This, however, was not to her liking. Quite the contrary! Maharishi also held a long-stemmed rose in his hand and, before we could react, our little daughter had energetically grabbed this second tempting gloriousness with her free hand—and did not want to let go of either one.

Everyone shared in Maharishi's pleasure when, smiling, he commented on this funny scene, "The fullness of live comes to another fullness" – an allusion to a Vedic quote from the Upanishads, which Maharishi loved a lot.

What a blessing for our little daughter! With an inviting gesture, Maharishi indicated the row of chairs just in front of him and asked us to sit. We chatted freely for a little while. He was benevolent like a fatherly friend, and I had the wonderful feeling that my wife was being welcomed into my family for the second time, this time into the big family in the center of this world-wide movement of which we both were a part.

As lovely these weekends together were, my life in Vlodrop during the week was quite a burden for Karin, which she accepted without complaint to make this precious time with Maharishi possible for me. But one thing did rankle her: "You know, it's fine with me that I have to do everything here by myself; I do it gladly. But I don't think it's right that on top of it I have to take care of the five of us financially; that does not feel right to me. I think you should ask Maharishi to have the organization pay you for your efforts." What nerve!

I knew that the many, many volunteer co-workers who were around Maharishi in Vlodrop got their housing and food free and that they got some small pocket money. Due to financial considerations, it wouldn't have been possible any other way; the money for salaries simply wasn't there. What held even more weight for me was that, in the Vedic tradition, the disciples lived with the master, and during or at the end of their training, they contributed to his livelihood. On the one hand, they did this as an expression of their gratitude and veneration, and on the other, to free him from worldly commitments so that he could dedicate himself completely to his spiritual tasks. I felt clearly that this harmonizing give-and-take in both directions was a universal law. The disciple submits to the master with devotion and a readiness to serve and, in turn, receives knowledge and an optimal development of his personality and with this, he is more richly rewarded than he would be with the highest salary. For all of us, it was an honor just to be near Maharishi and to help him with his great task. Of course, the costs of activities such as those in Tanzania or Kenya, for example, were borne by the Movement, but a salary? Completely absurd! Despite this I could understand Karin's point; she was not familiar with the customs around the spiritual Master. "Ok, I'll give it my best. I promise that I'll try to ask Maharishi about that."

But I did not feel good about it, and before my eyes, as if by themselves, the scenes in which I so often and fruitlessly had tried to speak to my Master about Tanzania came back to me....

I didn't have much hope, but, just in case, Karin and I agreed on an amount that we both thought equitable.

As already so often, Reinhard helped me. A few days later he arranged for a talk in a small group and, courageously, I brought up my wife's concern and her conclusive arguments. And what did my Master say? "But why does your wife need money when she has a rich mother?"

I could hardly believe my ears. Maharishi really did know everything. We had told nobody, really nobody, about this well-guarded secret. Even I only found out about this after I'd been with Karin for a long time. Truthfully, I answered, "Yes, that's true, Maharishi, but that money belongs to her mother. Right now, we are getting none of it."

"What's the minimum amount that you need?" asked

Maharishi, as if this were the most normal thing in the world.

I told my Master, who often was so lovingly interested in the smallest things, our personal costs of living and expenses and, a short time later, I got confirmation for the exact amount Karin had imagined. I got it in the whole time, month for month, for as long as I remained in Vlodrop.

For me it was an incomprehensible cosmic miracle, but I accepted it gratefully to create balance in my small family.

Thunder and Lightning

Back then, Maharishi now and again invited the European Ayurveda doctors to a conference in Vlodrop. Sometimes, he attended a few meetings himself. At the end of a meeting, I stood at the exit of the convention hall to say good-bye to Maharishi with the Indian greeting of folded hands, as did everyone else. When he got to where I stood, he unexpectedly stopped, looked into my eyes and said completely out of context, "Whenever the time comes and legal problems come your way in Germany for freely spreading Maharishi Ayurveda, then get in touch with me personally and directly because the law is very intelligent, and it will take my intelligence to deal with it."

He nodded towards me and immediately kept walking. His words however, with which I could do nothing in this moment, went deep into my heart.

A few weeks later, Karin, together with Dr. Hans Schäffler, led a one-week advanced training course in Maharishi Ayurveda for physicians in Schledehausen. These courses were designed coherently by Dr. Janssen and Dr. Jensen with Maharishi's personal guidance so that all Maharishi physicians world-wide could have access to the same standardized knowledge at the highest level. The two married physicians, the Drs. Kupferschmid, were participants, while I had fun with the kids at home on the last weekend. The course leaders, as well as majority of the participants, found the knowledge to be very good but found the transmission via video-taped lectures by physicians and scientists in English with simultaneous translation to be quite exhausting.

Gerd Kupferschmid wanted to lead these courses in East Germany for the foreseeable future and on a Sunday at the end of the course we spontaneously discussed some suggestions for improvements. All of us found these seminars for the dissemination of Maharishi Ayurveda to be so important that I spontaneously called Vlodrop to pass along these ideas. And just as spontaneously, Maharishi invited the four of us to a discussion with him. Hans was immediately ready to take over Karin's patients on Monday. In a countermove, he asked her to absolutely support the idea that they, in future, could lead a major part of the video-taped lectures themselves in German to make the advanced training livelier.

Once arrived at the suite, we felt the atmosphere of gently vibrating energy, and indeed even the holiness that always filled Maharishi's rooms. His closest co-workers, who often came and went, worshipped him. The more closely people knew Maharishi, the more gratitude and reverence emerged. The purer a person's heart became, the more they could perceive and value his unbounded greatness and wisdom. But in the lively discussion with Maharishi, when you put all your attention on a specific subject, you often forgot this or felt it only faintly in the background.

We discussed various possibilities to better present the contents of the advanced training courses for physicians. Especially Dr. Kupferschmid, who'd trained doctors worldwide in other fields, suggested several good ideas in his lively way. Karin was not to be outdone: "Maharishi, there are too many video tapes in this course, could we reduce them and replace those left out with lectures by the physicians leading the course?"

Maharishi turned to Dr. Janssen, who was part of the meeting. "How many hours per day are they? Is it really that many?"

Dr. Janssen looked over the hourly schedules for the courses he'd brought along, "Approximately five hours of a total of eight to nine hours' seminar time per day."

Maharishi thought that was fine and wanted to keep it that way.

But Karin was not satisfied, "But Maharishi, the videos all have to be introduced, and then questions need to be answered. So, every course day is already filled up with the videos. And Dr. Schäffler and I can present this knowledge directly in German."

Karin indulged her tendency to exaggerate slightly. Maharishi, however, responded to her argument perceptively. "I have to think for the whole world and I can't make any exceptions for exceptionally bright doctors. We need a standard for the whole world."

Karin, with the promise she'd made to Hans breathing down her neck, didn't let go just yet, though I, trying to hold her back, pulled at her sleeve. "I understand that, but in our case, can't we omit a few videos and replace them?"

Only when Maharishi declined for the third time did she give up.

A few weeks later, there was another meeting with physicians and Maharishi. Karin had stayed at home because of the children. Shortly before we all went into the suite, Hans crossed my path: "Well, too bad that Karin didn't succeed; in any case, I'm going to raise this subject myself today."

"Naw, Hans, I don't recommend this. Karin really tried,

but Maharishi was clear in his denial. I tell you, this makes no sense." But this did not convince Hans.

The physicians had sat down in the big lecture hall and were conversing quietly; Maharishi came in. All stood and were silent. For most of the doctors this was a special and exceptionally rare chance to experience Maharishi so close. Some of them reported their successes with healings. Then it went into expanding Maharishi Ayurveda and about the training of new doctors. Now, Hans' little moment had come. His hand was already up, and I was sure he'd now raise his point. Maharishi, however, shortly went within himself so Hans could not say anything. Suddenly Maharishi looked into my eyes sternly and, without any warning, he began to scold, "This girl thinks she knows better than I do!"

Oh, God, he meant my wife! Obviously, he'd understood that Hans, at this precise moment, wanted to bring up this topic and he nipped it in the bud. For a whole minute, he raked Karin over the coals. I'd never seen him this ticked off. I was totally shocked and paralyzed. Maharishi's gentleness and sweetness were often overwhelming, but so was the power of his anger in this moment. My heart was wide open for Maharishi. For me he was the greatest and the holiest person I knew; I worshipped him beyond measure. This tirade, that was coming down on me, was so intense that it cut me straight through the heart. In shock, I held my breath. Afterwards, I sat petrified, and it was deadly silent in the room. You couldn't hear a peep from Hans; his question had answered itself—once and for all. Then Maharishi kept going, cheerfully and on task, as if this incident had never happened.

I, on the other hand was so torn up with the whole thing that, even after the meeting, I was still sitting in my chair as if struck by lightning.

"Lothar, don't take it so hard; Maharishi only does this with disciples who are dear to his heart!" The compassionate voice of Maria* penetrated my ear. "Well" I only succeeded with a crooked smile, "I don't know…."

Her husband endorsed her, "That's really true; you have to understand that Maharishi has lifted a lot of karma off Karin and you."

In my state of shock, I'd never have thought of this. For many meditators in Maharishi's immediate surroundings, the teaching about karma and rebirth was a crystal-clear thing because, for a few, after years of meditation, some of the veils in their consciousness had lifted a little and had revealed memories of past lives. And others knew about positive karma, about lucky circumstances that could fall into your lap because some time ago you'd done something good that now comes back to you. The converse of this is negative karma that delivers an explanation for something that went totally wrong in this life, in that you are supposed to grow when you feel something personally that you've done to someone else in the past. My friends had obviously experienced something like that before and had read about it in the scriptures: the scolding of a master takes negative karma off the disciple.

I could only hope that this was true; but one thing was clear: Whatever the case, it must have been some powerfully evil karma—when measured by the severity of Maharishi's chastisement.

Yet More Projects

Maharishi regularly checked with me about the progress of the agreements to rent the spa at the corner where the Czech Republic, Bavaria and Saxony meet in Bad Elster. I often spoke on the phone with Mr. Altmeier. He discussed various details with his attorney, and finally I could convey the happy message, "Maharishi, the contracts are ready for signing. You can send Reinhard to Bad Elster to counter-sign them."

Overjoyed, Maharishi said, "That's very good. Invite the owner to come here. Then we'll sign them on the spot.

Happy, I called Mr. Altmeier who took the offer gladly. "Excellent, I'd love to come, but at the moment I've got my hands full. It would be better if someone from your organization were to come here."

And so, I conveyed messages back and forth. Maharishi wanted Mr. Altmeier to come to Vlodrop; Mr. Altmeier could not make time. The wires were running hot. Maharishi kept asking, and the nice Saxon could not find the time. Maharishis inquiries became increasingly rare; and so did my phone conversations with Mr. Altmeier.

For years, I'd noted peripherally that Maharishi was working with Doug Henning, a famous Canadian magician, as well as with a staff of others to create Veda Land. With a group steadily increasing in size, he developed the concept for an amusement park whose motto would be "Knowledge, Entertainment, and Enlightenment." Several international luminaries of the entertainment industry were involved, the director of special effects for the well-known movie *Superman* among them. By visiting Veda Land, hordes of fascinated people would admire the magic of creation while these attractions would make them aware of the full potential of the human spirit.

Our CDP work group took part of a meeting in the big assembly hall where we followed the development coming from the mouths of experts. There were dozens of technologies that were already fully developed. A special attraction would be a building that floated in the air above a lake, a building that the amazed visitors could enter! Two helicopters flying in parallel formation and in plain view for all would pull a rope stretched between them under the building. Nobody would know how the heavy building could stay in the air—it was a magic trick together with an aha-effect for the visitors—that would make them aware that there are things between heaven and earth that are outside the normal sense perception. In another attraction, a moving, life-sized figure of Dr. Triguna would read the pulse of visitors and would tell them something about their constitution and their characteristics in his voice. In a planetarium people would enter their birth data into a display, and just like magic, the exact planetary and star constellation at the time of their birth would appear on the domed ceiling while a computerized voice would name their character traits and would reveal future events of their lives.

After many years of intense groundwork, everything seemed almost finished: the design and the exact drawings for the various attractions, the implementation of the requirements of the fire prevention bureau, and a new system in which great numbers of people could get into the park and, once inside, could enjoy the various attractions without any unnecessary waiting. Even the economic calculations for such a huge undertaking were just about done. It could and should now get going. Various people were designated who, in their respective homelands, were to get the ball rolling. And Maharishi had already engaged me: "Lothar can go to Germany and find sites and building contractors for Veda Land."

Once again, I was doing research, along with my other projects—without the Internet it was a time-consuming undertaking back then —and I went for the phone. First off, I called one of the two owners of the biggest entertainment parks of Europe near Cologne. He was on fire to meet the world-famous magician, Doug Henning, and learn more about these well-guarded secrets—so much so that already on the following day, he came to Vlodrop. In Doug Henning's presence, I showed him the pictures of the various attractions and got him excited about the economic potential of such a park, but without, as is customary in this field, revealing too much. He immediately recognized the huge potential for the future of combining entertainment and spirituality.

After that, I invited Germany's biggest building contractors. Five of them showed up expensively dressed and registered in an equally expensive hotel. In much detail, I introduced the project and the following prospect: "Whichever one of you can arrange the financing with the banks gets the contract."

Highly interested in this project worth millions, they asked for the financial plan that several people in Vlodrop were working on at full speed. Some of the contractors stayed in contact after that and asked for the accounts. But Doug always gave the same answer, "We're still working out some details and so that's slowing us down a little."

On another front, the eight days we'd planned for the development of the CDP materials became weeks, and the weeks became months. In ever longer intervals, various CDP course participants called me and asked for the material that had been promised again and again, I had to console them. When, finally, the material that had been developed with much joy, vigor, and intense work was almost done for the TM teachers and the firms, Alois and the two Hartmuts and the others involved got new assignments from Maharishi.

I Get Stewed

Slowly but surely, I was dealing with more and more burning issues. A whole series of projects had begun according to Maharishi's wishes, but somehow it was all up in the air.

The project for the elimination of poverty in Tanzania that I'd begun with huge enthusiasm did not progress, despite many attempts to bring it up again to Maharishi. I could not understand why in the world he had very obviously put a big and promising project, which had already come so far, on ice. But I had no alternative but to accept everything. It weighed me down to have to disappoint the people who were full of enthusiasm to implement Maharishi's plans in their country and who had grown so close to my heart. Despite all this, the stubborn hope remained that my Master would take up this project once again—hopefully soon.

Maharishi did not release the CDP materials that were as good as finished; only t's to be crossed and i's to be dotted. Little by little, it dawned on me that the Master, despite the excellent work the team members, above all the Drs. Susie and Michael Dillbeck, had accomplished, as well as the enormous amount of time and the loving attention that the Master himself had invested in it, the moment for its publication seemed not yet to have come. But I wished that the TM teachers all over the world could soon rely on this excellent material.

The lease-purchase arrangement for the spa to build a big coherence group in Bad Elster had, little by little, fizzled out. Instead, the buildings, together with the magnificent park with its old trees, had gone for several millions to a big West

German funding agency. How could anyone just let go of such an opportunity handed to you on a silver platter? And the thing with Veda Land carried on in the same way.

I had successfully completed these and many smaller projects from my side, as much as I could. But shortly before concrete implementation, things just stalled.

Wherever I looked, all assignments had led me into some double bind. Now and then, I talked to others about that, how difficult it was for me not to be able to bring my projects to a satisfying conclusion. And little by little, I noticed that I was not the only one. I told Don, whom I'd admired since 1975 when he was still Maharishi's personal secretary for his gentleness and balanced nature, about all my troubles. For many years, he'd spent long periods in Maharishi's immediate surroundings. Now he'd listened to me patiently and compassionately before he said, "Lothar, if only you knew what we often have to go through around here!"

Another Purusha friend, who'd also worked closely with Maharishi, consoled me, "You know, Maharishi is a Vedic master. And, as is written in the scriptures, a Vedic master is especially concerned about the enlightenment of his disciples and not about the immediate success of any project. He does a lot only to develop his disciples and others concerned, and break their boundaries to let them grow. A project can be regarded as completed and successful when the Master is satisfied with the development of his disciple. That's the real success."

Another Purusha, knowledgeable in the scriptures said with all good intention: "In the Bhagavad-Gita, it says that you're free only when you're not attached to the fruit of action; just act and leave the success to nature." What a wonderful and wise statement, but even this only helped partially to calm me down.

Despite everything, I was most often extremely happy and grateful to be here. I felt good and protected near Maharishi and the uplifting company of his closest co-workers. Their selfless service and devotion to the great assignment to serve humanity touched me, as did their gentle radiance. I really liked each one of them very much.

One fine day, things finally got going. One of the secretaries called me and, to my great relief, I heard, "Maharishi wants to talk to you."

Thank God! Full of expectation I went up toward the suite in that same moment and sat down on one of the comfortable chairs in the waiting room. Various co-workers of his international organization were already sitting on other chairs. One after the other went in to see him. And I waited. One hour stretched into two...three...four. National leaders who wanted to discuss projects or coordinate them, even a stranger or two whom I'd never seen before, were asked to come in and came back out. I chatted with one or another of them. It was a pleasant, relaxing time. In regular intervals, one of Maharishi's secretaries came by, "Please stay, you'll be seen today."

So, I kept waiting all day. Late at night, I was still sitting there, had absorbed the good atmosphere directly in Maharishi's surroundings, and had completed a long meditation program on my upholstered chair. The last two visitors came out, it was around two in the morning. Then the secretary poked his head out the door and said, "Lothar, please come back tomorrow; it's gotten a little late today."

"When should I be here?"

"Just come back at nine, and you'll be the first."

Slightly lacking in sleep, I took my place again the following morning, when a rather big meeting was being scheduled in Maharishi's suite. Girish, for many years one of Maharishi's closest secretaries, a gentle Indian with huge, benevolent eyes and a long, full beard whispered lovingly: "Lothar, just go in, Maharishi will speak to you afterwards."

I enjoyed these meetings, Maharishi's knowledge, creativity, and humor. But serious things were discussed also. The second Gulf War had just begun with the invasion of Iraq in Kuwait, and Maharishi wanted to put together a peace group as close as possible to the action but also safe for the participants. "Do any of you have good contacts there?"

I spoke up, "I have gotten to know an influential professor from Kuwait a few years ago at the WHO main assembly of the year. I think he could open a door for us so we get permission to have many people do their group program on site."

As the secretaries learned over the phone, he'd meanwhile retired and was no longer in office. Maharishi smiled at me mischievously, "Well, you got lucky, this has kept you from traveling there." Other suggestions were developed and worked out. There were interruptions for meditations and meals. The group met till late into the night. And for me, there was no time left over.

On the following morning things started over again. I sat...and sat...and sat. For meals, I announced my departure, only to come back right after the meal—and to wait. This evening, too, the Master had me stay till the end of his day and to come back the next morning. The secretaries told me in regular intervals that Maharishi had asked if I was still there, and when they answered in the affirmative, he always said, "That's good."

After that, he'd dedicate himself to his various meetings that went like pearls on a string. But I sat, sunk into the velvety silence up here, and waited. On the following day, too, and on the one after that and after that. I learned unending patience and surrender to the here and now. I let things come to me as they were. Patience was not normally one of my exceptional virtues in many situations of every-day life. But in these days in Maharishi's sweet atmosphere that penetrated everything up here, patience came easily—and I practiced it.

Every morning, I sat at my post again, meditated, conversed with other visitors, waited, rested within myself, and continued to wait. One day followed the next and always with the same program.

Finally, however, the feeling that I simply had to sit here to be "stewed" took hold of me. For days now, Maharishi had no longer asked about me other than asking me to be here. I just had to get out! So, I treated myself to a time out and drove to the neighboring town. What a relief—after all that Ayurvedic food in Vlodrop—to indulge in a pizza at an Italian restaurant in the relaxed company of Reinhard and Hartmut, of course. As soon as we'd driven back to Vlodrop, Jürgen, one of Reinhard's assistants, stopped me at the entrance to the premises and yelled through the rolled-down window, "Man, Lothar, where have you been? Maharishi asked for you!"

Three hundred meters further in the next one, a secretary, "Lothar there you are! Maharishi sent me to look for you!"

And at the huge entry portal there stood the gentle Girish with his long beard and received me with almost the same words: "Lothar, where in the world have you been?

"Maharishi has asked for you several times and wanted to speak with you. Go straight up to the suite."

Oh, man, that was beyond embarrassing! Girish, who'd grown up in the traditions of India, would have waited there in full devotion and adoration come what may, as a good disciple of a Vedic master. But for me things were just not like that completely. Now, I had waited day and night for two whole weeks and had absconded just once, and then this!

In a hurry, I went up, but Maharishi was already in the next meeting. I sat down once more in my place and waited as before. When, that same evening, I went to a meeting in the big lecture hall, Maharishi looked briefly at me and smiled mischievously. At long last it was clear to me: he knew that I couldn't bear it any longer, and he had big fun with this situation and was playing with me. Even so, I never once dared again to leave my quiet post.

For more than a week more I sat from morning till night in my stuffed chair while different people, singly or in groups, entered the waiting room and then left again. And long after midnight, I'd hear each time: "Come back tomorrow morning; Maharishi wants to talk to you then."

Gradually, the feeling became a certainty: The Master was roasting me with every trick in the book. I was simmering on a low burner, while all my started and unfinished projects were going through my mind.

"Lothar, come, Maharishi has asked for you."

Finally! I was a little upset and self-conscious. For such a long time, I'd not seen my Master! I got up, a mixture of reverence and expectant love in my soul. I was led into the small reception room in Maharishi's suite; I sat down, and then Maharishi's voice, warm and soft, came from the intercom on the little table in front of me. "Lothar, how are you? I get the feeling that you're not so happy here."

"No, Maharishi, I feel great here. I am happy and extremely grateful that I can be here and work with you. The only thing that gets to me is that every time when a project is almost done, I get a new assignment from you and I can never successfully finish anything."

"I think you're happier at home with your family."

I felt it was all said and done. The Master knew the innermost corners of my soul and had decided.

But he added. "You have many great abilities and you can achieve anything you want in your life. But there's a small thing I want to tell you. It's just a little thing, and so don't take it to heart." His voice became yet another trace gentler, "You could be just a little more respectful towards me."

"Thank you, Maharishi."

He had hit the nail on the head. I accepted it, touched by the love that vibrated in his good-bye.

In the whole world, there is no one who is as independent of the respect, praise, or criticism of his fellow human beings, or as the completely grounded in the wholeness of life, as Maharishi. I thanked him within me for his words, for his fatherly and gentle encouragement of the disciple who does not understand his own small imbalance, and said, "Jai Guru Dev."

Slowly and thoughtfully, I stood up and went outside. It was July again, exactly twelve months after Maharishi's first call to our home, the call that sent me to Tanzania. My year with him was over. So, the laughing jyotishi had been right also with this part of his predictions.

Only many years later, when I had gained more distance from all of that and could again and again observe Maharishi's methods, could I understand the deeper significance of the big Tanzania project. Maharishi had shown my African friends a practicable way out of their crisis that they could have taken and implemented even without his help. It was not his task to insert himself into the implementation in detail. He could and would only show the way, which he did it concretely and to the smallest detail.

Don helped me, not for the first time, to see things from a bigger perspective, "You know, Lothar, Maharishi begins an untold number of projects and doesn't finish many of them. But each time a person with such a high and extremely coherent consciousness puts a big, cosmic impulse into the collective consciousness it's enough. Besides, everyone involved in it gets a big impulse towards growth. He does it often only for them, to develop them, and often this is his major focus. But anyway, sooner or later, when the time is ripe, these impulses will become reality and will be taken up by completely different people."

And that is how it went in this case. Certainly, the time had not been ripe back then. Today, a good twenty years later, there are, in some parts of the world, initiatives by Jesuits who implement in poor countries with good success parts of the methods that Maharishi developed back then. [57] In 2006, Muhammed Yunus, a professor of economics, received the Nobel Peace Prize for his Grameen Bank in Bangladesh for a comparable project with which he gave the poorest of the poor micro-credit without bank guarantees, and with the help of which they could build a livelihood. [58]

XI.

MAHARISHI AYURVEDA CLINIC

*The culture of the occident is determined more by reflection,
While the Asian cultures are determined more by meditation.
The meeting of the two sometimes seems to me to be the real
World-historical event of the present centuries.*

Carl Friedrich von Weizsäcker
1912-2007, German physicist and philosopher

Next to Maharishi

Back home, I understood the wisdom of my Master's decision. For my loved ones too, it was urgently necessary that I could be completely with them. For months Karin had had a furunculosis with recurring fevers, went to work anyway and, as usual, didn't get enough sleep. Physically, she was at the end of her rope. On top of that, the constant separation was more and more difficult for her and the older kids. Our 'Smiley' Lilian, was one year old and was overjoyed when I came through the door on Saturday but she clung desperately to my legs crying on Sunday evening as soon as I put on my tie and got ready to go to Vlodrop. It was good and right for us all that I was totally at home again.

In Schledehausen, I again held regular TM courses in the surroundings and spoiled my loved ones wherever I could. Their closeness felt good to me, and I enjoyed Karin, the kids, and family life with all that went with it.

But it wasn't long before Maharishi called me. A weight lifted from my heart! Secretly, I had worried a bit that my contact with him might have ended because I had not been respectful enough. Surprised and overjoyed, I got on the road.

Quietly so as not to disturb, I stepped into the big assembly hall at the back. Almost all the chairs were taken; in front Maharishi sat on his sofa. Just then, he was beckoning someone towards him from my area with his index finger. I looked around but didn't see anyone he could have had in mind. It took a moment till I realized that he meant me and was beckoning me towards the front. He had an arm chair put directly next to his sofa and offered it to me. Never had I sat directly next to Maharishi on the stage. Maharishi smiled mysteriously, bent towards me and whispered something confidential into my ear that had to do with plans for my future. My wife is the only one who knows what it was verbatim. If, in future, Maharishi's prediction was to come true, that would be the time to reveal it.

Then Maharishi turned once more to the audience and asked Klaus and Elke to sit in the first row with their almost grown daughter. I knew them. For several years, they ran a Maharishi Ayurveda Health Center in Sasbachwalden in the Black Forest. A familiar, relaxed dialogue ensued. Maharishi spoke with them about a few private matters and asked about the state of their business as well as about other projects. Klaus pulled out his narrow briefcase, "Maharishi, I've had many offers for opening new Ayurveda establishments; do you want to see some of them?"

He took a stack of pictures out and showed Maharishi the first big glossy print. My heart almost stopped. Speechless, I stared into the middle of the color photograph of the gigantic and magnificent building in Bad Ems, only a few kilometers from my hometown of Balduinstein; the same building which had drawn me into its spell since childhood. In this spa hotel, he wanted to establish an Ayurveda clinic? It was incomprehensible! When Maharishi showed interest in it, Klaus played it down: "Maharishi, I've been on the site and I think it's out of the question. In front of that house there's a loud street, and on top of that, we couldn't have our own kitchen there. And in that same complex, other therapies are being offered."

But, unimpressed, Maharishi said, "We'll do it anyway."

All the other projects that Klaus introduced went past me as through a fog; I was stirred up. What in heavens name was this all about?

In the evening, I drove back home. In the following months, Karin treated her patients in the Maharishi Ayurveda Health Center. I gave my TM courses and—as much as I enjoyed them—I'd have much rather worked together with my wife. Through the grapevine, we heard that Klaus had gone ahead with creating the Maharishi Ayurveda Health Center according to Maharishi's wishes in the magnificent building in Bad Ems, with which I felt mysteriously connected. But then, everything kind of fizzled out. Too bad!

Maharishi Ayurveda in Bad Ems

"Do you feel like driving to the spa hotel in Bad Ems?" Heiner's cheerful voice sounded on the phone. "Maybe you already heard? Klaus gave up on building a Maharishi Ayurveda Health Center in Bad Ems after a couple of months. I was part of some of the negotiations and I've met the director of the spa. And he called a little while back and asked if I could recommend someone else whom I'd trust to create an Ayurvedic clinic there." He made a brief but pregnant pause. "And now, guess who I'd recommended strongly? He has great interest in meeting you."

A few days later, Karin and I drove to Bad Ems, the picturesque little spa town in the heart of Germany, that lies on both sides of the Lahn River. Because of its more than a dozen mineral springs, the Emperor Wilhelm, I, Czar Alexander II, and many well-known composers and artists regularly spent their summers there in the 19th century. In its heyday, Bad Ems was known as the summer capital of Europe.

At first sight, Karin and I fell in love with the dreamy, wintry town with magnificent buildings and the spa districts on both sides of the peacefully flowing Lahn. We'd had our first long meeting with the spa director, Count Matuschka von Greiffenclau, a tall, gaunt man in his fifties with sharp features and a sarcastic, dry humor. As the CEO of the state spa, he was looking for an alternative therapy department for the spa hotel in the sunniest corner of the town, directly by the lazily flowing river. "During my last vacation, I did a test run of a panchakarma cure in Sasbachwalden and I'm impressed. I learned Transcendental Meditation there and got rid of the migraines I'd had for decades." With this he was certain that exactly this therapy should be introduced at the spa in Bad Ems, attract a stream of new guests, fill the empty spa facilities and make the hotel industry profitable again.

The Count closed our meeting with the words, "I got a very good impression of you two. I'll get back to you."

Certain of victory and exhilarated, we drove home that same night. We felt that here, finally, our shared professional future was spread out before us auspiciously. Day after day, Karin and I discussed this whole project from all sides and, on the feeling level, we agreed that we trusted this big undertaking despite all the risks it brought with it.

But the Count let us stew one week after another—the phone was totally silent. Despite this, it was unmistakable something had happened within us. Karin, too, saw meaning in it: "Isn't it strange? You know how much I love our house, the garden, the surroundings, and the community. But when I get up in the morning and see the little pond across the lawn, then I do miss the flowing water of the Lahn—really, every time!"

Together with our kids we went to the indoor swimming pool or skating on the weekends. Winter came and went; spring was near. When we slowly began to think that our intuition had deceived us, the redeeming phone call came. The spa director invited us for the next negotiation in Bad Ems. And at the end of it, it was clear: Together, we would launch a new Maharishi Ayurveda Health Center.

When Karin and I subsequently ambled across the magnificently beautiful old footbridge that stretched over the Lahn directly in front of the spa hotel while making plans, it suddenly hit me out of the blue: "Isn't it unbelievable that even when I was a kid, I felt an inexplicable attraction to this building without knowing why and now we'll open a big health center there."

At the invitation of the then spa director and managing director of the state spa town Bad Ems, my wife and I founded the Maharishi Ayurveda Health and Seminar Center in the Spa Hotel Bad Ems. Our treatment department of more than 1,200 square meters is located in the right-hand wing.

"Yes…" Karin turned to me, bubbling over with enthusiasm, "And isn't it almost unbelievable that Maharishi called you to exactly the meeting in Vlodrop and put you on the stage next to him when Klaus told him about the dream house of your childhood?"

She'd hit the nail on the head with that one. We both were amazed about the awesome synchronicity of creation with its mysteriously intertwined paths that had put all this together. We were equally impressed by the greatness and the wisdom of our Master because we were both sure that this just could not simply be a coincidence.

"Yes, Karin, and so Maharishi practically gave his blessing

for this project. That gives me a super great feeling for it all."

In the following months, we drove to Bad Ems many times. I did a detailed calculation of profitability, based on the numbers of the panchakarma department of Karin's clinic over the last few years. With this, we negotiated the conditions and the rental agreements. The spa director was a hard but fair negotiations partner but I was not to be outdone. I valued him and told him the truth about our reputation due to church and state as a "dangerous youth cult."

"Count Matuschka, please don't underestimate this. You'll have to deal with strong head winds when we take up our therapy business here. Think about whether you really do want to work with us. I don't want you to have any problems on our account."

He only laughed, "Mr. Pirc, I do believe you're exaggerating."

But I could not rest. I really did have to warn him because it was really clear to me what would come his way. And so, the next time I again pressed him, "We've endured quite a bit in Germany. They lie and do intrigues; you should really be careful. The church and the politicians will for sure give you big problems. It is even possible that you could lose your position for this."

"Aw, c'mon, I can't even imagine anything like that." Our slender spa director had broad shoulders. "On top of that, I have the best relationship to the highest government offices and I have an especially good connection to the bishop."

When I expressed my concerns again at the next meeting and the one after that, he shut me up with some force, "Mr. Pirc, I forbid you herewith to mention this topic ever again. Seriously, I don't want to hear it!"

And that's how it stood. The government-funded spa advanced three quarters of a million DM for the remodeling, that we'd have to pay back with the rent. Karin's mother secured the loan. We looked for an architect and I gathered in offers for comparison to save on costs. In the following months, I was once again separated from my family often, this time as the on-site overseer of up to forty tradesmen. From seven in the morning till late in the evening, I supervised the extensive building operations, to save as much on expenses as possible. Karin and I sold our home in Schledehausen and bought a new one in a town near Bad Ems, and then Karin, the kids, and me moved lock, stock, and barrel 300 kilometers further south. We developed brochures and circulars, conducted job interviews for staff, and browsed all the furniture stores in the surrounding area to buy all sorts of furnishings. We had the necessary treatment tables built and got all the other thousands of small things that were necessary for a well-functioning panchakarma therapy department, including telephones and computer network.

With all these various tasks and challenges, it could not be missed that a special blessing lay on this project. Much went down more than easily. An especially blatant example was the loan that we had to take out for the purchase of all the furnishings and the marketing that had been prepared ahead of time. We searched for a bank we could trust and found a sympathetic bank director. He obviously developed a seemingly unbounded level of trust for us. He not only extended a problem-free line of credit for several hundred thousand of DMs, but made the necessary funds available even before we had signed the credit agreement. "I want to wait till the interest gets to the lowest point so I can give you the most opportune conditions. I'm sure they'll fall further."

Every few weeks, I called him from my side because I hadn't heard from him. "Shouldn't we pretty soon sign the papers?" But he waved it aside with complete assurance. "Mr. Pirc, the interest rates will go down further; we'll just wait a bit more."

A few months later, only after we'd already spent a huge sum, his call came. "You should come to sign with your wife today; the interest rate is now really at rock bottom."

Words are not enough.

Many, many details luckily fell into place. At the right time, the right people crossed my path. Help and good recommendations came from all sides, a clear sign for Karin and me that with this project we were into something evolutionary that had the support of nature.

On the third floor of "The Emperor's Wing," the former summer residence of Kaiser Wilhelm I, we arranged the treatment section with much love, providing separate departments for ladies and for gentlemen. Ten generously-sized rooms flooded with light were created which, with their pastel colors and their high, stucco ceilings, radiated a simple elegance. Further, there were eight equally efficient and comfortable rooms for resting, including showers in which the guests could freshen up and rest undisturbed after their treatment. On this floor, our carefully trained technicians would soon implement the various panchakarma treatments.

On the fourth floor, we created the Ayurveda reception to personally receive and take care of the guests, as well as two beautiful seminar rooms for lectures and meetings. We furnished the two doctors' offices, the waiting room, a peaceful and bright yoga room, as well as a small, comfortable meditation room.

Somewhat exhausted but cheerfully, we opened the doors of the *Maharishi Ayurveda Health Center, Bad Ems* on the first of January in 1993 without having the slightest clue that, as promising as this beginning was, it would not be without some trials and tribulations.

Light and Shade

"What's going on here? Lothar, look down on the street. Do you understand this?" A little flabbergasted, Karin stood at the latticed window in our brand-new waiting room on the fourth floor of the spa hotel. From here, she had a glorious view of the little town, of the Russian Orthodox church with its shining, golden, onion-shaped roof, and the Lahn River. "Down there, cars are still driving, but today the street should be closed."

Very strange! I immediately called the spa director and got the devastating news. The main street that passed under the middle wing of the hotel initially should have been closed and all traffic from this effective date was supposed to run on the opposite side of the Lahn River. "Well, yes, Mr. Pirc, the residents affected by this could have toppled this decision by the city council through a legal process. I am sorry for you. The thoroughfare can now only be closed when the construction of the tunnel that will keep traffic out of the spa region is completed. That will presumably take five or six years."

We were shocked. Had we known this, we would never have taken on all this effort and financial risk. Our guests deserved a spa without street noise. But now, our boat had already left the harbor and, like it or not, we'd have to make the best of it.

Despite this downer, our 'baby' was off to a good start. From day one, the guests came, clients who'd followed my cheerful and competent Karin from her clinic in Schlede-hausen to our new place, as well as new guests we'd attracted with targeted advertising. With the choices that we'd made with our employees, we seemed to have been lucky. They were engaged and with our small crew of nine co-workers, we had a great work atmosphere from the get-go. Here's what was especially beautiful: We were all completely convinced of the efficacy of Maharishi Ayurveda therapies and we dedicated ourselves to the rewarding task of bringing more health and joy into the lives of other people.

In all my eventful life, I'd never had a project I loved as much as the creation and the management of this clinic. I enjoyed this independence with my whole heart and soul. Here, I could do as I wished and talk everything over with my most capable and committed wife. With great joy, we realized that we were a super team, even professionally.

As an entrepreneur, I could make decisions that were implemented immediately and could finish projects that had begun. It was fun to have my own brochures brought into being, specify the design, and decide who we'd employ, and how much to pay them.

Though it was extremely work-intensive in this development phase, I found it magnificent. I loved going into the clinic every morning, and every day this new life task unfolded a bit further. We began to contact the press, to invite them for interviews, and to try out the treatments for themselves, and, in return, we got many positive reports all through the land in newspapers and journals. Prominent people came, many wanting to remain incognito. Yet a whole slew of people, well-known and famous, were ready to personally tell the reporters we'd invited about their positive impressions and successful treatments, which brought in even more guests.

We developed circulars for our prospective guests, had them printed, and in the evening in the circle with our technicians, we stuffed envelopes while joking and laughing with one another. We filled in our co-workers about our successes as well as our new plans. We acted in concert with them, enjoying a spirit of optimism. Karin spoke at a medical congress. We both drove to health fairs for lay people in the surrounding areas and gave lectures there about Maharishi Ayurveda—with three kids in tow, of course. While their parents were busy, the kids went shopping joyfully at various stands and supplied themselves with samples and treats.

I had already twice experienced the blessings of a panchakarma treatment myself while I was on Purusha in Vlodrop and once in Schledehausen as well. To be able to see daily how guests blossomed under the loving care of the two physicians and our technicians was an enormous delight. All our staff noticed that guests who came to us for prevention or for the treatment of their chronic illnesses often looked smoother and more relaxed while becoming increasingly better psychologically after only a few days. And the doctors felt inspired when the complaints of their patients subsided or cures were successful.

For our guests, we had put together a lecture program: almost every night our doctors or I presented a lecture for them. In addition, we had brought a series of videos with the fundamental knowledge about Maharishi Ayurveda that Hans and Karin had recorded in Schledehausen. Guests could view these at any time so they would be motivated to continue at home what had begun here.

Our co-workers also blossomed. Most of us practiced Transcendental Meditation. But even those who didn't profited indirectly from it. Almost every week, I initiated guests into TM. This, despite our busy activity, further strengthened the velvety stillness and the good atmosphere that together we created here.

The young lady at the Ayurveda reception who could not be bothered with meditation became softer and lovelier. Even our cleaning woman, who did not meditate but who, with loving attention, cleaned our treatment rooms of all traces of oil became more radiant after some time because she took in the soft, peaceful vibrations of the department in which patients were treated in silence. Equally enjoyable was that our guests felt the positive atmosphere and frequently commented on it.

Despite all this, a lot went every way but smoothly. Guests complained about the noisy street and they complained about the food. Rightly so. The plan we'd worked out with the Count made sure that the chefs of the spa hotel would cook the special fare for our guests in their big kitchen, and they tried. They were, however, in part unwilling and in part too overwhelmed to fully acquiesce to our wishes and requirements. Even our employees to whom we offered a daily healthy lunch, in addition to one free panchakarma treatment per year, complained about the meals. Karin and I plunged into the solution of these problems with the help of the friendly hotel chefs but despite all efforts on our part it only got marginally better.

The hotel presented us with troubles just as big—a hotel which, at first sight looked so classy and well-managed. At a closer inspection, it was neither one, however. Our guests complained about the lack of cleanliness in their rooms, the hopelessly run-down baths, the dimness of the lamps on their nightstands, and the sometimes rude treatment from the badly trained receptionists of the hotel. My thankless task was to fix things, to mediate, to console, and somehow to save what could be saved—often for many hours per day. This was especially frustrating because we did all we could from our side to make everything run smoothly. If guests complained about any of our accomplishments, we immediately made every effort to resolve the matter and thus things got a little better every day. What made things difficult for us was that we had to watch helplessly when the substandard service of the hotel undermined the achievements we'd aimed at with great dedication.

Despite these shortcomings, many guests decided to come back simply because they were extraordinarily satisfied with the quality of the Maharishi Ayurveda treatments, with its effectiveness for their healing, and with the kindness of our team. But quite a few of them wanted to visit us again only when the failings of the hotel had been redressed.

A further challenge was that the number of guests fluctuated unpredictably. Regularly not enough guests registered but the rent and the salaries still had to be paid. Most guests booked with such short notice that I often didn't know in the middle of the month whether, at month's end, there would be enough money in the bank to pay for deliveries, taxes and duties, and the rent. For many months, it was constant nail-biting. Suddenly, it became clear to me how many responsibilities I'd shouldered with courage and with full trust in my well-founded profitability calculations, as well as the support of nature and the lucky coincidences that I'd been used to for years. But Karin and I grew because of the challenges and somehow it always worked out.

Even so, the workload of the first year was no picnic. We were still a small business that could not afford a lot of employees. A panchakarma department is a seven days per week operation. And if our only receptionist took the weekend she'd earned off, then I'd sit at the reception desk and take on her duties so that our guests would have someone to talk to. Within the week, we were at the clinic all day long—and then there were evening lectures. And in our free time, the planning, the decisions, or the development of ideas kept going at home with Karin, often even while we were brushing our teeth at the double sink in the bathroom!

With my multiple tasks, my eyes got opened. My whole, eventful life had secretly and quietly prepared me for these new responsibilities. In Maharishi's Movement, I'd received a customized training for all this. I was a hotel director, had taken over the management of the German National Center, became a TM teacher, and, on top of that, I'd got the basic training for Ayurveda and had accompanied vaidyas on their tours. All this now benefitted me, our employees, and our guests.

Only with this inner feeling that we were on the right path, that we helped many to better health and joy in life, and that Maharishi had wanted this establishment were we able to bear the deficiencies and the enormous workload of the first year. More important than ever for us was the daily energy input of our morning and evening meditations that helped us despite all the challenges to keep our engagement and the great joy of the work we'd chosen for ourselves.

All in all, we loved our work, we loved our employees, and we loved our guests. What could be better?

Much Ado about Nothing

Count Matuschka had followed the creation of our Maharishi Ayurveda Health Center with lively interest. Even after we'd launched our operation, he looked in on us now and again. His department, where he resided in the former work chambers of the Emperor, was two stories under ours. He took an active interest in the success of our clinic. Every time a new article appeared, I brought him the respective paper, chatted with him, and kept him current.

And he did the same for me. For things came as they had to. Shortly after our opening, the first comments fluttered into his apartment, comments in which the writers expressed their outrage in stirring words—that he had allowed this into the spa—a thorn in everyone's side—this "dangerous youth cult!" Without knowing anything about the situation, the authors of this slander assumed as a matter of course that we were the underlings of a dubious cult.

Count Matuschka always read me new letters, pointed with his long, narrow index finger at particularly drastic sentences and amused himself royally with these writers' attempts to create panic. After all, he'd thoroughly informed himself about everything before and knew that we were independent entrepreneurs who fully bore the risks ourselves. For him, the allegations were no problem. He answered in a friendly and gallant manner that he knew about all that, but that none of it corresponded with the realities, respectfully yours, etc. He also read me his responses with a derisive grin and his typically raised eyebrows.

More annoying for him, however, were the calls and visits of certain gentlemen who regularly, and equally zealously, solicited an audience to make their influence felt and to somehow remove this nuisance, these "cultish wing nuts" in a state spa! That could and should not be allowed; what an absurdity! Count Matuschka was an honest man with a profound sense of justice and showed something rare these days: a real spine. The visitors were treated in a friendly and courteous way and with great composure. The Count calmed them down and tried to take the wind out of their sails—and then they left. Afterwards, however, he made fun of them.

Soon, our enemies got bigger guns. The entire governing body of the state spa, who had, after all, agreed to our establishment, got all stirred up. It took such forms that discussions about the nuisance and the dangers in the state-owned hotel were the center of every board meeting for months, blocking all other subjects. As was to be expected, the spa director stood in the line of fire because he had been the one who had masterminded the whole thing. Count Matuschka raised his eyebrows and bore it calmly, though slightly fed up by this time.

He pulled all the strings with his good political contacts, traveled to Mainz, the capital of the province, presented himself in various places, and tried to calm down agitated souls. Yet all that time, the grapevine was overloaded: we were the bad guys who diverted innocent folks from the path of virtue and the true faith. For years, the faithful brethren, the politicians, and many journalists who copied from one another had this image fixed in their minds. In almost all German cities, there were "cult advice centers" back then, which were financed with government and church monies, and these centers propagated to the people their mistaken assumptions and twisted accounts, allegedly to warn the citizenry, but really to keep their own sheep in line, sheep who had started to leave the official churches in droves.

They didn't want to know, or hold as true, that we were running a medical establishment that helped people in gentle ways to get relief and that there were scientific research results that confirmed the successes of Maharishi Ayurveda.

In the middle of this heated phase, the spa director asked me to his office, "Sit down Mr. Pirc. You have no idea what's going on around here behind the scenes. You did warn me. But what's going down here, with all due affection and respect, I did underestimate things."

He put on his crooked smile with which he loved making fun of his contemporaries, "I've never seen anything like it in my entire career. And believe me I've been in politics for a long time and there are often evil intrigues in the background. But what's going down here…" he shook his narrow head, "… this has dimensions I've never experienced before. The secret service is nothing compared to this! I've done what I can. But nobody wants to hear that there's nothing behind all these accusations, that all this is nothing but a hot air balloon."

He bent towards me. And now his expression became a little more serious, and he lowered his voice, "I shouldn't be telling you this, obviously, but your telephone is tapped, even your home phone. They're trying everything to pin something on you. Despite my good political contacts, I've not been able to figure out who's behind all this. I have the best connections, you know, and I've tried again and again, but I couldn't get anywhere. The only thing I know is that it comes all the way from the very top. But who are the guys pulling the strings? In any case, they have huge influence, but are successful in staying totally in the background. I don't know what else I can do."

Aha, so our phones were tapped. I could hardly believe it. So much ado about nothing! In the following weeks and months, we did hear suspicious crackling when we used the phone. Karin took it lightly and made fun of it. "Those poor people! Imagine what they have to listen to all day long. All those boring business calls that you do. Never mind the irrelevant drivel when I chat with my friend. You can only feel sorry for these people. What a boring career. And then, they'll get nothing out of all that."

All this ran in the background while we, with love and care, led our health center while we grinned and bore it and kept it all quietly to ourselves. And in that way, we succeeded to save our innocent co-workers from feeling attacked by evil slander and not worrying about any endangerment to their job security.

Natural Law Party

Something from a completely different direction seemed to me to endanger the job security of our staff; this time, of all things, from Maharishi's side.

For this wise man had, not long before, begun to inspire meditators world-wide to found the Natural Law Party. As everyone knows, modern politics is almost always a balancing act between trial and error, a stony path that is paved with all kinds of failures and set-backs. The antithesis to this, the freshly baked political party—as its name already suggests—would govern using the intelligent power of natural law. This party was supposed to strengthen peaceful tendencies and progress in all areas of life through the systematic en-livenment of the consciousness of a small percentage of the population. It was supposed to implement programs that had already been shown scientifically to tackle the problems of modern civilization. Basically a really brilliant idea, if the governing bodies did not want to implement the Extended Maharishi Effect, to take initiative this way. But it was crystal clear to me that this endeavor—at least in Germany—would meet with a complete lack of understanding. Who, pray tell, would vote in this party? The propaganda against us that had spread all over the country for almost two decades and that had not failed in its endeavor would make it impossible for most citizens to grapple with this unusual approach to alleviate social problems.

So, I kept my distance. Reinhard asked me to participate and take on responsibility. This time, I had to pass: "I fear that these activities of the Natural Law Party could have a damaging impact on the business interests of our clinic."

For the first time in our lives together Reinhard was disappointed in me. But that didn't change anything. I simply didn't want to have anything to do with all that, even though I was fully behind its goals. Why get all warmed up about a hopeless thing?

Despite this, I landed in a meeting with Maharishi in Vlodrop, a meeting at which various people for the most different functions and areas of responsibility within the Natural Law Party were being proposed. I tried to make myself as small as possible on my chair. Maharishi's probing glance passed over me several times. He'd already spoken directly to every person sitting in the front. As sure as the amen in church, he would now address me. And, indeed, "Think about what would be best for your region."

Evasively, I suggested another candidate for our constituency because I really didn't want to do it. We had enough trouble with our clinic in Bad Ems; we really didn't need a position in the Natural Law Party to bring yet another strange thing into the line of fire. I could read in Maharishi's eyes that he had seen through me clearly and that he accepted it lovingly.

Before I drove home, I went into the MERU video library to look for a video with a short quote by Maharishi about Ayurveda for a new informative video about our health center. Doubts were still going through my mind that it would turn out that the TM Movement had done itself a great disservice with this Natural Law Party. And my gaze fell on an old audio tape from the sixties that attracted me somehow. I listened to it a little. Among many thousands of volumes that were being kept in many rows, I had picked exactly the one in which Maharishi said, "If someone were to ask you if you wanted to become the president or chancellor of a country, and you know that you have no chance to be elected, then it would be senseless to go into the elections as a candidate, unless you're doing it for some cosmic reason."

If that wasn't a clear answer! I thanked my Creator within myself for this small miracle—because it helped me to understand why Maharishi had called the Natural Law Party into life. And, with just a few picks, I then found the video volume I'd been looking for originally and drove home.

Even though in the following years we had only limited success in terms of numbers in Germany and the world with the Natural Law Party, the prospects of the Extended Maharishi Effect became known to the public in many countries through our election campaigns. Professor Hagelin, the presidential candidate of the U.S. appeared in hundreds of positive TV interviews and talk shows. Donald Walsh, the world-famous author of "Conversations with God" supported the Natural Law Party. There was a genuine sense of optimism. In a few countries, candidates became members of local governments. But despite the great support of thousands of meditators, it wasn't enough to establish big groups of people who would practice the TM-Sidhis—particularly the yogic flying technique together to help the troubled nations.

After a few years, Maharishi disbanded the Natural Law Party and established "The Global Country of World Peace," a land without boundaries that would create a unifying foundation for all countries of the world to uphold peace and well-being through the uplifting of consciousness. He thanked the active members of the Natural Law Party and said, "But don't think that the Natural Law Party was a failure. It just happens to be the case that sometimes you have to change roads to get to your goal faster."

Washington, D.C.

Once again, a call. This summer there would be for one last time a big world peace assembly whose effects would be scientifically monitored.

Maharishi was of the opinion, however, that the coherence effect had been demonstrated with scientific precision often enough. He wanted a permanent group without interruption to create coherence for the world. He didn't want the positive effects to stop as soon as the volunteer angels of peace drove back home. Naturally, this would be possible financially only if the government or big corporations took up Vedic techniques of consciousness—through the implementation of relevant programs in the world of work, in the military, in education, or in the prisons.

But, he finally agreed to an initiative of concerned mothers to implement a big demonstration project for the global community. In tune with the wishes of the Americans, it was to be monitored by independent scientists according to the highest standards of science. In the hopes that when the predicted outcomes took effect, this positive approach in the war against crime would finally be taken up by responsible parties.

In the U.S. there were far more violent crimes than in any of the Western European nations. There were seven times as many prison inmates as in the average of the European states.[59] The total costs due to criminality in the U.S. was almost 700 billion dollars annually.

Various government institutions had already tried to take counter-measures against this disastrous trend. But the analysis of 500 various programs used to prevent violence was devastating. Statistically, they had hardly any significant effects.[60] But with the Extended Maharishi Effect, we had a simple and repeatedly tested solution. And this would be shown incontrovertibly to be the case one last time with a large project.

In the years of 1981 to 1986 there had already been coherence creating groups of at most 400 Purusha and Mother Divine in Washington, D.C., which, depending on the size of the group, had reduced criminality up to 11% per year. The total criminality within those five and a half years dropped around 35%, which was not explainable in terms of other factors, such as the weather, police presence, changes in the age distribution of the population, or neighborhood watch programs. After the disbanding of the groups, the criminality started to rise again.

Just in the U.S. capital city of Washington, D.C. the expenses for containment of criminality from 1986 to 1992 grew to one billion U.S. dollars annually; violent crime in those same six years had increased by 77%. The Congress approved greater police presence on the streets and faster sentencing of criminals, for which the U.S. laid out enormous sums in the past years, but these did not result in any decline of criminality.[61] The situation had come to such a crisis that in the "crime capital," as the media had already dubbed Washington, D.C., several schools had been closed as parents refused to let their children walk to school due to the fear of many attacks and rapes on the way to school.

As soon as Karin heard about the world-wide call to participate in the summer project, she was on fire for it. She absolutely wanted to go to D.C. with me. But I hesitated; I didn't want to leave our health center after just half a year.

But she insisted, pleading, "Come on, Lothar, we've just had one vacation without the kids, and that was our 'pre-honeymoon' four years ago."

So, what does a committed father and caring husband do? Exactly! He bows down and organizes everything. Aurel and Elisa went on vacation with their father, while Lilian could live with her nanny. Finally, the two of us sat in the plane on our way to the last fourteen days of the eight-week event.

Washington, D.C. was sunny, and Washington, D.C. was hot. We got in touch with the volunteer help and discovered that we had hit the jackpot. At the same time as we were there, 4,000 other people participated in the conference. In the two-week blocks before that, the participants had continuously increased from 500 people at the beginning, and then 1,000 and, finally, 2,500 in the two weeks before our arrival. We knew, of course, the more the better, and that was also true for the subjective experiences in meditation—we rejoiced.

We were assigned to a simple hotel room near a big university campus that was empty during the semester vacation and was now available for the conference. To Karin's great joy, big, grey-striped lively squirrels jumped in great numbers on the mowed lawns between the big buildings. Twice a day we assembled in the big halls for the extended TM-Sidhi Program and attended the lectures offered in the afternoons and evenings.

At the first meeting in the packed auditorium, we were impressed with what enormous care this project had been prepared. Our Yank friends had really put together something admirable that took comprehensive preparation. The insights gained from the results of the extant studies on the Extended

Maharishi Effect had been developed to the point where scientists could calculate accurately which number of participants in the TM-Sidhi group program would reduce the criminality of a city like Washington, D. C. and by what percentages. With these calculations in their pocket, high ranking politicians and leaders of the police force were informed ahead of time, so that they could observe with open eyes what was taking place. Everywhere in America, and above all in Washington, D. C. the press reported almost daily about the steady reduction of criminality. The entire population could thus follow the results, especially as the demonstration project had been announced long in advance and had awakened the public's curiosity, which, initially, was no doubt skeptical. Huge ads, financed by American sponsors, brought additional attention.

A big success in terms of amusement for the public was produced by a speaker through the following anecdote. Shortly before the beginning of the experiment, the chief of police in Washington, D. C. was asked for his opinion about the predicted reduction of criminality through our programs. His succinct answer in broad American slang was, "The only thing that would reduce criminality would be a long snowstorm in the middle of summer."

He understand the statistics of his city because murder, rape, and other violent crimes did correlate with the average weekly temperatures—the hotter the outside temperature, the more crimes there were in these categories. The conference participants grinned anyway because, in the meantime, it was clear that the good man had been sorely mistaken and had greatly underestimated the Extended Maharishi Effect.

Karin and I spent the meditation times separately in the

rooms for male and female participants. Always when we met afterwards, Karin beamed, curious as always, "Well, my darling, how was it?"

And I'd answer grinning broadly, "Bulldozers rolled over me!"

She laughed because she understood. I was still in jetlag and still pretty worn out from the intense weeks of work in Bad Ems. My body used its inner intelligence to catch up with well-deserved sleep first. But the bulldozers came ever more rarely, and I soon enjoyed the super deep silence of meditation in such a big group and the enormous growth of energy though the group practice of the TM-Sidhis.

Since we all had the same program, we all had lunch at the same time. So, we stood at the end of the huge line that slowly and gradually moved forward before we got to the front of the line at the university cafeteria. So, there we stood all together, people of all skin colors, foreign languages from all parts of the earth, buzzing, all mixed-up. In the first few days, one or another of them still looked tired and crumpled up from the flight, the time-zone difference, or the work and life at home. But in the meantime, all were in a good mood and radiant and full of energy. And each one of those people had, like us, given his or her vacation time, and had paid for the flight and the accommodations from their own pocket and was happy to contribute their part to show humanity that new times with fewer problems were achievable.

While standing in line, we got to talking with the people next to us; most of the time, English was the language that connected us. It was all relaxed and joyful as if with long-time friends. As much as our outer appearance differed, inside, we hardly felt any boundaries. Soul touched soul; the meditation program enlivened the unified field, and the level of our cosmic selves united us in palpable ways. At the same time, it became clear to us what an outrageous insanity it was that everywhere in the world people constantly waged war against one another, and murdered one another, and what senseless, unnecessary sorrow was engendered through all this. Here we stood now, feeling intimately that all humanity could be one family. We held this simple, cost-effective, and peaceful solution in our hands and, on top of that, it was a lot of fun.

One of the following lectures was presented by the researcher who was part of the scientific monitoring process of the conference. We learned that the whole project had been planned by a team of scientists very thoughtfully so that it would meet the strictest standards and would stand against even the most persnickety criticism. To this end, the scientists at MIU had contacted many renowned researchers at universities in the U.S., to request their participation in the research study. As a result, a review board of 27 leading experts in criminology and statistics was formed, which included sociologists and criminologists and a member of the police department of Washington, D.C. Before the assembly began, the researchers at MIU developed a methodologically solid research protocol and stated the predicted results. This was presented to the review board for discussion and approval. The protocol was then deposited with a notary. The review board also later monitored the analysis of the data, and reviewed the results and conclusions of the research report. Moreover, all researchers signed a contract with a notary public to the effect that with their names they guaranteed the high quality of the study.

The researchers were busy in the background daily to

evaluate the newest data that came in constantly and they communicated the brand-new results to the public and to our group. And every new stat increased our elation. The rate of criminality sank more and more.

A few days later, one of the volunteers went to the podium. Beaming with joy, he told the assembly, "Before the next lecture, I wanted to tell you about a little event, a lovely by-product of your meditation. One of the people from the security firm who stands in front of the doors while you're meditating, talked to me a couple of days ago. He asked, 'What are your people doing exactly behind those doors? I've been suffering for years with deep depression, but every time when I stand watch in front of this door, my heart becomes totally light.' When I told him that we are practicing an es-pecially effective meditation and told him a little more..." He paused, "To make a long story short, he's starting to meditate today."

Huge applause followed his words. We were in high spirits, we were glad for the man and for ourselves. It was a terrific atmosphere full of optimism.

Quantum Physics and Consciousness

Dr. John Hagelin, world renowned quantum physicist and professor at Maharishi International University, presented a challenging speech about the newest insights of modern quantum physics and its relationship to consciousness.

He reported that many physicists had tried for centuries to trace back natural phenomena to ever simpler, more fundamental forces, and it had succeeded only in the 80s to summarize all the forces active in nature to a single field with an incredibly long formula.[L]

The Lagrangian of the Unified Field, as it is called, mathematically describes the characteristics of the unified field. One characteristic is that it is self-referral in its functioning; that is, it interacts only with itself in so far as modern physics is concerned. This explication by Professor Hagelin rang all kinds of bells with us in the audience because we knew from years of meditation practice that consciousness during the experience of the transcendent is conscious exclusively of itself without there being any kind of content. We were also familiar with the term "self-referral" from Maharishi's minute analysis of the same processes within human consciousness.

It was not difficult for Hagelin the physicist and experienced meditator to bridge the gap between the newest insights of physics and human consciousness. The field of pure consciousness at the basis of human thought creates everything to perfection from within itself in a permanent, unending process of coordination which, from time immemorial drives the course of evolution.

Physicists had discovered the existence of the transcendental field that lies at the foundation of all the various manifest forms of existence. For quantum physicists, it was only a fascinating theory—for us, on the other hand, a daily and lively experience.[M]

For years, Maharishi, as an enlightened Master, with a degree in physics, had probed and illuminated this subject with Professor Hagelin and a committee of other experts. In decades of detailed work, physicists had proven the existence of the unified field. And to all of us here, it was obvious that this was just another term for the all-penetrating, unmoved consciousness that creates everything out of itself and that we experienced daily within ourselves. Our universe consists only of the vibration or excitation of the unmanifest, non-material unified field. The layering of these vibrations consolidates increasingly until, finally, our sense perceptions and their further processing in the brain fool us into believing that all that we see, hear, smell, and taste has real substance and that we are surrounded by solid matter.

Modern physics knew, meanwhile, that, seen through the lens of quantum physics, there is no matter because on this level every subtle building block of the universe is, at the same time, a particle and a wave. The once so-solid matter turned out to be pure vibration without any real substance. And, too, the influence of consciousness on matter, demonstrated with a complicated experimental set-up, was a reality that physicists could no longer explain away. Many of them are still chewing on it to this day.

After this introduction, Dr. Hagelin let us see the foundations of Ayurveda in a new light, as he compared them with handed-down Vedic knowledge.

In the silence of one's own consciousness, the unified field of all the laws of nature can be experienced by everyone as absolute, unmoved, eternal, and unchangeable Being. The rishis who cognized Ayurveda within their own being, called it *samhita*; it is the "wholeness" that creates everything from within itself and whose coherence-creating power must be enlivened if one really aims at comprehensive healing. When Professor Hagelin—an enthusiastic, gifted speaker—began to compare the properties of quarks, bosons, neutrons, positrons, leptons, and all the other tiny building blocks of existence with the *doshas, mahabhutas,* etc. handed down through Ayurveda, I must admit it made my head spin! But by the end of this amazing lecture, all of us understood much better that what the rishis had seen spiritually within their own consciousness in Vedic times corresponded one-to-one with what modern physics had learned through the systematic observation of external matter.

Isn't that just plain incredible? The seers knew through the power of their own consciousness exactly the same thing, and even more, than what in modern times had been learned through enormous research effort and with the help of the most complex installations by the most intelligent minds. The physicists are right: the unified field really is the realm of all possibilities.

Numbers and Congress

A long and well-planned visit was to Constitution Hall, the biggest auditorium in the region of Washington, D. C. Here the preliminary results of the effects of our meditation would be introduced to members of Congress, high ranking representatives of the police, and the city council. On busses, we drove to the big building with its impressive pillars in front of the portals, in which we went through the many doors in the mezzanine of the big hall.

In the morning, Karin had said to me, "Too bad that Heiner and Charlotte are not on our campus, I would sooo love to see them." But to meet them here and now, that was naturally totally unthinkable with these masses of people.

Step by step and row by row, we went further down and finally sat down on two places just about in the middle of the U-shaped arrangement of seats. The Constitution Hall was so big and high that even from there the stage below us seemed far away. The room filled up until all the 4,000 participants of our world peace assembly had taken their places. We chatted with our neighbor to pass the time till the beginning of the official part. Karin's eyes went here and there and, suddenly, she pulled excitedly at my sleeve. "Lothar, look, that's not even possible! Look who's there!"

I turned around and there they sat, laughing and waving at us joyfully: Heiner and Charlotte, two rows above us, almost close enough to touch.

In these two weeks here, we had experiences of such wish fulfillment again and again, much more often than at home. Things like that happen when one is rested and meditates deeply with 4,000 friends.

Heiner and Charlotte told us about a nice event that reflected the mood in Washington, D. C. When they were riding in a taxi from the airport into the city, they got into a conversation with the driver. He asked about the purpose of their visit. "Oh, you're with the Maharishi group. That's great. But stay in town for a long time because we notice clearly in our daily lives that it's quieter and more peaceful in Washington since your demonstration is running. I've got no clue how you're doing it, but it seems to work for real."

The lectures by scientists and the speeches of politicians were rather dry. But the data numbers were impressive. We were a bit proud that we had accomplished such a big reduction in the crime rate. In the last two weeks, it had fallen by 23%.

Suddenly there was a loud and buoyant voice from the stage below. The governor of Ohio said with undisguised enthusiasm, "Many politician friends along with me have been watching the statistics reported in the press and in your ads with anticipation. That was the most important topic among us politicians. We were all fascinated."

He pulled his hand through his hair, "Even so, I can't give you much hope that your programs will be introduced everywhere because every politician wants to keep his post. Many would fear for their re-election if they were to propagate the idea of reducing criminality with meditation in their constituency. They'd be afraid to look ridiculous in the eyes of their voters."

How often I had experienced just this.

He raised his voice, "But I will make sure that your programs for lowering crime rates will be implemented in my constituency as soon as the final results of the research are published."

He got a standing ovation with thundering applause. Such statements could no longer floor me. Too much had happened, I'd seen too much—I knew, meanwhile, that this new thing obviously needed a lot of time before it would be generally accepted. Despite this, an incontrollable ray of hope rose within me—it would really be lovely if this came to be. Well, we'd see…

After the meeting, a few streets further, 4,000 people stood on a lawn beneath the blue summer sky for a group photo— Karin and I right next to Heiner and Charlotte—in the background was the White House, the home of the president.

With 4,000 participants at the World Peace Assembly, in front of the White House, which reduced the crime rate in Washington by over 20 percent, just as the scientists had calculated and predicted earlier

The scientists went to work directly on the voluminous statistics. They needed months to get through it.

In individual cases, backing up something statistically

can be a pretty unreliable thing, with which, in the worst-case scenario, you could show that the falling birth rate in Germany is correlated with the reduction in the number of storks. Therefore, a theory becomes solid only through many studies supporting the hypothesis with the same results. To be scientifically water-tight, a result is clearly validated when it confirms a prediction based upon prior research results. Exactly this had been obtained with the Washington, D.C. conference because the researchers could state before the beginning of the conference exactly how strong the expected Extended Maharishi Effect would be, relative to the size of the group.

It took six years until these research results appeared in a scientific journal, a paper of not quite fifty pages. If one compared the number with the statistically expected rise of criminality, the decline in the murder, manslaughter, robbery, and rape, because of the Washington, D. C. conference of 4,000 people, stood at 30%. The data had been collected and analyzed with great care and the hypothesis had been strongly supported; the almost one-third less crime could not be accounted for by factors other than the Extended Maharishi Effect.

The effect was cumulative, that is, it increased with the length of the demonstration project as the number of participants increased, and it sustained itself measurably up to eight weeks after the end of the group program. The researchers calculated that a permanent coherence-creating group of 4,000 could create a reduction of violent crime of about 48%.[62] That would amount to a savings of several hundred million dollars just for a city like Washington, D.C.

I never again heard anything from the enthusiastic congressman from Ohio. Without further ado, his visions for the future vanished from the scene.

Despite this, in the following years, I liked to include this study into my TM lectures. Afterwards, audiences always asked the obvious question again and again, "Why is this not being used when it's proven to avoid so much sorrow and expense?"

And I could give them only my own explanation. "The collective consciousness is not advanced enough for people to understand this—as sad as it is, the time is not yet ripe. But it will come."

Joy and Sorrow

A big wish, which had been our quiet companion for some time, got fulfilled: our second child for the two of us announced itself. Full of quiet anticipation and joy, we kept this sweet secret just for ourselves.

Then an unexpected storm broke over us. Our two big kids went to see their father for a week during the fall vacation—and did not came back. Just like that. Though our relationship with their father, who had married for the third time that summer, had always been open and friendly, we were confronted with this done deal without warning. The kids were already going to their old school.

The attorney we consulted only said tersely: "That's not right. You can have the police get the kids and bring them home today." But how could we do that to the children? On the phone, they had affirmed that they'd like to live with their father again, in their old neighborhood, with their former friends with whom they had deep-rooted connections. Police intervention would have been a shock for them and would not have been a solution anyway. For an untold amount of time, there would subsequently have been a lawyerly bickering back and forth and the children would be torn back and forth between the two fronts.

Karin was devastated. Despite this, we decided with a heavy heart to leave the children in peace. Karin felt as if a piece of her had been torn from her. She cried a lot and, a week after those evil tidings she came down with a bad case of pneumonia. In this phase of our lives, our meditation program was an invaluable help. But even with this, sorrow often overwhelmed my darling, but she always found a calming balance for her wounded soul. Gradually, Karin's sunny character won the upper hand. After all, Aurel and Elisa could come back any time. And on top of that, a small human being was growing within her, one for whom we'd been waiting for a long time and for whom we were boundlessly happy with anticipation.

Our Maharishi Ayurveda Health Center was running well. The guests were happy with their treatments and their healing successes. Many, however, still complained about the hotel and the street. All in all, it was not ideal, but we made the best of it and the good outweighed the bad.

Almost every week, I presented a lecture to our guests about the important role that spiritual techniques play in the prevention and the healing of illnesses. Many places in the classical Ayurvedic texts refer to the enormous healing power of the experience of pure consciousness. It enlivens the deepest levels of a person and harmonizes body and soul equally. Not for nothing is the Sanskrit world for health *swastha* in English is "To be grounded in the Self." Ayurveda is founded on the idea that perfect health appears only when a person rests in the Self, in pure consciousness, even while acting in the outer world.

It sounds good, but is it true even in our restless and stressful times? And once again, the answer came from our creative friends across the big blue ocean.

The biggest health insurance company in the U.S., Blue Cross/Blue Shield, had offered a better price to TM meditators across the country. When the statisticians of the health insurance company took a closer look at this group after five years, they could hardly believe it: These meditators had engendered 53% fewer costs in this time-frame than other clients.

This opened the doors wide to a desire for more research. The results of the following large-scale scientific study demonstrated how great the healing influence of consciousness really is. The researchers compared the illness-related expenses of 2,000 practitioners of the TM and the TM-Sidhi Program with the data of 600,000 non-meditating people who were nevertheless comparable in terms of age, sex, and occupation. It seemed almost too good to be true: the medical expenses for meditators up until their 40s were 50% below the controls. With those over forty, they were even better—more than 70% less, which is understandable since young people naturally are less often sick than older people, so that the positive effect is ever more noticeable with growing age.

These results were so phenomenal that the researchers wanted to know more. Dr. David Orme-Johnson and his colleagues then compared the data of Blue Cross/Blue Shield in eighteen different categories of illness. The biggest reduction of 87% showed up, of all things, in hospital admissions for the #1 killer of all industrialized nations, cardiovascular disease. Depending on the specific pathology in seventeen categories of illness, drastically lower costs accrued between 31% and 87%.[10] The probability that these data could be due to pure chance was seven in a million—a highly significant result.

---

[10] The real number is 9 and the text is: Specifically: heart and circulation illnesses—87%; nervous system illnesses—87%; general malaise with unknown causes—76%; nose-throat-and-lung illnesses—73%; metabolic disorders—65%; bone and muscle disorders—63%; benign and malignant tumors—55%; genetic illnesses—51%; digestive system disorders—49%; urogenital tract disorders—37%; blood disorders—33%; infections and psychological disorders—31%.

The only exception was the expenditure for gynecology. The researchers found the answer to the puzzle: pregnant meditators made use of the available medical check-ups even more conscientiously than non-meditators. Meditators, therefore, make use of medical care when necessary at least as much as other people. The enormous savings in the other categories were clearly the result of the fact that, through the healing power of Transcendental Meditation, they were healthier than others.

At the same time, the 2,000 meditators had saved their insurance company Blue Cross/Blue Shield more than two million U.S. dollars in a five-year span through the positive effects of regular mediation on their health.[63] It is difficult to imagine how much the practice of Transcendental Meditation would save for the combined health systems of all countries if, in the future, human consciousness were utilized extensively as a preventive measure just as Ayurveda recommends.

The team around Dr. Orme-Johnson in the following years continued its research tirelessly. They learned that meditators who had additionally included Ayurveda in their lives had adjusted their diets according to the recommendations of Maharishi Ayurveda, had done Panchakarma cures occasionally, or took Amrit Kalash—an effective rasayana which, with its elaborately prepared combination of herbs supports the immune system and general health—were 32% less in need of treatment than were meditators without these additional health-supporting measures.[64]

Most people were impressed with these numbers in my lectures. But someone always asked, "Well, those surely are people who've been meditating for a long time. How do things look with beginning meditators? Or with older people who already have some complaint or other?"

"Canadian researchers have studied 699 beginning meditators and, to make a long story short, with people over fifty, the costs for health insurance were reduced in the following three years by 19% after learning TM. And with this it is clear; it is never too late, regardless of what age you are when you begin. But you are right, the positive consequences for health do in fact increase continuously with the practice because, in the last year of the five-year Blue Cross/Blue Shield study, the expenditures for those TM meditators over 65 were almost 50% less than for the control group."[65]

I presented these and other studies to my audiences. Is it therefore any surprise that many of them decided during their panchakarma treatment to include this effective technique into their lives in the future? So, I always followed my most favorite calling to open the path to the transcendent for these people.

At the end of the year I was once again sitting in our lovingly decorated meditation room; a candle spread its soft light. The lady in front of me had closed her eyes. And in her gently relaxed face I could read that things were going well for her and that she sank into ever finer layers of her thoughts and was experiencing a feeling of inner peace and harmony.

And very suddenly, I knew that now the right moment had come to introduce Maharishi to our health center. It was a clear impulse. For ten months, Karin and I had successfully operated the clinic. Today was my one hundredth time I initiated someone into TM, and this seemed the right moment. With joy, I anticipated presenting all that we had accomplished to Maharishi.

As soon as the thought came, it was done. Spontaneously, I called Girish, who presented my wish to Maharishi. My impulse seemed to have been right—an hour later the call already came back: "Lothar, you can come, Maharishi will receive you both."

A few hours later, we arrived in Vlodrop and—without having to wait—we were shown into Maharishi's reception room. He already sat on his sofa and asked me to sit down on the soft carpet in front of him. Karin sat down on a small arm chair behind me.

"Maharishi, I want to report to you…" and I let him partake of the stages we'd gone through in the last two dynamic years. I showed him our brochures and pamphlets as well as the various articles in the papers that I'd collected and had brought along in a big portfolio. I told him about the difficulties with the street and the hotel and gave him the promotion video we'd had made about our health center. To our surprise, he wanted to see the film with us. And so there we sat, the Master on the sofa, me at his feet, Karin in the upholstered chair, and we watched the video together while I simultaneously translated the German words for him into English—all together we were surrounded by this unbelievably soft aura that was always around Maharishi. All around him there was a broad, softly glowing radiance of light.

The meeting lasted for more than an hour. And we could feel that Maharishi was very, very satisfied. Finally, I asked for his blessing. He smiled lovingly at us and said, his voice moved with joy, "Yes…yes…yes…!"

Full of gratitude, I bowed deeply before him. In that moment, my consciousness opened to unboundedness and my heart filled with bliss. I felt Maharishi's blessing in the depths of my soul and had the feeling that I could touch the wholeness of Maharishi, the deepest level of his personality in this one precious moment. Then he stood up and said, "Jai Guru Dev."

He gave each of us a dark red rose. Then he walked from the room with his inimitable gait, in which his feet seemed hardly to touch the floor.

Karin and I could scarcely speak. Moved by the power of his three-fold "yes," we felt the blessing we had received and the certainty for the future that lay within it. Everything felt whole and beautiful.

Karin, for the first time in her life, had intimately experienced the attention of the Master. She was touched and grateful, and my wife, who always put the welfare of her children and her patients first, exhorted me, "Lothar, I want to stay the night in the hotel and just remain within this silence. My cells feel as if I had soft cotton everywhere. It would be a sin to drive home now immediately and to plunge into activity and lose all this again immediately."

Even on the way home the next day we felt the after-effect of Maharishi's presence within us and we both were united, "It doesn't matter what will happen with the clinic in the future, it doesn't matter what kinds of difficulties will come towards us, just this one hour with Maharishi is worth all this."

We didn't have to wait long for the positive effects of our visit in Vlodrop. We succeeded in getting Dr. Triguna to visit Bad Ems for a few days and he advised guests who'd come from all over Germany and a few countries of Europe about their health.

Maharishi sent Dr. Hari Sharma and me on a visit to Japan. Dr. Sharma was a renowned scientist of Indian origin who did research at Ohio State University for the Food and Drug Administration. He had researched the effects of the herbal medicines of Maharishi Ayurveda for ten years, had published more than 100 scientific articles, had written three books, and could look back on a career of lectures given world-wide. Now he was presenting his results before 500 physicians at a medical congress in Japan—organized by the Japanese Ministry of Health in cooperation with the Sony Corporation. Afterwards, I summarized the results of a few actual panchakarma studies, showed the audience slides of our private clinic, and communicated an impression to them of what the holistic Ayurvedic health system is capable of in practice. I invited the crowd to visit us in Bad Ems so they could get the picture on site.

In our free time, we enjoyed the cherry blossoms in Japan and visited several of the touristic high points of Tokyo and environs.

I was glad and happy to be enjoying Maharishi's trust and to be serving the greater cause. Just as all the other times when I traveled for him into distant lands, I felt his blessings rest on me, which I experienced as a warm feeling of joy in my heart and which even here, on the other side of the globe and on the flight back, was my constant companion.

Soon after, two rather sizeable delegations from Japan, government representatives and academicians in healthcare, as well as some private business interests, came to our place in Bad Ems to experience panchakarma for themselves and to get inspiration for the construction of their own Maharishi Ayurveda facilities in their homeland.

1994, with Prof. Hari Sharma, Ohio State University, USA, on our lecture tour to a medical congress with 500 doctors organized by the Japanese Ministry of Health

Our house had become quiet with the absence of our older kids and Lilian was as always sweet and easy to take care of. Karin's belly became visibly rounder. In her free time in the afternoon hours during the weeks of her maternity leave, my active darling was writing her first book, "Ayurveda for Mother and Child." Months passed.

In May, the time had finally come. The midwife came to our home and while Lilian was sleeping through the night, Karin gave birth to our child a few hours later. The little fighter greeted the world with loud screaming before his exhausted mom nursed him and he calmed down.

I put my hand on him to welcome him and felt how my tiny little son spread an aura of heavenly sweetness around himself. In seed form, I felt the various facets of his personality combined with a loving respect for this little yet not fully expressed but still perfect being. And just as with the birth of our daughter, I was completely enchanted with him and deeply happy.

Birth and Death

Two days after Daniel's birth we welcomed high-ranking guests. A delegation of the Japanese Ministry of Health had come in response to my invitation to see our Maharishi Ayurveda Health Center for themselves and take home some inspiration. They were accompanied by the national leader of Japan's TM Movement. After two days, he gave Maharishi a report by phone: "The representatives of Japan's government are most impressed by the quality of the implementation and the entire facility in Bad Ems. Additionally, I have initiated some of them into TM, the highest science adviser of the Minister of Health among them, and Lothar's wife brought a son into the world the day before yesterday."

Maharishi's commentary was short and succinct, "Lothar's son has arrived to welcome the Minister of Health."

Even though it was just a tiny little sentence, Karin and I were delighted by this welcome for our newborn son.

Our nanny took sweet care of the little one. He got his daily oil massage and, for nursing him, Karin drove home in between appointments with patients so he would want for nothing.

Aurel and Elisa spent the summer vacation with us. Two weeks of vacation with excursions into the surroundings lay before us. On our first day together, my younger brother called, "Papa is in a coma at the Traunsteiner Hospital."

O my God!

Stressed out, Rainer, reported, "On his way home from vacation on the bus, he suddenly got really bad stomach pains. At the hospital, the doctors diagnosed an aortic aneurysm, a tear in the abdominal artery. They did emergency surgery. He's alive but he never regained consciousness."

We quickly rearranged to spend two weeks with all four children in a farmhouse at Lake Chiemsee. My loved ones made day-long excursions and swam in the clear waters of the lake, while I regularly travelled to the intensive care unit to be with my unconscious dad as much as possible, as did my brothers who traveled here. He lay there, motionless, with a feeding tube in his nose, an infusion bottle at his side, and connected to the heart monitor that beeped regularly. His eyes were closed and showed no reaction when I spoke with him. He was the very image of sorrow that cut me to the heart. The doctors didn't give us much hope for his recovery. When we had to go home, his body, strong as a bear's, was still keeping him alive.

As soon as the big kids had gone back to their dad's, another issue gnawed at me because, despite our efforts, the problems with the mediocre management of the hotel, the kitchen, and the street in front, were slowly but surely taking their toll. Many guests of the first year had not come back. The number of guests fluctuated critically and, with it, the necessary source of income.

But Karin was in a good mood. She enjoyed the little boy, nursing him and being a mother. I worried big time until my practically inclined wife finally said, "Why don't we do a jyotish consultation? Then, at least, we'll know what we're up against."

There was something to be said for that. On the first weekend Karin was free, we went to the Netherlands with the children to get professional advice.

In Valkenburg, our organization had acquired a former monastery building where Mother Divine did their long meditation programs in total seclusion. In a room on the first floor, an Indian jyotishi fathomed our immediate future based on my birth time. This was certainly devastating. "The best thing would be to close that health center down immediately, and the sooner the better. The stars are not only in a bad position now, but your problem is with the relationship to the hotel manager. With this business partner, you'll never have any luck, and it will remain that way. With this constellation, you will not recover."

How could that be? Hadn't Maharishi given us his powerful blessing less than a year ago? How could we just close shop? In my distress, I dialed the phone number of Maharishi's secretaries and described my dilemma to Reinhard. A few minutes later the return call came, "Come to Vlodrop; Maharishi will address the problem."

We described the situation in Bad Ems to Maharishi and told him the results of the jyotish consultation. When I was done, he sank into a long silence. We waited…didn't say anything, and waited…after one, two minutes Brahmachari Nandkishore, the only other person who was in the room with us, broke the silence and told us quietly, "I think we should delve a bit deeper into the jyotish analysis with our two pundits here in Vlodrop tomorrow morning. After that, we'll meet with Maharishi again and we'll see what's what."

On the following morning at the crack of dawn, Rainer called us at our hotel from the Traunsteiner Hospital, "Dad is dying. If you want to see him still alive, you have to come immediately. Presumably the time is up. The doctors said it's just a question of hours."

If that was true, we no longer had a chance. The trip to Lake Chiemsee by car was at least eight hours.

A little later and with an uneasy feeling in our stomachs, Karin and I drove to the MERU building for the jyotish consultation that had been promised. The two jyotishis looked not only at my personal horoscope thoroughly but also at Karin's and that of the clinic, and then gave us an all clear, "It's true what our colleague has said, but that was about the hotel manager that you've had 'til now. But since a new manager will take over the hotel now, this difficult phase will pass. You'll recover and will have much success."

We were relieved about the good news, but I was depressed about my father's critical condition. So, I used the opportunity and asked about that. After a brief look at my horoscope, the two Indians said straight out, "We're sorry, Lothar. But there's no chance for your father; he'll pass today."

A deep sigh escaped from me and I accepted the inevitable. When we thanked the jyotishis for their first-class consultation, my cell phone rang. "Lothar, Dad just now died."

We wanted to get home right away. So, I called Girish and asked him to inform Maharishi about the change in the situation. In just a few minutes, he called back and had us connected with Maharishi over the intercom. Maharishi asked about my family situation and my brothers. He kept making lengthy pauses, and I felt full of gratitude in these moments that he was giving my father a great blessing for his last journey. Finally, he said to me, "Go home, prepare the funeral, organize everything, and take care of your family. When everything is done in a few weeks, come back here to talk further about your situation in Bad Ems."

Maharishi, who was busy with the whole world day and night, who had thousands of close disciples, took time for personal family affairs! Karin and I felt it as a great gift and a little later we drove home with our children.

Vlodrop Once Again

We put our undiminished attention on growth for our health center and slowly but surely it ran a little better.

When, at the beginning of the year, Count Matuschka von Greifenclau announced his resignation as spa director, despite what the jyothishis had said a while ago, I got a slightly queasy feeling. At the end of the year, would he possibly be replaced by a hardliner who would give us problems? Up until now, things had been running smoothly despite the initial tempest in a teacup—on the surface the waves had calmed. Or did it just seem so?

In any case, the Count told us one day out of the clear blue, and as usual with his typically crooked grin, "Your phones are no longer tapped."

Karin countered immediately, "Great! But it was clear from the get-go that nobody would find anything of interest against us."

"But then, they secretly planted test subjects in your clinic, mostly the wives of politicians, who got treated in your clinic unrecognized."

"So?" Curious, I bent forwards on my chair.

"Well, Mr. Pirc," he smiled suggestively, "Things didn't go as one might have wished. The plants were impressed with the quality of the treatments across the board—by the thoroughness of the doctors and technicians, as well as by the entire atmosphere in your health center. Nobody felt pressured to learn to meditate, and everyone was more than satisfied." His grin deepened, "So you've found some unexpected advocates." And he finished, "I think the resistance will calm down now."

Well, we could only hope!

Meanwhile, Maharishi, unperturbed, insisted on expansion. At the end of November, he convened a big assembly at the MERU building in Vlodrop. He began to work on a new focal point in health care, namely, the treatment of serious, chronic illnesses. To that purpose, he had already won over several top-level Ayurvedic specialists from India who had come to Vlodrop, some of them bringing their families, to initiate this new project.

As the meeting was almost over, Maharishi once again turned my life up-side down, "Lothar, I'd like you and Karin and the children to come here to lead the building of the program for healing chronic illnesses. You can bring your nanny."

Completely unthinkable! "But Maharishi, I should take care of the clinic in Bad Ems, and Karin is the only doctor there now."

"That's not a problem. Let's think about who we can find to replace her, and for the rest, don't worry. I'll fill up your clinic with people suffering from chronic illnesses. Just come here. I'll give you office space and a few co-workers to be at your side."

Well, if that's how it is! It was an honor for me that I could come with my whole family to be responsible for this new project. In my joyous anticipation, I totally forgot in this moment what I'd experienced in my one year in Vlodrop. Karin, too, who even at the end of her medical training had wanted to work directly for Maharishi internationally, was enthusiastic for us both about this utterly unexpected prospect.

Despite this, she felt she was being drawn into a whirlwind because, as always, everything had to happen yesterday. Our flexibility was being challenged. Maharishi's attention was on this project and—as if it be otherwise—things just fell into place. Everything got organized with amazing ease. We entrusted our assignments in Bad Ems into good hands, and in December 1994 we moved into a suite in Vlodrop with Lilian and Daniel and our 60-year-old nanny, Sigrid. It was a little crowded and simple but we were joyful and expectant.

Shortly afterwards, the so-called Veda Intensive Program for the treatment of chronic illnesses was inaugurated. It combined all the approaches of Maharishi Ayurveda and included extremely complex treatments for which especially experienced vaidyas contributed their expertise. An astha-vaidya from a respected family tradition of southern India had joined. This honorific title indicated that he was familiar with all eight branches of Ayurveda (*astha* is the Sanskrit word for "eight"). So he was a highly-respected physician.

To my joy, I saw my beloved Dr. Raju just a little later among the group of vaidyas who had come specifically for this project from various parts of India. With pleasure, I introduced my wife and kids to him. He radiated, as always, from every part of his being, smiling and happy. The physician and vaidya team regularly went from Vlodrop to Valkenburg, almost an hour by car, to take care of patients in the clinic that had been outfitted there; Karin was always among them.

Dr. J. R. Raju, Ayurveda vaidya and world-famous instructor in pulse diagnosis, with his wife Dr. Devaki Raju, medicinal herb specialist, during one of his visits to Bad Ems

Soon after our arrival, Karin and I were invited to a meeting in Maharishi's suite. He greeted us personally and asked Karin with empathy, "How are you doing here?"

She beamed at him and, cool and free, she said, "Truthfully, I'm living the life o' Riley!" She meant the wonderful atmosphere in the whole complex that she'd experienced only briefly up to then was in what we could now luxuriate.

Everything went exceedingly well. In no time, I got freshly printed letterhead and business cards for the new project. The cards presented me as the "Director General of the Campaign to Create a Disease-free Society". Maharishi was a master in the assignation of titles. He always articulated the highest goals, even when—as in this case, according to his own statement—it would take at least three generations to implement, even under the best circumstances before genetically inherited illnesses would be eliminated from the human body.

Despite this promising beginning, we encountered some boundaries after just a few days. The office space that was promised turned out to be a single badly furnished room where just about everything was lacking. On top of that, some rather drastic economy saving measures were being introduced. Photocopier use was limited and we had no computer. Looking back, I'd romanticized my time in Vlodrop four years earlier. And above all, I'd forgotten that the projects with Maharishi were rarely about immediate success and outer perfection, but about the growth of the consciousness of the world—and of the disciples. For that, it was often enough to be concerned intensively about an idea, and, in that way, enliven it in the consciousness of the world. It wasn't long before the situation here seemed all too familiar. The Master rattled emphatically our solidly constructed boundaries that were as follows: we want to finish our assignment well, everything had to be structured in an orderly way, and we want to see success as much and as quickly as possible. The Master threw us for a loop because it was exactly that which didn't work at all. Karin and I fluctuated between devotion and estrangement, and we searched for answers. We gave our best with devotion and at the same time tried, despite all the limitations, to produce some sort of success somehow.

Despite all this, we enjoyed a wonderful time in Maharishi's atmosphere and the coherence of Purusha who pursued their intensive meditation program in the background. Lilian played with the children of the vaidyas, practiced Indian dance, frolicked through the halls, and was the little blonde star who was being spoiled by everyone during our communal meals. Daniel began to crawl and carried—tiny as he was—the move and the sacred surroundings with composure.

Many times, we could attend special events in Maharishi's suite, sometimes including the children. Here, we learned a completely new facet of Maharishi's character. One whole afternoon, he dedicated himself with a large group to the subject of what was the essential and the deeper meaning of various professions.

The audience named one profession after another and he gave his commentary. Finally, someone asked cheerfully, "And Maharishi, what is really the profession of children?"

Maharishi hesitated only briefly and then said with a mischievous look on his face, "To amuse their parents." Delighted laughter followed.

Often, one TM teacher was there with her son; her husband was traveling abroad for the Movement. Her son was hyper and aggressive and constantly in motion. In the lecture hall, the eight-year old jumped up and down continuously on an upholstered chair while the cameras were running and recording Maharishi's lectures. The boy clambered across the rows of armchairs and threw his pencils around. Despite this—or maybe because of this? —Maharishi always wanted Francesco* and his mother near him. At every meeting in the big hall, he had the two of them called to him. His mother suffered visibly and would get ready to leave the hall with her son when he got too obstreperous. Maharishi kept them back every time, wanting her and the boy to stay. When Francesco was once again too wild, Maharishi, winking, gave his calm commentary, "Little boys have to be naughty."

He was not put out in the least. On the contrary, he seemed to enjoy the kid. Completely unperturbed by the commotion, he still conducted his meetings.

One fine day, Francesco and his mother were sitting in the front row and, finally, after tireless jumping around, the boy became sleepy. His eyes fell shut, and his head began to sway to one side. And what did our Master do? He interrupted his talk for a moment and stretched his arm, lengthened by a rose, in Francesco's direction and, having fun, he attracted the boy's attention with the flower until the child was active once again and the jumping up and down started over. There was hardly anyone in the hall who could suppress a smile.

In regular intervals, Maharishi called me to his suite and asked about our progress. And with this, something started that wasn't new to me: I could once again evolve through waiting in his immediate environment. Many nights in a row, Karin got her good-night kiss from me, wearing a suit and tie as I got ready to sit in front of Maharishi's suite. One morning, I stepped into his meeting room as the first one—as Maharishi had directed me to do the night before. So now, he'd have time for me. Maharishi came in, looked at me, folded his hands in the Indian greeting and, smiling, said, "Jai Guru Dev," and sat down. Then, through the second door, Dr. Bevan Morris, the long-time president of Maharishi International University in the U.S., came in to discuss something with him. The empty rows of chairs filled up little by little. Maharishi indicated with his look that I should sit further back. So, I waited patiently in the last row till the end of the day and then once again left to leave to go sleep without having achieved anything.

When Dr. Triguna came to Vlodrop in 1995, I invited

this world-famous doctor to Bad Ems to advise patients there for the second time. So, our family took a trip home. When Dr. Triguna arrived at our health center, I introduced him to my loved ones.

Dr. Brihaspati Dev Triguna, for decades president of the All India Ayurvedic Congress, the world's largest medical association with 350,000 members, during one of his visits to Bad Ems in 1996, with his son Dr. Devendra Triguna, current president of the All India Ayurveda Congress

When he saw our eight-month-old son sitting on Karin's lap, he insisted on giving up his afternoon nap and, instead, he wanted to look at Daniel's jyotish chart. I was surprised, never had I gotten wind of the fact that he was an expert in jyotish. So, during the afternoon rest period, I drew Daniel's kundali, the position of the planets at the time of his birth, onto a flipchart and, soon after, Dr. Triguna interpreted his character and his future with many amazing details.

Travels

A few days later, I was to come to the suite early in the morning. When I got there punctually, Maharishi didn't have time for me and invited me instead to partake of the meetings in his seminar room. So, I sat there once again patiently hour after hour. Late at night, the room was emptying finally, and I thought that my moment had come. When Maharishi had sent the last ones to bed, I still sat faithfully on my spot. Then he looked over at me, seemingly amazed, "Lothar, there you are. But it's too late; come back tomorrow morning, and you'll be the first."

At some point, my moment really did come. Maharishi had a new assignment for us. He asked Karin and me to find hotels all around Germany that would want to integrate a Maharishi Ayurveda department. We drove on several trips across the German provinces, mostly in the company of Lilian and Daniel; we looked for and found prospective hospitals; we evaluated, made plans and negotiated. Finally, I drafted a few contracts.

When two of them were ready to be signed, one of them being with the best hotel in Aachen, a call came again, "Maharishi wants to talk to you."

I reported the state of things to him, and Maharishi was most satisfied. But instead of blessing the transaction, he said unexpectedly, "Lothar, I want you to fly to the U.S. for a while. We've bought a few hotels there in which Ayurveda departments are being set up. I want you to go there and arrange things and organize everything—can you take on this assignment?"

499

"Yes, Maharishi, of course, I'd love to do this."

"Go as soon as possible. Your wife can stay here with the children and continue to work with the vaidyas."

When I brought this news to my love, she swallowed quickly. But, of course, she was agreeable to it.

A little later, I sat in the plane. I traveled all over the U.S. and looked at various hotels that the TM Movement had acquired for a most reasonable price. When I evaluated these places on site, I was shocked. Who, in heavens name, had got the idea to buy these hotels? Just about without exception, they were in miserable condition. One of them had a leaky roof, another one was situated in the middle of three freeways, and a third was directly under a flight path and, on top of that, in a neighborhood where at the main entrance a few drug junkies were hanging out. American Purushas or TM teacher couples had the thankless task of managing these hotels. The Purushas who'd never managed a hotel were hopelessly overextended. They fought on all fronts as best they could. I was totally shocked. At the next phone call with Maharishi, he wanted to know, "Lothar, what is your impression of the various locations?" I told him point blank, "I think that the three hotels I've seen are totally unsuitable for offering Ayurveda treatments. Without some substantial investments, nothing will work there. The location is inappropriate for panchakarma. At the hotel where I'm at right now, three freeways are going right past. The insolation in the windows leaves much to be desired, and in some of the rooms, the rain is coming right in. The TVs don't work and dissatisfied guests are leaving. Something has to happen here fast."

Maharishi seemed really concerned and asked for my

assessment before the acquisition of the next hotel complex. This one was a truly beautiful hotel with a heavenly park in a good location, but there was water standing in the basement. When I told Maharishi about this, he cancelled the purchase.

After the conversation with Maharishi, I asked my friend, Dr. Barry Charles, a good-looking physician trained in Ayurveda and full of humor, for advice. He'd been living in the same hotel in Dallas for a few days because he was supposed to do the necessary preparations with me and take over the administration for the Ayurveda department: "Do you understand why the Movement bought and is managing these run-down hotels? It's making no sense at all."

Barry grinned, "You're not the first wondering about that. But I can tell you something because Maharishi's been asked about this several times. One time the answer was, 'I am making TM teachers weatherproof with this.'"

I was speechless. Never in a million years would I have guessed that, with this action, he was very purposefully training his closest disciples to keep their inner balance even under the most adverse outer circumstances.

Barry continued, "On another occasion with this question, he pointed with an outstretched arm to Brahmachari Nand-kishore and said laughing, 'I have a plan in my head that even *he* doesn't know!'"

Years later and to finance humanitarian projects in India that would guarantee world peace for the coming generations, Maharishi had these hotels, and particularly the land they were on, sold at a profit in a rising real estate market.

The next day, the phone rang in my hotel room in Dallas. It was Jochen, my deputy manager in Bad Ems. His voice sounded depressed, "Lothar, I hardly know how to tell you this. I am sorry, but we must close the clinic. During the last four months, we incurred a lot of debt and on top of that, the tax consultant made a mistake. If you can't raise 130,000 DM in the next ten days, we're bankrupt. The tax consultant advised me to shut down the clinic immediately. But I can't do that; only the owner himself can do that. You have to come back."

I was as if struck by lightning. Nothing had prepared me for this. With the few calls I'd had to Bad Ems, things didn't seem exactly great, but seemed to run normally. Where did this sudden bankruptcy come from?

I took the next flight to Europe.

After arriving in Vlodrop, Maharishi asked over the intercom, "What impressed you most in America?"

I said without thinking, "I was most impressed with the devotion of your TM teachers who are managing these hotels under extremely difficult circumstances."

In his voice, I heard how much this was making him happy, "That is very good—that is really very good," and after a short pause, "Lothar, I want you to fly back to the U.S. You'll get a much bigger but secret project. Please don't speak to anyone about it."

As soon as he'd described it to me, I told him first off about the dilemma in Bad Ems. In closing I said, "Maharishi, I'd love to be available to you further. But I can only do that if I could put the responsibility for Bad Ems into your hands."

Anxiously, I waited for his answer—first there was a long pause—and Maharishi was brief and concise, "You will fulfill all your obligations in an honorable way."

Then the connection was broken. Dr. Tony Nader, a close co-worker of Maharishi's was in the room with me and had heard the conversation. Clueless, he turned towards me, "What was that supposed to mean? Can you figure out what to do with that?" But to me the answer was unquestionably clear.

Hours later, Karin and I began to pack our belongings. My love took it with amazing calm. In the bottom of her heart, she wasn't all that sad that our time here had come to an end. The atmosphere of silence and holiness in Maharishi's surroundings was a precious gift and wondrously beautiful. But for the rest, she thought you had to be born to it.

Almost Bankrupt

Straight as an arrow, I went to the clinic to get a picture of the disaster. I greeted the employees like old friends and then went to my office and, first off, just sat down at my desk. And now, something totally unexpected happened. I had the feeling that my consciousness that had stretched over the whole globe through my work for Maharishi contracted quickly and systematically to the size of a grain of sand. From the great and all-encompassing back to the small; it was a strange feeling. It was clear to me that I had to roll up my sleeves and whip the joint back into shape.

Jochen had not been exaggerating; the situation seemed hopeless. The numbers of guests had declined, the debts of the health center had risen dangerously, and on top of that the tax consultant had overlooked a whole position in his calculations from the beginning of our existence. The tax office had demanded a gigantic back-tax payment within ten days. All in all, we had to conjure up a six-figure amount from our empty pockets. But where to get it?

"Lothar," It was the voice of my receptionist on the phone, "Mrs. Maxara wants to speak to you personally."

Mrs. Maxara, at first glance an intelligent, resolute woman with a good-natured face was getting our cure for the first time. Her humor-full façade hid a deep depression, triggered through her divorce a long time ago. Nothing and no one could help with her psychological exhaustion and depressed mood. Through the balancing treatments, she improved visibly. On the one hand, Karin prescribed calming *abhyanga* herbal oil massages and *shirodhara*, the Ayurveda oil flow onto the forehead that calmed innervated minds. Further, for

504

weight loss and detoxification she got *udvartanas*, massages with a rough paste containing activating herbal mixtures. Purifying nutrition did the rest. For the first time in many, many years, she felt the joy of life and the thirst for activity.

Evidently, she also had an enormous talent for observation. A day before she left, she sat in my office enthusing about Karin's qualities as a doctor and a human being and about the panchakarma treatments. After a few minutes, she put her head to the side, narrowed her eyes a little and said with her brisk voice straight out, "Is it possible that you need money? With one of my investments a big sum has become free. I'd love to make it available for you."

"Um, yeah, it's true," I said slightly embarrassed, "Financially we're in a tight spot right now."

"Yes, I somehow sensed that. I could lend you 130,000 DMs, of course with a small interest."

I almost fell off my chair. That was the exact sum we needed—to the penny. My God, what an act of providence. Immediately, a suspicion crept up. Could Maharishi have his hand in play? I'd told him of my predicament less than three weeks ago and he—as I'd experienced in Tanzania so often—could move mountains with his coherent awareness. Whatever the case, Karin and I took it as incontrovertible evidence that nature was supporting us and that we were on the right track with our health center.

We paid back the money in a few years. And we became good friends with Mrs. Maxara, who, a few years later, even worked for a time as a receptionist in our health center. The love for Ayurveda remains with her to this day.

The spa director, Mr. Schmitt, Count Matuschka's successor, had taken on his new domain. To him as well, I reported our precarious situation due to the small number of guests and the huge fluctuations in the booking that always had to be absorbed—and I noticed, with relief, that my initial fears were unfounded. Mr. Schmitt was indeed noticeably reserved with us. But this man with an honest and friendly face was fully motivated to support our endeavor. So, he considered with empathy, "If the costs are skyrocketing, why don't you do the treatments only with one technician?"

"Mr. Smith, I know you mean well, but that is out of the question for us! The special thing with Maharishi Ayurveda is precisely its high quality. That's how we started out, and that's how we'll keep going."

I was determined to grit my teeth and make it through, come what may.

Lunch with the children was sacred for us. The price, however, that our progeny had to pay for our presence was that their busy parents could not stop talking about their professional challenges while eating—which was most un-Ayurvedic. On this particular day, I told Karin about the conversation with the spa director and his suggestion. Karin totally shared my opinion: "No, that's out of the question. Then the best thing about it is gone. The deeper meaning of two technicians is that something happens in the conscious-ness of the patient. Do you actually know what happens when our technicians do their gentle stroking completely in unison as they've been instructed to do?"

"It synchronizes the activity of the right and the left hemisphere of the brain."

"Exactly. And that activates self-healing ability." She looked at me triumphantly, "And that's just the surface view. Since our technicians meditate, they begin to transcend in the silence of the treatment automatically; their nervous systems are used to that. And here's the thing: In his or her movements, one technician mirrors the other in this synchronized stroking. They are completely tuned in to one another and…" she smiled knowingly and went on, "that furthers the experience of Unity Consciousness. I know that from my own experience. And what's even better, the patient as the third one in this unity also dips into finer levels of consciousness on his or her own. That all this not only fires up self-healing, but also the development of consciousness should be obvious to you."

And she closed energetically with almost the same words I'd spoken that morning, "That's why it's absolutely out of the question that we depart from the high quality of Maharishi Ayurveda."

The high costs were only the surface of our problems. We had to eradicate the real cause of our small number of guests: the badly managed hotel, the bad food, the noisy cars.

I racked my brains on all levels. Karin, meanwhile, grabbed the bull by the horns and once again educated the cooks for an hour every day with infinite patience. But despite this, things advanced only in tiny steps. My patience wore down slowly but surely, but my tender-hearted love protected the hotel employees, "Let it be Lothar, this just takes its time. It'll come together; they're trying really hard."

Even with the best of intentions, there was no way to see that, judging by the food that we got for lunch. As a panchakarma treatment detoxes not only the cells, but also the intestines gently, the diet must be vegetarian and easily digestible. In order that that the patients got enough protein, we regularly served dahl for lunch. Dahl is a delicious, protein-rich legume puree. And ironically, four weeks after all her efforts, Karin fished out the remains of a sausage skin from her bowl. The cooks tricked us to get a better taste, in their opinion. It was the last straw!

I threatened the spa director with all the courage of desperation, "If we don't get our own kitchen immediately, I'll close down the shop."

Mr. Schmitt supported us completely, and within two weeks, what hadn't been possible suddenly was. We got a big room directly next to our dining room. However, we had to furnish it at our own expense; the finances of the state spa also were in the dumps. So, where would this money come from? God once again sent a saving angel. I got into a conversation with one of our patients—a super nice man in the construction business. He inquired about our situation. At the end of our conversation, he was glad to give us a loan for the necessary 80,000 DM.

With new fervor, we set up our own kitchen with used stainless steel appliances and furnishings, obtained from the surrounding area. We won over Frank to be the cook, whose excellent cuisine I already knew from the monastery in Boppard. From his first day on the job, our menu finally became a delight, despite the restrictions that came with a diet during a series of panchakarma treatments.

From this point on, things went up. The clinic became bigger and it grew and grew. We employed more people and rented additional rooms. Yet the financial nail-biters remained, but on a higher plane. Yet, somehow, we managed to pay all the bills right away. That was important to us. But at the end of the year, it was still tense—would we write red or black numbers? As it was, I could let go and meet these ups and downs with composure only four years later.

In our private lives, there was cause for joy as well. At the end of her summer vacation and just before starting high school, our Elisa came back to live with us. The little kids were thrilled and we parents too were more than happy about it.

Health Insurance Companies in a Tight Spot

"Why isn't my health insurance paying for the panchakarma treatments that helped me so much?" This very appropriate question was something I heard from satisfied guests with pleasing consistency.

"Conventional medicine is fully recompensed, no matter how expensive. For years, I cost them enormous amounts because of my asthma. But now that I got rid of it, I have to pay for the therapy that helped me—out of my own pocket—even though it would save the insurance provider a lot of money in the future."

Today, almost all insurance agencies follow this policy—which doesn't mean that it has to stay that way. What has to happen for people to be able to afford help through Maharishi Ayurveda?

In the first year of our official launch, we attempted to change something about the reimbursement method of German health insurance companies. As a start, we organized a symposium with the promising title "Cost Reduction in the Health-Care System." In writing, we invited almost two thousand registered health insurance companies, including their branches at the county and district level, as well as another almost fifty private insurance companies. Prior to the symposium, for two months we hired someone who followed up with them by phone.

I'd heard that a private insurance company in the Netherlands, Geové, had for a few years offered a special rate for TM meditators and reimbursed them for any kind of natural health care approach. What could be more obvious than to invite the CEO, Mr. Kegel, as the main speaker of this conference?

At the symposium, various physicians, all them pioneers of Ayurveda in the Western world, explained the foundation of Maharishi Ayurveda, also presenting a few pilot studies about the successes with chronic illnesses. In addition, they showed the numbers of the great American long-term study, according to which the costs of the insurance company for TM meditators on average were about 50% under those of the non-meditating population—a gigantic savings potential. If the people researched also made use of Ayurvedic treatments and herbal remedies, the savings for the insurance company shot up to an unbelievable 80%.

How would the numbers from the Netherlands look by comparison? All eyes were intent on the front. Mr. Kegel, a stocky, calm man in his mid-fifties began his presentation with the words, "First off, I want to say that I am not a follower of Transcendental Meditation. As the general manager, I owe my superiors accountability—and what counts for the corporation are facts and numbers." After his graphic presentation, we were nevertheless amazed. Why had meditators in the Netherlands only brought in 20% savings for Geové, not 50% as in America? Mr. Kegel had a fascinating answer, "When we analyzed the numbers more deeply, we saw that the meditators had a completely different health-related behavior than our other clients. For the use of allopathic medicine, they really were 50% under them. But since we offer natural healing methods for a special rate, they used these clearly more than the others—certainly also many preventive measures. That is the explanation why they only brought in a 20% savings. But for us, as an insurance company, this is highly interesting anyway."

I was enormously satisfied. This would surely and greatly impress our guests. They were professionals in the field and could calculate these numbers in their heads with the speed of light to see their annual expenditures.

Fifty physicians had come to this symposium, representatives of the press and TV were there, but despite thorough preparations, there were only seven decision-makers from various insurance companies. Every single one of them showed himself to be impressed by the numbers in the easy conversations afterwards.

"So now, what will you do about it?" I wanted to know. "Can you imagine that your company will initiate its own research so that we can use a similar model here in Germany?"

All of them without exception answered about the same way, "I'm personally totally impressed. If it were my decision we'd implement this. But if I did this, I'd risk my job."

At least, one private company subsequently took up Ayurveda into their range of products within the framework of a special rate for natural healing methods.

In the following years, we twice held similar symposiums in Cologne. In private conversation, we learned from the representatives of insurance companies that the law restricts the reimbursement by insurers and that Big Pharma has a huge influence behind the scenes and excludes almost all natural healing methods.

Despite this, we made a few more attempts with the CEOs of various health insurance companies and insurers in our neighborhood, gave them our data in presentations, and our successes in healing. Everywhere, Karin and I were received with friendly interest. But when it came to implementation, there were insurmountable obstacles. We learned that health insurers are not free. "Believe me," said Mr. Landmann*, department head of a big health insurance company near us, "I can no longer do anything like this. I'd be sent straight to hell. In response to patients' requests and on my own, I've recompensed alternative methods that had proven successful. But in two cases, the treating family doctor reported me because I recompensed for forms of therapy that allopathic medicine did not recognize. He'd lost his patient because of this."

Wherever we looked, we met with fear, social restrictions, and obstructing interrelationships.

I thought that is really too bad, as so many people could be feeling so much better if our methods became established in society but Karin remained hopeful. "I'm still sure anyway that things will turn around in the not-too-distance future. The treatment successes are so impressive that the good will no longer be suppressed and will win the day. Didn't Maharishi say, "You cannot fool all the people all the time?" You can't lead people around by the nose forever.

Leave out Maharishi

The politicians of the Rhein-Lahn region, the Prime Minister chief among them, had called for "a year of tolerance and peaceful coexistence and a year of growing closer together in Germany." Prime Minister Scharping was traveling around in the region to see to this. And lo and behold, it was seemingly all done with only lip service about coexistence and growing closer together. From credible sources, we heard that in the background he'd been pulling all the strings with great personal effort to exclude our health center somehow. But despite all his efforts he'd had to give up. We were told that the Prime Minister was having a tough time nullifying the contract between the state spa and our Maharishi Ayurveda Health Center.

It was solid, simple, and could not be terminated. Moreover, the German government does not allow an existing business to be terminated and to take away employees' jobs. When Karin learned about this, she said with an impish grin on her face, "Well, Lothar, unfortunately, your contracts are too good."

At last—what a great feeling that we were suffering no disadvantages for standing up for our conviction and were doing something good for our guests.

But the battle was by no means won. Over time, we had frequent business dealings with our new spa director, Mr. Schmitt. Sometimes it was about more rooms for our growing health center; sometimes it was about our mutual advertising for the spa town of Bad Ems. With all of it, we learned to value each other as reliable business partners and our friendship grew. He realized that we were okay, and, in the end, he was genuinely pleased to work with us. We loved his hearty sense of humor and we joked around together. With regularity, our meetings were topped off with a standard sentence in the Mainz dialect, "Leave out that Maharishi dude and we be best buds."

Karin and I would wink at one another every time and, in a humorful way, we told him no thanks. But the ice had broken.

The spa director wanted only the best for us. At a point in time, he demonstrated it. He went to Mainz, the provincial capital, to argue on our behalf that we were offering solid medical treatments, could demonstrate successful healings, and were fair, pleasant, business partners. He wanted to make sure that, as we were a medical establishment, they took us out of the classification as a cult. For support, he took along the acting mayor, Mr. Bilo. But the two of them had to come back empty-handed. "Nothing we can do, Mr. Pirc, we ran into a bunch of walls."

Germany's mills grind slowly.

Now and then, I took part in political gatherings. Karin and I met with the dignitaries of the town at the summer bridge festival or the flower carnival, when countless floats, decorated with flowers, were paraded through Bad Ems. We went to the Jacques Offenbach concert week, went to musical performances at the local theater or the marble hall of the state spa, a magnificent hall with dark red marble pillars and rich paintings on walls and ceilings. During an intermission I met our Mayor, Mr. Bilo, an active, older gentleman with clear, shining eyes, a headful of white hair, and an open, pleasant manner.

He took me aside briefly; we sipped at our champagne

glasses. "You know, for years the clergy of both denominations have come to see me regularly. They think of you as a dangerous youth cult. They'd come again and again. At some point, it got to be too much for me. I just asked the next one simply, 'Do you really believe that I'm harming our youth by doing nothing against that Ayurveda clinic?'

'Well, um, uh, not really.'"

He smiled at me mischievously, as he was remembering his answer, "Well, then, I think you don't need to come back about that."

Joyfully, the prankster in him flashed in his eyes, "So you see, Mr. Pirc, since then, they've let me be."

Little by little we became one of the figure heads for this charming health resort. The politicians were proud of us. Our guests played a big part in that when they shopped at various businesses, went to get their hair done or bought their Ayurveda herbal mixtures at the pharmacy next door while always praising us enthusiastically for our methods and their successful treatments with us. So, word got around, and, slowly but surely, the rumors and prejudices fell by the wayside.

Many celebrities of movies, TV, and sports, as well as foreign representatives of governments, came to us for cures— most of them, however, preferred to remain incognito. Some of those celebrities learned TM with us, but hardly any of them dared to let this be known to the public. Almost all of them wanted us to keep it secret—which was obviously our policy anyway.

Our establishment became more and more famous, even beyond the boundaries of our small county. Karin, as the leading physician, was invited to TV interviews, and the number of guests at our clinic grew. One day, after an extensive talk show appearance on ARD (the major German network), our phones went wild. Great! But one caller, from another local clinic, was not too enthusiastic about all this, "We're from the headquarters of the Paracelsus Clinic. We are totally overworked. All day long, people who've seen your wife on some TV show are calling us. The phones are ringing constantly—our whole operation is paralyzed. Please stop this."

That was unfortunately not within our power. The TV show had only mentioned Karin's name and "a clinic in Bad Ems," so as not to give us some unfair advertising. Interested folks had simply tried the numbers of various clinics in town. Almost 5,000 enthusiastic viewers called clinics in Bad Ems that day and the following days! To make amends, I sent gigantic bouquets and several boxes of pralines to the receptionists of all the clinics in Bad Ems on that same day.

These, and other broadcasts, were repeated in many programs. We were past the worst, and our 'fame' accomplished something almost overnight that all our good work hadn't been able to do before. The people were proud of us. And we got a good reputation as an indispensable, reliable partner in this resort town, one who could offer something truly special that other resorts didn't have.

All this made it possible for us to receive the official recognition as a private clinic at the beginning of 1996, with the corresponding hygiene requirements and the obligation for a 24-hour on-call service of our doctors, which we had already offered on a voluntary basis before. Soon delegations of other resort cities started to visit our "Maharishi Ayurveda Private Clinic;" they wanted to get inspiration from us to build such establishments in their towns. So then, the folks in Bad Ems were even more proud of us, since they had the prototype in their town.

In bigger intervals people from Russia, Japan, Thailand, and teams from the Netherlands came who wanted me as an advisor to build an Ayurveda establishment in their country, and in one or two cases to be a consultant for a cost efficiency analysis.

The resort's orchestral ensemble played music. For our five-year celebration, 300 guests showed up in the government-owned and festively decorated basement of our building, where the natural springs were. Among the diverse public, there were many physicians from the *German Association of Ayurveda*, businessmen and -women, and citizens of Bad Ems. The Indian ambassador from nearby Bonn took up the patronage. And the Adjunct Mayor of the city, as well as the Provost, stepped up to the podium and praised our establishment.

The tempest in a tea cup seemed to have calmed down.

Priests Break Their Boundaries

"Hello, Mr. Pirc, I'm glad I got you on the phone. My name is Cope*. I'm the ideological officer of the Church and would like to visit your Ayurvedic establishment together with 30 colleagues."

I was taken by surprise, and some mistrust reared its head. "Yes, and what is the purpose of your visit?"

"We'd like to get an impression of your place on site directly."

Spontaneously, a bad feeling took hold of my stomach—from painful experience, I knew only too well that most clergymen slandered us shamelessly. I did not mince my words, "I'm sorry Mr. Cope, in the past, we've experienced again and again that many Church officials are not ready to make any effort to get an objective impression due to their preconceived ideas. Over and over they've tricked us and—please understand—I don't want to receive such people at our clinic."

He remained friendly, "I understand your position, even though I find it regrettable. Could you please reconsider?"

Of course, I could do that. Karin and I consulted with each other if we could take this risk. If they'd treat us the way it was common in Germany now, we'd need quite a while before we could recover from their bombs of prejudices, evil insinuations, and invectives. On the other hand, we really would have liked some sort of rapprochement as we were ready to present our programs, especially in front of such a committee. We were still swaying back and forth when, a few days later, Mr. Cope was on the phone again. "I thought about your arguments again, and you are right. Many of my colleagues really do have rigid negative opinions. But I'd like to choose three or four people from my circle who are open and would like to initiate a genuine dialogue with you."

Who could say no to that? He sounded so sincere on the phone, so pleasant, that I agreed spontaneously and cordially. But a queasy feeling remained nevertheless.

Two weeks later the Reverend Cope showed up at our place with four of his colleagues. We'd just received state recognition as a private clinic, with all the attendant requirements, and were celebrating it.

Over some Ayurvedic tea in our conference room, initial inhibitions evaporated gradually. These churchmen were clearly intent on objectivity and open exchange. We were experiencing this for the first time in twenty years. Despite this, we were glad about it; better late than never. Maybe this was another portent for a change of mind in the Church? A bit earlier, we'd gotten an encouraging message. Cardinal Joseph Ratzinger, head of the Congregation for the Doctrine of the Faith of the Vatican and, later Pope, had written an official letter to the Catholic bishops. In it, he counted Transcendental Meditation among the "Genuine practices of meditation…. which prove attractive to the man of today who is divided and disoriented [and] constitute a suitable means of helping the person who prays to come before God with an interior peace, even in the midst of external pressures."[11] (66)

Our hearts rejoiced at his statement. That's exactly how it

---

[11] See Reference # 66 CONGREGATION FOR THE DOCTRINE OF THE FAITH
Letter to the Bishops of the Catholic Church on some Aspects of Christian Meditation
http://www.vatican.va/roman_curia/congregations/cfaith/documents/
rc_con_cfaith_doc_19891015_meditazione-cristiana_en.html

worked: almost always one's own religion deepened through the practice of TM. Would the tide turn, and would the unspeakable and unfounded hostilities from the Church come to an end?

During the guided tour through the 1,000 square-meters of the clinic, Karin explained to the Ideological Officers not only the special features of Ayurveda therapies but also about our successes in curing various illnesses. The five gentlemen were especially amazed at the many treatment and resting rooms as well as our numerous technicians, who we encountered everywhere in their white uniforms. They could see for themselves that our emphasis was on panchakarma, the classic Ayurvedic detoxification therapy for the elimination of internally and externally created deposits of toxins. This was in direct opposition to the distortions the churchmen and their sympathizers who—without ever once having seen our establishment from the inside first—were spreading the rumor all over the land that doctors in the Ayurveda health centers were using Ayurveda only to foist that oh-so-dangerous TM on unsuspecting patients.

Back in the conference room, the gentlemen sat down on our comfortable rattan chairs and began to question us openly about Transcendental Meditation—the real bone of contention. I explained briefly what TM is, where it comes from, and that in reference to a specific world view, it is completely neutral. I also cited a few of the extant studies. They seemed interested and completely open. I demonstrated objectively that with our 5,000 work-hours monthly, only 30 hours at the most were spent with teaching TM.

Afterwards, I was amazed at myself. Contrary to my usual ways, I began to list for the gentlemen in a strict and reproachful tone, the many insults and malicious defamations we had to put up with for more than two decades in Germany. "Your colleagues have hitched the politicians and the press to their cart and have systematically enflamed them—again and again spreading evil lies and slander against us."

I told them about the Church intrigues back in Wachendorf, when the intervention of the cult-watchers brought down the project through systematic defamation of TM to members of government and journalists. I also told them about my court case, in which I was treated like a leper because I fought against the fact that the hotel manager had, one day before my lecture, suddenly not wanted to give me the assembly hall that I'd already rented, and which was instigated by a lie the preacher told. "What kind of Christianity is this, in which we're stigmatized in public through presumptions and insidious perversions without ever being asked any questions? What do you think about local Church officials regularly showing up in Bad Ems in the offices of the Mayor and county politicians to depict us as dangerous, which lacks any sort of tenability, all that behind our backs obviously, and that at a time when we still had to put our business on its feet?"

The gentlemen looked embarrassed—and Karin looked at me astonished. But I was not yet done, "And what do you have to say about the cult commissioner in Koblenz, who, thank God isn't responsible for Bad Ems, who from a distance spreads negative gossip in the Koblenz papers as well as the local Rhine papers and on the SWR TV about our establishment? I don't think I need to tell you that this man has not stepped into our rooms even once and neither does he know what it looks like here or what we're doing. But he can judge it? Naturally!"

"An engaged journalist of the Rhein-Lahn papers wanted to write a balanced article, because here in this area we meanwhile had a good reputation. So, on the one hand she interviewed that preacher, but she also had read some scientific studies about TM for many days. She'd finished a series with three whole-page articles when her chief editor from Koblenz tersely told her, 'You can't write anything positive about them in my paper.'"

"Swept under the table, all that research. It knocked the woman's socks off, believe me, she'd never in her entire career as a journalist seen anything like this."

I took a breath. "I can list such things for you by the dozen. Take the consumer safety group *Stiftung Warentest*. For the edition *Herz-Kreislauf* (Cardiovascular System), the editor researched the natural reduction of blood pressure through TM and consequently wrote a recommendation for patients with high blood pressure.[12] [(67)] As soon as the book was off the press, Church representatives showed up at the publisher's office and raised hell with their CEO. And what do you think? In the next edition, nothing about that could be found anymore!"

"And it goes on like that. Last summer my wife was interviewed on the radio, and she spoke about better school performances through the increase in IQ, creativity, and attention span. We were glad to finally have a positive radio interview about TM—but then we heard that, in the following few days, the same station broadcasted three interviews with representatives of the Church in which they warned in the

---

[12] See reference # 67

strongest terms about the dangers of TM especially with young people."

Now Karin got into the conversation. "Can you understand that we slowly got so irritated, that we don't have any more enthusiasm to speak for something even though you know it's exceptionally great and could help a lot of people? And these are just a couple of examples that we experienced ourselves, and things like that are going on all the time all over Germany."

And I took aim for my final shot, "We're glad that you are finally looking for an open dialogue. But your colleagues should be ashamed for what they have done and are still doing. If they had not systematically stirred up politicians and the press with their unjust accusations, defamations, and distortions, then many thousands of people could have had much more positive and meaningful lives with better psychological and physical health. You have to accept the fact that you have obstructed people having a better life. How can you reconcile this with loving thy neighbor and with not bearing false witness?"

The compassionate Mr. Cope's eyes were full of tears. He was emotionally visibly shocked at my exposition. Deeply moved, he said, "I have to apologize for my colleagues. I fully understand your situation. I know that all this is true. But the people who are with me today are equally distressed about all that. I've already tried to correct the behavior of my hardline colleagues and I fell flat on my face. At the last conference of bishops, I suggested that the Church should not treat the so-called new religions and similar groups like this—that something needs to change right away. But they gave me to understand most definitely that I should hold back."

Aha, even he was not allowed to open his mouth and support the Christian doctrine of love thy neighbor—sad, but true. Even so, it was nice that these honest men had the courage to find us and to see both sides of the issue.

In a relaxed atmosphere, we answered their questions and were impressed by how we could value and accept each other person to person. When the gentlemen said their good-byes, I asked by way of closure, "If we're treated so badly again by representatives of the Church that it could be dangerous for the existence of our business, can we turn to you?'

Mr. Cope gave us a winsome smile, "You can call me anytime. But I know I can't really promise anything. Even so, you can be sure that I have great sympathy and understanding for you.

One of his companions shook our hands and, as he was leaving, he said, "We'll do what we can so our colleagues treat you more fairly. But we, too, don't have all that much hope that we can succeed. We have a few hardliners in the Church who make so much noise that many just follow them unsuspecting even though these guys are anything but representative. Unfortunately, the Bishops' Conference encourages them, but I'm sure they don't represent most of the clergy in Germany."

How right he was!

After the gentlemen had said their good-byes, my thoughts went back full of love to the first Reverend whose mediation I'd checked occasionally. He was an older, cultivated gentleman, the priest for the nuns of the cloister Schwalbenstein, north of my hometown, Balduinstein, the same cloister where as a kid in response to a dare one night, I climbed through a window into the department of novitiates, though without doing anything once inside. But I'd never confessed this prank to him. We'd both known one another well for many years, and so I got him enthused about TM.

Strictly incognito, he finally visited the four-week SCI course in Bavaria and learned TM there. "The knowledge was superb, and the people there were unbelievably open, joyful, and nice. The only things I have a complaint about are the eating habits of the course participants—barbaric!"

I chuckled amused; I could for sure understand that because his small table, always covered with a snow-white, starched tablecloth, was exactly the opposite. Every four weeks I was in the area, and I visited him and meditated with him. As sure as the amen in church, he blurted out every time, "Ahh, this is great, this freedom! But Lothar, right, you know, you won't tell the other preachers."

After our meditation together, he invited me now and then to a fine, spartan lunch and always lit the candles in a silver candelabra. He celebrated his meal times regularly, cut off every piece from his boiled potatoes and put them slowly and as enjoyably as possible into his mouth.

Not only because of this lovable old gentleman was I convinced that many preachers were fine souls who acted from the highest motives. They had nothing to do with the dirty intrigues of the Church and mostly didn't even know about them. In Bad Ems, too, I'd initiated seven or eight preachers into TM and had always experienced the same thing. Each of them was personally delighted about the depth that opened for them and that they'd missed for so long. But they were all worried that somebody could find out about it. In that context and before the time of the denunciations, a Roman Catholic priest had held a conference for clergy only, in which they exchanged experiences about personal growth through TM and its positive effects on their spirituality, as well as the increased intimacy of their prayers.[68]

XII.

HARD TIMES

The truth should always be repeated
because error is also preached all around us again and again,
and not just by individuals,
but by the masses.
In newspapers and encyclopedias,
in schools and universities,
everywhere error has the upper hand
and it feels good and comfortable
in the emotions of the majority which is on its side.

Johann Wolfgang von Goethe
1749-1832
German poet and natural scientist

Foul Play

"Hello, Lothar; it's Uli. I want to warn you. Just now an editor of the news agency *Frontal* called me and wanted to film us. I sent him packing because this Mr. Rohling* is a real shady character. He's known for his enthusiasm in destroying so-called cults."

It was Uli on the other end of the line; he was the leading Maharishi Ayurveda physician at the Parkschlösschen in Traben-Trarbach on the Middle Moselle. He had connections to the TV scene and knew his way around. "I think they'll call you. I can only advise you to stay away from him. Just don't let him film you, and then he can't do his thing."

On that same day, that same editor, who knew how to ingratiate himself, was on the line, "We want to make a balanced report and want to film at your place."

I'd been warned, "No, I'm sorry, but we're not interested."

But he didn't let go, showing me his friendliest self and imploring me "It really will be a completely neutral report and you, as a private clinic, can only profit from it."

He continued to insist, until, after a brief consultation with Karin, I finally agreed—but not without protecting ourselves with every trick in the book. As a precaution, we called in a professional, Mr. von Schönborn*, the owner of a paper and a PR agency, with whom we'd worked before. On the phone with an entirely too keen Mr. Rohling, we negotiated a written contract point by point. It stated directly that the editor could only mention points of criticism that we could counter at the same length and that he was prohibited from citing us out of context.

Relieved by the agreement, we faxed the contract to the

number of his editorial staff. Mr. Rohling called back immediately and jovially affirmed to our PR agent that *Frontal* would keep to those regulations, no problem. "I'll see you tomorrow morning. I'll be in Bad Ems at ten o'clock to conduct the interviews with Mr. and Mrs. Pirc. The people in the legal department of the ZDF are no longer here. But you can relax; tomorrow morning, they will sign and fax it to you on time before filming."

An hour earlier than expected, he stood in front of our door. A bit stocky, straight, reddish hair, an average face with eyes light as water. Smiling, he said, "I'm sorry, there are technical difficulties. The person who is supposed to countersign the contract did not come to the office this morning. So, we can't send you the contract." He nodded softly in a friendly way and continued, "But I'm telling you in front of witnesses [as backing, we'd also connected with our Mr. von Schönborn by phone] that I will fully comply with the agreement we've made."

Karin and I didn't trust him further than we could throw him. "We are sorry also, but in this case, we unfortunately can't let you film us."

Now he showed us the face Uli had warned us about, "If you do that, I have to inform you that I will then film the building from the outside—and I'll get additional film material from somewhere. This report will be made no matter what. If you won't let us film, then the report will be negative for you in any case because we'll just have to say that you've refused your opinion. I can only recommend that you give an interview now. Then you can tell it as it is."

A clear case of blackmail. After a brief war counsel with Mr. von Schönborn, we decided to answer Rohling's questions.

But Karin and I wanted to play it safe, "We'll just answer in brief and only with short sentences; then he can't take anything out of context."

After a slightly clouded mood at the outset, the interviews really were relaxed and friendly. Mr. Rohling seemed satisfied as well, and at the end he said with a handshake, "Well, you see—that turned out to be worthwhile for you."

Relieved, Karin and I nodded at each other afterwards, "Well, we pulled that off just like we planned."

Two weeks later came the broadcasts we'd been anticipating with much suspense. But the report was bursting with any number of insinuations, lies, and freely invented assertions, as well as the usual abuse for being a "cult movement" spread all through the thing. Since he couldn't find anything else, Mr. Rohling had taken a picture the size of a postage stamp off the back of a book in our little Ayurveda store and had enlarged to the size of a poster and then had claimed baldly, "Everywhere in this so-called clinic there are these pictures of Maharishi."

And the whole article was like that. It was scandalous. Mr. Rohling had lived up to his reputation. How had Uli put it so well, "A real shady character."

And we artless innocents had been taken in despite all warnings.

We were shocked. Not just because of the report, but above all because of the cunning of the editor who had so baldly lied right to our faces and had taken advantage of our friendliness. Next day, when I phoned those responsible at the ZDF, they got rid of me harshly. Mr. von Schönborn, who was no less taken aback, tried as a representative of the press to talk to a superior at ZDF. But the director and those responsible at *Frontal* outright declined even to let him get in touch with them. What to do?

In painstaking detail, Mr. von Schönborn and I prepared a legal document with an affidavit from him, in which we corrected the false claims of this 'investigative journalist'—supported with minutely detailed facts. Our work, which had taken hours, only got a short reply with the standard sentence about how everything in the televised report was correct.

We couldn't just let that go and become the final word of the day. We agreed to sue the ZDF and Mr. Rohling for damages to our business through slander. The tersely written answer from ZDF came a little later, "We are not the responsible parties; the editor is accountable."

So, we asked in another letter for the address of the editor. Not long after, another letter from ZDF fluttered into our house. "We regret to inform you that we do not know the address of Mr. Rohling. This is customary for the protection of our editors."

As we expected, this address couldn't be turned up in other ways. The lawyer we consulted affirmed that in Germany, you couldn't sue anyone whose address was not available.

How could it come to this in a state claiming freedom of expression, and in which most the citizens believed that, through the press, radio, and TV, they could be well and at least somewhat objectively informed? The neutrality of the state concerning world view is guaranteed in German constitutional law as is the self-determination of all religious communities. Despite this, there was a strong interweaving between church and state. Officially, they were separate, but the state did recognize the public role of the official church.

And this led to a system unique in the world: for one, the German revenue office collected church tax; moreover, the government paid the salaries of theology professors at the universities, as well as the education and the salaries of bishops. In addition, tax payers financed the major portion of religious schools, hospitals, kindergartens, senior homes, and social institutions. Of the 2,000 kindergartens in our province of Rheinland-Pfalz, 1,100 of them were financed by the churches. But it you looked closer, 85% of the personnel costs were paid for by the communities, the provincial government, and the parents. The church took over about 15% of these costs from the state—but they determined 100% of the content of the education.[69]

It didn't look much better in German schools. The agreement between church and state guarantees sovereignty to both churches. Germany is predominantly Catholic and Lutheran, and religion is a required subject in all schools. The church has control over the materials taught in religion classes. Because of this, the Catholic and the Protestant churches determine autonomously what our children are taught. And that is the case even though the education, as well as the salaries of religion teachers is paid 100% by the state. One of the explicitly stated educational objectives, as formulated in the "officialese" of these churches, is this: "The ability to distinguish real religiosity from any false manifestations of it."[70] By now, about two generations of children—mostly without the knowledge of their parents—have undergone an indoctrination through which they have been "inoculated" against so-called cults. In this context, TM is mentioned to this day, and, of course, without pointing out that it is a technique of meditation that is free of ideological or philosophical beliefs, and is practiced by people of all religious communities and that hundreds of scientific studies bear witness to its beneficial effects. Without being informed, all taxpayers thus finance the clerical apparatus that has always and is still determining the transmission of values in our land—yet with the difference that it is more cleverly disguised today than it has been in the past.

The official churches have thus succeeded in hitching the state to their wagon, through exaggerations, distortions, and falsehoods, in such a way that the state contributes in high style to the costs and the work with which the churches keep imagined competitors off their backs.

And the media? Representatives of the churches sat in decisive positions on broadcasting councils and on TV committees, and, in this way too, they asserted their influence on public opinion. Meanwhile, many potential clients, made insecure because of the ZDF broadcast, canceled their appointments with us. In my dismay, I called the Reverend Knoop who'd shown himself to be so sympathetic at our house among his colleagues.

"Is it possible for you to make a positive statement for us in this context?"

But his hands were tied. "I'm really sorry, but this would be too dangerous for me. I'm too far out on a limb already. I wouldn't just lose my job, but there would be other consequences for me. So, I'm in no position to help you, even though I would really love to."

We could fully understand his dilemma. All too often we'd experience it for ourselves that it doesn't pay to go up against incalcitrant stubbornness and prejudice.

Were there legal options? Even if there were, as Karin

reminded me, in their education at the academy for judges, German judges took courses about "cults in modern times"; she also mentioned the futile battles for law and justice my friend, Dr. Christoph Reusch, had fought for our cause.

So, we finally swallowed this bitter pill and found consolation with Arthur Schopenhauer: "Anything new goes through three phases before it is recognized: in the first one, it is ridiculed; in the second, it is fought; and in the third is recognized as self-evident." Hopefully, the third phase wouldn't make us wait for it too long.

And so, after this distasteful interlude, we again dedicated ourselves to our real life's work—to bring health and the joy of life to people.

I Manage the Spa Hotel

The hotel continued to give us trouble. In six years, believe it or not, three different operating companies with seven different hotel managers had been in charge. The hotel employees, with a few exceptions, were badly educated. The managers tried to save money with every tiny detail. The four stars we'd had at the start were denied by the German Hotel and Guesthouse Union due to all the uncertainties and deficient performances.

Now, the Hotel Management Company of Cologne* managed the place, and the conditions were worse than ever before. A former photocopier salesman was acting as the hotel manager, a man who talked big when it came to suggestions for improvements but other than that, was incompetent. He took complaints from the hotel guests but no action was ever taken. Our clinic guests, who stayed in the hotel, went and bought their own lightbulbs for their bedside lamps, and complained about spider webs in the hotel rooms and un-cleanliness of the bathrooms.

Every day, I had to calm down our upset guests. When it became clear that the new hotel manager couldn't be counted on, I complained in writing to the CEO of the Hotel Management Company of Cologne. When that proved to be of no avail, I wrote him again. This time, I included copies of dozens of complaint forms filled out by dissatisfied guests—and still no reaction. Mr. Müller* came about every few weeks to the spa hotel unannounced to see to things. Before I even figured out he was here, he was most often already gone. This just could not keep going on. We were tilting against wind mills! There was no question that we offered good service in our clinic but, due to the poor conditions in the hotel, we couldn't get repeat customers or recommendations. We were at the end of our rope.

Karin and I often looked for a way out, examined every detail inside and out, and had to admit defeat—there was just no solution to be found. A change of venue was out of the question due to the investments we'd already made, and, as for the hotel, we ran repeatedly into a stone wall. In our distress, we could think only of one way out, and that was to address the problem from a completely different level—the level of consciousness. We scratched together our meager finances and ordered a very special yagya, a traditional Vedic technology handed down for ages, with the intent to activate life-supporting influences for our business and, especially, to solve the current problems in the hotel.

After the pundits in India had been reciting their Vedic hymns for a couple of hours on the morning of the second day, someone knocked at the door of my office. Surprise! Before me stood the CEO of the Hotel Management Company of Cologne, Mr. Müller, with whom I could almost never connect. "Mr. Pirc, I have to ask your forgiveness. I've been unfair to you and your business. I couldn't sleep all night and have been thinking about the situation in this house. I've decided to quit managing this hotel. You know, the Hotel Management Company of Cologne has taken over this hotel in conjunction with three other convention hotels—our emphasis is to host conventions. We had to take all four hotels as a package even though the spa hotel didn't fit into our concept at all. Last night it became clear to me that this hotel needs a completely different management from the other ones. It should be run as a family business with a lot of close attention."

A bit theatrically, he pulled a bunch of keys, the hotel keys, from his pocket and held it in front of my nose, "This very day, I'm going to the mayor and to the spa director, and I'll give them these keys. I will not take responsibility for this facility for another day even if I must pay a fine. And I will suggest to these gentlemen that you and your wife should take over the management of this hotel, and that will do justice to this place."

What a total turn-around in no time at all! It came literally overnight and seemed like a miracle. It's exactly this kind of thing that a yagya should do: a total support of nature in an evolutionary direction.

Mr. Müller did not give over the keys. But, two hours later, the completely blind-sided spa director, Mr. Schmitt, asked me to come to his office, where, long ago, the Kaiser had resided. "For God's sakes, Mr. Pirc, what are we to do now? The best thing would of course be to close the spa hotel until we can find a new manager. But we have to keep going for the sake of your patients."

"Yes, of course, nothing else will do."

"Mr. Müller suggested that you and your wife should manage the hotel. Can you see your way clear to doing that until we find another solution?"

"Yes, that would be possible. In fact, many years ago, I did manage hotels and I know this place pretty well."

"Well, then, I think this would be the best solution. OK, I'll call the board of supervisors to a special meeting, and I'll inform those gentlemen about the new situation, and we'll see what can be done."

All this was highly explosive, of course. Mr. and Mrs. Pirc, who, together with their Maharishi Ayurveda Private Clinic were to be kicked out by the prime minister personally not too long ago are now to be the managers of the state-owned spa hotel? That this would make waves was not hard to guess. Despite initial prejudices, the manager of the spa and the mayor trusted and supported us wherever they could. But what would be going on behind the scenes?

This we learned not too long after from Mrs. Hatzmann, an assemblywoman of the FDP (a smaller political party) who was from a neighboring town and who had met with us several times already and had supported us, that a big meeting had been scheduled, and the regional politicians of all stripes had assembled and were deliberating.

"What are we doing to ourselves politically if we support Mr. and Mrs. Pirc? What happens if reporters from the *Bildzeitung* (a German tabloid) get wind of this, and articles spread around the country: "Scandal at a State Spa—Politicians Employ a Cult?"

They had not been entirely wrong with their fears, though the political wind in Germany had begun to turn a little. In the same year that we'd opened our Ayurveda clinic in Bad Ems, the German government created a non-partisan commission inquiry into "so-called cults." To be sure, the originally harshest cult persecutors were called to this committee, but after intensive protests from the ranks of targeted groups, the people who were practicing these denounced methods were interviewed personally for the first time and could therefore speak from their own experience. After four years of examination and evaluation, the inquiry commission concluded with the long overdue summary that "At the present point in time the new religious and worldview associations do not, all things considered, constitute any danger to the state or to society."[(71)]

Indeed, the troubled scene calmed down somewhat after that. Since then at least, the German government no longer published official reports on cults in which Transcendental Meditation was mentioned. As ordered by the appeals court, there had since been no official negative announcements. But how long would it be until the fomented and deep-rooted fears and prejudices in the public and in the press subsided? Especially since there were a few influential religiously oriented persons within the anti-cult sphere who still unswervingly tried to defend their untenable position and carried on with their propaganda.

Even if some day all this belonged to a less than honorable past, it was clear to all members on the board of supervisors of Bad Ems that my management of the spa hotel was still a hot topic. No one wanted to stand up for it alone. So, they shrewdly agreed to a feasible way out: they assured each other not to shout it from the rooftops and stand behind it in closed ranks. A little later, I got the official cleaned-up version from spa director Mr. Schmitt: "Mr. Pirc, we have discussed the matter, and we'd be glad if you could manage the hotel until we can find a new tenant."

Things did get a little complicated anyway. As I would manage the hotel only for a limited time, I could not take over the responsibility for marketing and the costs for up-keep by myself. With this, too, we reached an agreement with the spa manager on a workable contract. I employed Mr. Sikora as the hotel manager because I thought him to be very competent as he had led the hotel for some time years ago under another manager. But despite the relief he offered, this task was not easy. It was fun to motivate the employees and to educate them in the ways to improve the service of the hotel. I was proud and happy that, under our leadership, we succeeded at the next evaluation through the German Hotel and Restaurant Association to get back the four stars for the hotel.

Yet there were problems everywhere you looked. Only now, I realized fully the extent of the backlog of renovations for this old building and its consequences. In the long run, the hotel would attract more guests only if a private investor would put several millions into it because the tills of the state spa were yawningly empty.

I laid out my view of things to the spa director and informed him of the amounts it would take for urgently necessary renovations and I offered, "Mr. Schmitt, I would be glad to assist you in finding someone suitable for this."

"Well, Mr. Pirc, there really is no other way. In view of the costs, the board of supervisors has already thought about whether it wouldn't better to privatize."

Soon after, the search for a buyer for the state-owned enterprise began. The spa owners rubbed their hands together gleefully. With the sale of this magnificent real estate right by the river, it would certainly be possible to improve the ailing cash box of the state. But despite all efforts, no fish would bite. And so, the asking price sank in direct proportion to the unwillingness of those who were possibly interested in the purchase. Time was short because the numbers in the red grew month by month.

Finally, I got the glorious idea to contact Mr. Jagdfeld, the co-owner of the Fundus Group, one of the biggest real estate enterprises in Germany. He had just bought the Adlon

Hotel, and, with expensive renovations, had made it into a number one destination in Berlin. Wouldn't that be great for our spa hotel also? Mr. Jagdfeld came and succumbed to the magic of our baroque building that had largely been maintained in its original condition. The negotiations came to a successful conclusion. The appointment with the notary was made. He chose a prospective hotel director, a cultivated, charming gentleman in his sixties with a lot of experience, who was glad to re-awaken this gem on the Lahn River.

All the government representatives who heard about this were over the moon about it. Finally, finally, things would pick up again with the heart of Bad Ems. I'd already been working with the prospective hotel director for a few days, when the appointment with the notary fell through. Mr. Jagdfeld had more urgent business. The second appointment with the notary was postponed for the same reason. For the third one, Mr. Jagdfeld brought his wife, who had helped the Adlon to its impressive standard of luxury and timeless elegance with her tasteful design. She was interested in what we were offering, enjoyed an Ayurvedic test treatment, and was extremely impressed. Everything went well, we dined together in the hotel restaurant and, immediately afterwards, they drove to the notary. And now, there came something incomprehensible. Anne Maria vetoed the thing! And Mr. Jagdfeld followed the intuition of his wife.

Dream, over!

What to do? But our spa director had an idea. "Mr. Pirc, can't you imagine buying the hotel together with your wife, renovating it and then keep running it?"

Of course, I could imagine it.

Karin and I once again discussed the situation at length.

The hotel had meanwhile become dear to our hearts. We would have loved to restore it back to the glamor that this marvelously beautiful building deserved. I went to the bank president and, after laying out the numbers and our ideas, I got confirmation for the eight million DMs required for the necessary renovations.

Things could move ahead. Mr. Schmitt was happy; Karin had the first plans in her head, and on paper, about how we'd transform the building. And in our minds, the whole thing took form. "Lothar, I think that we're both well-suited for this, and I can see how we'll renovate the hotel and make it successful. But one thing is sure. We'll have no time in the coming years for a private life, and what's worse, our kids will see much too little of their parents."

She'd hit the nail on the head. Daniel was five years old, Lilian was eight, and Elisa was fourteen. All of them were too young in our opinion to leave them to their nanny most of the time. And I got further worries. "I'd love to take over the hotel, but I'd much rather use my energy to the expansion of Ayurveda." What to do? I hesitated only briefly. "Hmm, what do you think about asking Maharishi for his opinion?"

"Good idea. Try getting hold of him."

I called Tony in Vlodrop, described our situation to him, and only hours later I got the call back with Maharishi's opinion. "You can buy the hotel and you'll be successful, but it would be better to find another investor because the building doesn't have good *vastu*. And if you own it, this would have an unfavorable influence on you."

So, the die was cast for us. Vastu designates an aspect of Vedic architecture that prescribes the orientation of a building and its rooms with respect to their compass directions, as well as their proportions, so that the house would have a propitious influence on its residents. Maharishi had given his attention to this aspect of Vedic Science for a few years now to return it to its original significance. Karin and I only knew a few basics. We knew that an east entrance brought good luck. A south entrance and a gloriously wide south-facing façade, as well as water to the south, such as our Lahn River, were all seen as inauspicious and promote disputes. Well, that was the third and last argument to back off from purchasing the hotel.

For Mr. Schmitt, this was a bitter setback initially. For months, he searched all over the country for an interested buyer. And without the urgently needed renovations, it was still difficult to offer our guests a great stay at our spa. When nothing seemed to go forward, Karin and I once again ordered a yagya in India for an improvement of the conditions within the hotel. And, after that, the complications finally began to resolve themselves. Through the minister of finance, Mr. Schmitt found the Häcker family, a hotel-owner family who, in a short time in another spa town had rebuilt the run-down Hotel *Fürstenhof* (Courtyard of a Prince) with equal amounts of effort and good taste to become a five-star hotel. Additionally, the Fürstenhof had a fabulous occupancy, and with this Mr. and Mrs. Häcker seemed the most ideally suited candidates for Bad Ems. Mr. Häcker committed himself to invest far more than eight million in the house in the following years and make it become once again a real grand hotel.

With this, and after fourteen months of my time as a temporary hotel manager—which should have lasted only a few months—was finally over.

In Court

Only sparsely the winter light came through the tall windows before which the dark silhouette of a barren branch with a few greyish-brown dead leaves swayed. Karin and I sat on a long dark-stained wooden bench in an austere court room in Koblenz. To the left of me sat our attorney, Mr. Bittner*, who had become an indispensable help to us this past year. This small, roundish man with an almost feminine and gentle face was a specialist in German advertising law for pharmaceuticals and medicinal products. He understood his field well. And we truly needed him urgently.

A year earlier, the blue letter had come from the court. There it was in black and white, "It is forbidden to make assertions about the healing successes with your patients in your publications." The passages we were not allowed to use were cited in their exact wording. At the end, it said, "Violations are punishable with a fine up to 250,000 Euro or imprisonment up to six months." As it turned out after some brief research, this letter had been initiated by an organization to watch against unfair practices. It was one of many whose self-proclaimed assignment, according to their attorneys, was to find doctors and clinics whose advertising went beyond the legally permitted limits. And then to sue them—to rake in good money for themselves—obviously.

With much love and over time, we had developed a brochure and a folder for people interested in Ayurveda. After all, people didn't get the idea on their own that they could spend their vacation in an Ayurvedic clinic if they'd never heard of it. And patients wanted to know what a treatment would do for them before they'd go for it and spend a not exactly small amount of money for it. With fiery enthusiasm, Karin and I had been on this task to develop appealing informational material. And this material, which contained nothing that didn't correspond to facts would now not be allowed?

A few phone conversations later, it was clear that German law really did not allow all that was warned against in the letter.

It took only a few seconds of shock till it dawned on me that we'd have to shred all our printed material. Ignorance of the law does not protect you from punishment. But didn't the letter say that we had a grace period of eight days? That was exactly the way out!

With lightning speed and with all our employees, we prepared a mailing of all our existing materials. Thousands of previously unplanned letters informed our target audience of the blessings of Ayurvedic medicine. To be sure, this entailed some cost, but it was better than feeding all those lovely brochures into a shredder.

But now, how to create a new brochure in compliance with the law? Mr. Bitter got the thankless task to check that the next brochure was unassailable and to delete anything about which we'd been admonished. Frequently, we struggled about every formulation. With a heavy heart, we removed all medically relevant statements from the printed interviews of our guests. That they loved the food and that our employees were friendly could stay. But that their illnesses got better or were healed—that we had to take out. Soon, the restricted brochure left the press. That whole episode cost us "a measly" forty thousand DM! Our time and the losses due to the reduced number of guests, as we had no materials to send out for a few weeks, was not included. And that was during a time when we truly did not write any numbers in the black. It was a heavy burden, but we'd make it work despite even this. The main thing was that we were on the safe side. That gave us a good feeling.

At least until, after a few months, when the next letter came—once again from the same organization. "In your publications, you are forbidden from citing scientific studies that document successful cures with the therapies you use."

Once again, we were threatened with a significant fine or time in prison. Come again? This was getting better and better! Those were scientific studies, well thought-through results that one could rely on better than any reports of personal experiences. I called Mr. Bittner. But nothing helped. "It's true, Mr. Pirc. Scientific results can only be given out to experts in Germany, to doctors and other members of the medical profession."

So, patients in our free country cannot be informed about verified medical facts—to this day. The only exceptions were specialized books in which doctors could present their expertise to lay persons.

For a couple of days this situation had me a bit depressed because wouldn't we suffer massive losses in the number of guests if we were disallowed just about any kind of attractive advertising? And then the scales fell from my eyes. Didn't Maharishi tell me, totally unexpectedly, years ago that, "If legal problems come up for you in spreading Maharishi Ayurveda in Germany freely, contact me personally and directly"? And I was certain that he had foreseen exactly this situation back then. In a fax to Maharishi, I quoted his statement and sketched out the details of this whole disaster.

Ten minutes later, Nankishore called and gave me Maharishi's answer, "Lothar should take it easy! Even if he can't make these statements in the future, it will not affect his success significantly."

It was so good to see the whole thing through his eyes from a higher perspective and to feel his attentions and his blessing!

So, now we sat in the courtroom on a hard, wooden bench, a bit tense; next to us sat a big box with five thick volumes full of scientific studies.

The judge stepped into the room wearing his black robe, a burly man with a red, square face, whose life had engraved deep furrows in his features. Another health practitioner was ahead of us, who'd described some of the special therapies he offered in his practice on his website—presumably, he was as clueless as we were. The judge made short work of him. He shouted at him roughly several times and finally gave him a fine of over 7,000 DM. The poor guy—what a gigantic sum—given such a harmless infraction!

Karin and I got smaller and smaller on our hard bench for poor sinners. Heavens alive, that judge was worked up— and we, "from the cult," were about to get our comeuppance. For starters, he looked cantankerously at Karin and asked me caustically, "Who's that woman?"

"She is our leading physician."

"We won't need her here. You are the solely responsible CEO. And what are those boxes with file folders and books—what do those have to do with anything?"

I explained to him that we had the results of scientific studies with us, that we'd referenced in our brochures. "We don't need that stuff. You know, on the high seas and in a courtroom, you are in God's hands."

Then he turned to the right abruptly, to where the smug attorney for the organization that was suing us was sitting, and snarled at him, "I must point out that you have not done your homework, young man! You have accused a private clinic. But in your organization, there are only members of the pharmaceutical industry—therefore, you are lacking any sort of legal basis to sue a clinic. Case closed!"

He got up, bowed in a friendly way in our direction and left the room. Karin and I were totally flabbergasted. Mr. Bittner had to explain to us what had just happened. Within a few minutes this grumpy man had decided the case in our favor. Nothing would happen to us; we really were in God's hands.

Despite this, however, we were not yet out of trouble. A little later, we were sued again by the same organization who—hard to believe—had won over a few clinics to be members. But our good Mr. Bittner was up to every trick in the book also. He fought back bravely, so that this time we only had to make a few changes. "Why, in heaven's name didn't they mention everything the first time?" I complained to him. "In our profession, we call this the "salami tactic", he said, calmly, "With that, you defeat people slice by slice and you can make in more money each time."

A half a year later, a new letter came. This time it was from the Center for Combatting Unethical Advertising. The penalty for any violation was a laughable 10,500 DM. Nevertheless, this letter packed a punch: No more scientific studies, no statements by patients about successful healings, and no technicians or doctors in professional attire when they are shown in connection with therapeutic treatments.

And so, the spectacle began anew, and, this time, we'd just had few thousand brochures printed. For the third time, we sent out the remaining editions and then followed the usual walk on eggshells in the grey zone between what was and wasn't allowed, all while under the eagle eyes of Mr. Bittner.

Thank God, our attorney was on the ball. He got agreement that we would at least be allowed to use the graphics of studies that showed the preventive effects of panchakarma because this, as we learned to our amazement, was indeed allowed. We showed how panchakarma lowered cholesterol and ratios of arteriosclerosis and thus could protect from heart attacks and strokes. Further, we showed that this ancient therapy breaks down environmental toxins and the damages through free oxygen radicals and therefore helps to prevent the occurrence of various illnesses. On the other hand, we had to take out that this gentle therapy is extremely effective to mitigate or heal asthma, chronic bronchitis and sinusitis, to reduce psoriasis, neurodermatitis, as well as treating adult-onset diabetes and high blood pressure with exceedingly positive results.

Indeed, Maharishi's assessment proved to be right over time. Even with this pared-down material, our clinic grew and prospered unhindered. Evidently, the recommendation of satisfied guests was more important than any raw information.

The law on Advertising in the Health Care System was a joke for us: totally old hat. So, a little later, I went to visit Mr. Winkler, our government representative of the Green Party in the House of Representatives. "Can you do something politically so the Law on Advertising in the Health Care System is changed? Our patients are educated people. Why shouldn't they be able to see the scientific studies about the therapeutic successes that affect them personally, especially since they have to pay for the treatment themselves?"

Mr. Winkler tried. His petition to reformulate the Law on Advertising in the Health Care System was welcomed unanimously by the Greens and the Left—and shot down by all other parties.

Mozambique on the Upswing

Maharishi European Research University (MERU) in Vlodrop opened its doors only a few days per year to outsiders. One of these times was *Guru Purnima*, the first full moon in July when the tradition of Vedic masters is honored as the source of wisdom. Every year Maharishi allowed the representatives of the world-wide TM Movement to present their successes in the spreading of Vedic knowledge. It was a way to thank his master, Guru Dev, for everything that had become possible through him. This ceremonial meeting was transmitted to almost all the countries of the world via satellite, and for many it was the high point of the year.

Our children roughhoused together with many others in the big on-site park; they went high up in the air on the swing hung in an old tree, and had fun. Karin and I stood at the edges of the drive that was decorated with international flags, when an escort of the Netherlands government accompanied several diplomatic vehicles to MERU. The president of Mozambique exited one of those cars, together with many of his cabinet ministers. They disappeared into the huge entrance portal. Originally, the president had wanted to participate in a European UN conference that had been cancelled with short notice. Now, he used the time slot that had become open to accept a standing invitation from Maharishi. That it coincided with the first full moon of July made it possible for all of us to participate in this event.

We sat in the huge assembly hall in Maharishi's suite. There were no empty chairs. Various speakers reported the positive effects of their activities.

"Do you think that he's the president?" Karin pulled at my sleeve and, with an unobtrusive nod of her head, indicated a tall man standing amid a group of other Africans on the speaker's platform. He had a pleasant, friendly, and round face. His whole appearance radiated great authority.

"Presumably," I didn't know either. Shortly thereafter, he was the next speaker introduced: Joaquim Chissanó, President of Mozambique.

For years, teams of Purusha had spoken to heads of state in many countries and introduced them to the TM programs. They had presented the background and the scientific studies which showed that a new approach was available to peacefully address the problems on the most diverse levels of any country.

President Chissanó explained, "I was fascinated, but also careful. First, I and my family learned TM and practiced it for several months. After that, I knew for sure that it was a good thing. Only then did I speak with my Ministers face-to-face to win them over gradually. They too first tested it for themselves and their families and were as pleased with the positive changes in their lives as I was. Slowly and carefully, we spread it until most of my cabinet practiced TM. Only with the next step did we then introduced it to the officers of our armed forces and then to our plans to build up a big and permanent peace-keeping force. These officers had already been convinced by the positive effects in their personal lives. And then, last year, we subjected the endeavor to thorough tests to see if we wanted to give this thing a chance."

He laughed a boyish laugh. "And we decided to do it. Many thousands of people in Mozambique have meanwhile learned TM; 12,000 of our soldiers practice TM, and most of these also practice the TM-Sidhis as a group."

We were touched. Finally! The first head of state in the world, who implemented Vedic techniques for the development of consciousness exactly as Maharishi had suggested they should be. Mozambique was the first country to reward its soldiers for real peace-keeping.

President Chissanó continued: "As soon as this group of soldiers had started to meditate, we got plenty of rain after a prolonged drought, which led to record-breaking harvests in Mozambique and neighboring regions."

Well, didn't that sound familiar somehow?

Like no head of state before him, Joaquim Chissanó had understood the laws about the influence of consciousness and had used them in a targeted way to solve problems. He told us about the peace negotiations with his political opponents to end the civil war which had been ongoing since 1975, and which had broken out immediately after the termination of Portuguese colonialization, when Mozambique had entered the fight against the rule of the white minority in neighboring South Africa and Zimbabwe.

About these peace negotiations, he told us, "I had a group of meditators in an office right next to the conference hall, and the whole time during this meeting, they created coherence. When the representatives of other organizations came to me, they all expected massive quarrels and altercations. Yet the atmosphere was totally relaxed; we were like old friends who met after a long absence!"

Indeed, he accomplished what had earlier been impossible. In 1992, the conflict had been resolved, a conflict that had killed almost a million people through war and famine in the past 17 years. Six million had been uprooted, and the farmland had been mismanaged so that, in the end, the country was 70% dependent on foreign aid. In the meantime, however, things looked very different. Already in 1993 there was a noticeable reduction in crime and in traffic accidents, while the economic growth was 19% instead of the expected 6%.[72]

On this full moon in July, Joaquim Chissanó was given an honorary doctorate from Maharishi Vedic University in Holland for the creation of the Maharishi Effect in his country.

With gracious humility, he expressed his gratitude: "Who is responsible for all the good things that happened in Mozambique? It could be our people who meditated there; but it's also all the people on this planet who meditated for a better world. That is why the honor bestowed on us should go to all those who practice Transcendental Meditation."

During the next intermission, our voices buzzed with excitement and happiness. That was excellent good news!

"Do you know what I think is best in this whole thing?" Karin's voice was sunny and her eyes were bright, "I think it's great that it's Africans who are the first to implement this. They usually come last in the affairs of the world, and now they're in the front as a good example!"

I could only agree with her, but would it continue? I was no longer the wide-eyed young man I'd been maybe ten years earlier. Back then, such news would have put me into an overabundant state of ecstasy. Brimming over with certainty, I would have gone with the assumption that the fate of humanity would turn toward the good after we could show a well-functioning model project. In the meanwhile, however, I'd seen that even brilliantly successful projects could come to nothing if the attention or the means behind them fizzled out. So, I just hoped deep in my heart that this thing would last.

Unnoticed by the peoples of the world, the peace wing of Mozambique's military practiced the TM-Sidhi Program every day. But we, who knew what the potential inherent in this project was, waited with bated breath for further development. A while back, we had learned at a similar conference that of the four million New Zealanders, 40,000 had learned TM. There, too, we had followed the results of the 1% effect in the news and were happy that amazed reports showed up in the newspapers about the decline of unemployment and the improvement of the economy. We believed we knew the reasons for that on subtle levels. What would we be hearing about Mozambique?

About half a year later, there was a series of detailed reports about the remarkable changes in Mozambique. In one of Germany's major newspapers, the conservative *Frankfurter Allgemeine Zeitung* we read: "The contrast between the former colonies of Portugal in the south of Africa could not be greater. A decade ago Angola and Mozambique both were immersed in civil wars. Angola had vast resources of oil and diamonds. Mozambique, according to the statistics of the World Bank, was the poorest country in the world. Ten years later, the war in Angola became worse... Mozambique, on the other hand, is a model case of a peaceful conflict resolution in how the respected government settles disputes in the region. The economy shows a growth rate of more than ten percent and an inflation rate of zero percent; the currency shows a growth rate on the free market, even when compared to the American dollar... That Mozambique is

on a path of instituting one of the few governmental con-
stitutions—and not just on paper—is evident, even now,
as it upholds freedom of the press."[73] Four years later, the
International Edition of the New York Times confirmed the
noteworthy transformation that had taken place in the fate
of its population: "For the first time in years, Mozambique
produces enough food to sustain itself. Refugees of the civil
war have come back to their farms, and, in the fertile north,
after the most severe draughts in the history of south Africa,
the harvest is most bountiful. The inflation rate fell from
70% to 5%.... The country that was regarded as one of the
poorest in the world is starting to look like an African success
story....The authority of UN in the termination of the civil
war and the resulting general election was an exceptional
African success story for this organization. International aid
was, at one time, the only source of growth of industry in
Mozambique, but today, there are many more private cars in
Maputo (the capital city of Mozambique) than those of the
relief organizations."[74]

A follow-up article a few months later, held that the
transformation in Mozambique had its roots in something
more humane than just politics. "The people are characterized by a peace that is impelled by a general refusal to
continue the conflict, as well as an unshakeable determination to live a normal life. ...What really drives Mozambique's
rise is the energy of individuals to tackle problems at their
inception."[75]

Joaquim Chissanó knew where these amazing transformations in the collective consciousness of his people came
from. And it was crystal clear to him how to duplicate these
transformations. He loved his country and he also loved his

neighboring countries. So, what could be more obvious than to tell them how they could turn around their bad luck with little investment or cost? He was tireless at political meetings with other African statesmen to explain the Vedic defense strategy and to offer his experience in building these peace troops.

At the end of 1999, he once again affirmed the continuing success of his coherence-creating group. He conveyed how he had succeeded in ending the 20-year civil war in his country, and how, since then, in the past seven years, peace, stability, and democracy of his country had been maintained, for which results he'd implemented the programs Maharishi had given to the world. In his speech, this great and unconventional thinker said, "The culture of war has to be replaced with a culture of peace! For this reason, something deeper in our spirit and our consciousness must be changed to prevent the rekindling of hostilities."

Chissanó, the statesman, emphasized that people who had always lived in a peaceful country could not understand the effects of war on the daily life of a nation. "In Mozambique, we know very well what we are talking about when we say, 'No more war' and 'Peace forever'." He gave expression to his deepest conviction: "Stress is the ultimate cause of fear and conflict. Stress in the family brings domestic abuse; Stress in government causes false perceptions and power struggles and loss of success for the whole country."

Not long after, the inevitable happened.

At a small meeting in Vlodrop, Joaquim Chissanó, the great beacon of hope, turned to Maharishi with all eyes on him: "Maharishi, in the last few weeks I experienced massive resistance. The heads of state of rich, Western countries are everything but enthusiastic about my support of Vedic theories about invincibility in other African nations. The UN threatened to cancel all financial aid to my country if I don't stop talking at political functions about the potential of the TM-Sidhis for the military. They demand that I disband the detachment of soldiers who are practicing TM in Mozambique."

A breathless and tense silence followed his words.

"Maharishi, I am very sorry. I know what you have done for our country, and I am most grateful for it. This is not what I want. But I don't see any other possibility. I must disband that group. We are not yet ready to make it without these subsidies."

Maharishi tried to encourage him: "If the soldiers continue to practice the sidhis in such a big group, your country will become so strong that Mozambique will continue to grow even without international support."

But Chissanó could no longer stand the pressure: "Of course, I'll continue to meditate and many of the members of my cabinet and my people will too. But we have no other alternative; we have to back down."

At the end of the conversation, Maharishi warned: "If you disband this detachment, you'll have to be very careful with water—there is a danger that your country will be flooded."

The die was cast: Joaquim Chissanó, the great and strong man with an innovative mind surrendered to the Superpowers.

In February of 2000, Mozambique once again made headlines—this time, negative ones. Heavy rains had led to catastrophic floods that cost numerous lives.

In appreciation of his accomplishments, the democratization of his country, the drafting of a constitution for a multi-party system, and the normalization of the relations with his neighboring country, South Africa, Joaquim Chissanó received the "Mo Ibrahim Foundation Prize for Excellent Governance" at the end of his presidency in 2007.

Peace for Yugoslavia

At the beginning of the Easter vacation in 1999, we visited our friends Norbert and Mary in southern Germany with our children. My Purusha friend had meanwhile married a nice American woman whom Karin had taken into her heart at first meeting. The six of us spent a relaxed weekend in their comfortable apartment, went for walks, chatted, and, together, enjoyed the laughter and the spontaneity of our youngest.

In the evening, we turned on the TV and, snuggling innocently on the sofa, we learned terrifying things. For years now, the civil war between the Serbians and the Kosovo-Albanians over the independence of the Serbian province of Kosovo had been smoldering in the multi-national state of Yugoslavia. Since 1998, the weaponized disputes between the Yugoslavian police, together with the troops and the Albanian rebel organization, the "Kosovo Liberation Army," had been getting more intense. Both sides had destroyed several towns and had killed their civil populations. At least 1,000 deaths were being mourned, and 300,000 Kosovan Albanians had fled. The UN Security Council had intervened. In response to pressure from the U.S., Russia, Great Britain, France, Germany, and Italy, direct negotiations between the Serbian government and representatives of the Kosovan Albanians had been conducted, which, at the end of 1998 had led to a ceasefire. But already in January, combat had flared up again. In March, the on-going peace talks through the mediation of NATO had broken off without success. On this evening, there had been an uproar. NATO had threatened for months about attacking and now, without a mandate from the UN, they had bombed five air defense facilities in Serbia. Russia criticized these attacks and threatened military countermeasures. The Yugoslavian army was mobilized and a state of emergency was declared that same evening. Petrified, we sat in front of the TV. There was war here, directly in Europe!

Already on the following morning, we got a call. Maharishi asked that as many meditators as possible drive to the tormented country. A hotel in Croatia had already been rented to get as strong a group-meditation program together as possible to prevent the worst. We already had a two-week vacation in the south before us. We convinced our youngest and drove further south to do our part in calming things down.

When we arrived after a seemingly endless drive through the hills of the Istrian Peninsula, we were pleasantly surprised to find many friends and fellow campaigners already there in Rabac. At the same time, there was a slightly depressed mood because the tension erupted here in the south of Europe in a massively hostile confrontation. More and more people wandered in from Europe in the following days. For our kids, we found a sweet student who played with them at the shore during our meditations. In the hours we were not meditating, we strolled through Istria's small, dreamy vacations spot in the welcome spring sunshine, enjoyed the turquoise blue water in the calm bay, and played with Lilian and Daniel on the sparkling pebble beach.

Back at home, we followed the events in Yugoslavia with some tension. To our dismay, things got much worse. Fourteen NATO member states finally participated in the air war. A total of 1,200 war planes attacked the entire territory of the Yugoslavian republic of Serbia. In a targeted way, the attacks destroyed the civil infrastructure of Serbia, together with the centers of the cities, including their electrical systems, the thermal power stations, the water supply, the schools, and the hospitals. The number of civilian deaths soon exceeded that of the armed forces.

From our friend Branko, the national leader of the TM Movement of Yugoslavia, we learned that Maharishi had motivated him and the other TM teachers by phone. Across the country, he'd asked them to create the biggest possible group programs in all the cities and insisted that as many people as possible should aim for as powerful an impulse for coherence in their country to bring about an end to these combat operations. But it was difficult to get the necessary numbers for long periods of time from volunteers who had normal professional and family duties to keep up. The TM teachers knew that they had the means to end this war in their hands. They did their best, introduced representatives of government to the proven programs of Vedic defense strategies, but their talks fell on deaf ears despite all efforts.

Finally, they chose the Serbian city of Zrenjanin, located 70 km north of Belgrade, a city with more than 120,000 residents in which already 1% of the population had learned TM. Here, they hoped to lay down a positive example for the future and rescue at least one city from the unavoidable bombing raids. Jozef, a local TM teacher, went to the general headquarters of the civil defense and got their support. After that, Branko could appear live on TV and radio to introduce the Vedic defense. "We offer the residents of Zrenjanin a 100% certainty that no more bombs will fall if they decide to come together and form a coherence creating group that is big enough. As unrealistic as it may sound, please come and save your city."

The people reacted in a most positive way. There were 1,200 meditators already there and 200 more people learned TM in a short time. At the public university, group programs were organized in which about 20 people practiced the TM-Sidhis and 120 people meditated every morning and evening.

During the entire conflict, hundreds of thousands of residents of Kosovo became refugees. One after another of about 650 towns were attacked from the air, and, frequently, great numbers of civilians died who, in the international press, were tersely dismissed as "collateral damage." In Serbia, too, the biggest of the Yugoslavian state, most buildings were destroyed through the air raids of NATO. Cultural monuments and historically valuable structures were irreparably destroyed. The bombing of several chemical plants led to massively harmful environmental damage, as great quantities of poisonous chemicals polluted the rivers and the soil. Over 15,000 people lost their lives in air raids—almost exclusively Yugoslavians.

In the fragmented land, attacked by NATO, the TM organization established world peace courses with meditators who spent their vacation directly at the Adriatic, doing the TM-Sidhi Program to create peace. In the first months, hundreds came but the numbers were not enough to end acts of war. Only when the number of meditating vacationers of Dubrovnik and the group in Zrenjanin exceeded 500 people, and with this the number of participants equaled the square root of one percent of the population of 25 million Yugoslavians, did the acts of war diminish. The Serbian Parliament and President Milošević finally agreed to the peace plan proposed by the G8 States, after which NATO ended the bombings at the end of June and, a few days later, the Serbian parliament decided to end the state of war.

Zrenjanin had indeed been spared. It seemed like a miracle. While every single one of the other Serbian cities had been attacked from the air, Zrenjanin remained completely untouched for the duration of the entire war. Not a single bomb fell on this city.

At the beginning of July, the women and the men of this meditating peace group were honored in an especially moving ceremony in the local hall of the parliament and in the presence of the press as well as TV and radio stations. They were given a golden plaque of gratitude for their patriotism that had saved this beautiful, old city with its historic buildings in the north east of Serbia.

Human Physiology: Expression of Veda

Maharishi worked tirelessly—always at a dozen projects in many countries on this Earth at the same time. Daily, he brought new impulses to life to spread Vedic knowledge and, through it, to bring happiness, health, and peace to mankind. Parallel to this, he unceasingly pointed out connections between the tradition and practical applications of Vedic knowledge and modern science.

When Karin and I came to Vlodrop one time with a real estate investor who was planning a large Ayurveda establishment in one of his hotels, we met Professor Tony Nader there, the doctor and neurophysiologist whom I already knew well from his TM teacher training course and international projects. Enthused, in his work room he shared with the three of us his brand-new research. "Maharishi has told me that the human nervous system has the same structures as the various aspects of the Vedas because both are based on the same eternally unchanging laws of nature. And I work with his support to isolate and quantify them."

Already thirty years ago, Maharishi had talked about this during my time in Switzerland and in France. It just seemed so abstract to me back then that I couldn't do anything with it. But now, Tony's explanations peaked my interest.

"I'm on this for a few years now and for many hours per day. I research the Vedic literature about its structure and contents and look for parallels in the human body."

"Can you explain this in more detail; what exactly do you mean?" As a physician, Karin wanted to understand this more deeply

"Of course. So, for example, I'm looking at a certain area of the brain and its functions that are known in modern medicine. Then I look for the relevant Vedic texts that describe this same function in life. And, believe it or not, up till now, they correspond exactly one to one."

I interrupted him, "In plain language, does this mean that Vedic literature is an expression of the same laws of nature that structure and drive the human organism, just as Maharishi has explained so often?"

"Exactly," Tony agreed, "It really is fascinating— sometimes it tears me out of bed early in the morning because I just have to know if it is congruent with the area that I'm just now researching. Then, I analyze the structure of the Vedic literature, count the number of chapters, verses, and syllables and, often, I'm so excited. And when it fits exactly, I feel inspired."

Slowly, the meaning of what he was explaining to us sank into me, "Maharishi always explained that Sanskrit is the only language in which sound and meaning are one. The sound frequencies of a Sanskrit syllable carry a meaning within itself, that one understands automatically, given a subtle perception of consciousness, just as a specific seed produces a specific tree, or how an architect's plan reflects the house to come. So far, so good. Do your insights mean that the forty different aspects of Vedic literature have the same building plan as the human body; is that the way it is?"

"Yes, that is really true. Both correspond to the field of cosmic intelligence that controls the entire universe. So far, it really does look like that. But I am not by any means done with this huge task."

In the year 2000, Dr. Nader published his groundbreaking work, *Human Physiology: Expression of Veda and the Vedic Literature*. In it, he explained in detail, how the various physiological functions of the human organism correspond in their structure down to the smallest detail to the forty aspects of Vedic Literature.[76]

Maharishi was so pleased with the successful conclusion of this work that he honored him for his enormous merit in the re-establishment of Vedic science. He was awarded his weight in gold.

That summer we participated in the Guru Purnima festival in Vlodrop, where, within the framework of his celebratory speech, Dr. Nader presented many details of his discoveries with brilliance and yet easily understandable. Once again, Maharishi expressed his great respect and joy about it. "Dr. Nader is the greatest scientist of our time. I am very grateful to him for his wonderful work. He has discovered the relationships between the subtle structures of the Veda and of Vedic literature to the human body and has shown that consciousness—Veda—is the foundation of the human body as well as of all other matter. This whole time, I have been thinking about how we could honor Dr. Nader for this. That is why I want to ask all those assembled here to make a suggestion for the greatest conceivable reward and write it down on a piece of paper."

Without having to think about it much, I wrote on my piece of paper, "Maharishi should appoint Tony to be King, and he should lead the TM Movement." This idea came to me all on its own, and just as spontaneously, I wrote it down without hesitation. It wasn't so far-fetched at all because, occasionally, some TM friends and I had been thinking about how things would go for the TM Movement after

Maharishi, now that he was way into his eighties. Furthermore, Maharishi now and again spoke about the advantages of the time of the Vedic kings, a time, when the regents thousands of years ago had an enlightened awareness and therefore led the fate of their countries in tune with the laws of nature in such a way that their citizens could live in health and in harmony.

In the fall, we used the usual family vacations to once again go to the Croatian coast on the Mediterranean Sea to do our modest part with the extended meditations and TM-Sidhi Program to create peace in the embattled region because, despite the cease fire, peace in Serbia-Croatia was anything but stable. For that reason, the world peace assemblies near Dubrovnik were being continued to prevent a new escalation of hostilities. Depressed, we noted a number of bullet holes in the concrete walls of the hotel. It was one thing to follow this in the news, but it was another thing to see the results of the war on site and with our own eyes. When we made excursions with our youngest children in the surroundings, we were distraught about the visible results of war everywhere.

One day at noon, our course leader presented us with a surprise. "We just learned that Maharishi will crown Dr. Tony Nader as King of the Global Country of World Peace according to ancient Vedic custom. It will be broadcast via satellite. Anyone who wants to, can watch it from here."

Except for his closest co-workers, we meditators were all totally surprised, and I was doubly so. Unconsciously, I'd taken up something and put it on paper that summer in Vlodrop that Maharishi was already planning back then.

Of course, we immediately discussed Maharishi's decision.

"I think, he couldn't have chosen anyone better" Karin said, "Tony is highly intelligent, an accomplished scientist who'd done his doctoral dissertation at MIT, the famous Massachusetts Institute of Technology, and has shown that he can hold his own in the world."

"Yes," I added, "And he's been close around Maharishi for many, many years and knows his thinking and his way of working very well."

Karin played with the children outside. Inside, the broadcast was running, and I was stuck to the TV. There were Vedic recitations en masse. I closed my eyes and sank into deeper and deeper levels of my awareness, really the home of us all that we so often forget with our outwardly directed lives. I was so impressed by the images on the screen and the power of the ceremony that two days later at the end of our vacation I dropped my loved ones at home, did what was most urgently needed at the clinic, and the next day drove to Vlodrop. I didn't want to miss out on experiencing the last days on site.

For the first time in my life, I enjoyed the thousands of years-old traditional Vedic crowning ceremony in all its purity and that stretched over days. During the recitations, I sank with my eyelids closed deeper and deeper day by day; it was like meditation, until I could hardly feel my body and was just consciousness filled with light. I felt that this yagya of the crowning ceremony, as well as the mantras that were being recited, created the powerful impulse in Tony's awareness that helped him to fulfill the royal dignity that was being bestowed on him and the responsibility that came with it for the good of all.

Maharishi's house in Vlodrop, the Netherlands, which still hosts many courses and conferences, as well as guided tours for the public

The quite-literal crowning achievement of the whole festivities was reached when Maharishi, slowly and with full dignity, put the crown on Dr. Nader who was clothed in a floor-length, ivory-colored robes. Never had I seen Maharishi so emotional. He was deeply moved as he said, "Govern the Country of World Peace according to Vedic principles."

That Maharishi was very, very happy couldn't be missed. He gave the freshly chosen king the honorable title of *Raja Raam*, King Raam, the name of the divine king who lived three thousand years ago, and since then, was revered as the embodiment of the highest ideals of Vedic governance. In the *Raam Charit Manas* one can read: *Raam Raj duhkh kahu na vyapa*—no sorrow in the kingdom of *Raam*.[77] During the reign of Raam, the inhabitants of his country were happy and healthy, and no one suffered.

This expresses precisely the vision that Maharishi had

given voice to already back then, at a time in which most people believed in a dark prospect for our blue planet, and only a small minority dared to dream of this glorious future for the earth and her inhabitants.

Dark Prophesies

In the summer of 1999, when the peace group in Mozambique, Africa was in full swing, and the Kosovo war had just ended, we drove to Vlodrop once again for Guru Purnima to learn the news from all over the world about our Movement. I enjoyed my time in my adopted homeland of the Netherlands; these were moments which had become more and more infrequent in the last years, and they were a welcome change from my intense dedication of our Ayurveda clinic in Bad Ems, which usually took all my time. With joy, I anticipated hugging one or another of my Purusha friends from the old days, meeting many friends that had become so dear and again to let myself be enveloped by the deep silence in Maharishi's house.

Yet today, it was something different. A whole series of presenters had already given their talks, when Maharishi began to speak. Instead of offering his usual wise and uplifting commentaries to open new correlations for us between our consciousness and life, he seemed highly worried. With a serious tone, he painted a scene as we had never heard it before. "All the countries of the earth are in great danger. Soon, terrorists will bring fear to the earth world-wide if we don't create big coherence groups quickly enough."

Maharishi launched into the darkest of prophecies. We were a bit taken aback and touched in an unpleasant way. We had never heard Maharishi speak such a threatening way. The end of his speech culminated in taking the assembled TM teachers to task. He accused us of sleeping and that we'd have to put in a bigger effort to avoid the danger. He spoke with great authority and certainty, "You have to mobilize all your strength because it's in your hands to avert this fate from humanity with the help of our programs and through the power of your consciousness. The whole earth is in the gravest danger. A web of terror will spread across all nations. There is hardly one of them that will remain safe."

On our drive home, his words stayed on our minds. What had gotten into him? Why this sudden negativity? Who could know what such a Maharishi had in mind, what purpose he had for scolding us? Soon, we shook off that bad mood that had infected us. We didn't take him by his word and could not imagine the scenario he'd conjured up. It all seemed too far-fetched for us.

Soon after, Maharishi initiated a new institution: a weekly global press conference with the subject "A Scientifically Proven Preventive Measure Against Criminality, Terrorism, and War." These press conferences were sent via satellite from America or Vlodrop. Reporters the world over tuned in. Maharishi answered the questions of the journalists regarding Vedic techniques of invincibility with the help of human consciousness, and about the actual world situations. Every week he denounced the failings of various governments and—we'd never seen him like this—he minced no words, "We can apply the same law of nature that organizes the universe without problems to end criminality and terrorism in the world in a peaceful way. But I don't have much hope that the politicians responsible will accept my offer. The reason: the stressful life of each head of state, in combination with their lack of forward-looking scientific knowledge, has produced leaders who are too incompetent to deal with the necessary new solutions for the current global problems."

With a harsh and impatient voice, he continued, "I have

informed political leaders about the ways they could bring their governments in tune with natural law for the last ten or twenty years. But now, I am convinced that this is a waste of time. These leaders with their stressful lives have 'functional holes' in their brains, as neuroscientists call them."

This was the most up-to-date medical knowledge in the recently developed photon emissions computer tomography with which areas of the brain with deficient blood circulation can be made visible and from which a doctor could diagnose a dysfunction of the cerebral cortex. Maharishi continued, "Their brains don't function properly, so that they cannot understand this knowledge."

Hard words from a Master who'd always been uplifting and loving to everyone. Maharishi berated the heads of state, Bush and Blair, who had even promoted the use of boots on the ground in the Yugoslavian war, and he also criticized the Germans and other nations as war mongers, not excluding the gun lobby. When Mr. Schröder, the German chancellor, later distanced himself from the war in Iraq, Maharishi again left out the Germans. With razor sharp analysis, he criticized the darkest, most hidden machinations of the politicians on this planet, which we, in the audience, could in part no longer follow. In between times, Dr. Hagelin and other scientists explained the rationale for the systematic implementation of the coherence of consciousness as a practical solution for all these problems. Maharishi called on journalists to spread this information via the media and thus do their part to improve the lot of humanity. Week after week, he warned of the specter of the threat of terrorism and more warfare. He tried to rouse humanity and appeal to their hearts to avert this evil fate in time through our programs.

Once a week these press conferences flickered across TV screens. I'd rather have deepened my Vedic knowledge as in earlier broadcasts and enjoyed the positive world-wide developments through various TM activities. Instead, we got these scolding tirades for politicians and pessimism about the world situation. When I turned on the TV now and then for press conferences, I often thought, "Oh darn it, not again!"

It was just too much for me. What had gotten into him? God knows it's not news that this planet has a lot of shadows. If I want to know about that, all I have to do is watch the normal news on TV. But from an enlightened Master, I want to hear the counterweight to this, namely a positive perspective, something uplifting. Or is there something wrong with me because I no longer want to listen to Maharishi?

One afternoon, it got too crazy for me. 'Does he always have to get mad and excited like this?' went through my head, 'That's downright discouraging.'

In that same moment, Maharishi interrupted himself in the middle of the conference, and, completely out of context, he said, "I am sorry that I have to speak so harshly. For me, too, it's everything but pleasant. If someone is sleeping deeply and you must wake him to save him, and he won't wake up with gentle means, then you have to get loud or even shake him."

Was this sudden interjection a coincidence or did he read my thoughts? No way to know, but in any case his explanation felt good. I was calmed and then could at least bear it more easily.

The intensity with which Maharishi appeared increased exponentially and culminated finally in the dark prophecy: "The high-rise buildings in America will burn; they'll collapse in rubble and ashes."

When I heard this, I was shocked. How could he say something like that! It sounded like a threat with which he frightened and upset people. I doubted his statements and found them unpleasant and embarrassing. But it didn't last long and history, dark and cruel history, took its course.

A week after this statement, Dr. Hagelin invited everyone to a big press conference at the National Press Club in Washington D. C. to urgently offer President Bush the effective alternative of Vedic consciousness technologies to his ballistic missile defense system. One of the main speakers was Major General Kulwant Singh, a high-ranking army general who'd been involved with the fight against terrorism in India for almost three decades. The quintessence of his experience was presented at the beginning of the conference. "Military and diplomatic solutions will never achieve lasting peace because enmity festers in the heart of humanity. The ongoing crisis in the Mid-East is evidence of the incapacity of treaties on paper and it underlines the necessity for a groundbreaking new effort."

But it was already too late.

At that same time, TVs all over the world showed how, on the 11th of September of 2001, two fully occupied airplanes crashed into the Twin Towers, and a third plane into the Pentagon. In the space of a few hours, 3,000 people lost their lives. Tens of thousands died in the following months and years from the consequences of a huge cloud of poisonous dust full of hundreds of tons of asbestos, PCB, cadmium, thallium, lead, and dioxin that floated over New York City. In reaction, America intervened in October of 2001 in Afghanistan which, in the following years, led to tens of thousands more deaths. "9/11" led to the second Iraq war with more than a hundred thousand deaths. Both these wars led to a total cost to American taxpayers alone of in excess of three trillion dollars US.

Once again, our programs and the foresight of Maharishi had not been taken seriously enough, not even by all TM practitioners—including Karin and me. The horror scenes Maharishi had painted back then just seemed too unbelievable.

Only in retrospect, could we understand Maharishi's efforts and admired all his courageous co-workers who, together with him, had tried everything to avert the coming disaster. It was depressing but true: Maharishi had once again been right.

Only then, it became clear what had happened with me. For years, I'd been around Maharishi only sporadically and had followed his thoughts and actions only from afar. Only rarely in direct contact with his uplifting field of consciousness that he spread around him, I had become entangled automatically, and without my noticing, into the web of the collective consciousness of my daily surroundings. I had begun to judge him from this narrowed perspective, had doubted and just forgotten that a human being in Maharishi's state of consciousness can clearly see on his inner canvass what has been and what will come. And from this distance, it had slipped away from me over what far-sightedness and immeasurable dedication to the welfare of humanity Maharishi had command.

The Wondrous Synchronicities of Nature

The intensive commitment in the clinic absolutely took its toll. Karin, especially, was at the end of her strength from time to time. We had three wonderful, lively, rambunctious children at home. They had to be awakened and driven to school, or to the train, and in the afternoons to their riding or music lessons. We gave them support and help with their homework, as well as small and bigger problems—everything that active parents do so that their offspring are well taken care of and are supported in the best ways possible. Thank God, we had household help, but despite this, Karin carried too much on her shoulders and could never get enough sleep. And now, the time was ripe once again, as Daniel was eight years old. Karin needed some time out desperately. With a friend, she flew to Delhi, to the Indian Maharishi Center to Dr. Raju, for a major overhaul of body and soul far from home.

I once again got an unexpected phone call, this time from Roman, an Armenian TM teacher. "Lothar, here in Delhi there will be the "International Conference on Medicinal Plants and Ayurveda." The organizers would like to hear from you as a speaker about the successes of your clinic and the implementation of Ayurveda in the West. But there's a catch: There are already many speakers, and so you've only got five minutes for your talk."

"Five minutes? And for that I have to go to India at my own expense? The organizers could get Karin as a speaker; she happens to be in Delhi right now."

"OK, I'll check with them."

A little later the answer came. "The organizers already

have many doctors as speakers. They've heard that you are especially successful in marketing and have done a lot to make Ayurveda known in the West. So, they are inviting you to be a main speaker. That means you get fifteen minutes. For that they're offering free transport from the airport, free overnight stay in a government guest house, as well as free meals. But you have to pay for the airline ticket yourself." I thought about it. A few days later, I landed in Delhi. At two in the morning, I took Karin into my arms.

She had a loving surprise for me. "For tomorrow morning, I've ordered a yagya for you. You can drive there and take part personally."

After only three hours of sleep, I experienced a yagya directly for the first time in my life. I sat in the middle of a group of eleven pundits with crossed legs on the hard floor of a small temple, outside the city gates of Delhi. Over decades, Maharishi had built up pundit schools in various parts of India. He had structured and refined the eight to ten years of education, and, above all, had reintegrated the lost element— the regular experience of pure consciousness in deep meditation, without which the effects of the recitations would be shallow. In the Rig Veda, it already says that the hymns of the Vedas spring up from pure consciousness and that the Veda, absent from the direct experience of the transcendent, has little effect.[78]

The recitations of the synchronized voices by these eleven pundits called up waves of bliss; I was dog-tired and closed my eyes. The pundits wanted the best for me, and so to strengthen the effects of this yagya, they led me through the performance all the actions together with them. I poured ghee into the fire, waved incense sticks, flowers, and the traditional camphor light in the air; I offered flowers and holy water. It was an incredibly long ceremony, but I enjoyed it. My fatigue had dissolved into the air with all that spiritual energy. I was allowed to choose the *sankalpa*, the purpose of this yagya, and among other things I wished that my speech at today's congress would be crowned with success.

The congress took place at the India International Center, one of the most prominent cultural institutions of India. There were about 200 people present, almost exclusively Indians. Crowded together, they sat in a medium-sized hall of this classy building. The patronage of this event belonged to Swami Maheshwarananda who was revered as a saint; he was a big, powerful man, wearing orange robes; his eyebrows were bushy, his beard long and white, and his long hair stood out from his head in all directions—truly an impressive appearance. He shared the chairmanship with two other gentlemen and sat on the stage with them. Karin and I sat in the first row in the audience.

One speaker after another presented various aspects of Ayurveda. There were practicing physicians among them, as well as researchers, heads of clinics, and manufacturers of Ayurvedic products. After each presentation, there was a short discussion. And things went predictably. In the tightly organized program, each speaker took a little too long and the schedule got delayed more and more. Until now, only men had spoken. Shortly before the lunch break, an attractive, opulent, middle-aged Indian woman stood behind the lectern; she'd developed a line of Ayurvedic cosmetics and had been successful with them for years. And now we experienced the Indians' most charming behavior towards women: no one interrupted the lady to remind her of her time limit. The men were glued to her words, and I looked at my watch because, slowly, but surely, the fifteen minutes that were allowed me shrank significantly. From then on, it went beat by beat; the remaining speakers got only two minutes for their speeches. Even Dr. Triguna Jr. the son of the famous Dr. Triguna who'd been in Bad Ems twice, and who was the head of the All India Ayurvedic Physicians' Congress with over 350.000 members, only got two minutes. After that, it was my turn.

In that same moment, a small, older Indian with grey hair came into the hall and said with a loud, authoritative voice, "Everyone must leave the hall right now. The Vice President of the Indian government is on his way, and we must follow through with his security checks. The remaining presentations are herewith cancelled."

Karin looked at me somewhat aghast, "And your speech that you've traveled to India for?"

"Well, let's just wait how things go after the break."

We were pushed through the doors and into a small, green inner courtyard where there was a cold buffet. While we were enjoying the Indian delicacies, I felt an inner desire to turn to the impressive Swami. As soon as I'd taken the first steps in his direction, he also stepped towards me and asked about our background. I told him about our clinic in Bad Ems and the situation of Ayurveda in Europe. We got into an animated conversation, and he, from his side and beaming with bliss, told about the spreading and the successes of his yoga schools all over the world. And he assured me, "I really want to hear your presentation."

"Well," I said mischievously, "And I really want to give it."

The people from security were done. After a body search, all participants were allowed back into the hall. When everyone had sat down, Swami Maheshwarananda said with a thundering voice, "I want this man here to speak!" and with his strong, muscular arm he pointed at me with authority.

The skinny security guard in charge protested energetically, "That's no longer possible. Nobody can speak anymore. The Vice President will be here any moment!"

"Then he can speak until the President gets here!" His word seemed to be an order. The security officer complied.

Always with the expectation to be interrupted by the arrival of the Vice President, I nevertheless presented my speech as if I had the whole time available. Afterwards, Karin explained several scientific studies about Ayurveda on the spur of the moment. Still no trace of the Vice President. So, we reported several impressive successful healings and about experiences in running an Ayurveda clinic in Germany. The Vice President was taking his sweet time. Finally, the first interested questions came from the audience. Karin and I stood at the podium completely relaxed with the feeling that we had all the time in the world. Without any time pressure, we could really go deep. For a whole 45 minutes, we presented material and answered questions, and, at the end, used the opportunity to talk about all the programs that Maharishi had brought to life world-wide in Ayurveda and Vedic disciplines, including the training of tens of thousands of pundits who upheld Indian culture. Just as we had the feeling that we'd said everything and had answered all questions, there was a voice from the door, "Attention, the Vice President is coming!"

He gave a speech about the future of Ayurveda in India and the planned expansions and scientific studies. Then he congratulated all the participants for the successful congress and their contribution to this ancient Indian healing methodology, and then, swiftly left the hall for his next state appointment. Around us there formed a crowd of business people and physicians who wanted to keep up contact and have business relationships with us.

Meanwhile, a jostling crowd formed outside. Somehow the people seemed unable to get out of the hall. Then there was a voice at the door, "Come, please come, the Swami wants to see you."

"Us?"

"Yes, please come right now; otherwise he won't leave."

As Karin and I were pushed through the crowd with loud, imperious calls by the watchman, we saw the reason for the crowd of people. The Swami sat in the driveway in his car, but still wanted to say a few nice words to us as a good-bye and wanted to wish us much success in the future and to say his soothing "Namaste" to us personally. But why this crowd, all these people, all this excited chatter? We learned it immediately. The protocol was that the saint would drive away first; only then could the Vice President leave in his state car. So, without knowing it, we had been holding up the whole thing.

That was a prime example for the power of a potent yagya. At first sight in the morning, the congress had looked like a fiasco that didn't seem to justify the expensive flight and the attendant effort. But if I'd held my speech according to the plan, I'd have had at best ten minutes or even less and could never have accomplished as much as through the wondrous intervention of the Swami and the unpredictable and enormous lateness of the Indian Vice President. The wisdom of nature is infinite and perfect in organizing and synchronizing everything optimally.

Vedic Architecture

"Bye my Love; be well!" A last kiss at the railroad tracks
and the doors closed. Smiling, Karin waved through the
window as the train slowly started to move. She was going
to Oebisfelde for the yearly summer World Peace Assembly.
I stayed home, for I wanted to keep working in Bad Ems. I
was stubborn.

Most years, our family went to the Maritim Hotel in
Bad Wildungen for two relaxed weeks during the summer
vacation. In this wondrously beautiful, five-star hotel directly
next to the spa park, we took part several times in the large
German summer World Peace Assemblies held there. Long
meditations in a group of up to 500, yoga and breathing
practices, delicious vegetarian food, and great outings for the
group of children, as well as a big indoor swimming pool
for our little water rats, in combination with the luxuries of
a first-class hotel—all that was ideal for adults and kids. In
other family vacations, we were there only for the children
and our own desires were second place. But on these assembly
vacations, the parents too were allowed some recuperation.
"When I come from Lanzarote, the effect is gone after a few
days of work," Karin would muse, "But Bad Wildungen is
always impressive. My body recovers so much through the
group program that I can still feel it for weeks afterwards."

I would have loved to go there again this time, but...

A few months earlier Maharishi had insisted that in
future our World Peace Assemblies could only be held in
facilities that met the criteria of Sthapatya Veda architecture.

For many years, he had been working with a group of
Indian and Western experts to also uplift Vedic knowledge in

this area to its original level by removing the inaccuracies that had crept in during many centuries. The Vedic health programs he'd created were to use all the coherence creating powers of all areas of the Veda and of Vedic literature to further the inner intelligence of the body and to systematically enliven its power of self-healing. In tune with these measures to promote enlightenment, the most external aspect should not be missing—a harmonizing structure of the homes in which we live.

The protection of a home according to Sthapatya Veda can only be complete when the outer walls run parallel to the compass directions and thus correspond to the laws of nature that govern our solar system. Vedic architecture observes the timeless laws of nature and connects individual life with cosmic life.

A few basic concepts of Sthapatya Veda were familiar to me. The situation and orientation of the property, the correct placement of the house within it, the orientation and placement of the entrances as well as the proportions and the arrangements of the various rooms, the kitchen, and the bathroom, with all of them arranged following the path of the sun so that the laws of nature support the respective activities of the residents optimally at various times of day.

An important feature of Sthapatya Veda is the *Brahamasthan*, the exact geometric center of the house. It should be free of obstruction from walls, pillars, furniture, etc. In the ideal case, it goes through all floors and is lit by a central light above or a skylight in the roof. It is a center of absolute peace that has a calming and coherence-creating effect on everyone in the house. Of course, for such a house, only natural building materials are used.

For years, Maharishi had emphasized the special worth of an east entrance that is touched by the first beams of the morning sun. "These farmers must have known this years ago. The entrance doors of our old farm houses point to the east, and the churches, too, were oriented according to the compass directions so that the preacher would stand looking toward the east when performing his sacred acts" is what my initially skeptical wife told me. "It's totally great how these things come together because in Sthapatya Veda they say that the orientation toward the east brings abundance and fulfillment, supporting the inhabitants in all areas of life and—well, that's always the most important thing for us—it naturally furthers enlightenment. In many old cultures, this was somehow also known."

A north entrance is also advantageous, promoting prosperity and happiness. All other entrances are not advantageous for the residents. A west entrance produces losses over time, losses in creativity, vitality, and money. A south entrance destroys all these areas of life permanently.

In a whole series of assemblies and conferences on this subject, Maharishi had urgently asked the participants again and again to take to heart and make use of the life-supporting influences of such a house as quickly as possible because disregarding cosmic rules in city-planning and building of homes was tantamount to a breach of natural law which would, over time, lead inevitably to health concerns or other problems. If one can't live in an ideal house, then one should at least change a south entrance into an east entrance. This alone would bring noticeable relief for health and success.

Five years earlier, Maharishi himself had moved with his closest co-workers in Vlodrop from the old brick monastery into a wooden structure which had been built by a generous donor. During the construction of this spacious wooden house, all the criteria of Sthapatya Veda had been followed exactly. Even the generous gardens had taken perfect symmetry and harmony into account.

Now, Maharishi wanted to expand his exemplary act. From now on, our World Peace Assemblies would be held only in ideally situated buildings—for the maximal facilitation of coherence. From my side, there would have been no objections, if a suitably beautiful building had been available. For years, I'd felt good all-around in the Maritim Hotel, and now we'd have to go to Oebisfelde instead. There, in East Germany, an engaged TM teacher had bought an unadorned box not long ago, a typical East German building of prefabricated concrete slabs that was used by the military in the past. With a lot of his own personal contributions, he'd rebuilt it according to the criteria of Sthapatya Veda and had furnished it for the courses. The entrance was moved to the east, the windows got the right proportions, and all the bathrooms were properly oriented. Even the kitchen and the restaurant were adjusted. And despite all the work had just all been finished, I didn't need much imagination to envision how austere things still probably looked there. "No thanks, this summer it can go on without me." I'd much rather take care of our Ayurveda guests in Bad Ems.

As a faithfully caring husband and with the two kids in the back seat, I drove to get Karin at the end of the two weeks. The plan was clear: a nice weekend together in the country, visit with a few of our friends, and then to get out of Dodge with the whole family.

The facility was not different from what I envisioned

but super clean, lovingly furnished with Ikea furniture, and serving delicious food, but the meditation rooms were in the basement for reasons of space and had only small skylights. I was glad that I didn't have to spend two weeks in this place.

Obviously, I was not alone with my assessment. In earlier years, several hundred people had come to Bad Wildungen. But Oebisfelde had attracted only ninety determined folks. Within myself, I argued with my Master. What was more important, the orientation of the house with an east entrance or the number of meditators for the Maharishi Effect?

Upon arrival, Lilian and Daniel had rushed outside immediately to play with a few old and new friends. I took my wife into my arms briefly and then our paths parted again—she went right to the room for ladies, and I went a little further down the dark hall into the room for men. As soon as I sat on my mat, I felt better. It became lovely, peaceful; I dove with my group into an ocean of profound silence. Immediately, I once more felt at home in this deeply trusted inner realm. After a while, there was a rushing and gurgling sound. Involuntarily, I looked up. Aha, someone, a floor higher had flushed the toilet. I saw the naked, freshly installed drain pipes that had not yet been soundproofed. Oh, well; resigned, I again closed my eyes.

I sat with legs crossed. Suddenly, my spine went bolt upright while a crystal-clear feeling spread in my brain and got increasingly stronger. The top of my head suddenly felt permeable and my consciousness opened upwards like a funnel and kept opening more and more. In this expanding movement, I first perceived the coherent structure of the large house in which I sat. My consciousness expanded even further upwards, and I felt a direct connection between the coherence of the universe and the coherence of this building. This experience did not last long, but it left behind a gentle happiness and was so crystal clear that it continued to impress me. I was amazed, delighted, and grateful at the same time. So, this was Sthapatya Veda, the experience to be in a house that furthers such experiences instead of blocking them. Once again, I felt blessed and asked my Master for forgiveness for my unjustified opposition—as if I knew better!

I did an about-face of 180 degrees. While Karin drove home to her work and her patients, I stayed for another week with my little darlings who didn't want to leave because of their friends from years back.

Saul had become Paul! And the latter remembered now some of the information he'd heard in presentations years ago.

Medical science waited with a plausible explanation for the advantages of correctly oriented houses. Due to neurophysiological research, it was already known that every person has an inner compass of certain nerve cell groups in the brain that tells him the cardinal direction in which he happens to be looking. Other nerve cell groups are calibrated to the position of a given room. If the two indications do not agree because the house or the road system does not follow a compass direction, our brain sends the signal: "Not right!" Due to this, a subtle area of tension is created, which, in the long term, negatively influences and restricts our creativity, our thinking, action, and well-being.

Building on this knowledge, an American physician had a hundred of her patients fill out a questionnaire to assess their psychological health, with the result that those who slept with their heads pointing north had worse psychological health and greater financial problems than those who slept in any other compass directions.[79] A California cardiologist had found that 50% of his heart patients lived in houses with south entrances; the other 50% were divided among the three other compass directions.[80] Manic depressive hospital patients could be released on average of almost four days earlier if their rooms were arranged so they got eastern rather than western light.[81] But I was most poignantly impressed by a statistic according to which break-ins occurred 75% more often in houses with southern entrances![82] And finally, the amount of profit of a business was highly significantly correlated with the extent to which the building was oriented to the more favorable compass directions, according to the position of the entrance door and the amount of eastern light that shone onto the building.[83]

These early studies were not even done with houses built completely according to Maharishi Sthapatya Veda—only a few rough criteria corresponded. In any case, I was waiting intently for the time when more and more such buildings were built and their positive effects could be studied.

I enjoyed this unexpected and relaxed week. And, naturally, a new desire haunted my mind: "One day, I want to live in such a house with my family."

Not long after, we once again experienced the feeling in a Sthapatya Veda house. Lieutenant Colonel Gunter Chassé was in process of moving into a just built house with his wife. It was just an hour's drive from Bad Ems and so the two of them invited our family for a tour on a Saturday. Immediately, I was reminded of the experience in Oebisfelde: as soon as we came in, we felt a special gentleness and lightness as if the house were permeable and had no walls; we felt connected with the fields and meadows around it. At the same time, we felt sheltered and protected.

Soon, I would have the chance of seeing many of these auspicious homes from the inside. And for me, it was always newly astonishing with what gentleness such a house surrounded you, how relaxed and good you felt in it as soon as you entered. You have to have experienced it yourself to feel the difference.

Again and Again TM

Besides our activities for the Maharishi Ayurveda private clinic and our family life, I never completely forgot my great love: the spreading of Transcendental Meditation. One day, Brahmachari Nandkishore called, "Lothar, back when you were on Purusha, you took care of a successful expansion of the German Movement. Could you create a team with your friends for the professional expansion of TM?"

I didn't have to think long. I called my friend Norbert, the one with whom I was in the expansion team when he was on Purusha and who continued to be active as a TM teacher in southern Germany after his marriage. We developed a strategy. With phone calls all over Germany, we invited all the interested TM teachers, meditators, and sidhas to a founding event in Bad Ems. At festively set tables with candle light, classical violin music, and gourmet Ayurvedic food, old friendships were deepened. In this mood, and inspired by the project, the friends who were present that night donated 200,000 DM as start-up capital. We won over the professional marketers and PR people among them, as well as designers, and other creative folks who, with joy for the project, gave their know-how and their labor free of cost, or at a friendship price. We founded the "Maharishi Veda Ltd.", and a few weeks later, the first flyer was printed with an attractive logo. Meanwhile, many people were on the job with fiery enthusiasm and ever new ideas.

In the rooms of our clinic, a film was being made of short interviews with meditators who were being questioned about the changes in their lives since beginning the practice of the TM technique. Everything was well prepared. Fifteen people had signed up—twenty-eight showed up—young and old, simple people, as well as some highly educated professionals.

"Great, then we have more choices." I was enthused.

The film producer, Mr. Engel, on the other hand, was all but: "There's no way we can pull this off in a life time. They're all lay persons. Such people are always terribly nervous and insecure in front of a camera. You have to do too many takes. Please just choose fifteen people. We absolutely don't have the time for twenty-eight. Oh, well, let's just do it, and we'll see how far we get."

Eight hours and twenty-eight live interviews later, we heard this: "Those folks knocked my socks off. I've never seen anything like it. Those people just talked off the top of their heads, just about all of them."

The camera men nodded in agreement, "Yeah, they were totally relaxed and we could just about always just film them. That was pretty unusual. We've got good material we can put together for a great thing."

They were obviously and deeply impressed. When the film was done, the producer and two of his cameramen learned TM. In fact, they were very relaxed already, but things can always get better.

Inspired by our progress, Karin got busy in her free time going through the fascinating international studies about the effects of TM in the English originals and writing summaries of them in German for our TM teachers. For more than half a year, she sat, tireless and almost daily, in front of her "Folder for TM teachers". Michael, another active TM teacher, made beautifully designed colorful graphics for it. [84] The crowning glory was a seminar in which fifty TM teachers from all over Germany spent a whole weekend under Karin's humor-filled guidance, grappling with scientific terminology, and making the content of these summaries their own.

Towards the end, Karin pulled the trump card out of her pocket: "Now we'll do the last studies in the folder. I'm warning you, they're dry as dust, but for me, they were the high point. I think they'll be that for you also. And why? In two experimental designs, Fred Travis, the famous brain researcher from the U.S., together with his colleagues [86], has examined enlightened Americans, people who through meditating for years are in Cosmic Consciousness permanently."

She took a brief but pregnant pause. "Now you all want to know if this is for real, right?"

"It is," she said, answering her own question, "The criterion for the selection of these experimental subjects was that they had witnessed deep sleep for at least a year; that is, during every hour of the night they rested in their beds fully aware in deep transcendence. And," Karin continued, "Naturally, I counted right away how many people in Cosmic Consciousness he'd studied. There were at least seventeen persons. In the second study, there were eleven who'd had been fully conscious during deep sleep for even five years."

"People in Cosmic Consciousness were measurably more effective and more relaxed during tests of reaction-time than other meditators who were not yet established in this state[85] This is not too exciting for us, but the real bang for the buck is that TM practitioners are verifiably enlightened for years."

Karin smiled happily. "Nobody shouted it from the rooftops. The consciousness of these meditators quietly and secretly merged with unboundedness. Isn't that great?"

The state of enlightenment had become real, not only for some chosen few from deep in the Himalayas, but for totally normal Westerners who had released deep stresses and tensions twice daily for years and had cultivated their nervous systems. Was this not a milestone for humanity? One of the research subjects described his condition succinctly, "The impulse for action during the waking state comes and goes; the lethargy during deep sleep comes and goes. Despite this, during these changing states of wakefulness and deep sleep—I am never lost to myself."

As Maharishi had always predicted, this subjective experience was objectively measurable in terms of precisely defined physical changes. The brain waves of these people were as coherent and orderly in daily life during the day as they were during deep meditation with closed eyes. Moreover, their brain activity during deep sleep showed not only the usual delta and theta waves, but along with these alpha waves—well known to indicate a relaxed state with closed eyes—that had never yet been seen during deep sleep. And there was yet another sign of physical rest which was unique. When the researchers evaluated the surface electromyogram (EMG) of enlightened subjects, a measurement which records the electrical activity of the musculature, they found markedly reduced muscle activity. At times, it was reduced so much that instruments could measure no tonicity at all—a condition that had never yet been found during the delta phase of sleep.[86]

XIII.

FAREWELL AND NEW BEGINNING

Those who are one with the Tao,
Can safely go wherever they want.
Even in great sorrow,
they perceive the all-encompassing harmony
because they have found peace in their hearts.

Lao-Tsu

Chinese Philosopher

c. 6th to 4th C BCE

Government of Consciousness

Restful awareness is so great in a person in the highest state of human evolution that his or her perceptions go beyond the habitual and lead to decisions and actions that are perhaps difficult to understand in an unenlightened state of awareness. Maharishi was infinitely flexible in his state of consciousness. Again and again, he broke the boundaries of our preconceived opinions and concepts. In this, he allowed himself to be guided by the natural impulses of his own consciousness. For all who'd experienced Maharishi up close, there was no question that he perceived all levels of creation, even if he rarely spoke about it. He knew about the golden future of mankind which he could already see, while we could often only guess.

In 2004, Maharishi surprised us once again. "I am beginning to educate Rajas, administrators as regents of the Global Country of World Peace. In the future, they will take over the responsibility of the Movement. To this training, I am inviting all those who feel called to spread all branches of Vedic knowledge and maintaining it in its purity as well as creating heaven on earth."

However, some rather big hurdles for aspirants were involved with this invitation. Every future Raja had to give many months of his time and, afterwards, had to be prepared to dedicate his life to the great task of realizing this lofty task. On top of that, he had to help to secure the global Maharishi Effect for the future—a financial feat of significant strength. The financial contribution expected from every participant was one million U.S. dollars, in order to be able to put Maharishi's ambitious plans into practice, and to build up and maintain the funds for peace-making groups. But as improbable as it seemed to us at first, the almost impossible happened–people were found who not only somehow raised this amount but were willing to devote their lives to this great task.

Once before, in the two years from 1988 to 1990, and through the generous financing of a large donor, 8,000 Vedic pundits in India had daily practiced the TM-Sidhi Program and yogic flying together, as well as yagyas for peace in the world. Surprisingly during this time, the Berlin Wall fell. The cold war ended; the Warsaw Pact dissolved. The biggest standing army in the history of the world with 30,000 nuclear warheads and 12 million solders was simply disbanded, and the Soviet Union broke up without bloodshed into fifteen different countries. China and India approached one another after a long silence.

After this time-frame, the financing of that big group was no longer possible. It shrank down to 2,000 pundits, and the spring wind of this global transformation that had just filled the Earth with great optimism died down.

But Maharishi did not lose sight of any of his goals. And now, Raja training would begin.

As one can imagine, his announcement did not leave me unmoved. Since my youth—as much as it was possible for me—I'd tried to help to make this Earth a better world. Wasn't it a logical move to engage more intensively in this great task as a Raja? But to spend a million dollars, this, God knows, was beyond our private possibility. When the first Raja trainings ran, Maharishi also offered this training for a half a million, and I secretly began to do some figuring. Karin was crystal clear about it: this would be on my mind a lot.

So, this subject was debated at the table in the circle of our loved ones. The children looked at us with critical expressions on their faces. Elisa, now seventeen years old, wrinkled her sweet little pug nose: "Well, if you ask me, I think it's verrrry weird!"

Our seven-year-old Daniel trumpeted with his little child's voice, "Papa, I think it's totally dumb. I don't want you to run around here as a king—it would be sooo embarrassing!"

And Lilian, eleven, topped it off, "So, if you walk around in Koblenz with a light-colored gown and a crown, I won't know you anymore!"

From the mouth of babes—clear and succinct. I grinned to myself. I could understand them. It was a little weird to me also, when I imagined it. But practical considerations tipped the scales for me. It would really be difficult to conjure up a half a million dollars somewhere. And above all, even if the thing did tempt me, our clinic just could not cope with its CEO just vanishing from the scene for a few months to get training as a Raja and then dedicate himself completely to this new task.

So, I stayed where I was.

In 2005, the time had come. Maharishi had the first fourteen graduates he'd trained personally crowned as Rajas. With this, I once again saw in my mind the impressive crowning ceremony of Dr. Nader. Not personally a participant, I still at least wanted to be present at this unique event and experience once more this great yagya with its ancient, powerful recitations. I granted myself a special vacation from my intensely busy life as CEO and head of a family and drove to the corner of the three countries of Germany,

Belgium, and Holland, to spend a whole week there and once again dipped into a completely different world. Almost. In the morning in a hotel room in a neighboring town, I conducted business, and did emails and phone calls. Then, I enjoyed the traditional Vedic crowning ceremony performed exactly in the form it had been done for thousands of years in a white and richly decorated pavilion erected specifically for the purpose. It was broadcast via satellite and Internet so that thousands of people everywhere on Earth could follow the event from their homes.

I heard that Maharishi had invited representatives of the press and I immediately got slight stomach cramps. If you knew all the background and were well-disposed to this sort of thing, then what would be experienced here was not only wondrously beautiful, but infinitely precious. But what if you weren't? How would the public react to it? Would the Vedic recitations and the Rajas in their cream-colored gowns and the modest crowns that Maharishi had designed, would all that damage anew our image that had already been tarnished? And above all, could such a scathing review damage our clinic in Bad Ems again?! Understandably, I wasn't exactly sad when I heard that no representatives of the press from Germany had accepted the invitation and, consequently, no articles would appear.

Unencumbered thus, I could now indulge in this royal consecration. A big group of Vedic pundits from India was connected to us through video conference and they performed the *rajyabhishek* yagya. Automatically, memories of studying Vedic scriptures during my time on Purusha in Boppard and in Vlodrop were awakened. We learned that during the flowering of Vedic culture, the great rishis with their enlightened consciousness stood by the side of the acting rulers. They advised them throughout their lives in spiritual and worldly matters. Additionally, the rishis supervised and led the education of the young princes from their earliest youth and, when they were ready to assume the throne, conducted the same ceremony that all of us here in the *Dreiländereck* ("three-country-corner") could experience in its authentic form in 2005.

With closed eyes and resonating with the ceremony, I felt that this is not just an old, beautiful ritual celebrated for its own sake. Instead, the new Rajas were uplifted through it on the level of their consciousness—just as Dr. Nader had a few years ago before when he became a Maharaja.

At the end of this coronation ceremony, Maharaja Nader Raam said, "The significance of this coronation is the renewal of the administration that rests on the enlightenment of man." He closed his speech with words of thanks for the holy tradition of Vedic masters who were embodied for this generation in the person of Maharishi. He thanked him for his life's work, "So that today, after fifty years, we see the flowering of the seeds of *Sat Yuga* (the golden age). Despite all the events that we might see on the surface of life our joy grows with the feeling that our world will be enlightened and our world will be peaceful."

Three-Fold Joy—Veda, Family, and Professional Awards

In my personal life, I felt richly endowed. Since learning TM and the TM-Sidhi Program, I practiced both, once in the morning and once in the afternoon or evening—now preferably together with Karin. As a warm-up, I did yoga asanas and pranayama, the calming breathing exercise. Given my active life, the meditations didn't lead me to absolute silence every time. Especially in times of difficult professional or familial situations, I sometimes fell asleep or had many thoughts—yet still subsequently always felt more energy than before. I refueled and came back to myself. These hours belonged only to me and freed the joy of life and creative ideas that I could make good use of in daily life. Without a doubt, my life would have been less joyful, less fulfilling, and less successful without this regular contact with the more silent realms of my inner self.

My children were part of the most fulfilling experiences of my life. I felt a ray of light of their personalities from the first second of their lives, and that continued into their grown-up life and just simply unfolded increasingly. I felt a deep love and respect for these lovable and, in a way, already finished, unique and completely special personalities.

Daniel, our youngest, enchanted us through his intelligent, radiant charm with which he could wrap especially us parents around his finger. He was almost always on the ball, smart, and articulate, the center among his friends—and only with difficulty did he let go of anything he'd set his mind on. Despite this, he was gentle and loving toward his parents.

Our cheerful Lilian captivated us through her harmonizing empathetic personality. She was strong, independent, self-aware, loving, and understanding. She was fervently caring, always there for a friend loaded down with problems, and she was great at arbitration.

The affectionate and highly sensitive one in our quartet was our musically talented Elisa. She was a good-natured buddy who needed a lot of love. Even now, as a young woman, she was for me still the sweet princess whom I want to protect and spoil a little.

And what would we be without the dry as dust humor of our handsome Aurel, who could make the whole family laugh, and yet he was a loving philosopher, empathetic and social at the same time. He was honest, fair, and an all-around genuine human being.

Even though I worked a lot, I could watch our children mature, and I almost always enjoyed their lively, radiant presence—especially once or twice a year on vacation under a southern sun. I was grateful for every hour that I could spend with them, but, like any busy father, would have liked to have more time for the children.

These wonderful beings would certainly not have been so strong and balanced without my dear Karin and her enormous kindness. In addition to her intellectual clarity, she is empathetic and humane. She takes pleasure in building up others and she can inspire people in almost any of life's circumstances with her positivity and her quick-witted humor. The trust in life that Karin and I have developed transferred itself automatically to our children. All of us experience an especially lucky providence in our lives, that again and again makes us pause with gratitude. Almost always we have the feeling to be on the sunny side of life that the constant contact with the silent levels of creation brought into all our lives.

When the children were small, Karin and I, or one of us, meditated with them in the morning. That was always a beautiful, peaceful start of the day. During puberty, the children thought their friends and normal teenage life and enjoyments more important.

But there were almost no arguments. The atmosphere at home was always characterized by affection, appreciation, and mutual trust. Through Vedic knowledge, we had a common basis. The children were interested in the interpretations of their personal horoscopes and in healthy food (within boundaries, obviously!). They all knew that life has a deeper meaning than just learning a profession, earning money, and raising their own children.

Of course, we, too, went through some heights and depths of life and sometimes felt shaken by the ups and downs of fate. We parents, and each of our children, had our own very personal rough edges that made life difficult for us and that had to be balanced. I am sure that the years-long practice of the TM programs furthered the gentleness and liveliness that bound us all together.

My profession was my calling. Our many years of tireless engagement in the Maharishi Ayurveda Private Clinic began to bear fruit.

In 2006, the clinic had received its first award from Russia. Karin and I got a completely surprising invitation to the Academy of the Sciences in Moscow. There, we were to receive an award for our work in the Maharishi Ayurveda Private Clinic from the respected Russian International Charitable Foundation—Art Patrons of the Century. We flew to Russia and enjoyed a wonderful celebration with rock, pop, and ballet. The moderator was a charming, older gentleman and a TV star known for his animal programs, films, and publications, and had been recognized with multiple awards internationally. Sixty-eight TV teams filmed the event with 500 VIPs, who crowded onto the benches of this festively decorated hall. Not only did we receive our certificates and medals, but, as the sole prize recipients, we could give a brief presentation about our clinic, Maharishi Ayurveda, and Maharishi's world-wide programs.

Professor Nikolay N. Drozdov, a famous personality as a television presenter throughout Russia, awarded my wife and me the Silver and Gold Medal for "Honor and Efficiency" in 2006 for the International Charitable Foundation Patrons of the Century at the Academy of Sciences, Moscow.

Next morning, we went to the TV studio of "Domashniy," whose broadcasts were watched by sixty-three million Russians. This live interview was picked up by thirty-five other TV stations. Subsequently, a few Moscow TM teachers contacted us, which opened more doors for us. There followed a presentation of several hours with the director of Natural Healing Methodologies at the Ministry of Health. He and his closest co-workers had us explain in detail the advantages of Maharishi Ayurveda and our therapeutic successes with chronic illnesses. At a big congress, we advertised for naturopathic physicians and talked shop with interested doctors. Karin and I were excited and happy about the openness of the Russians. They were far more open about holistic health than we were accustomed to in buttoned-up Germany.

We spent a last inspiring evening in the private residence of a charming professor and his son, a meeting arranged by the Moscow TM Coordinator Milovan. The two of them were interested in creating Ayurveda establishments in Russia, together with the Ministry of Health, and they wanted to profit from our experience. I was so impressed by everything that, on the drive to the airport, I asked Milovan, "Please write down everything I'll dictate to you. When Maharishi calls, you can tell him in detail what we've done here and how the people in Moscow reacted to it."

"Nonsense, Lothar, Maharishi has no longer been calling here for years."

"It doesn't matter. Write it down anyway. You never know."

As soon as we got home, Milovan called, "You won't believe it but when your plane took off Maharishi called me on my cell phone and asked out of the blue, "Is there something new going on in Moscow?" I had to read him your whole report three times in a row—that's how happy he was about everything."

Two weeks later the mayor of Bad Ems, Mr. Canz, organized a celebration for us, to honor us in our home town for the Russian tribute we'd received. A member of the Bundestag, Mr. Winkler, and the municipal mayor, Mr. Oster, and other representatives of the city council were there. The Russian Consul Mr. Stankevič wanted to congratulate us personally. A whole series of articles appeared about this event in the local press.

And that was just the start. Soon an acquaintance, a jyotishi, told us after a brief look at my horoscope, "There will be many more."

"Yet more awards?" I replied, "I really can't imagine it. Where would they be coming from?"

They did indeed come. It began when Karin, a few months later, got the Indian "Global Hakim Ajmal Khan Award" as "The best Ayurvedic doctor of 2006." This distinction is given annually by the renowned Indian physicians' association *Hakim Ajmal Khan Memorial Society* (HAKMS) which advocates for the popularization of the traditional Siddha-, Unani-, and Ayurvedic medicines.

Holidays should be celebrated as they come. For her day of great honor, we held an evening reception in the baroque marble hall of Bad Ems that had been festively decorated. Several hundred guests from Bad Ems and all of Germany filled the rows of chairs to the last seat. Dr. Aslam Javed, the General Secretary of HAKMS had expressly flown to Germany and, in his laudation, he said, "Dr. Pirc has been working for twenty years exclusively on the spreading of

Ayurveda in Germany and the world through Panchakarma, consultations, books, speeches and through the presentation of courses for physicians, and has therefore been elected unanimously by our committee for awards."

He gave Karin a certificate and a big glass trophy and the traditional white Indian shawl. We learned that this distinction was given for the first time in Europe and only for the second time outside of India. Subsequently, there were celebratory speeches by the mayor, the county commissioner, as well as the executive of the *German Association of Ayurveda*. To my and Karin's great joy, the event was framed by the music of our Elisa, who was meanwhile twenty-two years old and studying music, and her friend, a young singer, whom she accompanied on the piano. After that, our guests, in a super mood, enjoyed a festive banquet of Ayurvedic cuisine. These friends, colleagues, and relatives, who'd come from all over Germany, were unanimous that Karin had more than earned this distinction for her life's work. She had treated more than 20,000 patients with Maharishi Ayurveda and, through her medical competence and cheerful nature had helped them and given them courage. It was a wonderful, successful evening followed up by diverse interviews and articles in the press.

After that, one thing followed another.

Some of our offerings of the Maharishi Ayurveda Private Clinic, Bad Ems, were honored by the German Spa Association with the coveted seal of approval, "Wellness at the Spa", which the spa administration of Bad Ems had proposed for us.

Shortly afterwards, we were given a newly launched seal of approval at the suggestion of the state government, an award which had been developed as a joint project of industry and the Chamber of Commerce, as well as various tourism associations. After we had demonstrated our quality standards and continuous performance improvements according to set criteria, the State Secretary of the Ministry of Economics awarded our private clinic the certificate "Service Quality, Rheinland-Pfalz".

The Honorable Sheila Dixit, Chief Minister of the Indian State of New Delhi, presents me with the Global Hakim Ajmal Khan Award 2007 for Organizational & Social Vedic Services in front of 250 invited guests in the ballroom of the Ministry of State.

Next, the *Ajmal Khan Memorial Society* once again approached us, this time to award me in India a distinction in the category of "Organization and Social Achievements." Sheila Dixit, the Chief Minister of the Indian State of Delhi, gave me the "Global Hakim Ajmal Khan Award, 2007"in a festive setting before 250 invited guests in the ballroom of the State Ministry. In his laudation, the General Secretary, Dr. Aslam Javed spoke about my efforts with the research, the implementation, and the dissemination of Vedic science in Europe, in the Middle East, in Africa, and in Russia. "With this award, the Commission has especially wanted to highlight the thirty-year activity of Lothar Pirc in the areas of health care through Ayurveda, the psychological health through Transcendental Meditation, and the efforts towards creating peace through Vedic approaches."

The celebratory brochure printed my article, "Ancient Vedic Science for the Solution of the Problems of Modern Society."

After the celebration that the media had broadcast, I used the opportunity to set up a program running several days for an exchange of knowledge and experience. I gave a speech to the medical students at the Hakim Ajmal Khan Tibia College, led conversations with the Minister of Health of Delhi together with several Indian Ayurvedic doctors, as well as representatives of various medical authorities, and visited Ayurvedic and conventional medical establishments and hospitals.

Slowly but surely, we acquired an excellent reputation at home and abroad. Surprisingly, the Indian Minister for Health came to visit us one day, as she was intent on being informed in some detail about the extent and the quality of Ayurveda in German establishments. She had us show her the treatment rooms, explain the therapies we used thoroughly, and she looked with great interest at the training programs for the continued education of physicians of our *German Society for Ayurveda*. A meeting with the mayor and the local press was part of the plan. She was so impressed by everything that she called a government colleague in Paris and warmly recommended that she also come to Bad Ems to get an idea on site of the quality and authenticity of this German establishment.

The Indian Government Minister for Rural Development, Suryakanta Patil, came a few days later, and, after a visit of several hours, she wrote in our guestbook: "I am very impressed after visiting the Ayurveda Clinic, especially about the fact that our Ayurveda is practiced in its purest form in Germany."

And not least, we were distinguished during the following months and years as an especially recommended establishment by diverse and prestigious leaders in the field of wellness. Some of the authors had taken treatments with us incognito to scrutinize us and to be able to judge us from personal experience.

Visit of the Indian Minister of Health, the Honorable Panabaka Lakshmi, 2007 in front of the Maharishi Ayurveda Private Clinic, Bad Ems; (from left to right) Shantanu Banerji, Gudrun Buchzik (Maharishi Ayurveda Europe), City Mayor Ottmar Canz, Panabaka Lakshmi, Ashok Kumar, Consul General of the Indian Consulate in Frankfurt, Dr. Karin Pirc, and Lothar Pirc

We had put up with and attenuate the problem of street noise for twelve years until 2007, before a bypass road rescued us from it.

We had built up our own dining room, and, finally, through the great commitment of the Häcker family we also got hotel services, which made the stay for our guests a real recuperation in which every detail was perfect.

The relationship with our co-workers—their number had climbed continuously from nine to eighty—was so good that Karin and I loved going to the clinic every day.

The staff team of the Maharishi Ayurveda Private Clinic Bad Ems in front of the historic walkway of the Bad Ems spa gardens

Conflicts that came up now and then, even with so many people who are meditating, fortunately could be solved with mutual effort. In a nutshell, even after twenty years, my work still gave me great joy. In it, nothing inspires me more than to see relaxation and greater peace, as well as increasing joy in life, on the faces of people who had just learned TM. I knew from experience that those who maybe came back after a year, would say a sentence to me that I'd heard often from people of all ages: "This meditation is the best thing I've ever done in my whole life."

We were happy about the results we'd achieved and took them as a reward for our personal and years-long engagement as well as that of our co-workers. Their loving and competent dedication to their work had ultimately made possible the healing and the satisfaction of our guests, and with this, the many awards.

Success does not fall from the sky. For years, I was on the job 365 days a year; a weekend was just more workdays, I went to greet guests or looked after things when something went awry somewhere. When on vacation in the first years, my sometimes-grumbling family had to get used to my first-off looking for a phone booth to make pending decisions. In later years, a cell phone and a laptop were my indispensable companions, and day trips could happen only when the organization of the clinic was done long-distance.

With success, tasks did not diminish. Meetings with co-workers and the coordination between therapy, kitchen, restaurant, reception, bookkeeping, individual interviews, employment contracts, and the implementation of always new improvements in the organization of our accomplishments, as well as marketing, advertising, external contacts, and greeting newly-arrived guests constantly kept me on the go.

In recent years as the CEO of the business, more and more international tasks were added to my workload. I also started a new enterprise of clinic consulting to help those who are planning to start a new Maharishi Ayurveda health center so they can benefit from our professional know-how and operate with full success right from the beginning. With that, I got around in the world and got to know interesting new people, felt stretched, and enjoyed a variety of new ideas, growth, challenges, and successes.

Through the course of my life, I became more realistic, and in many things, I stood more firmly on the ground with both feet. And sometimes I wondered how, as a young man, I could believe that the transformation of world consciousness could happen quickly and smoothly. I must have been completely supported by Maharishi's inner strength and my boundless trust in the all-knowing nature of life, whose voice he was for me. Meanwhile, I had to learn that everything takes its time and that humanity needs a long time—as sad as this is—to warm up to this new thing and implement it.

Despite this, I felt supported overall by the feeling of being able to do something good for humanity, to do my small part to help people, to make them able to better control their lives, and to be happier and healthier. I felt in the flow of life and in tune, knowing deep within that nature carried me and my loved ones and often fulfilled our desires in wondrous ways.

And gradually, as if by the way, even during activity, the experience of unbounded consciousness just happened. Especially when I spoke about Maharishi's knowledge, I felt uplifted and lost no energy—in fact, I gained it. Then, I didn't not act; "It" acted; I did not speak, "It" spoke while I just remained within silence, expanded awareness. I rested in unboundedness and looked, relaxed, and often amazed, sometimes even amused, at what came out of my mouth, what impulses rose from within, and what I did in the external world. The result was always perfect, even when in the first moment I did not understand it with my small, limited mind.

Mahasamadhi

When Maharishi had ended his seven days of silence in January of 2008, as he did at the beginning of every year, Karin and I watched his first speech on the Maharishi channel in which, as always, he outlined the course of that year. But it wasn't long before he said, "I close my activities, I close the days of my life."

Karin and I looked at one another: Would this be his farewell speech to us?

In calm words Maharishi spoke about the fact that he had completed the assignment that his Master, Guru Dev, had given him. "We want to emphasize—when we shall see the administration of the universe as a living reality for all future generations—from what source it happens. It happens from everywhere, everywhere, everywhere, really everywhere. It is not an individual person who does this. It is the big Self that acts."

He expressed once again and for the last time that everything he had done had come from the transcendent realm, that he was not an ego, but one with the divine breath that is everywhere and creates everything out of itself. And that all that he had strived for in his life and had achieved was ultimately not the work of a single person, but the Divine Will, the power of evolution, that expressed itself through him.

With everything that Maharishi did, he was, in his greatness, infinitely humble. The Shankaracharya of Jyotir Math, Swami Vasudevananda Saraswati, a successor of his Guru Dev, said about him later: "He, who really was a *Jagatguru*, a world teacher, who didn't just bring individual disciples to enlightenment, but was there for the welfare of the whole world, kept nothing for himself alone; he always gave everything away to others."

Never did he designate himself as Guru. He always felt himself to be a tool of nature and he brought all successes in humility and dedication to his Master, Guru Dev, who was for him the source of all his knowledge. When a journalist in the Sixties asked him at the close of a beautiful interview, "Maharishi, for what should the world remember you in the future?" after a pause and with an indescribably deep expression in his eyes the answer came: "...for nothing!" This always was and remained for me a moving testament of a human being who was grounded in absolute freedom in the Absolute!

And now, he put the coming fate of his decades-long efforts in the hands of Maharaja Raam and his forty-eight Rajas and international ministers, together with the national directors of his movement, as well as thousands of teachers of Transcendental Meditation the world over. He expressed his conviction that more than enough experts of his peace-creating techniques had been trained to uplift every nation to invincibility through the organizing power of consciousness to guarantee peace and prosperity for the world, and that his global organization was now ready to create and maintain this permanent peace.

But he wouldn't have been Maharishi had he not, as a precaution, created something new for the future. He founded the *Brahmananda Saraswati Trust*, a foundation located in India, that carried the name in honor of Maharishi's beloved Guru Dev. The Shankaracharya of Jyotir Math holds its patronage, the current spiritual head of Northern India. This foundation was called into life by Maharishi to support big groups of 30,000 Vedic peace-creating pundits in all of India for all times. Maharishi had had more than a hundred-thousand Vedic pundits trained in an almost ten-year intensive program. In the Brahmasthan of India, the geographic midpoint—which, according to vastu science is the most auspicious location for the spiritual and worldly administration of any country—Maharishi had inspired the creation of a small city out of thin air. In this vastu settlement in the heart of the subcontinent, already 1,500 pandits regularly performed the TM Sidhi group program and yogic flying together and did daily special yagyas, Vedic recitations and actions to strengthen the peaceful tendencies in the world. They kept building to get closer to the goal of 9,000 pundits in this place of power, which could produce the Extended Maharishi Effect for the whole earth. When I heard this, a light went on within me. So that is where the money went that Maharishi received a few years ago from generous donors in the rich West.

The Brahmasthan at Jabalpur, Madhya Pradesh, at the geographical center of India. By 2008, 1,500 Maharishi Pandits were regularly practicing Transcendental Meditation and the TM-Sidhi group program there, as well as Vedic yagyas to strengthen peaceful tendencies in the world.

Maharishi closed his speech with the words that comprised his whole life's task, as well as the goal of the Vedas: "I can only say, may the world live long in peace, happiness, prosperity, and freedom from suffering.... The Brahmananda Saraswati Trust will guarantee the glorification of life on earth for individual human beings and the nation in a permanent way. For all future millennia, the world will be a peaceful, happy world. The world has a bright future—that is my joy—*The future of the world is bright and that is my delight!*"

When Maharishi said this, his certainty, and the feeling of deep joy associated with it, sprang directly over to me and struck a chord within me. On a deep level, I knew that this would come to be exactly as he'd said and that we already stood at the threshold of this golden age that many prophets and wise men had foretold in the past and in the present.

At the same time, I felt a little depressed; his retreat into silence carried the sorrow of a farewell. I felt that soon he would leave his body. We all gladly granted him this rest with all our hearts because, for as long as we'd known him, he had worked unceasingly. Only at the start of each year was he in silence for himself; other times Maharishi worked a seven-day week all year long since the founding of the TM Movement in 1957. If anyone expressed amazement about this, he often said, "Nature did all this. I am always just a tool."

He rested only a few hours during the night and worked twenty hours each day; truly, he demanded a lot from his body. Already seventy-five years ago, when he was still a young disciple of his Master, he'd had the spiritual intention (*sankalpa*) to dedicate his life to the task of carrying Guru Dev's knowledge into the world and spread it everywhere on this earth. And he had not lost this inner calling for a single moment of his life.

When he stayed in Africa in 1983 for a few weeks, he was so tirelessly busy that his personal chef finally complained to the then Shankaracharya, "Maharishi has not touched his food in three days!"

When the Shankaracharya subsequently spoke to him about that, Maharishi was surprised, "Oh, yes, that's true. I totally forgot to eat." And the older Shankaracharya kindly admonished him, "We also have to take care of our bodies because we are able to bring the highest knowledge to the world only through it."

Other people also worried about him sometimes. "Maharishi, I am so sorry that you sacrifice yourself and have left the silence of the Himalayas for us." Maharishi's succinct answer was, "I have never left the silence of the Himalayas."

At a similar comment, he played it down smiling, "No problem, I am more relaxed during my most intense activity than you are in your deepest meditation." Another time it was, "Don't worry about my activity; it is more restful than your deep sleep."

He carried eternal silence within himself and realized it everywhere. He, in his very Self, was the embodiment of silence. Even so, I have never in my whole life experienced anyone who came even close to completing a physical marathon as Maharishi did.

Three weeks later, Karl called from Vlodrop, "Maharishi left his body yesterday evening."

It would not be the only call. Like a wild-fire, the official news spread everywhere: "His Holiness, Maharishi Mahesh Yogi, the famous wise man of the Vedic Tradition of India, who, more than fifty years ago, introduced his program of

Transcendental Meditation to renew mankind spiritually and create world peace, has passed away peacefully on Tuesday, February 5th, around 8:00 p.m. at his international headquarters in Vlodrop, Netherlands."(87)

Many of us had known this was coming; despite this, however, mixed feeling went through me. For Maharishi's sake, I was relieved that he could now go to Heaven, whose realization on Earth he had worked for with every fiber of his being. At the same time, I was a little anxious: How would the future look? Would we, his disciples, now be able to take on this gigantic task without his enlightened consciousness?

I was certain that Maharishi had made a very good choice when he had trained Dr. Tony Nader as the Maharaja. The latter was not only deeply familiar with Vedic knowledge and Maharishi's vision, but he was also as highly intelligent as he was realistic and, in combination with his warm-hearted and balancing nature, he brought the best qualifications for bringing the seeds Maharishi had sown to sprout and blossom and flourish in the future.

I had the desire to drive to Vlodrop to see Maharishi one more time. What a blessing that we lived only two hours by car from Vlodrop. When Karin and I arrived, there were already many people in the yard. The mood of many was depressed and sad; on some faces, tears glistened.

As if nature had once again guided our steps, we crossed paths shortly with Girish on the grounds, and he fulfilled our unspoken desire. He put together a small group of people who'd put special effort into Maharishi's Movement and led us to Maharishi's house. On the way there, a friend whispered to me, "In the evening, Maharishi sat down on his sofa in lotus position and then went into mahasamadhi."

If that was true, then it went just as it had with Guru Dev. He'd sat up straight and, very consciously, had left his body in the way it had been told many times of enlightened masters.

Girish silently led us up the stairs into Maharishi's private rooms where we'd never been before. And there he sat, upright, on his sofa with a white cloth under him—and silent and unbelievable power emanated from him. A group of Indian musicians sang praises to God strong and loud. Some of Maharishi's closest co-workers sat silently next to him and meditated. We looked at Maharishi for a couple of minutes and absorbed his radiance. Within myself, I thanked him for all that he had given me and bid him farewell, while a tender, yet clear feeling of bliss rose within me. After a while, Girish gave us to understand with a look that it was time to go. For closure, we bowed silently in the beautiful Indian greeting that had become habitual for us in Maharishi's presence and which expressed the unity that Maharishi had lived since his enlightenment in his youth. As silently as we had come, we left the room, grateful that we could see him and could absorb once more the impressive atmosphere around him. His consciousness filled the room as it had in life, and I thought I could perceive, the gentle and, at the same time, powerful presence of many heavenly beings around him.

On two of the following days, his disciples and guests could observe the occasion and, in this way, say their farewells to him.

Not long after, I learned from a Raja friend that Maharishi, in the last days of his life had planned the exact details of his funeral celebration with a trusted few. And above all, he had pointed to a completely new direction. "When I am no longer here, focus on success in the future and lead the Movement like a business. You can determine the course fees for learning TM as you see fit."

The time of testing seemed to be over. As if all by itself, an event of more than thirty years ago showed up in my thoughts when a TM teacher asked at an internal meeting shortly after Maharishi had announced the Dawn of the Age of Enlightenment: "Maharishi, why are you always doing something new that many people don't understand and that ultimately impedes the spreading of TM?"

Smiling impishly, Maharishi answered him, "We were always impossible, and we'll always be impossible."

How true! He simply was infinitely far ahead of his time. Some of what he said and did was only understandable on his highly evolved level of consciousness. Much of what he spread expressed the absolute truth in a way that would perhaps be understood in the golden age. And it demanded more than a surface level engagement with the background and scientific facts; it would need freedom from preconceived ideas or a complete rethinking of and an ability to let go of deeply ingrained world views.

Only in retrospect could I understand that Maharishi had been under an enormous time pressure in the last years. He used his limited life span tirelessly to make the Veda in its wholeness and depth once again available and to develop countless programs, courses, and structures for the coming generations. What is special about cosmic intelligence, whose enlightened expression he was, is that all actions are evolutionary and good for the individual and good for the cosmos. And in that way, this great Master had optimally trained at the same time those disciples from all over the world who wanted to work with him, even when, in the last years, it wasn't always a cakewalk—at least not for me.

Measured against the greatness of his endeavors, there were only a limited number of co-workers available during his life time. In terms of numbers, they'd never have been enough to accomplish the oft-times gigantic projects that he designed. If, for example, he had permitted the Tanzania project, in which I could evolve along with all the others involved, then all the people from his world-wide movement would have been tied to it for years, and nothing else could have grown during that time. Instead, he had delivered for hundreds and thousands of projects a detailed layout. He used his consciousness and that of his disciples to implant these ideas in the collective consciousness, so that often people who had nothing to do with him came up with those same ideas somewhere in the world and implemented them or will implement them in the future.

In that way, he ensured that, beyond his death, what he had already seen decades before the actual implementation: Humanity stands at the threshold of a new spiritual age, and the techniques of the Vedic tradition of masters contribute the decisive part of this turning point.

A Great Man Goes

"Lothar, have you heard? Maharishi's body will be transferred to India. He'll be buried there. Do you want to come along? But if you do, decide now because there's bound to be an onrush. It's gonna be difficult to get airline tickets later. Tens of thousands of people from all over the world will want to fly there. Should I try to get a ticket for you?"

Karl, erstwhile flight captain for Maharishi, had been living in Vlodrop for a long time. In the last few years, we'd done tours by motorbike with one another or met for the weekend. Karl was my unofficial line to Vlodrop when it came to news.

"Of course, I'll come with you, that's not even a question. Luckily, I still have a valid visa for India."

Two days later, the two of us flew to Delhi. From there, we needed a flight to Allahabad, a town with over a million inhabitants, the "City of God" in the state of Uttar Pradesh in North India. But the gentleman at the ticket counter just shook his head: "Nothing doing, Gentlemen, we're sold out."

We knew that nature would support us—in such an important thing.

So, Karl and I insisted, "We're disciples of Maharishi Mahesh Yogi and we want to go to his funeral. Why don't you take a look-see if there isn't something you could do?"

He vanished, and was back in a jiffy. "We have two tickets for you in a very small plane."

The small plane had about thirty seats, and whom did we see there? We sat in the same plane with the members of Maharishi's closest family!

In that plane, we met Zoran, a Yugoslavian TM teacher whom we knew well.

"Hi, how are you doing? Do you already have a hotel room?"

"No, we still have to find one."

"I thought so. You know, it's really hard now to still find anything there. In Allahabad there's a huge spiritual meeting. Thousands are flooding the town already; it's crawling with pilgrims and saints and Maharishi's people on top of that." He was happy, "I already have a really good hotel by Indian standards," and now he grinned impishly, "so in wise foresight I have booked an additional double room. Do you want it maybe?"

Did we ever! When we arrived, we saw how well providence had taken care of us. The hotel was exceptionally beautiful and almost totally booked with our people: Mother Divines, Ex-Purushas, TM teachers from all over the world. We had hit bull's eye once again.

After our extended evening meditation program, we went to the Ganges and rented a boat to go to the *Triveni Sangam*, the holy junction of the Ganges, the Yamuna, and the subterranean Saraswati. That was an experience of a very special kind. There was a magical atmosphere—crystal clear gentleness—outside and inside.

My soul acquired wings: "It's like Heaven on Earth here!" Karl nodded dreamily and pointed to hundreds of white seagulls on the water, "That's not just your perception. Indians believe that this spot is so sacred that the devas, the subtle impulses of nature, take on the form of birds just to be able to be in this place."

A grandiose sunset, the subsequent dusk, and the

following moonlight on the water enchanted us as well.

On the following morning, we took a taxi to the ashram of Maharishi's master in Allahabad, near the confluence of the three rivers. Guru Dev had spent every winter there after accepting the office of the Shankaracharya, the highest spiritual representative for North India, one he'd accepted only after there'd been long pleading. When it got to be too hot in the summer, he moved to the more northern Uttar Kashi.

Upon entering, we saw a grassy inner courtyard and tall trees, all surrounded by four whitewashed walls; two white cows were nibbling leisurely. Everywhere there sat and stood Indian sadhus, begging monks with staffs and begging bowls, who'd obviously come from afar. In the ashram, there were placed whitewashed statues of Guru Dev and the current Shankaracharya in lotus position. We saw the current Shankaracharya of Jyotir Math, Swami Vasudevananda Saraswati, the fourth successor of Guru Dev. He was surrounded by his closest disciples and many people who knew Maharishi in his initial phase in India and who had come to honor him this last time. One of them told us in which rooms Guru Dev and Maharishi had lived and, from the outside, pointed to Guru Dev's room on the first floor as well as to Maharishi's right next to the entrance.

It was impressive to see the Shankaracharya with his major disciples sitting in this courtyard in their orange dhotis. The entire ashram vibrated with spiritual power.

Soon after, we saw a big wagon come along the street. Directly behind it, at walking speed, drove a truck whose bed was decorated with flowers and on it was the glass coffin in which Maharishi could be seen sitting straight up. Indian brahmacharis squatted beside the coffin on the same level, which was overflowing with flowers. There was no trace of the grief that is customary with us; things were lively, loud, and exuberant. The truck forced its way through the narrow passage in the courtyard of the ashram, behind and beside it a procession of people who would not all fit into the courtyard. Maharishi's mortal remains were being brought back to the place where his work had begun. The Shankaracharya did not miss the opportunity to climb onto the truck with some of Maharishi's older brother disciples and offer flowers to Maharishi.

When the truck finally left the courtyard, Karl and I joined the huge procession that moved at walking speed through Allahabad to Maharishi's ashram on the other side of the Ganges. Karl and I snagged a taxi and went along, enclosed in a seemingly unending crowd. We saw all sorts of sadhus with their staffs and bowls, uncut beards and wrinkled orange robes. The dust on their feet bore witness to the fact that they'd walked here from afar to give their last honors to this great Vedic Master. When we finally got to the goal, we were amazed to find buildings for several thousand Vedic pundits. There were about 1,500 pundits there. Their recitations sounded over the whole area from the loudspeakers that had been set up along the streets. The TM people from the West were totally impressed by the size of the ashram. Not even the insiders knew that Maharishi had built up such a big group here.

It continued into one of the big halls, in which the body of Maharishi had been set on a platform. We got into the long line of people moving forwards slowly so we could walk all around him once. It took more than half an hour till we finally got to the front. Many sat down to meditate. I did my whole meditation and sidhi program there, and, during the day, walked around Maharishi many times.

Toward evening, I bid him my last farewell. I knelt before him, bowed with my hands folded together in front of my heart and closed my eyes. In that moment, my consciousness opened to infinity and my heart filled with bliss. I felt the reverberation of Maharishi's blessing in the depths of my soul and had the feeling that in this one precious moment I could touch the deepest level of his personality. A stream of love flowed through me, uplifted my soul and imbued every fiber of my being. It was the same fulfilling experience I'd had when Maharishi, many years ago in Vlodrop, gave Karin and me a blessing and some flowers for Bad Ems. In this moment, I knew with absolute certainty that it made no difference whether Maharishi was in his body on this Earth or now acted from a different plane. The blessing from him was still here, as deep as ever. I felt is as an unexpected, gentle grace.

A few hundred meters from the hall, big tents had been set up in which several thousand guests were being treated to an Indian buffet. I met Purushas who had been living for years in a remote Shtapatya Veda ashram near Uttar Kashi. I'd been with many of them for years in Boppard and Vlodrop. They'd aged, but nevertheless still had radiant eyes and bright vibes; there was a connection between us, as ever.

On the next morning, Karl and I drove to Maharishi's cremation ceremony. From far away we saw hundreds of pundits on both sides of the street forming an honor guard while reciting the Vedas. Today in the procession, many thousands were there, including high government officials in their suits, high-ranking military officers and soldiers in

Allahabad, India, February 2008. Maharishi is India's first and only
spiritual leader to date to be honored with a state funeral.

The pundits began their recitations. And Maharishi's
body, wrapped in white cloths, was carried in a procession
from the great hall across the area and laid on the stacked-up
sandal wood. Indians dressed in white poured ghee, clarified
butter, over the thick logs and Maharishi's mortal remains
and then lit the fire according to a specific ritual. The shining
flames crackled, and flared up high. Again, and again, the
men poured more ghee to keep the fire alive.

Maharishi was honored by the Indian State as, to date,
the first and only spiritual leader of India with a state funeral
that included military ceremonies.[88] The government of
Uttar Pradesh had organized it; the soldiers, lined up in rank
and file, fired a rifle salute. The Shankaracharya directed the
proceedings. The pundits recited the Vedas through the entire
time, and the fire burned. Most in attendance watched, were
silent, went inwards, and let it all take its effect. The Sadhana

TV Channel broadcast the whole ceremony live over Eutelsat 1 and the Internet worldwide.

When the fire had burned down after a few hours, Karl and I stayed with many others in the area for our evening meditation program. Afterwards, we went a few kilometers on foot along the street to the shore of the Ganges. The bright red glowing evening sun dipped all that water of the wide stream into gleaming red-gold light. An unforgettable view! Later, we strolled through the city and enjoyed the evening cool before a taxi brought us back to the hotel.

Around noon on the following day, the two of us rented a small boat to sail with about a thousand others from the TM Movement in various canoes and barges also sailing to Triveni Sangam. There, all of us crowded around the boat of Maharaja Raam from whom the recitations of the pundits wafted towards us. There was such a crowd on the water that Karl and I could only occasionally catch a glimpse. Maharaja finally scattered some of Maharishi's ashes into the Ganges according to old Vedic tradition. It was a blaze of color beyond compare: the brightly painted boats, the various colors of the saris of the women, and, in the middle of all that, Karl and I in our newly bought airy-white Indian dress, a kurta, the collarless long shirt buttoned down the front and the pants that went with it.

With such crowds of people there were no kinds of announcements, since all of them had come spontaneously and on their own and had to organize everything by themselves somehow. The program was known to only a few insiders. Here everything seemed to be a race with time and a test for how much nature support you had. Karl was glued to his cell phone again and again and tried to get information from friends. He learned that some of Maharishi's ashes would be spread into several sacred rivers of India, as well as into the ocean at Kanyakumari, the southern-most tip of the Indian subcontinent. Tomorrow, it would certainly go to Varanasi, which was 125 km further east—and with Indian traffic, at least two hours away by car. There, too, we had to get a hotel room—not so easy when three to four thousand people invade a city unannounced and at the same time. All the hotels were full in no time. We once again had luck on our side, and we found a room in a small, simple hotel in the middle of town, directly next to the Ganges. Varanasi is honored by Buddhists, Jains, and Hindus equally as a sacred city. Even though the filth was in your face everywhere, a silky soft gentleness pervaded the city that you just have to experience to know it. It was indescribably beautiful.

In the bright light of day, we went for a boat—they were becoming hard to get. Somehow, all our pilgrims were taken care of, and so we bobbed up and down in front of the dream-like scenery of one of the oldest cities in India with its crowded-together houses on the hillside and the numerous *ghats* (flight of steps) devout Hindus take to go down for a cleansing bath in the sacred Ganges. Exactly as the day before, the pundits chanted on Maharaja Raam's boat while he, according to ancient rites, gave a second part of Maharishi's ashes to the river. The place for this had been chosen precisely, because it was exactly in this spot where, more than five decades ago, Guru Dev's *jal samadhi*, his water samadhi had taken place. In this ceremony, the mortal remains are given to the Ganges; it is a ceremony that is restricted to sacred Brahmins.

Varanasi, India. Maharishi's ashes are scattered into the Ganges River during a traditional Vedic ceremony, accompanied by many of his disciples paying their last respects.

The sadhus sat at the shore, and many men and women sat on the steps leading down to the river and dipped into the Ganges to get a little closer to their enlightenment with this ritual. Later, we joined them and jumped into the lukewarm water. Then we sauntered through the old town where I got a finely patterned shawl of Varanasi silk for Karin. In the evening, we enjoyed our extended meditation program in this special city and, afterwards, saw that everywhere along the river shore altars had been set up. The evening pujas for *Ganga Devi*, the songs of praise and invocations of the goddess of the Ganges, began. Before the beginning of the pujas, the greatest Vedic masters were called upon, and I was glad to hear Maharishi's name among them. Once again, we rented a boat and let the beauty of the play of the light and the synchronous songs of the pujas, that came from countless voices have their effect on us. The high point was the *arartikyam*, the swaying of camphor light, as an expression of pure consciousness, which, like a chain made of lights, was mirrored in the water that had meanwhile become dark.

On the following day, we flew from Varanasi to Delhi and then back home.

Those few, intense days remained as deep impressions within me and left a feeling of gratitude for all I'd been able to experience. Had I not gone there, I'd presumably felt a little thorn prick for having missed something important. As it was, it was flawless and so much supported by nature that it was the perfect farewell to my Master.

But how would it go on without him? Once, when Maharishi was asked at a press conference how the future of his movement would look when he was no longer there, he answered directly, "Then the Movement will be very successful because the people who are close around me now will go out and carry Vedic knowledge throughout the world."

Indeed, today countless people in all parts of the world are working on this.

Even though there are still wars and conflicts on our planet, people are starving, and immeasurable suffering occurs in many parts of the world, it can't be missed that at the same time a shift is happening on this planet. In all cultures, more and more people are opening to their inner riches and are becoming increasingly more conscious of their responsibility towards their fellow human beings, the plant and animal kingdom, and our environment. Many millions of people are now contributing their personal input to further the spiritual awakening of mankind.

How had Maharishi expressed it so beautifully in his farewell speech?

Farewell and New Beginning

"The future of the world is bright
and that is my delight!"

Jai Guru Dev

XIV.

Maharishi's Worldwide Programs Today: Overview and Links

*We have the golden sight to see only right things
because we know that the power of good is greater
than any other kind of power,
and we see the power of good increase in the world.*

Maharishi Mahesh Yogi

Total Knowledge about Natural Law

For the entirety of his life, Maharishi worked to combine modern science with traditional Vedic science to form complete knowledge about natural law—he tied the objective path of knowledge to the subjective path of it, making it possible for man to live in accordance with natural law.

Six Million People World-Wide

Since Maharishi began the first of his ten world tours in 1957, more than five decades ago, more than six million people from almost all countries on Earth, from all levels of education, and from all religious traditions and world-view backgrounds have learned the technique of Transcendental Meditation. In almost all countries of this Earth, there are TM teachers and TM teacher training centers.
https://www.tm.org/ ;
https://tmhome.com/transcendental-meditation/

Studies and Professional Publications

Since the 1970s, the extensive, positive effects of the various Vedic programs Maharishi has revived have been documented with more than 700 scientific studies which were conducted in 250 independent research institutes in thirty-three countries; 350 of these studies, which were independently peer-reviewed, were published in more than 100 scientific journals.

The National Institutes of Health (NIH), the government ministry of health in the U.S., has spent a total of twenty-four million dollars just for the studies on the efficacy of Maharishi's Transcendental Meditation for the prevention of heart and circulation illnesses, the lowering of hypertension, and the reduction of arteriosclerosis, as well as the improvement of health and optimal brain function.

In an official statement in 2013, the American Heart Association (AHA) recommended the practice of Transcendental Meditation as an effective method for the prevention and treatment of high blood pressure after a committee of experts of the association had examined the most current clinical studies of all meditation and relaxation methods. It concluded that Transcendental Meditation was the only method that could lower blood pressure permanently, while all other forms of meditation could not demonstrate any sufficient effectiveness to date.

www.truthabouttm.org

www.tm.org

https://www.sciencedaily.com/
releases/2009/11/091116163204.htm

https://www.ahajournals.org/doi/10.1161/
JAHA.117.002218

The Foundation for the Promotion of TM in Risk Groups

In 2005, the David Lynch Foundation was established by the film director of that same name to help underprivileged people learn TM (and partly other methods, such as the implementation of Vedic agriculture). The foundation helps war veterans with post-traumatic stress disorder and their families (see below), impoverished Native Americans on reservations with diabetes, cardiovascular illnesses, and high suicide rates, the homeless with addictions, prisoners, and children with ADHD (Attention Deficit and Hyperactivity Syndrome) or other learning problems, anxiety, depression, or abuse of drugs.

Many successful business people, musicians, and Hollywood stars of TV shows and movies who had been practicing TM for years and even decades and knew about the good effects have come out in support of the foundation with charity concerts and large donations in their names, including such notables as Paul McCartney, Ringo Starr, Clint Eastwood, Tom Hanks, Oprah Winfrey, Martin Scorsese, Jerry Seinfeld, Russel Brand, Katy Perry, Dr. Mehmet Oz, Ali Stephens, British chess grandmaster Jonathan Rowson, among others.

www.DavidLynchFoundation.org

https://www.thedailybeast.com/oprah-and-more-stars-who-do-transcendental-meditation-photos

War Veterans with Post-Traumatic Stress Disorder (PTSD)

Clint Eastwood and David Lynch, in cooperation with a committee of researchers, veterans, and active servicemen, founded "Operation Warrior Wellness" to donate the funds to teach TM to 10,000 veterans and their families. By 1986, a study by an American veterans' center had shown that former active duty servicemen who had just learned TM showed remarkable improvements in all the areas of life tested within only three months, while by comparison, weekly psychotherapy sessions proved to be ineffective for these serious disorders (89).

Approximately 30-35% of the 1.64 million active duty personnel serving in Afghanistan and Iraq since 2001 have PTSD. "When I heard that eighteen veterans per day commit suicide and more soldiers died from suicide than in the wars in Afghanistan and Iraq…I knew that the foundation had to do something to help," said David Lynch. Operation Warrior Wellness currently works in partnership with veteran groups, the "Doe Fund for Homeless Veterans" in New York City, the "Tragedy Assistance Program for Survivors" (TAPS), "Hope for the Warriors", and "Urban Zen". Based on the extant scientific studies, the Veterans Administration pays for instruction of TM upon request.

In 2016, the research institute of Maharishi International University in Fairfield, IA, together with the San Diego Veterans Administration Medical Center of the US Department of Defense, received 2.4 Million dollars for further research of TM in post-traumatic stress disorders (PTSD) in war veterans.

https://www.davidlynchfoundation.org/veterans.html
www.globalgoodnews.com/health-news

750,000 Students use "Quiet Time"

As of 2019, there are 700 mostly state-run schools and 60 universities and institutes of higher learning in which a total of more than 750,000 students and teachers regularly practice the technique of Transcendental Meditation daily within the framework of their studies; about 250,000 of them practice the TM-Sidhis, including Yogic Flying. Students show exceptional improvement in academic achievement as well as psychological well-being and an immediate reduction of violence and absenteeism.

Secondary and Elementary Schools

There have been schools, some for decades, in the US, Mexico, Columbia, Ecuador, Brazil, Bolivia, Chile, Peru,

New Zealand, Australia, China, Mongolia, Kyrgyzstan, Bali (54 schools), Thailand, Nepal, and India (169 public schools with over 145,000 students and teachers in sixteen Indian states, of which 47,000 in 40 vastu halls practice the TM and TM-Sidhi Program in groups, partially assisted by the corresponding group programs of their parents). Further, there are schools in Iceland, Sweden, Denmark, the Netherlands, Moldavia, Ukraine, Armenia, Israel, Uganda, South Africa, Denmark, the Netherlands, Great Britain, Ireland, Belgium, Spain, Portugal, France, Moldavia, Ukraine, Armenia, Israel, Uganda, Tanzania and South Africa. Altogether, Consciousness-based Education, using TM programs as part of the school curriculum, is implemented in 47 countries worldwide.

Group meditation as part of the lessons at a girls' school in Botswana, Africa

The director of the San Francisco Unified School Districts received the distinction of "U.S. School Director of the Year" after he'd introduced the program, and violent behavior among the students decreased by 78% within two years.

In the last few years, the David Lynch Foundation has made it possible for several hundreds of thousands of under-privileged schoolchildren in the U.S. and in Latin America to learn TM. Within the framework of a "quiet time," group meditations are done in public schools. For his philanthropic endeavor, David Lynch not long ago received the Smith-sonian American Ingenuity Award, a distinction for great innovative initiatives for the betterment of the life-situation of many.

TM group meditation of 700 students from public middle and high schools in San Francisco, USA, who had already participated in their schools' Quiet Time program for six years; on the occasion of a lecture with film director and foundation founder David Lynch

In Latin America, there are currently 479 schools that have established this "quiet time"; there are also 45 universities where 232,000 students use these programs—74,000 of them practice the TM-Sidhis in groups.

The 840 girls of the Dhammajarinee Witthaya School in Thailand have been creating the Extended Maharishi Effect for the whole country since December 2019, and the numbers of girls are continuously increasing. The school is building a 6,500 square meter vastu flying hall for 2,000 girls, not only to create coherence and positive trends for Thailand, but also to extend these effects for the whole of Southeast Asia.

The government of Brazil has authorized a program to promote TM in all 50,000 public schools in the state of Rio de Janeiro as well as financing the training of more TM teachers. The governments of Peru and Mexico are beginning state financing TM programs in many schools.

Within the framework of the "British Free School Programs" since 2011, the government supports the Maharishi School in Skelmersdale and shall also for any newly created Maharishi schools, due to the extraordinary accomplishments of this private school.

When teachers, students, employees, and parents began to practice TM in Auckland, New Zealand, crime rates in South Auckland City, where the school is located, declined from 805 to 254 within six months while in the neighboring city they continued to climb.

A school in Israel that implemented Consciousness-based Education received second place for the "National Education Award" in 2008 and third place in 2009. This was the first time that a school in Israel received this honor two years in a row.

As of 2016, the European Commission in Brussels has financed a two-year major project for the scientific validation of the changes implemented through the integration of the TM technique in the school day to see to what extent this approach can counterbalance the increasing radicalization and aggressive tendencies of the students. To that end, twelve hotspot schools with socially disadvantaged students were chosen in Portugal, Sweden, and the Netherlands—schools that had a high percentage of drop-outs compared to other schools. A total of 520 students, 350 teachers and co-workers, and 120 parents learned the TM technique in this project. The evaluation of the data showed the same positive results in Europe as in other parts of the world: greater creativity and ability to concentrate, more self-confidence, reduced absenteeism, 86% fewer drop-outs, around 10% higher rate of scholastic accomplishment, 40% less psychological stress of all concerned, as well as a 65% reduction of delinquency, gang involvement, and violent behavior.

www.maharishischool.com

www.cbesa.org

https://consciousnessbasededucation.org/

www.maharishividyamandir.com

https://en.wikipedia.org/wiki/Transcendental_Meditation_in_education;

https://europe-project.org/results/

https://friends-project.eu/

Universities

More than sixty universities or tertiary educational establishments in over sixty countries, with a total of approximately 150,000 students, make TM a permanent part of their curriculum; among them are the U.S., India (98,000 students in 10 institutions), Sri Lanka, Malaysia, and Thailand (3,000 students in fifteen institutes accredited by the state with the lowest national termination rate of their studies), a total of 39,000 students at the Maharishi Vedic University in Madhya Pradesh and the Maharishi University of Management and Technology in India.

The Maharishi Institute for neglected young Africans in the business district of Johannesburg in South Africa recently received the "Best Seedling" award at a global conference for education and training in Bahrain, at which 500 educators participated. The Maharishi Institute won first prize for its innovative educational techniques, which can be replicated in other countries.

The positive influence on the environment of such establishments is always fascinating. In Fairfield, IA, Maharishi International University was established in 1974. According to the statistics, Fairfield is one of the safest cities in the U.S. Before 1974, the crime rate was on the level of other U.S. cities of the same size. Since 1974, that rate has declined. Between 1991 and 1998, it was 34% less as that in comparable cities. With violent crimes, it was even between 38% to 85% lower than comparable figures. (90)
https://en.wikipedia.org/wiki/Transcendental_Meditation_in_education
www.mum.edu
http://www.mahamediaonline.com
http://www.rajapark.ac.th/

Street Children in Columbia

The Catholic priest, Father Gabriel Mejia Montaya, the former president of the Latin American Federation of Therapeutic Communities, has built up 60 youth centers in Columbia for neglected street children and orphans and has already helped tens of thousands of children. For this work, he enjoys world-wide recognition. He was recognized by the Queen of Spain for his humanitarian work and received an award from the World Federation of Therapeutic Communities as well as the World's Children Prize of the Swedish government. With the help from the David Lynch Foundation, more than 3,600 children have learned the TM technique in his shelters and more than 700 practice the TM-Sidhi Program. Right now, a school for 1,500 children, planned according to the vastu criteria of Sthapatya Veda, is being built. The statement by the "Saint of Columbia," as Maharishi called him, speaks for itself, "The basic therapy is love. Love is the imperial medicine for any illness or disorder....When a child closes his eyes and begins to meditate, it opens itself to the field of all possibilities.... The world opens for the child. And then the child discovers his or her essential nature, which is love... That is why we must insist on the globalization of love."

The success of the rehabilitation of street children is so great that, meanwhile, centers in all Latin America are following his example, and have up till now taken a total of 60,000 children off the streets. They receive not just food, protection, education, and a roof over their heads, but the initiation into TM and the TM advanced techniques of the TM-Sidhis form the central core of the therapeutic rehabilitation program.

https://www.tm.org/blog/meditation/catholic-priest-transcendental-meditation-orphans-latin-america/

Prison Projects and Rehabilitation

With a total of four issues in 2003, the Journal of Offender Rehabilitation dedicated the major part of its annual edition to the subject of "Transcendental Meditation in Rehabilitation and Prevention of Crime".[91] This journal is one of the leading American academic publications for research about rehabilitation programs and their influence on prison inmates and drug addicts. These special editions present a large area of research, which shows that the practice of Transcendental Meditation significantly reduces criminal aggression, violence, recidivism, terrorism, and even national conflicts while, at the same time, developing higher states of consciousness.

A scientific study on 181 traumatized prisoners in two prison in Oregon, U.S.A., published in 2016, showed a decrease of fear, depression, sleep and perceptual disorders of around 45%, and a reduction of the symptoms of severe trauma of around 56% — all within four months. Two prisons in Columbia use the TM technique for all prisoners, as does a juvenile prison in Mexico.

www.istpp.org

https://tmhome.com/benefits/new-study-relieving-trauma-symptoms-in-prisoners-with-transcendental-meditation/

Maharishi's Vedic Defense—Reduction of Poverty in Latin America

Dr. John Hagelin, world renowned quantum physicist and executive director of the International Center for Invincible Defense: "The Maharishi Effect, known in the scientific literature, was confirmed by more than fifty studies. Many of them were published in leading scientific journals after being vetted by experts. This [the TM-Sidhi group program] is an extremely practical technique to prevent conflicts and reduce them, to prevent terrorism, to strengthen national security and invincibility, and even to end open combat operations in warzones."

In five Latin American countries, as well as in Nepal, security forces within the military have established "Prevention Wings." These are prevention associations in which soldiers practice the TM and TM-Sidhi Program and, additionally, may take intensive courses in which they study the knowledge and the background of this new form of defense. Large groups of the police as well as rehabilitation centers and prisons have implemented comparable programs.

Altogether, approximately 178,000 people in Latin America practice the technique of TM, and approximately 28,000 of them do the sidhi program together.

Units of the Prevention Wing of the military of Ecuador practice the Transcendental Meditation technique as a preventive defense strategy for their nation.

A well-regarded economic research institute published statistics in 2011 about the situation of poverty in Latin

America. In the year 2010, according to this report, forty-one million people were lifted above the poverty line and 180 million experienced a general reduction of hardships. The initiators of the local TM programs attribute these positive effects to the huge increase of groups of yogic flyers in these countries.

www.gusp.org

www.globalgoodnews.com

2,400 Pandits at the Brahmasthan of India

At Jabalpur, Madhya Pradesh, the geographical center point of India, a Sthapatya Veda settlement for thousands of pundits was built. More than 2,000 experts today perform the TM-Sidhi Program, as well as Vedic recitations and yagyas daily to further evolutionary tendencies on this earth. This project is financed by contributions collected world-wide and should increase continuously to 9,000 pundits to assure world peace and a better quality of life through the Extended Maharishi Effect for all the people on this planet. Meditators can spend their vacations there to profit for themselves from these powerful impulses while also strengthening the global effect.

Today, a total of 5,000 Maharishi Vedic pundits live in thirty-eight different establishments in India and daily practice their TM-Sidhi group programs and yagyas. In India, there are 29,000 student pundits who are not only learning the Vedic recitations and the performance of yagyas, but are at the same time receiving a complete secondary school education.

www.vedicpandits.org; www.maharishiindiacourses.com

Promotion of Vedic Cultural Heritage in Nepal

The foundation of this name, created by my wife and me together with a lawyer couple, has been funding the training of Vedic pundits in Nepal since 2011. Shortly afterwards, several committed colleagues have joined us, contributing significantly to the enormous expansion of this project. By 2020, eighty-four pundit schools with about 3.0000 had adopted Maharishi's programs structured especially for the training of pundits. A four-months intensive curriculum enables new pundit trainers (*pundit acharyas*) to each take care of a pundit school (gurukul) after their training.

As of 2021, around 400 pundits have been performing their Vedic recitations and yagyas in newly-constructed vastu buildings specifically designed for this purpose. All gurukuls are connected via the Internet to perform their TM and TM-Sidhi Program and their recitations simultaneously and thus create a gigantic coherence effect together.

My address to 8,000 participants at a cultural conference on Maharishi's contribution to the revival of Vedic culture in India and Nepal and on the activities of our Foundation for the Promotion of Vedic Cultural Heritage in Nepal

https://stiftung-vedische-kultur.de/english/index.html
(English version is not found)

3,000 Buddhist Monks

More than 3,000 Buddhist monks in 100 different monasteries in Southeast Asia learned TM in 2011 at the suggestion of the Reverend Koji Oshima who has practiced this technique for many years and is a teacher of Transcendental Meditation. The monks at all levels of training and age practice this technique as preparation for their prayers and spiritual exercises and feel that the effectiveness of their traditional spiritual practices is intensified through it.

Peace Project Reduces Violent Crime in America

From 2006 to 2012, between 1,400 and almost 2,000 people from sixty countries did the TM-Sidhi group program twice daily in one place in the U.S.: Additionally, almost 1,000 Indian pandits conducted daily yagyas, Vedic recitations which promote evolutionary and peaceful tendencies for all of America. A big-hearted entrepreneur family donated a million U.S. dollars per month for the maintenance of this peace initiative in that time frame. In 2006, the creators published the prediction that the "Invincible America" assembly would reduce the crime rate in the U.S. significantly.

Subsequent statistical analyses showed that the sudden increase of positive tendencies began in July of 2006, the same month the assembly began with initially 1,200 people. The Washington Post reported in May of 2010: "The national violent crime rate rose between 2005 and 2006...but violent crime began to fall in 2007; it fell 0.7% in that year and then an additional 5.5% in 2008. The trend accelerated in

2009 with a 5.5% reduction in overall serious crime..."
According to the Global Peace Index (GPI) of the Institute
for Economics and Peace, the U.S. experienced the largest
improvement in the category of peaceful tendencies since
2007 during that time. Indeed, in this same period, America
had the lowest crime rate in forty years. These crime statistics
of the U.S. government exceeded all expectations and were
commented on in the world-wide press. Already in 2010, in
an article entitled, "What's Behind America's Falling Crime
Rate?" in Time Magazine, one could read: "No one can
explain convincingly how the crime problem was solved."
In the spring of 2011, the New York Times reported in their
article, "Constant Reduction of Violent Crime Puzzles the
Experts" that the violent crime rate in 2010 had reduced by
40%, which, in a period of recession is completely inexplicable. In comparison with the early 90s, the probability of
being a victim of murder has fallen by half...in cities with
fewer than 10,000 inhabitants, the number of murders has
reduced by 25% within one year.[92]

www.permanentpeace.org; www.istpp.org

Every Month: 55,000 Meditate for World Peace

Once a month, TM meditators meet in small and big
groups to meditate for world peace together; people, who
cannot meet because of distance, practice their individual
meditations at the same time. This world peace meditation is
performed sequentially at the same local time in twenty-four
different time zones. Every month such a wave of silence and
bliss moves around our whole planet—24 hours long—and
it enlivens the positive qualities of the collective consciousness that connects all humanity.

At the last world-wide TM group meditation, more than 55,000 people from forty-two countries of our earth joined this powerful impulse. It is a rising tendency because the participants are moved not only by the deep connection that they feel to our planet and to other people, but they also feel inner peace, bliss, and gentleness in the meditation more intensely than they do when they practice TM alone and for themselves.

The Global Union of Scientists for Peace

Created in 2005, the Global Union of Scientists for Peace is an initiative for the prevention of terrorism, wars, and social violence. This union of leading scientists, politicians, and decision-makers advocates for reducing the use of force as a means of conflict resolution as well as stopping the proliferation of nuclear and other weapons of mass destruction. It propagates only approaches that have been tested through practice and have been scientifically validated in the areas of conflict resolution, national security and peace. It offers answers for the prevention of social tensions that lead to terrorism and social conflicts. In addition, this union promotes the exploration of evidence-based, non-violent methods to prevent conflicts, to support national security and the creation of global peace.

A congress, held in 2017, with more than 600 scientists, Nobel Peace Prize holders, educational experts, politicians, and military leaders from twenty-one countries presented new solutions for security from conflicts and for the creation of world peace as they adopted a unanimous resolution to implement these programs.

www.gusp.org Ukraine Symposium ergänzen?

Programs for Managers and Entrepreneurs

An increasing number of businesses use TM to further creativity, the improvement of mental and physical health of employees, as well as the increase of job satisfaction and a reduction of absenteeism.

https://www.tmbusiness.org/

https://www.meditationtrust.com/category/transcendental-meditation-in-business/

Livestream Deepens Knowledge about Consciousness

The YouTube channel and the FaceBook page of Dr. Tony Nader, Maharishi's successor, offer current knowledge about consciousness as well as lectures by various scientists. 4.2 million viewers watch Dr. Nader's free livestreams per month.

https://www.youtube.com/user/DrTonyNader

https://www.facebook.com/DrTonyNader

Residential areas with Vedic Architecture World-Wide

There are, by now, Sthapatya Veda buildings in many countries. Larger settlements can be found in the U.S. (private residences and office buildings in Maharishi Vedic City and Fairfield, Iowa, as well as in Kentucky), in Canada, New Zealand, Serbia, Ukraine, Turkey, France, the Netherlands, England, and Ireland, as well as in the Brahmasthan (the geographical center) of India, and in continental India.

The 2000 Tower Oaks Office Building in Rockville, Maryland, a 18,000 square-meter nine-floor structure flooded with light, was built 100% according to Maharishi Sthapatya Veda, as well as according to the strictest criteria for organic building methods and energy-efficiency (41% less energy costs; 48% less water costs than conventional office buildings; every fifty-one minutes, the air in the entire building is exchanged 100%, etc.). For its innovative concept, the 2000 Tower Oaks Office Building was awarded the "Platinum Certificate LEED" by the committee for the evaluation of sustainability of buildings.

www.maharishivediccity.org; www.maharishivastu.org;
http://www.rendlesham.suffolk.gov.uk/_UserFiles/Files/
Rendlesham%20Sales%20Brochure2018.pdf
www.toweroaks.com

Vedic Organic Agriculture

Together with agricultural experts, Maharishi has enlivened and newly organized Vedic agriculture in detail. Vedic organic agriculture makes use of the cycles of nature with the exact determination of the most suitable jyotish times for sowing, fertilizing, watering, and harvesting. Vedic sounds activate and strengthen the plants in their various stages of growth. Often, organic farmers have to deal with the fact that their yields are less than those who use chemical fertilizers. As field tests have shown, however, Vedic organic agriculture yields even greater harvests than conventional methods, and the vitamin and mineral content of the plants is distinctly higher.

http://www.mvoa.com
www.globalcountry.org/wp/agriculture-2/

Maharishi Ayurveda

Through Maharishi's initiative, Ayurvedic medicine has spread world-wide since the beginning of the 80s. Many hundreds of Western doctors have been trained in Maharishi

Ayurveda and dozens of Ayurvedic establishments have come into being. There are Maharishi Ayurveda panchakarma centers in the U.S., Japan, Thailand, Austria, Switzerland, France, Germany, the Netherlands, Demark, Norway, and England, among others.

Maharishi Ayurveda herbal medicines are available in many countries of the world. One of Maharishi's last projects was the detailed planning of large medicinal centers built according to the principles of Sthapatya Veda. These integrated health centers, with modern medicine and diagnostic techniques in combination with all the natural healing methodologies, would do comparative scientific studies to sort out the most effective therapies dependent on the given pathology.

Many international professional Ayurveda congresses bring physicians and scientists from all over the world together to exchange new insights as well as the current state of research on Ayurveda.
www.internationalayurvedacongress.com; www.imavf.org;
https://ayurveda-badems.com

My Vision
In addition to leading the Maharishi Ayurveda Health Center, Bad Ems, I am internationally active to integrate Ayurveda as a solid part of our healthcare system. I regularly travel to various countries, make presentations, speak at congresses, give TV interviews, contact health insurance companies, as well as Ayurveda universities and colleges in India and Nepal. Moreover, I am involved as a consultant in the establishment of new Maharishi Ayurveda clinics.
https://lotharpirc.com/

APPENDICES

GLOSSARY

The Absolute, Absolute Reality from Latin *absolvere*; detached Self-referential reality; pure Being; pure consciousness that penetrates everything and from which everything emerges; the unified field of the quantum field in its ground state.

Ashtavaidya (Sanskrit) *ashta* eight; *vaidya*, an Indian expert of Ayurvedic medicine; name of an ancient tradition of Ayurveda experts in Kerala who make use of all eight branches (*ashtanga*) of Ayurveda.

Atma (Sanskrit) our Self, the innermost transcendent core of the personality that in the Vedic literature is designated as "the realm that never gets sick."

Ayurveda (Sanskrit) *ayus* life; *veda* knowledge; Ayurveda is the science of life, or the science of long life. The teaching about life in Indian high culture as cognized by seers (*rishis*). Ayurveda emphasizes prevention through the development of consciousness and right action in tune with the laws of nature; it offers natural healing methodologies for all illnesses while striving to achieve balance in body and mind.

Brahmachari (Sanskrit) he who walks in Brahman; Brahma is the absolute, the all-pervading. A person who dedicates his or her life completely to spirituality and has sworn to be celibate with the goal of attaining Brahman (see below).

Brahman (Sanskrit) the all-encompassing, all pervading. In Maharishi's Vedic science, Brahman is the wholeness of the relative sphere of creation and the Absolute.

Brahmananda Saraswati the name of Maharishi's Master (see *Guru Dev*).

Brahmasthan (Sanskrit) *Brahman* (see above) *sthan* place; place of wholeness. The geometrical center of a house. It is designed as a center of silence that is free of walls, pillars, furniture, etc. and is not used to live in. This area has a coherence-creating, harmonizing influence on the inhabitants. The Brahmasthan of a country is the geographical center point, which—used appropriately—brings a coherence-creating influence of wholeness and silence, which is especially effective in the collective consciousness of the population.

CDP Program (Corporate Development Program): CDP is a special program in which TM is used for the improvement of performance and the quality of life of companies, company leaders, and staff.

Cosmic Consciousness, the fifth state of consciousness (see States of Consciousness below). The experience of transcendence (the blissful silence and unboundedness without thoughts—see below) is maintained along with activity, as well as during the dream state and deep, dreamless sleep. The person rests completely in the profound silence of pure consciousness. In Cosmic Consciousness one is the constant witness, the uninvolved observer, of the actions that one experiences as the actions of nature.

Enlightenment the continuous experience of a higher state of consciousness (see also States of Consciousness) in contrast to transient experiences of enlightenment, which are temporary experiences of higher states of consciousness that may come and go.

Extended Maharishi Effect the measurable effect of the group dynamics of the collective consciousness of a group of people. This group effect is created when a required number of people practice the TM and TM-Sidhi Program together in one place. According to experience, the square root of one percent of the population of a given country is enough for the coherence-creating effect on the entire population of that country through those group dynamics.

Global Maharishi Effect the measurable effect of the field of collective consciousness on the global level: the square root of one percent of the world's population is enough to create the coherence effect in all the people of this planet if this is the number of people practicing the TM and TM-Sidhi Program in one place.

God Consciousness the sixth state of consciousness (see States of Consciousness)
The experience of Cosmic Consciousness has deepened further, the senses and their perceptions are more refined. A person in God Consciousness can perceive the heavenly aspects of creation as well as all-pervading divine love. He or she can, for example, see into the past and the future and can see light-beings as well as the auras of people.

Guru (Sanskrit) *gu* darkness, ignorance; *ru* removal, destruction; spiritual master who explains to his disciple the meaning and purpose of life and shows him or her the path to self-realization. He removes the last remaining ignorance that separates the awareness from the realization of the wholeness of reality (Brahman).

Guru Dev (Sanskrit) *div* radiate, glow. Guru Dev is an addition to the name of enlightened people who have realized divine consciousness. In the TM organization, it is the loving abbreviation for Maharishi's Master, Swami Brahmananda Saraswati, a renowned Shankaracharya of Jyotir Math, North India.

Guru Purnima (Sanskrit) *purnima* full moon; In the Vedic tradition the first full moon in July is the day on which the guru is venerated.

Jyotish (Sanskrit) inner light, heavenly light, star; Differing significantly from Western astrology, Vedic astrology (jyotish) takes into consideration the movement of both the sun and the moon through the constellations (relative to the Earth).

Karma (Sanskrit) deed, act, activity; The law of action and reaction. This especially refers to the retroactive effects of actions or thoughts which stem from this or a previous life and which construct the individual. In higher states of consciousness, human beings act in accordance with natural law; they experience greater joy and fulfillment. Retroactive effects are then no longer experienced as a burden.

Maharishi (Sanskrit) *maha* great, *rishi* seer (see Rishi); A seer who not only has the highest insight into life, but, beyond this, can implement this knowledge for the benefit of mankind and to lead others to enlightenment.

Maharishi Effect the measurable effect of the collective consciousness of individuals who practice Transcendental Meditation for him or herself; however, if one percent of the population of a city practices TM, a phase transition occurs, whose effect is that all the people of this city become more harmonious; negative events such as accidents, hospital admissions, and criminality decrease measurably.

Maharishi Mahesh Yogi (Sanskrit) *maha* great, *rishi* seer (see *Maharishi* above and *rishi* below); *Mahesh* Maharishi's given name, *Yogi* from the Sanskrit root *yuj* to unite; a yogi is realized person or someone who practices various yogic methods with the goal of realization.

Mantra (Sanskrit) *man* mind, *tra* instrument; a mantra is an instrument of thoughts, or of speech; Specifically, during the TM technique, it is a sound without meaning, which is used to meditate. It allows the mind to enjoy increasingly finer states of mental activity and to experience the ground state of the mind—transcendental consciousness.

MERU acronym for Maharishi European Research University

Mother Divine The name of a group of women who live together in a secluded environment to practice Maharishi's advanced programs for development of consciousness and to study the Vedas.

Panchakarma (Sanskrit) *pancha* five, *karma* action; The classical system of the five therapeutic methods of Ayurveda to rejuvenate, prevent, and treat chronic illnesses through the mobilization and excretion of metabolic waste and toxins for the creation of balance in body and mind.

Purusha (Sanskrit) human being, eternal human being, absolute, pure consciousness; he name of a group of men who live together in a secluded environment to practice Maharishi's advanced programs for development of consciousness and to study the Vedas.

Rajabhishek (Sanskrit) **raja** king; **abhishek** consecration (yagya, see below); The traditional Vedic crowning ceremony

Rishi (Sanskrit) seer, one whose spirit is grounded within the Self, in the unbounded; A rishi can clearly perceive the original impulses of creation and impart them correctly to others (see Maharishi above).

Ritam Bhara Pragya (Sanskrit) the intelligence that knows the truth. The mind is so solidly grounded in the transcendent that it can have impulses without losing the eternal silence of the unbounded, the Absolute.
Sama Veda slow and melodious recitations from the Rig Veda; They are calming and expand the awareness.

Samskaras (Sanskrit) old impressions and experiences within the nervous system, which must be dissolved so that the awareness can free itself and can experience higher states of consciousness.

Sankalpa (Sanskrit) will, desire, thought, intention, purpose

Sanskrit perfected, prepared, constructed, refined; Sanskrit is the language of Vedic high culture and classical Indian culture. Sanskrit belongs to the Indo-Aryan branch of the Indo-Germanic family of languages and thus has a common ancestry with almost all modern European languages, but also with the classical languages such as Latin and Greek, and with ancient Persian and thus, with all languages that developed from this in the Near East. A unique characteristic attributed to Sanskrit is that sound and meaning are one.

SCI (Science of Creative Intelligence) a discipline established by Maharishi Mahesh Yogi; Knowledge about natural laws of life, especially those related to the development of coherence, perfection, and higher states of consciousness.

Shankara (Sanskrit) Name of the greatest saint and philosopher of India (788-820 CE); Shankara revived the Vedic tradition and created a position in all four compass directions for the preservation of the spiritual knowledge of India.

Shankaracharya (Sanskrit) *Acharya* spiritual teacher, master; Title of the representative of the Vedic tradition going back to Shankara. Each of the four learning centers founded by Shankara in the four corners of India is headed by a Shankaracharya who is democratically elected by the spiritual great men of India.

States of Consciousness
There are seven states of consciousness which are physiologically and psychologically clearly distinct from one another:
1-3. Relative states of consciousness: waking, dreaming, sleeping (deep, dreamless sleep)
4. Transcendental Consciousness: the subjective experience of restful alertness without thought
5-7. Higher states of consciousness that develop through the regular experience of the fourth state of consciousness (transcendence) alternating with the three relative states of consciousness (waking, dreaming, and sleeping)
5. Cosmic Consciousness: (I am That). The experience of transcendence pervades the alternation of the three relative states of consciousness.
6. God Consciousness: (Thou art That). The perception of celestial realms is added to "normal" sensory perceptions.
7. Unity Consciousness (All this is That). There is no longer anything that is not perceived as one's own Self, the unified field of the all-pervading silence (see Unity Consciousness below).

Sthapatya Veda (Sanskrit) knowledge about the art of building; Vedic architecture encompasses the building of residences as well as land and city planning. For example, Sthapatya Veda arranges the rooms of a house in accordance with the position of the sun and the compass directions, making use of the principles of cosmic geometry.

Transcendence from Latin *trans* beyond, *scandere* to climb, to cross over.

Transcendence is the fourth state of consciousness (see States of Consciousness) or the simplest or the ground state of consciousness in which the conscious mind rests completely within itself. Subjectively, it is the experience of perfect silence, absent of sensory objects and thoughts.

Transcending (see Transcendence above); Increasing refinement of thoughts in meditation until the practitioner finally leaves the realm of thought and experiences the absolute, pure Being, transcendental consciousness without thoughts (see Transcendental Consciousness under "States of Consciousness" above).

Unified Field (the unified field of natural law); It is a concept from quantum physics of the most fundamental level of existence, from which in a sequential manner all natural laws and all matter unfold.

Unity Consciousness the seventh state of consciousness (see States of Consciousness above); The perception of the Unified Field, the absolute reality of silence and unboundedness, which is one's Self, in every object. The finer perception of God Consciousness remains present, along with the person feeling connected with everything and being one with everything. It is the experience of the oneness of everything, of being the master of all natural law (All this is That).

Vastu (Sanskrit) place, property; vastu vidya is the knowledge about the art of spatial planning and creation based on natural law. A branch of Vedic architecture and city planning (see

Sthapatya Veda), which constructs all buildings and living spaces in accordance with nature; for example, it situates them according to compass directions.

Veda (Sanskrit) pure knowledge; The Vedas are tonal presentations of the cosmic order. Recitations of sound and meaning are connected to one another in the Vedas. The Vedic recitations have an immediate effect on the consciousness of the speaker and the listener.

Yagya (Sanskrit) offering; A Vedic ritual that has a coherence-creating effect on a person through the enlivening of the finest impulses of natural law and its original sounds. It has been used for thousands of years to create fortuitous occasions during phases of difficulty or to strengthen positive aspects in the life of a person.

ANNOTATIONS

(A) page 85
The Fourth Major State of Consciousness
The fourth major state of consciousness is the original ground state of human nature because each one of us experiences it daily many times, specifically when we change from one of the three major states of consciousness into another—for example, when we fall asleep or wake up and when we change from the state of deep sleep into the dream state or the other way around. Indeed, this transitional state, the so-called *hypnagogic* state, is normally so brief that most people do not notice it consciously. In modern medicine, it has not been ascribed any great significance, but Maharishi explained to us that this experience of completely silent awareness makes possible the deepest regeneration of our nervous system. If this state is experienced systematically and regularly, then our brain begins to develop the higher functions that it is endowed with.

This ground state or 4th state of consciousness is distinguished by the fact that the body is significantly more relaxed than it is in deep sleep, yet the mind is wide awake without having any thoughts. The researcher Robert Keith Wallace, a young physiologist from the U.S., who was the first to have measured and described it, called it *restful awareness* [6]. The fascinating conclusion of all this is that a person who allows this ground state to just lie fallow while directing his attention only to the external aspects of life and who lives, as most of us do today, with all the restrictions, mental and physical constitution that we generally consider to be a self-evident part of human life. Yet when we begin to cultivate that state and to intensify it, then we activate the enormous power of regeneration that is inherent in it and with it we can open totally new dimensions of our consciousness that sleep in all of us.

(B) page 86
Higher States of Consciousness Through the Release of Stress

Maharishi explained to us that the real purpose of every human being is to live in these higher states of consciousness. These states develop totally by themselves when stress and tension, those burdensome imprints that life brings with it, dissolve little by little. Our bodies have a built-in healing mechanism that no one has to learn because it comes with a regenerative mechanism: deep rest. Just as one recovers from an infectious disease when the body rests, so the mind releases deeply ingrained blockages from past situations that are stored in the mind-body system. Exactly this is accomplished through TM—it provides extremely deep rest which breaks down these blockages and makes our nervous system permeable again so that our mental abilities may grow by themselves.

(C) page 88
The Third Law of Thermodynamics— Order through the Reduction of Activity

The lower the temperature is in any system, the more orderliness takes place: in hot steam, the individual molecules rush around completely chaotically; in liquid water, they are connected to one another reversibly and form orderly structures, while, as ice, they form highly organized crystals. The same universal law also applies to the human mind: the more it comes to rest, the more ordered the thinking process becomes.

(D) page 96
Collective Consciousness

Already at the beginning of the sixties, Maharishi began to explain that there is a field of collective consciousness in which all human beings participate. Every thought, every emotion, of every single human being contributes to the collective consciousness, to the quality of the spiritual atmosphere of our planet. Elevated stress in the life of individuals increases the stress in the collective consciousness. Much stress in the collective field of consciousness leads to a higher tendency to violence, crime, and multiple social problems for the individuals of a society.

This concept was completely new and it turned the predominant materialistic world view upside down—especially in the Western world. Even more remarkable in this context was the ancient Vedic assertion handed down through time that this field of collective consciousness could be balanced through meditation. If meditation were successful in uplifting the level of coherence, of orderliness and harmony in the collective consciousness, then this would also influence individuals positively. This was a completely new approach to improve the quality of social life and to solve social problems—diametrically opposed to the thousands of years old customary strategies of exclusion, punishment, revenge, and wars.

Maharishi explained the exact mechanisms according to which this is possible. The decisive factor is transcending, the state of total silence without thoughts. With this is meant the complete absence of thoughts while the mind is fully awake, resting within itself regardless how this experience manifests. With the technique of Transcendental Meditation, this restful alertness occurs especially quickly and frequently so that most beginners experience this consciously even in the first meditations. The atmospheric influence of rest and coherence is so powerful that it "cleanses" the collective consciousness, especially when many people do this together.

(E) page 97
Effect of Coherence—Simple Examples from the Natural Sciences

In a normal piece of iron, the electrical positive and negative poles of the atoms are disorganized and point in all directions. To make the iron into a magnet, an electrical current is sent through the iron, which forces the electrons of the iron atoms to align parallel with their north and south poles. What's fascinating about this is that only a small percentage of the iron atoms have to be oriented in the same direction— in that moment, in which the critical number is reached, the rest of the iron atoms follow by themselves.

But this is by no means the only example of an ordered system showing completely new characteristics. In a laser, all the light waves travel completely parallel and the laser beam scatters only "in infinity." Through this, a laser has completely different qualities than the disorganized light waves from normal light sources, whose disorganized wavelengths scatter in all directions. The coherent laser is so powerful it can be used as a precise tool for cutting tissue or even metal, which as everyone knows is simply not possible with an ordinary light. The amazing thing here is again that to create such a focused aligned light beam of a laser, only a small percentage of atoms need to be stimulated to emit photons to create the laser. The effect is strengthened through the additional resonances between the photons that interact with one another or with themselves.

The same principal can be found everywhere in the natural sciences: the coherent elements of a system have a stronger influence overall than do disorderly components. To put it simply: order prevails when it is big enough.

(F) page 99
The Field Effect of Human Consciousness

An obvious question would be: how is it even possible that the consciousness of an individual person has such a strong influence on that of other people since this is about separate individuals?

Scientists explain this in terms of the field effect. The field effect in physics generally means that one doesn't have to influence the individual parts of a system but instead, that at one go, one can manage the system with the field that lies at its basis. Thus, if one knows how to influence a field, one no longer has to change the components individually. Instead one simply uses the more abstract and much more effective level of the unifying field.

Electromagnetic fields, such as radio, TV, and mobile phone networks are produced by countless stations at the same time and traverse countries everywhere: this is completely understandable and real for us—even when we can neither feel nor hear this dense field of vibrations. Only when we tune an appropriate receiver to a specific frequency through the radio, TV, or mobile phone are the vibrations in the field transformed into sounds and pictures. No one can see what happens, as if guided by the hands of ghosts, yet despite this we make use this phenomenon as a matter of course. Is it then so far-fetched that human brains, that constantly produce electromagnetic mini-streams and send out subtle information day in and day out, could weave a field in which we are all connected with one another and through which we influence one another positively or negatively?

Something as ground-breaking and unprecedented as the Maharishi Effect substantiated through sociological studies can only function according to this principle—as the field effect of human consciousness. With the many thousand-fold repeated experience of unmoved silence within them, meditators imperceptibly produced a dense field of coherence, peace, and harmony in their city. And through the field of consciousness connecting everyone there spontaneously arises a coherent behavior by the people in the city—as long as the number of "coherence generators" is enough.

(G) page 117
The Support of Nature
Since the silent, unmoved field of consciousness is *the* field of life that underlies everything and from which everything emerges, it is, logically speaking, a field in which all possibilities are contained. When a person is active from the level of this silent field, then the entire power of nature supports him or her with its unbounded possibilities. That is, all the laws of nature with their unbounded creativity, which allows

a whole universe to function frictionless, support individual desires with a much greater intelligence and energy than would be possible with less contact to this subtle field.

(H) page 132

Third Law of Thermodynamics— Purification through the Reduction of Activity

Everywhere in nature, this is true: When the activity in a system is reduced, its orderliness increases at the same time. Physicists have formulated this well-known principle as the third law of thermodynamics, while observing that impurities are expelled at the same time.

When water cools significantly, for example, with the reduction of the temperature the disorderly movement of the water molecules reduces concurrently. Their movement reduces more and more until, finally, a coherent new condition is created, namely an ice crystal. Furthermore, if a salt water solution is frozen, the resulting block of ice is only water molecules, that is, fresh water, because as the water freezes, the lattice structure of salt does not fit within the lattice structure of the water molecule and the salt molecule is squeezed out. This same principle is used in a targeted manner in some seawater desalination facilities.

In an analogous way, the human mind-body system expels "impurities" in a completely natural way when it is exposed to profound rest. For that same reason, a doctor or a mother prescribe bed rest to a seriously ill child. It is a simple but effective principle: rest increases order; illness is disorder.

(I) page 132

Cosmic Consciousness—the Beginning of Enlightenment

In Cosmic Consciousness (restful alertness maintained during any of the three other states, waking, dreaming, and deep sleep) a person is so deeply restful within himself that he or she accepts everything as it is. The person is so satisfied with the silence and unboundedness that always accompanies all thought and behavior that one could assume one had already realized everything that is possible. However, Cosmic Consciousness is only the beginning state of enlightenment. That is why a Maharishi sees to it that his disciples can also develop the states of consciousness that are based upon Cosmic Consciousness and for which their nervous system is created.

(J) page 180

Maharishi Patanjali—Unified Consciousness Creates Peace

The state of unified consciousness described by Maharishi Patanjali can be systematically produced as if at the touch of a button by many, many people because unified consciousness, the experience of resting in pure Being, arises in an especially profound way during the TM-Sidhi Program and Yogic Flying. It has therefore become possible for the first time in our age to test scientifically the validity of Patanjali's statement that hostile tendencies disappear in the vicinity of unified consciousness.

(K) page 180

Meissner Effect—Invincibility Through Coherence

Already on the TM teacher training course, we learned that this effect is not as unusual as it seems at first glance because similar phenomena are quite well known as laws of nature: A magnetic field can penetrate an ordinary power line completely unhindered because of the incoherent, disorderly movement of the electrons within this electrical conductor. This is completely different with the Meissner effect of a super conductor because its electrons, which are vibrating in unison, form a protective field, so to speak: The disruptive magnetic field can simply no longer penetrate.

This immense coherence of its electrons protects the superconductor from outside influences—just as a sufficiently large number of coherent brains could protect a nation from foreign enemies. As surprising as this may sound, with this method victory would be guaranteed before any war could even break out. Conflicts that result in violent confrontation, just no longer escalate. The emergence of enmity is prevented from the outset—without enemies, a nation thus becomes invincible.

In the so-called superfluids or superconductors there exist totally coherent realms of atoms in addition to incoherent ones. The ordered ones increase the collective coherence of all particles so much that the entire system is protected from internal and external disturbances according to "the square root of n" law. However, the minimum number of the coherent particles must approximately amount to 1% of the total number of all present particles. Scientists around Maharishi had analyzed these scientific phenomena with him and had concluded that the same law should be applicable to macro-social improvements.

(L) page 468

The Discovery of the Unified Field of all the Laws of Nature

James Maxwell succeeded at the end of the 19th century to unify magnetism, and light to electromagnetism, a unified energy field. At the beginning of the 20th century, Albert Einstein worked for years to unify electromagnetic energy with the force of gravity, but without success. Only decades later, bright minds described supersymmetry in which all the energies of matter were unified: electromagnetism, weak and strong atomic energy and gravity. A formula first published by Hermann Nicolei and Bernard de Wit in 1982 was received in the scientific literature as the Lagrangian of the unified field of supergravity. It is an incredibly long and highly complicated mathematical presentation of all the energies active in nature and combining them to a single field.

(M) page 469

A Paradox: Particles and Waves are One

Professor Hagelin had worked in the European Organization for Nuclear Research (CERN) where member physicists observe in the gigantic particle accelerator in Geneva how particles are created out of the vacuum state and again vanish into it. The physicists who, like all scientists had learned to be exactingly mindful in bringing to light only objective and systematically verifiable laws of nature, faced a paradox that made life difficult for them. Even an electron behaves sometimes like a particle, and sometimes as a wave, depending on the experimental set-up. The evident conclusion is this: at an un-manifest level that underlies creation, wave forms transform into particles and vice versa; one can merge into another.

With the discovery of the unified field, these surprising insights could be expressed more precisely: All particles that build up creation are wave forms of certain omnipresent fields that can be described precisely in terms of their characteristics and that, together, form the unified field. When thus an electron is sometimes a wave and sometimes a particle, depending on the experimental design, and the result is, moreover, dependent on the observing consciousness, is this not tantamount to evidence that the unified field is consciousness—and with this everything is ultimately a form of consciousness?

For Professor Hagelin, this was no longer a question.

REFERENCES

1. Robert Keith Wallace, R. K. Benson and H. Wilson: "A Wakeful Hypometabolic Physiologic State," *American Journal of Physiology* 221, no. 3 (1972): 84-90.

2. Michael A. West: "Changes in Skin Resistance in Subjects Resting, Reading, Listening to Music, or Practicing the Transcendental Meditation Technique," in Orme Johnson, D. W. Farrow, J. T. (publisher): *Scientific Research on the Transcendental Meditation Program*: Collected Papers, vol. I-VI*, vol. 1, p 224-229.

3. Christa Knifki: *Transzendentale Meditation und Autogenes Training* (Munich: Kinder Verlag, 1979).

4. Maharishi Mahesh Yogi: *The Science of Being and the Art of Living* (California: Meridian Publishing, Inc., 1995).

5. F. P. Sandahl: "Inverkan av tm-utövnin pa neurotiseringsgrad," *Läkartidiningen, Journal of the Swedish Medical Association* 77 (34): 2808, (1980). Based on Jaan Suurküla: Forschung über Transcendentale Meditation (TM) bei der Schwedischen Luftwaffe. www.tmdoctors.info/DMTger.htm

6. Wallace: "The Physiological Effects of Transcendental Meditation: A Proposed Fourth Major State of Consciousness." Ph.D. Thesis, Department of Physiology, University of California, Los Angeles, CA, 1970.

7. M. C. Dillbeck, et. al: "The Transcendental Meditation Program and Crime Rate Change in a Sample of Forty-Eight Cities." *Journal of Crime and Justice* 1981 4: 25-45.

8. Aaron and Aaron: *Der Maharishi-Effekt*, (Heine Verlag, 1991).

9. C. Borland and G. Landrith, III: "Improved Quality of City Life through the Transcendental Meditation Program: Decreased Crime Rate." In: Collected Papers, vol. I-VI*, (vol., 1, p. 639-6480).

10. Tat Twam Asi' (skr.): "I am that, thou art that, and all this is that." In Chandogya Upanishad 6.8.7., in *The Chandogya Upanishad of the Samaveda: With the Commentary of Shankaracharya and the Gloss of Ananda Giri* (1873; 2010).

11. Hans Selye: *Stress without Distress* (New York: Lippincott Williams & Wilkins, 1st edition 1974).

12. P. Gelderloos, K. G. Walton, D. W. Orme-Johnson: "Transcendental Meditation and Substance Misuse: An Overview." *International Journal of the Addictions* 26: 293-325 (1992).

13. Donald E. Miskiman, Graduate Department of Psychology, University of Alberta, Canada: "The Treatment of Insomnia by the Transcendental Meditation Program," (1972).
    Donald E. Miskiman, Graduate Department of Psychology, University of Alberta Canada: "Long-Term Effects of the Transcendental Meditation Program in the Treatment of Insomnia" (1975).
    Both in: Collected Papers, vol. I-VI*, vol. 1, Paper 41 and 42, p. 296-299.

14. A. F. Wilson et, al.: "Transcendental Meditation and Asthma." Respiration 32: 74-80 (1975).

Clinical Research, 21, p. 278 (1973).

Respiratory Therapy: The Journal of Inhalation Technology, 3, p. 79-80, (1973).

All three studies reprinted in: "Collected Papers, vol. I-VI*, vol. I, Papers, 36, 37, and 38, p. 279-286.

N. Wolkove et. al. "Effect of Transcendental Meditation on Breathing and Respiratory Control." *Journal of Applied Physiology: Respiratory, Environmental and Exercise Physiology*, 56: 607-612 (1984)

Karin Pirc: *Asthma ist heilbar* (Lübbe-Verlag, 1999, ISBN 378 58 09 7220).

15. *Hypertension*, 1995, vol. 28, no. 2, p. 223-237.

Hypertension, 1996, 28, p. 228, p. 228-237.

Journal of the National Medical Association, 1997, 89: p. 464-476.

American Journal of Hypertension, 2005, 18: p. 88-98.

The Journal of Alternative and Complementary Medicine, 1995; vol. 1, no. 3, p. 263-283.

W. Schachinger and E. Schrott: *Ayurveda bei Bluthochdruck und Gefäßkrankheiten*, Mosaik Verlag, 1997, ISBN no. 3-576-10736-3.

16. *Journal of Criminal Justice*, vol. 15 (1978), p. 211-230 in Collected Papers, (vol. V, p. 3123-3135).

17. C. N. Alexander et al.: "Treating and Preventing Alcohol, Nicotine, and Drug Abuse through Transcendental Meditation: A Review and Statistical Meta-Analysis. *Alcohol Treatment Quarterly* 11: 13-87 (1994).

18. Orme-Johnson et. al.: "Intersubjective EEG Coherence: Is Consciousness a Field" *International Journal of Neuroscience* 16:203-209 (1982).

19. Patanjali: Edwin F. Bryant, *The Yoga Sūtras of Patañjali: A New Edition*, Translation, and Commentary with Insights from the Traditional Commentators; illustrated. (New York: North Point Press, 2009).

20. Robert Keith Wallace, et al.: "Decreased Drug Abuse with Transcendental Meditation: A Study of 1,862 Subjects." In Drug Abuse: Proceedings of the International Conference, ed. Chris J. D. Zarafonetis (Philadelphia: Lea and Febiger), p. 369-376 (1972).

21. H. Schenkluhn and M. Geisler: "Eine Langzeitstudie über den Einfluss des Progamms der transcendentalen Meditation auf Drogenmissbrauch," in Collected Papers, vol. I-VI*, vol. I, p. 524-536.

22. E. Stutz: "Transzendentale Meditation in der Behandlung Drogenabhängiger." Das öffentliche Gesuntheitswesen 39: p. 759-766 (1977).

23. W. T. Windquist: "The Transcendental Meditation Program and Drug Abuse: A Retrospective Study" in Collected Papers, v. I-VI*, vol. I p. 497.

24. *Journal of Criminal Justice*, vol. 15 (1987), p. 211-230. In Collected Papers, vol. I-VI*, vol V, p. 3123-3135.

25. Albrecht Schöll, 19th ed. In: *Vereinigung Meditierender Juristen in Deutschland e. V.*: "Verfolgung im Rechtsstaat, Die Rufmordkampagne gegen Transcendentale Meditations—Fakten und Hintergründe." (Unpublished copy, 1993) .

26. Ibid.

27. Judgment of the OVG Münster of 12.18.1985, Az.: 5 A 1125/84.

28. Bundesverwaltungsgericht (Federal Administrative Court) BVerwG 7 C 2.87 of 23.5.89.

29. *Vereiningung Meditierender Juristen in Deutschland* (See note # 25 above).

30. „Orsakssamband mellan vissa aktiviteter och psykisk sjukdom – redovisning av en rundfraja jämte vissa rekomendationer". 09 09 1975, Socialstyrelsen byrä, SN 3 D: no. SN 3–9–204.

   "Transcendental Meditation: An Evaluation" by Jan Otto Ottoson (1977). Socialstyrelsen, D: no. 3–9–1194/73.

31. Guy D. Hatchard, Ashley J. Deans, Kenneth L. Cavanaugh, and David Orme-Johnson: "The Maharishi Effect to Reduce Crime in Merseyside Metropolitan Area"; *Psychology, Crime and Law,* vol. 2, p. 165-174 (1996).

32. – W. H. Burgmans, et. al: "Sociological Effects of the Group Dynamics of Consciousness: Decrease of Crime and Traffic Accidents in Holland." In: Collected Papers, vol. I–VI*, vol. 4, p. 2566–258.

   – M. C. Dillbeck, et. al.: "The Effect of the Group Dynamics of Consciousness on Society Reduced Crime in the Union Territory of Delhi, India." In: Collected Papers, vol. I–VI*, vol. 4, p. 2583–2589.

   – M. Dillbeck, et al.: "A Time Series Analysis of the Relationship between the Group Practice of the Transcendental Meditation and TM-Sidhi-Program and Crime Change in Puerto Rico." In Collected Papers, vol. I–VI*, vol. 4, p. 2679–2687

   – J. L. Davies, C. N. Alexander: "The Maharishi Technology of the Unified Field and Improved Quality of Life in the United Sates: A Study of the First World Peace Assembly, Amherst, Massachusetts, 1979". In: Collected Papers, vol. I-VI*, vol. 4, p. 2549–2563.

33. – "Taste of Utopia" – *Journal of Offender Rehabilitation* 36: 283–302, (2003).

Summary in: Collected Papers, vol. I–VI*, vol. 4, p. 2472–2473.

– K. L. Cavanaugh, D. W. Orme-Johnson, and P. Gelderloos: "The Effect of the Taste of Utopia Assembly on the World Index of International Stock Prices" Department of Management and Public Affairs and Department of Psychology, Maharishi International University, Fairfield, Iowa, U.S.A. (1984).

– D. Orme-Johnson, K. Cavanaugh, C. Alexander, et al.: "The Influence of the Maharishi Technology of the Unified Field on World Events and Global Social Indicators: The Effects of the Taste of Utopia Assembly" in: Collected Papers, vol. I–VI*, vol. 4, p. 2730–2762.

34. Performance improvement of students in all age groups:
– *Education* 107: 49–54 (1986).
– *Education* 109: 302–304, 1989.
– In: Collected Papers, vol. I–VI*, vol. 1, p. 396–399 (1977).
– *British Journal of Educational Psychology* 55: 164–166 (1985).

35. Improved IQ:
– *Gedrag: Tijdschrift voor Psychologie* 3: 167–182 (1975).
– *Dissertation Abstracts International* 38 (7): 3372B–3373B (1978).
– *College Student Journal* 15: 140–146 (1981).

– *Perceptual and Motor Skills* 62: 731–738 (1986).

– *The Journal of Creative Behavior* 19: 270–275 (1985).

– *Journal of Clinical Psychology* 42: 161–164 (1986).

– *Personality and Individual Differences* 12: 1105–1116 (1991).

– *Intelligence* (September/October 2001, vol. 29/5, p. 419–440).

36. Improvement in reading, mathematical abilities, language and work behavior:
   – *Education* 107: 49–54 (1986);
   – *Education* 109: 302–304 (1989).

37. Brain waves in all parts of the brain become more settled and more coherent:
   – *International Journal of Neuroscience* 15: 151–157 (1981).
   – *International Journal of Neuroscience* 13: 211–217 (1981).
   – *Journal of Moral Education* 12: 166–173 (1983).

38. Improvement of creativity:
   – *Dissertation Abstracts International* 38(7): 3372B–3373B (1978).
   – *The Journal of Creative Behavior* 19: 270–275 (1985).
   – *The Journal of Creative Behavior* 13: 169–180 (1979).

39. Improvement of the ability to concentrate:
   – Broader Comprehension and Improved Ability to Focus Attention –Increased Field
   Independence (4, 13, 15).
   – *Perceptual and Motor Skills* 62: 731–738 (1986).
   – *Perceptual and Motor Skills* 65: 613–614 (1987).
   – *Perceptual and Motor Skills* 39: 1031–1034 (1974).

40. *Anxiety, Stress, and Coping: An International Journal* 6: 245–262 (1993).

41. Kam-Tim So, David Orme-Johnson: "Three Randomized Experiments on the Holistic Longitudinal Effects of the Transcendental Meditation-Technique on Cognition." *Dissertation Abstracts International* (1995).

42. R. A. Rabinoff, M. C. Dillbeck, R. Deissler.: "Effect of Coherent Collective Consciousness on the Weather." Departments of Physics and Psychology, Maharishi International University, Fairfield, Iowa, U.S.A. (1981). In: Collected Papers, vol. I-VI*, vol. 4, p. 2564–2566.

43. F. K. Anklesaria, M. S. King: "The TM Program in the Senegalese Penitentiary System," *Journal of Offender Rehabilitation*, 36: 303–318 (2003).

44. Systeme Intégré Maharishi de Rehabilitation, *L'Imprimérie Nationale du Sénégal Rufisque*, Dakar (1988).

45. C. Bleick, A. I. Abrams: "The Transcendental Meditation Program and Criminal Recidivism in California," *Journal of Criminal Justice*, vol. 15 (1987) p. 211–230. In: Collected Papers, vol. I-VI*, vol. 5, p. 3123–3135.

46. – Orme-Johnson, C. T. Haynes: "EEG Phase Coherence, Pure Consciousness, Creativity, and TM-Sidhi Experiences." International Journal of Neuroscience 13: 211– 217 (1981).

   – Dillbeck, and E. C. Bronson: "Short-Term Longitudinal Effects of the Transcendental Meditation Technique on EEG Power and Coherence." *International Journal of Neuroscience* 14: 147–151 (1981).

47. – Dissertation Abstracts International 49, 1988, 2381A
    – J. L. Davis, C. N. Alexander: presented at the 85th
    Annual Meeting of the *American Political Science Association*, (Atlanta, Ga., August 1989). In: Collected Papers,
    vol. I–VI*, vol. 5, p. 3260–3262.
    – Orme-Johnson, et al.: "Time-Series-Impact Assessment Analysis of Reduced International Conflict and
    Terrorism: Effects of Large Assemblies of Participants
    in the Transcendental Meditation and TM-Sidhi-Program." Paper presented to the 85th Annual Meeting of
    the *American Political Science Association*, (Atlanta, GA
    USA, 1989).

48. Compare with:
    – Klaus Kairies: "Stress bewältigen durch Kreativität,"
    Arbeitshefte Führungspsychologie, ed.: Ekkehard Crisand,
    Wilhelmsfeld, vol. 40.
    – K. Kairies, E. Schrott: "Soft Skills haben einen großen
    Einfluss auf den Unternehmenserfolg." *Betriebswirtschaftliche Blätter*, 02/2002, p. 62–68.

49. – *Journal of Criminal Justice*, vol. 15 (1987), p. 211–230
    In: Collected Papers, vol. I-VI*, vol. V, p. 3123–3135.
    – Overview of 8 studies on this subject: I: Collected
    Papers, vol. I-VI*, vol. V, p. 3415–3426.
    – *The Journal of the Iowa Academy of Science*, vol. 96,
    1989, p. A32, / In: Collected Papers, vol. I–VI*, vol. V,
    p. 3141–3149.

50. *Japanese Journal of Industrial Health* 32 (7), 1990, p. 346.

51. *Japanese Journal of Public Health* 37 (10), 1990, p. 729.

52. M. Kriele: "Die faschistischen Züge der Sektenjagd," in *Zeit-Fragen*, no. 52. of 01.11.98, also see: www.zeit-fragen.ch.

53. – *Dissertation Abstracts International* 49, 1988: 2381A.
– J. L. Davis, C. N. Alexander: presented at the 85th annual assembly of the *American Political Science Association*, (Atlanta, Ga. August 1989). In: Collected Papers, vol. -VI*, vol. V, p. 3260–3262.

54. *Journal of Conflict Resolution*, vol. 32, no. 4, p. 776–812, (December 1988).

55. Patanjali: Edwin F. Bryant, *The Yoga Sūtras of Patañjali: A New Edition*, Translation, and Commentary with Insights from the Traditional Commentators; illustrated. (New York: North Point Press, 2009).

56. Maharishi Mahesh Yogi: *Dhavanatari Lecture* (2004).

57. Entwicklungshilfeklub Österreich: www.eh-klub.at/projekte/index.php?detail=1893

58. Nobel Prize 2006 for Prof. Muhammed Yunus and the Grameen-Bank: www.nobelprize.org/nobel_prizes/peace/laureates/2006/press.html.

59. International Criminal Police Organization, (1994). United Kingdom Prison Service, (1994).

60. Sherman, 1997 in: Social Indicators Research 47, p. 153–201, (1999).

61. ibid

62. ibid

63. Orme-Johnson, R. E. Herron: "An Innovative Approach to Reducing Medical Care Utilization and Costs." *Psychosomatic Medicine* 49: (1987), p. 493–507.

Hans Schäffler: "Kostendämpfung und Maharishi Ayuveda im Gesundheitswesen," *Therapeutikon*, (1989).

64. *Journal of the Iowa Academy of Science* 95(1), (1988), A56.

65. – *Dissertation Abstracts International.*53/12-A (June 1993), order number 93–10427.

– R. Herron, S. Hillis: "The Impact of the Transcendental Meditation Program on Government Payments to Physicians in Quebec," *American Journal of Health Promotion*, 2000, 14 (5), p. 284–291.

– Herron, Cavanaugh: "Can the TM-Program Reduce Medical Expenditure of Older People?" *Journal of Social Behavior and Personality*, (2002).

66. J. K. Ratzinger, in: *Herder Korrespondenz*, (1990).

67. *Handbuch Herz und Kreislauf*, 2. aktualisierte Neuauflage (1996), Stiftung Warentest, Berlin, p. 97.

68. Publisher: A. B. Smith, OSB: *Transzendentale Meditation – eine Methode für Christen*, Helmut Felder Verlag, (1985).

69. – After Klaus Hartmann: *50 Jahre Verfilzung von Staat und Kirche*, Freidenker 3, (1999).

– Matthias Holzbauer: *Der Steinadler und sein Schwefelgeruch*, Verlag das weiße Pferd.

70. Norbert Thiel: *Der Kampf gegen neue religiöse Bewegungen*, (Mörfelden 1986), p. 138.

71. Ortrun Schätzle, MdB: "Pressemitteilung vom Deutschen Bundestag, Enquete-Kommission, sogenannte Sekten und Psychogruppen," 19. (June 1998).

72. Programs Advocated by the Natural Law Party Successfully Applied in Mozambique, www.btinternet.com.

73. Frankfurter Allgemeine Zeitung of 9.04.99: Ausführlicher Bericht über den erstaunlichen Aufstieg Mosambiks (Detailed report about the surprising way up of Mosambique).

74. "Country Profile of Mozambique," published in the international edition of TIME Magazine, August 1997.

75. Article in TIME Magazine: "Africa Rising", March 30, 1998.

76. Tony Nader: *The Human Body: An Expression of the Veda*, Vlodrop, Maharishi Vedic University Press, (1994).

77. Ram Raj duhkh kahu na vyapa – No Sorrow in the Kingdom of Ram. in: Ram Charit Manas, Uttar Kand, 20.1.

78. Translation of Maharishi Mahesh Yogi, Maharishi Vedic University, 1985, p. 101.

79. F. Travis, V. Butler, M. Rainforth, et al: "Can a Building's Orientation Affect the Quality of Life of the People Within? Testing Principles of Maharishi Sthāpatya Veda," *Journal of Social Behavior and Personality*, October, 2004.

80. J. Zamarra: Oral description of an overview of 100 patients recently treated by him.

81. F. Benedetti: "Morning Sunlight Reduces Length of Hospitalization in Bipolar Depression." *Journal of Affective Disorders* 62 (2001), p. 221–223.

82. F. Travis, V. Butler, M. Rainforth et. al: Study Conducted on 110 Burglaries Reported in Fairfield, Iowa: A preliminary, unpublished study in 2000 by student Jar-El

Cohen at MSAE, Fairfield.

83. O. Christiansen, University of the Faroe Islands, Denmark. Oral presentation by Christiansen in August of 2001 to the faculty of the business school at Maharishi International University, Fairfield, Iowa.

84. K. Pirc, "TM-Lehrermappe," 2005. Unpublished Summary of English-Language Original Studies in German.

85. F. T. Travis, J Tecce, A. Arenander and R. K. Wallace: "Patterns of EEG Coherence, Power, and Contingent Negative Variation Characterize the Integration of Transcendental and Waking State." *Biological Psychology*, 2002, 61, 293–319.

86. L. I. Mason, et al: "Electrophysiological Correlates of Higher States of Consciousness during Sleep in Long-Term Practitioners of the Transcendental Meditation Program." *Sleep*, 1997, 20(2), p. 102–110.

87. News Release of 6.02.2008, Global Country of World Peace Press Office, 6063 NP MERU, Netherlands.

88. *Hindustan Times* 11.2.2008.

89. J. Brooks, T. Scarano: "Transcendental Meditation in the Treatment of Post-Vietnam Adjustment." *Journal of Counseling and Adjustment*, 1986, 64, p. 212-215, in: Collected Papers, vol. I-VI*, vol. 4, Paper 313, p. 2446–2452.

90. The dates for Fairfield can be found in the Uniform Crime Reports Communications Unit staff, Washington D.C. From: www.truthabouttm.org
– Fairfield Crime.

91. Hawkins, M. A. (2003). Effectiveness of the Transcendental Meditation program in criminal rehabilitation and treatment of substance abuse: A review of the research. *Journal of Offender Rehabilitation*, 36 (1-4), 47-65.

92. *J Offender Rehab 36 (1–4), 2003.*

93. The dates for the U.S. cities can be found in the FBI Uniform Crime Reports, www.fbi.gov/ucr/ucr.htm.

94. "What's Behind America's Falling Crime Rate?" *TIME Magazine*, 22. February (2010).

95. "Steady Decline in Major Crime Baffles Experts," *New York Times*, 23. May 2010 p. 493–507.

CPSIA information can be obtained
at www.ICGtesting.com
Printed in the USA
LVHW081456231021
701306LV00002B/81